ANNUAL REVIEW OF WOMEN'S HEALTH

Volume II

ANNUAL REVIEW OF WOMEN'S HEALTH

Volume II

Edited by

Beverly J. McElmurry
and
Randy Spreen Parker

National League for Nursing Press • New York
Pub. No. 19-2669

ISBN 0-88737-636-3
ISSN 1073-1695

The views expressed in this publication represent the views of the authors and do not necessarily reflect the official views of the National League for Nursing.

Cover illustration: *Spirit of the Winds,* by Maxine Noel-Ioyan Mani.

This book was set in Aster and Trump by Publications Development Company. The editor was Maryan Malone and the designer was Nancy Jeffries. The cover was designed by Lauren Stevens.

Printed in the United States of America.

To all of our colleagues—faculty, students, and community women—who help us create a better vision of health care for all women.

Beverly J. McElmurry

To the memory of Randolph Ernest Spreen, whose lifelong commitment to teaching, compassion and respect for others, and continual celebration of the differences among people, touched the lives of many who loved him and shared his passion for life.

Randy Spreen Parker

Contributors

Doris E. Ballard-Ferguson, PhD, RNC
Associate Professor
College of Nursing
University of Arkansas for Medical Sciences

Linda A. Bernhard, PhD, RN
Associate Professor
Department of Adult Health and Illness
    Nursing, and Center for Women's Studies
The Ohio State University

Catherine Ingram Fogel PhD, RNC, (OGNP),
    FAAN
Associate Professor
School of Nursing
University of North Carolina at Chapel Hill

Patricia A. Geary, EdD, RN
Dean and Professor of Nursing
School of Nursing
University of Southern Maine

Marie Hastings-Tolsma, PhD, RNC
Assistant Professor
School of Nursing
University of Southern Maine

Jeanne Beauchamp Hewitt, PhD, RN
Assistant Professor
School of Nursing
University of Wisconsin at Milwaukee

Karyn Holm, PhD, FAAN
Professor and Chair
School of Nursing
Loyola University, Chicago

Donna Huddleston, PhD, RN
BHM Health Associates, Inc.
Crown Point, Indiana

Tonda L. Hughes, PhD, RN
Assistant Professor
Department of Psychiatric Nursing
College of Nursing
University of Illinois at Chicago

Susan R. Johnson, MD
Professor
Department of Obstetrics and Gynecology
College of Medicine
University of Iowa

Jackie B. Labat, RD, CDE
MS Candidate
Food Science and Nutrition
University of Minnesota

Carol Leppa, PhD, RN
Assistant Professor
School of Nursing
University of Washington

Pamela Fox Levin, PhD, RN
Assistant Professor
College of Nursing
University of Illinois at Chicago

Lucy Martinez-Schallmoser, PhD, RN
Assistant Professor
Niehoff School of Nursing
Loyola University, Chicago

Theresa Lawlor McDonald, PA-C, MA, NP
Clinical Director
Hillcrest Family Services
Dubuque, Iowa

Beverly J. McElmurry, EdD, FAAN
Professor
College of Nursing
University of Illinois at Chicago

Susan Terry Misner, MS, RN
Research Specialist
College of Nursing
University of Illinois at Chicago

Ellen Sullivan Mitchell, PhD, RN
Associate Professor
School of Nursing
University of Washington

Jeanette Norris, PhD
Research Scientist
Alcoholism and Drug Abuse Institute
University of Washington

Amy C. Olson, PhD, RN
Associate Professor of Nutrition
Department of Nutrition
College of Saint Benedict

Randy Spreen Parker, MSN, RN, C
Doctoral Candidate
College of Nursing
University of Illinois at Chicago

Sue M. Penckofer, PhD, RN
Associate Professor
School of Nursing
Loyola University, Chicago

Barbara Jones Warren, MS, RN
Doctoral Candidate
School of Nursing
Ohio State University

Joan L. Woods, MPH
Doctoral Candidate
School of Public Health
University of Illinois at Chicago

Nancy Fugate Woods, PhD, RN, FAAN
Professor, Parent Child Nursing
Director, Center for Women's Health Research
University of Washington

Contents

Preface

Given the history of my involvement with this publication in its various forms and titles, I bring a certain propriety to this series and to this volume. What began as an idea to put into written form the expert resources that I had available as a graduate student at the University of Illinois at Chicago, "Women's Health Concentration in Nursing" has evolved into an authoritative reference series on women's health issues. It is critical that women's health experts collaborate in the dissemination of current knowledge about women's health concerns.

As a consumer of women's health information, I am grateful for the success of the *Annual Review of Women's Health*. I eagerly anticipate each volume as I struggle to make sense of the flood of health information that appears daily in the professional and popular press and media. Like all women in our culture, I am bombarded with information and subliminal messages in advertising. Women are targeted for huge amounts of health information that reflects our primary role in family health care decision making—for example, ask Dr. Mom about the best cough remedy (Leppa, 1994). In wading through this flood of information, I have found it helpful to think of two types of health information.

First, there is what I call Health Information Given to Women. The best example of this information is the cover story of a recent issue of *Harvard Women's Health Watch* (Mertz, 1994). The goal of this publication is "to interpret medical information for the general reader in a timely and accurate fashion" according to the publication information listed in each issue. The banner of the publication claims to provide "information for enlightened choices from Harvard Medical School." The cover story of the July 1994 issue summarizes a study of antioxidant vitamin supplements and lung cancer in smokers, published in a medical journal. What is missing in the presentation and discussion of the study is any mention or comment on the fact that the study was conducted on 29,000 men. No women were included. Yet, the impression in this summary is that the study's results are applicable to women. The authority of the Harvard Medical School is seductive, yet the information in the report is seriously limited. It is time that women's health researchers gain the recognition that is justly due them. The authors in this annual review provide readers with a significantly different perspective.

The second type of health information is what I call Women's Health Information. This volume of the *Annual Review of Women's Health* is an excellent example of this type of information. The authors and editors of this volume are not only experts in women's health, they are conscientious educators providing entry into the world of women's health information. With their expert guidance and interpretation of what the literature is saying— and what is missing—both the general reader and the health practitioner gain an understanding of the issues and concerns of women. This type of women's health information is honest about the limitations of current research and keeps women and their concerns in the forefront. It is interesting to know about the first type of health information, but I rely on this second type. Women's health information in the tradition of this volume makes sense of the flood of health information.

Health information will only increase in volume and complexity under the congressional mandate to address gender in all federally funded health research. This volume of the *Annual Review of Women's Health* guides the reader in evaluating the research that has been published. It also educates women, as health care consumers and providers, as to what questions to ask and what to look for when given any health information. I use this group of trusted professional researchers to advise and guide my personal and professional health care decisions. I welcome this volume and thank the authors and editors for their continued efforts in producing quality women's health information for all women.

REFERENCES

Leppa, C. (1994). Women as health care providers. In C. Fogel & N. F. Woods (Eds.), *Women's health*. San Francisco: Sage.

Merz, B. (Ed.). (1994). Antioxidants re-examined. *Harvard Women's Health Watch, 1*(11), 1.

Carol Leppa

Introduction

Beverly J. McElmurry
and Randy Spreen Parker

It has been wonderful to work with Allan Graubard and Nancy Jeffries in putting together this volume of the *Annual Review of Women's Health*. Consistent with NLN's vision for health care reform, they challenged us in this, the second *Annual Review*, to write about women's health concerns for a dual audience of health professionals and interested lay readers. As editors, we welcomed this challenge; after all, feminists value the ideal of inclusive language that is understandable not only across disciplines but also among laypersons. Yet, when we contacted contributing authors, we realized that the majority of them had written primarily for professional audiences. Authors found that writing to both professional and lay readers was a formidable challenge. Nevertheless, this challenge has served to test one of the fundamental beliefs of many feminist researchers: research, theory, and practice should mutually inform and refine one another, to create knowledge that empowers women. If this goal is not achieved, then, we believe, what we write about women's health will have little impact on women's daily lives.

The aim of women's health research is to generate empirically grounded theoretical knowledge and to disseminate these empirical and theoretical insights in a language that is meaningful to women in all walks of life. Ironically, we have yet to break down such communication barriers across different disciplines. Each scientific discipline, nursing included, uses a unique vocabulary that is often foreign to scientists in other disciplines. Some literature has attempted to bridge the language barrier, but we have not realized an inclusive language. In the *Annual Review*, we have not fully reached our goal of inclusive language but we believe we are moving in the right direction.

Along with the language, we remain concerned about the classification of knowledge of women's health. Readers will note that we have retained the framework of certain categories of women's health that were presented in the previous volume. These include development across the life cycle; health promotion and maintenance; delivery of health care to women; health and work; reproductive health; physical diseases and health problems; health/illness; economics, ethics, policy, legislation; and research/theoretical issues. As we gain greater understanding of women's health issues, we know these categories may change. However, the framework stimulated us to solicit authors who could address racial, cultural, and economic diversity among women. The sequential editions of the *Annual Review of Women's Health* share some common topics but they do not duplicate information. Given here are additional topics of concern to women's health: AIDS/HIV, women's reproductive options and rights from an international perspective, depression in African American women, postpartum depression in Hispanic women, and prostitution. Thus, the *Annual Review* works in tandem to provide readers with comprehensive coverage of current issues related to women's health.

The chapter authors consistently offer women information that can make a difference in their health. In this vein, an important question facing midlife women is whether to use hormone therapy for preventing diseases associated with aging. As Nancy Fugate Woods and Ellen Sullivan Mitchell illustrate so ably, this complicated decision is not made any easier by the variety of positions advocated in the literature. It is helpful to learn of the historical development of hormone therapy and to have the chapter authors distinguish between hormone replacement and hormone therapy. Given the medicalization of menopause that has occurred over recent years, women must use their knowledge of self to carefully weigh their options when considering hormone therapy. These authors provide a comprehensive overview of what is known about hormone therapy at this point. Women have recently been included in clinical trials relevant to midlife health concerns, but we lack sufficient data to determine the long-term effects of hormone therapy. The revelation that women often obtain most of their information about hormone therapy from popular women's magazines is disturbing. We ask our readers to give serious thought to how researchers share their findings with women and how we might ensure better dissemination of research findings over time.

The topic of women's sexuality is treated sensitively, albeit with frustration, by Linda A. Bernhard. After years spent in conducting research and reviewing the extant knowledge in this area, Bernhard still finds that insufficient attention is paid to the diversity of women who should be included in the study of sexuality. As she evaluated the extensive literature reviewed in her chapter, she asked two important questions: (1) Is the information needed? and (2) Does it benefit women? The information included in her review can be used in practice, research, teaching, and activism on women's behalf. In musing about Bernhard's comment that some researchers seem not to read across disciplines in their subject area, we are inclined to wonder whether tying research funding to the inclusion of women in research does not also mean that women researchers should be cited in the references provided for funding proposals. The review and criticisms of this area of women's health are cogent and thought-provoking.

A new author, Doris Ballard-Ferguson, presents a new topic for the *Annual Review:* the health-promoting behaviors of African American elderly women. In the past two decades, little has been written about this subject, and much of what has been written emphasizes deficits in health rather than positive health measures. After defining health and health-promoting behaviors, the chapter identifies constructs that are crucial to understanding and promoting health outcomes for this population. Consistent with her regard for older African American women, Ferguson advocates use of the acronym DEARS to capture the areas of concern to their health. The DEARS framework represents the personal health practices that promote health: diet, exercise, activity, rest/relaxation, and support. The wisdom in this chapter illustrates what we can learn from older women.

Amy Olson and Jackie Labat's review of women, diet, and heart disease is a much needed resource for women who are trying to sort out all of the recent findings on the relationship of diet to coronary heart disease. These authors make the point that some things can be done to modify this leading cause of death for women, and a primary way in which women can take charge of their own risk status is to become knowledgeable about dietary factors that affect blood lipids: alcohol, antioxidants, calories, dietary cholesterol, and the quality and quantity of fats in the diet. There is an urgent need to continue the clinical trials and other research studies related to women and nutrition. Recent research suggests that the serum cholesterol levels that place women at risk are different from those for men, yet most women are counseled to attain the norms established for men. Olson emphasizes that, compared to total cholesterol levels, other measures of blood lipids are more sensitive indicators of coronary disease risk for women. The chapter offers numerous ideas for dietary changes that women can consider.

To profile the key developments in the care of hospitalized women, Patricia Geary reviews the literature about the care of women with breast cancer, cardiac problems, and lung cancer. Geary believes that, since the last review of literature on acute care, progress has been made in the treatment of women with cardiac disease. However, real progress in the future will depend on working to establish standards of care for acutely ill women. During her review of the literature, Geary paid special attention to how gender differences are depicted in the discussion of comfort, expressions of anguish, caring, well-being, and pain. A sense of urgency is conveyed as she develops the thesis that making women better recognized as consumers of acute care is a means of reducing the barriers to their receiving quality care.

The authors of the occupational chapter, Susan Terry Misner, Jeanne Beauchamp Hewitt, and Pamela Fox Levin, remind us that the increasing numbers of women in the work force require a broad perspective on occupational issues. Accordingly, they caution that some of the areas of concern are: changing gender roles, how public and private work is defined, the devaluation of women's work as evidenced in wage differentials, role expansion, and workplace health risks. Further, they draw our attention to special female worker groups such as women in cottage industries, women with disabilities, and older women. Another occupational issue is the societal expectation that women will act as caregivers for children and older family members while trying to maintain their employment status. An enduring topic of social debate—mothers, employment outside the home as a factor in the health of their children—diverts attention from the effect of work and multiple roles on the health of mothers, an important focus that has received insufficient research. One of the challenges noted by the authors is how to create supportive environments in the workplace for women who wish to maintain breastfeeding. The extensive discussion of workplace hazards covers topics such as temperature extremes, sexual harassment, and chemical, physical, and biological agents. The importance of future research on occupational health concerns for women is revealed in the number of areas about which little is known. These authors continue to break new ground and offer information that is useful to all women, regardless of their employment status.

New knowledge about childbearing continues to focus on technological and scientific advances. Marie Hastings-Tolsma and Patricia Geary caution us to observe what literature is *not* available. Childbearing experiences for women from diverse ethnic and cultural groups receive minimal attention. To facilitate a comparison between the material included in this chapter and the areas discussed in the 1993 *Annual Review*, the authors use the same categories: issues in childbearing, women with special needs, pregnancy, health and illness, teen pregnancy, intrapartum, postpartum, cesarean section, and breastfeeding. The breadth of topics covered and the sheer number of reviews underline the importance of ensuring safe childbearing experiences for women. Control over the childbearing process and financial resources to obtain desired care are continuing issues in this area.

The authors of the chapter on contraceptive options are Theresa Lawlor McDonald, a nurse practitioner, and Susan Johnson, a physician. They present a strong case for the involvement of health professionals in the politics, economics, and education that impinge on modern contraceptive knowledge and practice. They are clear about the importance of education for women and the global evidence that better education for women results in an improved quality of life and increased use of birth control practices. Also, they are articulate about the importance of examining the hazards of pregnancies that are too early, too close, too late, or too frequent. Untimely deaths of women are a serious drain on any country, whether classified as developed or developing. These authors select articles on new developments in reproductive technology, the management of contraception when women have risk factors associated with chronic disease, and the continuing need for adequate education of health professionals about contraception. McDonald and Johnson emphasize the importance of fully informing women about the correct use of new technologies and about recent developments in fertility control and in the prevention of sexually transmitted diseases. Among their recommendations for the future are the involvement of teens in discussions of adolescent sexuality with their peers, and the management of contraceptive issues for women with behavioral disorders.

Karyn Holm and Sue Penckofer detail the life-style changes women can make if they want to reduce their risk for cardiovascular disease. Compared to their research for the previous *Annual Review*, these authors found an increased emphasis on the cardiovascular health of women. The publications reviewed are grouped according to demographics (educational level, race, and socioeconomic level), the prognosis for women with cardiovascular disease, risk factors (family history, smoking, cholesterol, alcohol, diabetes, obesity, and physical activity), psychosocial factors, diagnosis and treatment, and hormonal and reproductive factors. The authors conclude with a discussion of the implications for education, research, and practice. Examples of some questions that need to be addressed are: Do older women with coronary disease receive care comparable to that provided to younger men? Are there alternatives to hormonal therapy that are beneficial to cardiovascular health? What early prevention strategies would be effective for women of color? How can we help health professionals to better understand the clinical differences between men and women in cardiovascular risk factors and disease symptomology? In general, early attention to the promotion of cardiovascular health is important to enhancing the quality of women's lives as they age.

The chapter on sexually transmitted diseases is extremely important because, as Catherine Ingram Fogel reminds us, these infections are found in every socioeconomic class, culture, ethnicity, and age group. Reflecting on that statement, one might wonder how often women discuss such infections with one another. Such confidences are not common because of women's varied emotions when they are diagnosed as having an infection. Fogel presents staggering facts and figures, to help us understand why women are vulnerable to these infections and why some are more vulnerable than others. This chapter is a call to action. It is difficult to comprehend the fact that syphilis rates in a five-year period increased 230% for black women and 10% for white women. The chapter offers a variety of ideas for dealing with the STD problem and pleads for studies of the lived experience of women and their sexual behavior over the life span. The author states the questions that guided her selection of articles for review. One of the criteria for inclusion was whether a particular source would enrich readers' understanding of prevention and self-care practices related to STDs. When the same criterion is applied to this chapter, we are confident that readers will find this material very useful.

The importance of recognizing AIDS/HIV infection as a serious women's health concern is stressed by Donna Huddleston as she calls for more studies on women and the promotion of their health. She urges an end to the public silence surrounding the threat posed to women by AIDS/HIV, and she addresses various concerns about the reliability and validity of the current studies conducted with women. The young age at which females are drawn into prostitution, and the recruitment of the girl-child are reprehensible situations with which our society must deal more actively as we sort out the social issues that influence AIDS/HIV. Huddleston proposes that future research on AIDS/HIV in women should be based on self-care, the provision of information, and attention to the women's lived experience. Self-care can include care of self and care of others either as a professional or as a family member. Both laypersons and professionals will find this chapter useful for its definitions of terms, resources for further information, and articles that touch on the variety of ways in which AIDS/HIV can affect women.

Both the topic, postpartum depression, and the author, Lucy Martinez-Shallmoser, are new to the *Annual Review* series. As a Hispanic nurse scientist, this author has a special interest in enhancing the general understanding of the perplexing phenomenon of postpartum depression, especially in Hispanic urban mothers. The costs of postpartum depression are profound for the mother, infant, and family. Martinez-Shallmoser stresses the importance of defining this condition, seeking ways to identify its presence, and continuing research on how to prevent the depression and/or provide early intervention. The chapter covers the period from 1959 to 1994; topics are: recognition, parity, age, socioeconomic considerations, life events, cognitive style, child–parent relationships, reaction to pregnancy/fertility, and social support/relationships.

Another author who is new to the series, Barbara Jones Warren, is a self-defined womanist and mental health expert. She offers a comprehensive and sensitive treatment of the topic of depression in African American women. Our readers will be grateful for the breadth of this discourse: it covers the experience, definitions, diagnostic criteria, theories, risk appraisal, and interventions. Depressed African American women face social, physical, emotional, and interpersonal challenges and are assisted in solving problems and dealing with crises by their social support network, whether family, friends, and/or church members. Warren highlights chapters, books, articles, dissertations, videos, popular magazines, technical reports, teaching pamphlets, and mental health associations.

Tonda L. Hughes and Jeanette Norris provide a ground-breaking chapter on women's use and abuse of alcohol, with particular emphasis on how research about sexuality, sexual orientation, and violence might help us understand these women. Little research has been done about women and alcohol or how to treat women who abuse alcohol. An area that ties all of these topics together is women's intimate relationships. The authors introduce the beliefs and myths relative to the use and abuse of alcohol by women, and indicate whether any research supports those beliefs. For example, there is no conclusive evidence that women who drink are likely to engage in increased sexual activity. Further, data are insufficient to determine whether the influence of a problem-drinking partner is stronger on a lesbian than on a heterosexual woman. The difficulties in studying the effects of childhood sexual abuse on the later abuse of alcohol are developed, along with what is known about the consumption of alcohol as a factor in acquaintance rape and violence. These authors deal with difficult, sometimes taboo topics and provide authoritative guidance for understanding women's use and abuse of alcohol.

Related to the chapter on contraceptive options is Joan Woods' international perspective on reproductive options and women's rights. It is important to link the two ideas, options and rights, to the insistence on safe, sensitive family planning services for all women. Woods offers readers a historical perspective on the population control movement and the reproductive rights response. Discussion of risks and barriers to reproductive options leads easily to a survey of the international human rights laws that justify the importance of achieving women-centered reproductive policy. If societal expectations are that women bear the burden in fertility regulation, then it is essential that women have a voice in creating the policies that affect fertility. The articles selected for review are consistent with the view that reproductive rights are human rights. The literature offers an analysis of legal theory, reproductive options, and women's health, as well as cultural and geographic considerations. Woods' work in other countries has developed her global perspective on the link between the rights of women and their exercise of these rights in the area of reproductive decisions. This chapter helps readers address a critical question: Should family planning clinics exist to control population growth, or are they a means for helping women exercise control over fertility?

The chapter on prostitution by Susan T. Misner, Randy Spreen Parker, and Beverly J. McElmurry represents a struggle to come to terms with a difficult topic. One of the authors' first decisions was what ages to cover in this discussion. Adolescent prostitutes were included because prostitution is a widespread, difficult, and tragic life-style for young women. It was heartening to find some literature that described effective interventions for adolescents. Although some of the health risks for prostitutes overlap with topics covered in other chapters, information was included on sexually transmitted diseases, drug and chemical abuse, and physical and emotional abuse, all of which are serious threats to the health of prostitutes. The issue of decriminalization of prostitution without sanctioning such behavior led to the recognition that feminist literature is needed in the area of social ethics. The authors' encourage dialogue between health professionals and prostitutes in order to better understand their health situation. Aside from celebrity cases, most prostitutes have not been heard or given a voice in depicting their lived experience. No definitive short-term solutions are offered, but the authors suggest some recommendations for progress toward the goal of eliminating prostitution.

To assist readers in moving through some of the more dense material, we have appended a glossary of commonly used research terms. As editors, we are grateful for the patience and diligence demonstrated by the contributing authors, especially in response to our request to address a dual audience. By accepting the challenge of translating the research literature reviewed in each chapter into a meaningful communication of research findings, our contributors strove to serve both audiences. A great deal was learned through this process, and we look forward to making subsequent *Annual Reviews* even more inclusive on issues of women's health and more accessible to all interested readers.

Part I

Development Across the Life Cycle

Chapter 1

Midlife Women: Decisions about Using Hormone Therapy for Preventing Disease in Old Age

Nancy Fugate Woods
Ellen Sullivan Mitchell

As the baby boomers enter their middle years, they exhibit a predictable surge of interest in midlife and menopause. As a group, midlife women are one of the most rapidly growing populations in the United States. The health of this population has significant consequences because of the cost associated with health care. Preventive measures to reduce morbidity in this group warrant attention of clinicians and researchers alike. One preventive measure, use of hormone therapy (estrogen or estrogen plus progestin), has captured the attention of many women. There is a plethora of research about the short-term consequences of estrogen or combined hormone therapy. Two large studies evaluate the effects of hormone therapies on cardiovascular risk factors in women (the Postmenopausal Estrogen and Progestin Investigation, PEPI); the long-term consequences of hormone therapy for heart disease and osteoporotic fractures are studied in the Women's Health Initiative trial. There is little information about women's decision-making processes in adopting and continuing to use hormone therapies. This review summarizes what is known about women's decisions and the factors that support their continuing use of hormone therapy for preventing morbidity in old age. Papers abstracted for this review focus on women's perspectives about hormone use. Abstracts of several papers illustrate a range of professional positions about hormone use for prevention of disease.

HISTORY OF HORMONE THERAPY

Women's use of hormone therapy is not a new phenomenon. Estrogen replacement therapy for postmenopausal women has been part of medical practice for four decades (Bush, 1992; MacPherson, 1993). The term "hormone therapy" in this review distinguishes our position from advocacy of hormone therapy as "replacement therapy," since the dosage administered is in excess of natural physiologic levels in midlife. Over time, patterns of prescribing estrogen and combined hormone therapy, types of hormonal preparations, and indications for use of hormone therapy have changed dramatically. Although estrogen was first approved for use by postmenopausal women during the 1940s, the prevalence of estrogen use did not increase substantially until the 1960s, when clinicians prescribed estrogen replacement therapy for relief of menopausal hot flashes and urogenital symptoms. Some advocates of estrogen therapy (e.g., Wilson, 1966), promised women eternal youth, beauty, and femininity. During the mid 1970s, evidence for increased incidence of endometrial cancer associated with estrogen therapy and worries about increased risk of vascular disease (as had occurred with oral contraceptives) led to a decrease in the prescription of estrogen therapy (Bush, 1992; MacPherson, 1993). During the 1980s, the additions of progestin (a synthetic form of progesterone) to prescriptions of estrogen therapy to reduce the risk of endometrial cancer predated a subsequent increase in prescriptions for hormone therapy (Gambrell, 1987; Hemminki et al., 1988). Recently, the Food and Drug Administration approved the use of postmenopausal estrogen for the prevention and management of osteoporosis (*Physician's Desk Reference*, 1993) based on evidence supporting its effectiveness in reducing hip and vertebral fractures (Weiss et al., 1980). Evidence linking the use of estrogen therapy to a reduction in the incidence of heart disease has introduced yet another indication for hormone therapy—the prevention of disease by use of estrogen or estrogen/progestin therapy (Bush et al., 1987; Henderson, 1988; Stampfer, 1985).

GUIDELINES FOR THE USE OF HORMONE THERAPY

Despite the possible new evidence for the protective effects of estrogen and combined hormone therapy, caution pervades discussion of recommendations for its use. The American College of Physicians recently published "Guidelines for Counseling Postmenopausal Women about Preventive Hormone Therapy," in which they advocated careful and separate consideration of benefits of short-term use of hormone therapy for managing menopausal symptoms and use of hormone therapy for disease prevention (1992). The College advises a limited course of therapy (1 to 5 years) for women seeking relief from symptoms such as hot flashes associated with menopause. In the absence of data from randomized clinical trials to provide definitive estimates of benefits and risks, the College recommends that women of all races should consider preventive hormone therapy. Those who have had a hysterectomy are likely to benefit from estrogen therapy and have no need for combined hormone therapy (estrogen and a progestin). Women who have coronary heart disease or who are at increased risk of coronary heart disease are likely to benefit from hormone therapy. They should receive combined therapy if they have a uterus unless careful endometrial monitoring is performed (e.g., endometrial biopsies, aspirations). Risks of hormone therapy may outweigh the benefits for women with increased risk of breast cancer. The College Guidelines conclude that "for other women, the best course of action is not clear" (1992, p. 1038).

The Guidelines were based on a review of the most recent data available (Grady et al., 1992). They include consideration of the following potential benefits and risks as outlined in Table 1.1.

Although conclusive information about the benefits and risks of long-term use of estrogen or combined hormone therapy awaits further research, data currently available indicate benefits for managing symptoms such as hot flashes, night sweats, and urogenital symptoms; reducing the risk of osteoporosis; and reducing the risk of heart disease. Increased monitoring by a health professional may also contribute to the early detection of other treatable diseases, thereby having a net positive effect on women's health. Possible risks associated with the use of estrogen and/or combined hormone therapy include increased risk of endometrial cancer in women who have a uterus and who are using estrogen alone; increased risk of breast cancer; resumption of menses, or spotting related to progestin therapy; increased risk of gallbladder disease; growth of uterine fibroids; and the necessity to adhere to a medication regimen for an extended period of one's life (Grady, 1992).

Two large clinical trials, the Postmenopausal Estrogen and Progestin Intervention (PEPI) study and the Women's Health Initiative trial are

Table 1.1
Benefits and Risks of Hormone Therapy

	Estrogen	Estrogen/Progestin
Potential Benefits		
Reduced risk of heart disease	Reduces risk by about 35%	Data limited, cannot estimate
Reduced risk of osteoporotic fracture	Reduces risk of hip fracture by about 25% and vertebral fractures by about 50%	Data limited, cannot estimate
Increased life expectancy	Probably will increase life expectancy	May increase life expectancy, but perhaps not as much as estrogen alone; less protection from heart disease than estrogen alone; women at high risk of breast cancer may have decreased life expectancy
Potential Risks		
Endometrial cancer	Increased risk of endometrial cancer is 8-fold for 10 to 20 years' use	Risk not increased; symptoms related to progestin use unpredictable; endometrial bleeding for 6 to 8 months
Breast cancer	Evidence inconsistent, use for <5 years probably does not increase risk; use for 10 to 20 years increases risk by about 25%	
Endometrial monitoring	Endometrial evaluation at baseline and yearly intervals to detect endometrial cancer	Endometrial evaluation if no withdrawal bleeding occurs, or if heavy or prolonged or frequent or persistent bleeding occurs
Need for hysterectomy	20% lifetime probability of hysterectomy for endometrial hyperplasia or cancer due to therapy	Probably no increase in risk

*Data abstracted from American College of Physicians, 1992; Grady et al., 1992.

underway. The PEPI trial results will be informative about the consequences of using estrogen or combined hormone therapy (estrogen with a progestin) for heart disease risk factors. The Women's Health Initiative study will assess the long-term consequences of hormone therapy in postmenopausal women for heart disease, osteoporosis, and breast cancer. In addition, the use of a low fat diet with calcium and Vitamin D supplementation will be compared with the effects of hormone therapy on several disease endpoints. Among the many important contributions of this trial will be the comparison of interventions that women, themselves, can initiate—the low fat diet and use of vitamins and minerals—with the use of hormone therapies (National Institutes of Health, 1992). The PEPI trial will yield information within 1995, about effects of hormone therapy on risk factors for cardiovascular disease, but results from the Women's Health Initiative trial linking hormone therapy to disease endpoints—cardiovascular disease, osteoporosis, and breast cancer—will not be available for 12 years. Thus, women must make decisions to use or not use hormone therapy in the face of incomplete information. Because women have historically been excluded from clinical trials, information about the short-term risks and benefits is largely limited to retrospective studies, with their problematic bias in selection of who used and who didn't use hormones. The absence of information about the long-term risks and benefits gained from clinical trials comparing the consequences of using estrogen alone or combined hormone therapy awaits completion of the Women's Health Initiative study.

FEMINIST CRITIQUE

As the medical indications for hormone use and prescribing practices have changed, so has the tenor of feminist critique of hormone therapy. Early critics of those advocating use of estrogen for women from "womb to tomb" alleged that use of hormones without long-term assessment of side and hazardous effects represented dangerous experimentation with women's health. Many asserted that the medicalization of women's health events, such as birthing, menstruation, and menopause, transformed natural events to diseases needing treatment (Bell, 1990). To many, the use of hormone therapy for menopausal symptoms represented additional evidence of the medicalization of women's lives. Critics asserted that the early focus on symptom management included prevention of osteoporosis and heart disease, diseases defined increasingly as part of menopause, and thus menopause was viewed increasingly as a disease state (MacPherson, 1981, 1985, 1992, 1993).

Understanding women's beliefs about hormone therapy and their actual practices would be incomplete without consideration of the social and historical context. Women who were part of the baby boomer birth cohort are now attempting to sift through the available information about hormone therapy. In the 1960s, women were encouraged to remain "feminine forever" by using estrogens. Most will remember the news reports of the 1970s linking estrogen therapy to an increased incidence of endometrial cancer. Some find the current attempt to assess the benefits and risks of hormone therapy yet another attempt to medicalize the menopause. At the same time, breast cancer awareness is ever present in public media. Some women are waiting for the results of the PEPI trial to become available before deciding about therapy. Results of the Women's Health Initiative study will not be available for another decade. Women who once asked, "What is the risk of using hormone therapies?" are now asking, "What is the risk of *not* using hormone therapies?"

DECISION MAKING ABOUT HORMONE THERAPY

Despite intense interest in the use of hormone therapy for prevention of osteoporosis and cardiovascular disease, there have been few studies about women's decisions to adopt hormone therapy for this purpose and to adhere to the therapy once they begin using it. Adherence to hormone therapy regimens is low: 20% to 30% of women participating in the Massachusetts Women's Health study never had their prescription filled and 20% stopped treatment prior to completing nine months of therapy. Women's primary reason for stopping treatment was fear of cancer. Moreover, women tended to use hormone therapy inconsistently. Of those receiving their first hormone prescriptions, 10% took the prescription sporadically (Ravnikar, 1987).

To date, most studies of hormone use have involved women who are perimenopausal (noticing changes in the regularity of their menstrual bleeding patterns), and likely to be using hormone therapy for managing hot flashes or other symptoms instead of for preventive purposes (Ferguson et al., 1989; Ravnikar, 1987). Moreover, studies that have focused on women's decision-making processes have involved simulated cases rather than a decision process pertaining to their own actual situations (Rothert et al., 1991; Schmitt et al., 1991). Nonetheless, the published studies about women's decisions to use hormone therapy provide an important perspective for clinicians who are studying the use of hormone therapy in midlife.

Estimates of hormone use from other countries illustrate a wide range in prevalence, from 3% in Italy to 25% in Germany (Oddens et al., 1992), 13% to 24% in Australia (MacLennan et al., 1993), and 22% in Denmark (Koster, 1990). In North America, there is also wide variation. In Canada, 18% of women experiencing natural menopause used some form of hormone therapy, but 27% of those who had a hysterectomy did so (Kaufert, 1986). Estimates of use in the United States range from 12% to 32% (Scalley & Henrich, 1993). Women who are perimenopausal or postmenopausal are more likely to be using hormone therapy than women who are still cycling regularly (Harris et al., 1990; McKinlay, Brambilla, & Posner, 1992; Topo et al., 1991).

Factors Influencing the Use of Hormone Therapy

Women's use of hormone therapy can be partially understood by considering factors associated with adherence to prescriptions in general. Factors accounting for adherence to treatment include: accessibility of the treatment, attitudes toward the treatment, threat of illness, knowledge about the therapy, social norms, demographic characteristics, and self-efficacy (Becker, 1990). Factors associated with women's use of hormone therapy additionally include threat of future disease, knowledge about the therapy and its relationship to diseases that can be prevented, social influences about hormone use, current health status, health practices (including self-care and preventive service use), and self-efficacy. Each of these factors will be discussed in turn.

Access to therapy includes the ability to purchase and refill prescriptions—a function of income, insurance, and geographic proximity to a pharmacy. Women with middle to upper incomes are more likely to use hormone therapy than poor women (Draper et al., 1990; Hemminki et al., 1988).

Attitudes toward treatment derive from assessment of the benefits and risks of treatment, the quality of care provided, and the influence of information about the treatment. Benefits of treatment might include beliefs about the effects of hormone therapy on osteoporosis, cardiovascular disease, symptom relief, and physical appearance, in contrast to risks of treatment such as uterine or breast cancer, blood clots, fibroids, gallstones, elevated blood pressure, and lipid changes. In addition, women's perception of the quality of their health care (such as trust in their care provider) could have an important influence on adherence. Completed studies reveal that women who used hormones were more likely than nonusers to believe that women should take hormones for hot flashes and that the natural approaches to managing menopausal symptoms were less preferable than medical treatment (Ferguson, 1989). Over 1,000 women participating in a Norwegian opinion poll had a positive attitude toward hormone therapy if they had a high level of self-assessed information. More than half believed that hormone therapy increased the risk of heart infarction, stroke, breast cancer, and cancer in general. Their negative attitudes toward using hormones were associated with a belief in an increased risk of serious disease. Women were more positive about the use of hormone therapy for the prevention of osteoporosis and the alleviation of postmenopausal urogenital symptoms and hot flashes (Hunskaar & Backe, 1992). A Gallup poll sponsored by the North American Menopause Society (NAMS) revealed that 60% of the women surveyed believed hormone therapy would help resolve symptoms related to their menopause, 38% believed it would help prevent osteoporosis, and 34% believed it would help prevent heart disease (Utian & Schiff, 1994).

Threat of disease or future disease refers to perceptions about the seriousness, susceptibility, and consequences of the diseases being prevented. In addition, attitudes toward aging (aging as a natural phenomenon vs. aging as a disease to be treated) and symptoms women link to aging may help account for their willingness to adopt hormone therapy. Studies of hormone users demonstrated that viewing menopause (and perhaps aging) as a medical condition was associated with estrogen use (Ferguson et al., 1989). Little information is available about how women perceive the threat of osteoporosis, heart disease, and aging in general, although women mention the threat of breast cancer in many of the studies of hormone use (Utian & Schiff, 1994). Women participating in the NAMS poll indicated concern about their increasing risk of heart disease (57%), osteoporosis (56%), and depression (48%) in association with their menopause (Utian & Schiff, 1994).

Knowledge about the therapy and diseases it could prevent is another component of adherence. Women using estrogen therapy were more likely to be aware that lower estrogen levels were associated with osteoporosis than those who were not (Ferguson et al., 1989). In other populations, better educated women were more likely to use hormones (Barrett-Connor, 1991; Cauley et al., 1990). Education probably influences women's ability to obtain information about the therapy and gain access to health services.

Social influences about hormone use include social interactions and social norms about hormone therapy. Women not using hormones were more likely to have had relatives with uterine cancer than those using hormones (Ferguson et al., 1989). Aside from the Norwegian poll referenced earlier, no other studies focused on women's social networks and media influences on their use of hormones.

Self-efficacy refers to perceptions about being able to carry out the prescribed treatment. No studies provide data about women's perceptions of self-efficacy in adhering to hormone therapy. This is surprising, given the variety of regimens prescribed for women—for example, the cyclic administration of estrogen and progestin.

Several other factors have been linked to women's use of hormone therapy, including their health status, health practices, and past experiences with use of the therapy. *Health status* refers to perceptions of health in relation to others of a similar age, the accumulation of chronic illnesses, and changing functional status. In studies of several populations, women in better health were more likely to use hormone therapy (Barrett-Connor, 1991; Egeland, 1991; Pettiti, Perlman, & Signey, 1987). Women who were thinner were more likely to use hormones (Barrett-Connor, 1991). Women with a recent diagnosis of certain health problems that resulted in their contact with health professionals were more likely to be using hormone therapy. Findings from two different populations suggest an association between depression scores and hormone use (Egeland, 1991; Matthews et al., 1990).

Health practices include self-care activities to promote health and prevent disease as well as the use of preventive health services. Women who used hormone therapy were more likely than nonusers to exercise regularly or to have increased their exercise frequency (Barrett-Connor, 1991). In addition, they were more likely to have decreased their dietary fat and salt intake (Barrett-Connor, 1991). Indeed, these findings prompted Barrett-Connor to suggest that biases of self-selection, penchant for using preventive services, and increased opportunity for ascertainment of disease could be confounding the relationship between hormone therapy and the lower incidence of heart disease and osteoporosis. Healthier women who tend to use preventive and early detection services take hormone therapy and appear healthier on a variety of indicators when they are compared with women who do not use hormone therapy. The relationships between smoking and alcohol use and the use of hormone therapy are less clear. Egeland and associates (1991) found no difference between hormone users and nonusers in smoking, but greater alcohol use by hormone users, whereas Cauley and associates (1990) found that hormone users were more likely to be smokers and to use alcohol than nonusers of hormones. Harris and associates (1990) found that hormone users were more likely to use alcohol, but less likely to be smokers.

Use of preventive and early detection services are more prevalent among hormone therapy users than nonusers (Barrett-Connor, 1991). Women who were using hormones were more likely than nonusers to have had preventive health care within the past 1 to 2 years, including physician visits, cholesterol screen, blood pressure check, stool analysis for blood, rectal exam, mammography, and pap smears (Barrett-Connor, 1991; MacLennan et al., 1993).

Use of other medication or supplements such as vitamins is associated with hormone use, suggesting that women who are inclined to use other medications are more likely to use hormones (Matthews et al., 1990; Palinkas & Barrett-Connor, 1992). Use of alternative therapies, such as herbal teas, or special dietary modifications for menopausal symptoms, has not been explored.

Characteristics of one's health care provider may also influence the use of hormone therapy and adherence. Women who use hormone therapy were more likely to receive health care from a gynecologist than from other types of providers (Ferguson et al., 1989).

Women's past experiences with hormones are also important. Women may have had experiences using oral contraceptives and/or hormone therapy to treat menopausal symptoms. Those experiences may enhance women's willingness to use therapy or predispose them to anticipate problems and side effects of the therapy. The inclination to use medications, such as vitamins and oral contraceptives, has been associated with hormone use (Egeland et al., 1991). In addition, women who had hysterectomies will be likely to have been treated with estrogen therapy and to continue using estrogen therapy (Ferguson et al., 1989).

Finally, *current experiences with the therapy* are likely to be important in women's adherence to hormonal therapy. Women rated the recurrence of menstrual periods as the most unfavorable aspect of hormone use (Ferguson et al., 1989). Other problematic side effects include breast tenderness, vaginal irritation, headaches, edema, bloating, weight gain, irritability, cramping and dysmenorrhea, and nausea (Nachtigall, 1990; Utian & Schiff, 1994).

DECISION-MAKING PROCESSES

Most published studies of women's decision-making processes about hormone therapy have predated the recent emphasis on prevention of heart disease. Most earlier research focused on hormone therapy for preventing osteoporosis and symptom management. Moreover, most studies have involved women of perimenopausal rather than postmenopausal age. Studies have been oriented to theoretical rather than actual decision-making processes. For example, Rothert and associates (1991) studied women's decisions to use estrogen therapy through the use of simulated case studies. Community women who met the criteria of being 45 to 55 years of age, having an intact uterus, and not taking hormone replacements volunteered for the simulation study. This group of women largely based their decisions on relieving distress associated with hot flashes and to a lesser extent on risk of osteoporosis and other side effects of estrogen therapy. Although health professionals tend to emphasize risk reduction, women were more concerned about relief of symptoms. In a study of midlife women's decisions to use estrogen or combined hormone therapy to alleviate menopausal symptoms, again based on hypothetical cases, women's decision patterns sorted into four distinct groups who: (1) based their decision to take hormones on the severity of their hot flashes; (2) would use hormones if their hot flashes were severe, but also would consider the risk of osteoporosis and cancer in making their decision; (3) were most influenced by the unpleasant effects of adding progestin to the hormone therapy because they did not want to resume menses or spotting; and (4) considered health risks, particularly the risk of cancer, as the most important factor in their decision. These groups were distinguished by educational level, perceived stress, attitudes toward menopause, and use of medications. Women in the second group had the most formal education, higher stress levels, and more use of vitamins to control menopausal symptoms. Women in group 3 had the most positive attitudes toward menopause. In all cases, prediction of willingness to take estrogen was related to knowledge about menopause and its effects on women and the perception that hormone treatment might be helpful in controlling menopausal symptoms. Expectations that menopause would be difficult were related to lower likelihood of taking hormone therapy. Current comfort level, as indicated by hot flashes, was an overriding concern in women's decisions (Schmitt et al., 1991).

Implications

Few studies address how women make their decisions about adopting hormone therapy and adhering to the therapy. Moreover, women find that information is available, but are uncertain about the long-term consequences of their decisions. What remains ambiguous is how women weigh the risks and benefits of hormonal therapy in light of the potential for osteoporosis, coronary heart disease, breast and endometrial cancer, discomforts associated with using hormone replacement therapy, cost of the prescription and monitoring of adverse side effects of the therapy. Moreover, little is known about alternative treatments for menopausal symptoms. Adequate information is not available to women about the risk of *using* or *not using* hormone replacement therapy. Aside from a single research program focusing on how women make these decisions (Rothert et al., in progress), researchers are dedicating little effort to understanding the dilemma women face. A concerted effort is needed to understand how women make their decisions, for in the final analysis, women, themselves, will decide whether to use hormone therapy.

REFERENCES

American College of Physicians (1992). Guidelines for counseling postmenopausal women about preventive hormone therapy. *Annals of Internal Medicine, 117*(2), 1038–1041.

Barrett-Connor, E. (1991). Postmenopausal estrogen and prevention bias. *Annals of Internal Medicine, 115,* 455–456.

Barrett-Connor, E., Wingard, D., & Criqui, M. (1989). Postmenopausal estrogen use and heart disease risk factors in the 1980s. *Journal of the American Medical Association, 2061,* 2095–2100.

Becker, M. (1990). Theoretical models of adherence and strategies for improving adherence. In S. Shumaker, E. Schron, & J. Ockene (Eds.), *The handbook of health behavior change* (pp. 5–43). New York: Springer.

Bell, S. (1990). Sociological perspectives on the medicalization of menopause. In M. Flint, F. Kronenberg, & W. Utian. *Multidisciplinary perspectives on menopause.* (pp. 173–178). New York: The New York Academy of Sciences.

Bush, T. (1992). Feminine forever revisited: Menopausal hormone therapy in the 1990's. *Journal of Women's Health, 1,* 1–4.

Bush, T., Barrett-Connor, E., Cowan, L., et al. (1987). Cardiovascular mortality and noncontraceptive use of estrogen in women: Results from the Lipid Research Clinics Program Follow-Up Study. *Circulation, 75,* 1102–1109.

Cauley, J., Cummings, S., Black, D., Mascioli, S., & Seeley, D. (1990). Prevalence and determinants of estrogen replacement therapy in elderly women. *American Journal of Obstetrics and Gynecology, 163,* 1438–1444.

Draper, J., & Roland, M. (1990). Perimenopausal women's views on taking hormone replacement therapy to prevent osteoporosis. *British Medical Journal, 300,* 786–788.

Egeland, G., Kuller, L., Matthews, K., Kelsey, S., Cauley, J., & Guzick, D. (1991). Premenopausal determinants of estrogen use. *Preventive Medicine, 20,* 343–349.

Egeland, G., Matthews, K., Kuller, L., & Kelsey, X. (1988). Characteristics of noncontraceptive hormone users. *Preventive Medicine, 17,* 403–411.

Ferguson, K., Hoegh, C., & Johnson, S. (1989). Estrogen replacement therapy: A survey of women's knowledge and attitudes. *Archives of Internal Medicine, 149,* 133–136.

Gambrell, R. (1987). Use of progesterone therapy. *American Journal of Obstetrics and Gynecology, 256,* 1304–1313.

Grady, D., Rubin, S., Petitti, D., Fox, C., Black, D., Ettinger, B., Ernster, V., & Cummings, S. (1992). Hormone therapy to prevent disease and prolong life in postmenopausal women. *Annals of Internal Medicine, 117*(12), 1016–1037.

Hahn, R. (1989). Compliance considerations with estrogen replacement: Withdrawal bleeding and other factors. *American Journal of Obstetrics and Gynecology, 161,* 1854–1858.

Harris, R., Laws, A., Reddy, V., King, A., & Haskell, W. (1990). Are women using postmenopausal estrogens? A community survey. *American Journal of Public Health, 80,* 1266–1268.

Hemminki, E., Kennedy, D., Baum, C., & McKinlay, M. (1988). Prescribing of noncontraceptive estrogens and progestins in the United States, 1974–1986. *American Journal of Public Health, 78*, 1479–1481.

Henderson, B., Paganini-Hill, A., & Ross, R. (1988). Estrogen replacement therapy and protection from acute myocardial infarction. *American Journal of Obstetrics and Gynecology, 59*, 312–317.

Hunskaar, S., & Backe, B. (1992). Attitudes towards and level of information on perimenopausal and postmenopausal hormone replacement therapy among Norwegian women. *Maturitas, 15*, 183–194.

Kaufert, P. (1986). The menopausal transition: The use of estrogen. *Canadian Journal of Public Health, 77*(1), 86–91.

Kennedy, D., Baum, C., & Forbes, M. (1985). Noncontraceptive estrogens and progestins: Use patterns over time. *Obstetrics and Gynecology, 65*, 441–446.

Koster, A., (1990). Hormone replacement therapy: Use patterns in 51-year-old Danish Women. *Maturitas, 13*, 345–356.

Lindsay, R., Hart, D., MacLean, A., Clark, A., Kraszewski, A., & Garwood, J. (1978). Bone response to termination of estrogen treatment. *Lancet, 1*, 1325–1327.

Logothetis, M. (1991). Women's decisions about estrogen replacement therapy. *Western Journal of Nursing Research, 13*, 458–474.

MacLennon, A., MacLennan, A., & Wilson, D. (1993). The prevalence of oestrogen replacement therapy in South Australia. *Maturitas, 16*, 175–183.

MacPherson, K. (1981). Menopause as disease: The social construction of a metaphor. *Advances in Nursing Science 3*(2), 95–114.

MacPherson, K. (1985). Osteoporosis and menopause: A feminist analysis of the social construction of a syndrome. *Advances in Nursing Science, 7*(4), 11–22.

MacPherson, K. (1992). Cardiovascular disease in women and noncontraceptive use of hormones: A feminist analysis. *Advances in Nursing Science, 14*(4), 34–49.

Matthews, K., Wing, R., Kuller, L., Meilahn, E., Kelsey, S., Costello, E., & Caggiula, A. (1990). Influences of natural menopause on psychological characteristics and symptoms of middle-aged healthy women. *Journal of Consulting and Clinical Psychology, 58*, 345–351.

McKinlay, S., Brambilla, D., & Posner, J. (1992). The normal menopause transition. *Maturitas, 14*, 103–115.

Nachtigall, L. (1990). Enhancing patient compliance with hormone replacement therapy at menopause. *Obstetrics and Gynecology, 74*(4), 77s–80s.

National Institute on Aging. (1993). Workshop on menopause. Bethesda, MD: National Institutes of Health.

National Institutes of Health. (1992). Opportunities for research on women's health. Bethesda, MD: Author.

National Women's Health Network (1989). Taking hormones and women's health: Choices, risks, and benefits. Washington, DC: Author.

O'Leary Cobb, J. (1994). Why women choose not to take hormone therapy. *Women's Health Forum, 3*(3), 1–3.

Oddens, B., Boulet, M., Lehert, P., & Visser, A. (1992). Has the climacteric been medicalized? A study on the use of medication for climacteric complaints in four countries. *Maturitas, 15*, 171–181.

Office of Technology Assessment (1992). The menopause, hormone therapy and women's health. Washington, DC: Author.

Palinkas, L., & Barrett-Connor, E. (1992). Estrogen use and depressive symptoms in postmenopausal women. *Obstetrics and Gynecology, 80*, 30–36.

Pettiti, D., Perlman, J., & Signey, S. (1987). Noncontraceptive estrogens and mortality: Long-term followup of women in the Walnut Creek Study. *Obstetrics and Gynecology, 70*(125), 854–859.

Physician's desk reference. (1993). 47th Ed. (p. 2625) Montvale: Medical Economics Data.

Ravnikar, V. (1987). Compliance with hormone therapy. *American Journal of Obstetrics and Gynecology, 156*, 1332–1334.

Rothert, M., Rover, D., Holmen, M., Schmitt, N., Talarczyk, G., Kroll, J., & Gogate, J. (1990). Women's use of information regarding hormone replacement therapy. *Research in Nursing and Health, 13*, 355–366.

Scalley, E., & Henrich, J. (1993). An overview of estrogen replacement therapy in postmenopausal women. *Journal of Women's Health, 2*(3), 289–294.

Schmitt, N., Gogate, J., Rothert, M., Rovner, D., Holmes, M., Talarczyk, G., Given, B., & Kroll, J. (1991). Capturing and clustering women's judgment policies: The case of hormonal therapy for menopause. *Journal of Gerontology, Psychological Sciences, 46*(3), 92–101.

Spector, T. (1989). Use of estrogen replacement therapy in high risk groups in the United Kingdom. *British Medical Journal, 299*, 1434–1435.

Stampfer, M., Willett, W., Colditz, G., et al. (1985). A prospective study of postmenopausal estrogen therapy and coronary heart disease. *New England Journal of Medicine, 313,* 1044–1049.

Thorne, S. (1990). Constructive noncompliance in chronic illness. *Holistic Nursing Practice, 5*(1), 62–69.

Topo, P., Klaukka, R., Hemminki, E., & Uutela, A. (1991). Use of hormone replacement therapy in 1976–1989 by 45- to 64-year-old Finnish women. *Journal of Epidemiology and Community Health, 45,* 277–280.

Utian, W., & Schiff, I. (1994). NAMS-Gallup survey on women's knowledge, information, sources, and attitudes to menopause and hormone replacement therapy. *Menopause, 1*(1), 39–48.

Wallace, R., Heiss, G., Burrows, B., & Graves, K. (1987). Contrasting diet and body mass among users and nonusers of oral contraceptives and exogenous estrogens: The lipid research clinics program prevalence study. *American Journal of Epidemiology, 125,* 854–859.

Weiss, N., Ure, C., Ballard, J., Williams, A., & Daling, J. (1980). Decreased risk of fractures of the hip and lower forearm with postmenopausal use of estrogen. *New England Journal of Medicine, 303,* 1195–1198.

Wilson, R. (1966). *Feminine forever.* New York: Evans.

Woods, N. (in press). Midlife women's health, use of health services, and hormone therapy. *Analyses of the Commonwealth Fund Survey of Women's Health.*

Wren, B., & Brown, L. (1991). Compliance with hormonal replacement therapy. *Maturitas, 13,* 17–21.

American college of physicians guidelines for counseling postmenopausal women about preventive hormone therapy. (1992). *Annals of Internal Medicine, 117*(12), 1038–1041.

This brief article includes the current guidelines for counseling asymptomatic postmenopausal women about using hormone therapy to prevent disease and prolong life. The article emphasizes that an understanding of the probable risks and benefits of hormone therapy is necessary to assess the potential effects of therapy and participate in the decision about using hormone therapy. It includes four recommendations, with the caveat that they could change with the results of clinical trials.

1. Regardless of race, all women should consider preventive hormone therapy.
2. Women who have had a hysterectomy can use estrogen alone without adding a progestin.
3. Women with coronary heart disease or at increased risk for coronary heart disease are likely to benefit from hormone therapy.
4. Risks of hormone therapy may outweigh the benefits in women with increased risk of breast cancer.

5. For other women, the best course is unclear (see Grady et al. (1992) regarding women with a uterus and women with increased risk of hip fracture).

Recommended hormone regimens, management strategy for evaluation and risk assessment, estimation of benefits and risks of long-term hormone therapy, patient information and education, and the management decision are outlined. Methods of endometrial evaluation include outpatient biopsy, transvaginal ultrasound, and dilation and curettage. Recommendations for surveillance for breast cancer are included. This paper outlines clear guidelines for prescriptive policy, providing information that women will wish to review in making decisions about hormone replacement therapy.

Avis, N., & McKinlay, S. (1991). Health-care utilization among mid-aged women. In M. Flint, F. Kronenberg, & W. Utian (Eds.), Multidisciplinary perspectives on menopause. *Annals of the New York Academy of Sciences, 592,* 228–238.

The investigators compared predictors of utilization of health services for preventing of disease and resolution of problems. Menopause did not increase overall utilization of health services, but did increase problem-oriented use. Because women sought health care for a variety of complaints, it is not possible to conclude that menopause, itself, caused the women to seek health care. Of women 45 to 54 years of age in this population-based study, 9% were using hormone therapy.

Bush, T. (1992). Feminine forever revisited: Menopausal hormone therapy in the 1990s. *Journal of Women's Health, 1,* 1–4.

The author reviews the history of menopausal hormone therapy from the 1960s to the 1990s. She cites studies that support both benefits and risks associated with hormone therapy. This article is an interesting companion paper to MacPherson's (1993) paper, illustrating the differences in interpretation of the history of hormone therapy in the United States.

Cobb, J. (1994). Why women choose not to take hormone therapy. *Women's Health Forum, 3*(3), 1–3.

The author identifies reasons why women choose not to take hormone therapy, noting that little research is published on this subject. The author bases her comments on approximately 7,000 letters received at the publication of *A Friend Indeed,* a newsletter for women in midlife or menopause. She notes that women for whom menopause is a nonevent or who cannot afford the therapy did not write. The majority of women correspondents were knowledgeable about hormone therapy yet they rarely discussed the rationale behind their decisions with their health care provider. The reasons women do not take hormones include the following:

1. Women believe menopause is a natural transition and not a disease to be treated.

2. They do not perceive osteoporosis as a personal threat although they think it may be for other women.

3. Side effects they have experienced or other women whom they know have experienced, discourage them from taking the therapy.

4. Women do not view the use of hormones as a preventive strategy in the same way they view diet and exercise.

5. Women are concerned about the adverse effects of hormones.

6. Breast cancer is perceived as a major threat, given the uncertain effect of estrogen and progestins on breast cancer.

7. When weighing heart disease and breast cancer risk, women wonder if hormone therapy will enable them to live long enough to get breast cancer.

8. Women are not convinced about the value of prolonging life with hormone therapy.

9. Women are concerned about the unexpected long-term consequences of treatment.

Draper, J., & Roland, M. (1990). Perimenopausal women's views on taking hormone replacement therapy to prevent osteoporosis. *British Medical Journal, 300,* 786–788.

Midlife women (84) between 50 to 52 years of age responded to a questionnaire mailed to members of an urban medical practice about using hormone for prevention of osteoporosis. More than 75% were interested in using hormones, but most wanted more information. More than 75% agreed it was important to prevent osteoporosis. More than 50% worried about potential side effects. A few said that continuing menses would dissuade them from using hormones.

Ferguson, K., Hoegh, C., & Johnson, S. (1989). Estrogen replacement therapy: A survey of women's knowledge and attitudes. *Archives of Internal Medicine, 149,* 133–136.

This study examines factors influencing postmenopausal women's decisions about estrogen therapy. Women volunteers recruited from a university community responded to questionnaires about estrogen therapy, menopausal status, knowledge, attitude, and information gaps related to hormone use. Women using estrogen therapy were more likely than nonusers to have had a hysterectomy (61%), to receive their medical care from a gynecologist (57%), and to have a Pap smear at least every two years (76%). These women resembled nonusers with respect to history of birth control pill use, knowledge of friends or family with hip fractures, and concerns regarding osteoporosis. Hormone users were less likely than nonusers to have relatives or friends with uterine cancer. Women using estrogen were more likely than nonusers to believe that a lack of estrogen was related to osteoporosis (89%) or that family history and inactivity were related to osteoporosis. Unfortunately only about 25% of women were aware of the effects of smoking on osteoporosis or that smoking cessation would reduce the risk of osteoporosis. The most unfavorable factor women identified about using estrogen was the onset of menses. Knowing someone who was having difficulty with an estrogen therapy regimen was rated negatively by women regardless of their use of hormones or menopausal status. Women using estrogen were more likely than nonusers to believe that menopause is a medical condition and that women with distressing symptoms should take estrogen. They were more likely than nonusers to disagree that psychological problems were due to life changes and not hormonal changes, that the risks of estrogen therapy outweigh the benefits, and that natural approaches were better than estrogen.

Grady, D., Rubin, S., Petitti, D., Fox, C., Black, D., Ettinger, B., Ernster, V., & Cummings, S. (1992). Hormone therapy to prevent disease and prolong life in postmenopausal women. *Annals of Internal Medicine, 117*(12), 1016–1037.

This article critically reviews risks and benefits of hormone therapy for asymptomatic postmenopausal women who are considering long-term hormone therapy to prevent disease or to prolong life. The authors review literature since 1970 regarding the effect of estrogen therapy and estrogen plus progestin on endometrial cancer, breast cancer, coronary heart disease, osteoporosis, and stroke. Using meta-analytic techniques, they pool estimates from studies, identify relative risks for selected diseases in hormone users, and develop methods to estimate changes in life expectancy related to hormone therapy. The results suggest that estrogen decreases risk for coronary heart disease and hip fracture, but long-term estrogen therapy increases risk for endometrial cancer and, to a smaller degree, breast cancer. Although the use of progestin probably decreases the risk of endometrial cancer, effects of combination therapy on risk for other diseases have not been studied adequately. This article provides a thorough review of the potential risks and benefits of hormone therapy and thus would provide useful information for women considering hormone therapy.

Hunskaar, S., & Backe, B. (1992). Attitudes toward and level of information on perimenopausal and postmenopausal hormone replacement therapy among Norwegian women. *Maturitas, 15,* 183–194.

When Norwegian women over 17 years of age (1019) were interviewed as part of a national opinion poll of women's attitudes and information about hormone therapy, 34% of the sample identified women magazines as the most important source of information on hormone therapy. Only women over 45 years of age mentioned their physician as an important source of information. Friends or relatives and physicians were mentioned at a similar rate (19%). Women who believed they had a high level of information had a positive attitude toward hormone therapy. Women who received information from a physician were more positive about hormone therapy than those who received information elsewhere. The majority were unsure about potential adverse effects of hormone therapy, but approximately 22% to 24% believed hormone therapy increased the risk of heart attack, stroke, breast cancer, and cancer in general. Women who believed that hormone therapy increased risk of serious disease were more likely than others to have a negative attitude toward using hormones. Women felt more positive about using hormones for preventing osteoporosis and for postmenopausal urogenital complaints than for treating menopausal symptoms such as hot flashes.

Johnson, S., & Ferguson, K. (1993). Making a reasoned choice about hormone replacement therapy. In J. Callahan (Ed.), *Menopause: A midlife passage* (pp. 136–144). Bloomington: Indiana University Press.

This thorough discussion of the long-term use of hormone therapy includes a review of risks and benefits in easily accessible terms. The authors summarize the results of their earlier study (see Ferguson, Hoegh, & Johnson, 1989). Their presentation of the risks and benefits is from the perspective of a physician (first author) who has been involved with large clinical trials.

Kaufert, P. (1986). The menopausal transition: The use of estrogen. *Canadian Journal of Public Health, 77*(1), 86–91.

Questionnaires from a community-based sample of 2,500 Canadian women 40 to 59 years of age were analyzed to determine the rate of estrogen use and its relationship with menopausal status, menopausal symptom experience, and patterns of use over time. While 27% of women who had a hysterectomy were given a prescription for estrogen, only 10% of those who were perimenopausal and 18% who were postmenopausal had received a prescription. Having hot flashes and reporting them to a physician was associated with estrogen use. Followup over 4 years revealed that some women used estrogen intermittently, and the majority who used estrogen on one occasion reporting they were not using it on the next. The women's reasons for discontinuing their estrogen therapy merit further attention but are not presented in this report.

Lichtman, R. (1991). Perimenopausal hormone replacement therapy: Review of the literature. *Journal of Nurse-Midwifery, 36*(1), 30–48.

This review article about HRT use includes an overview of the history of estrogen alone and HRT use in the U.S. and therapeutic uses. Specific uses discussed are for hot flashes, genital tissue changes, skin changes, and affective symptoms. Also reviewed are potential benefits such as prevention of osteoporosis and cardiovascular disease. The issue of mixed findings relating breast cancer and

HRT use is addressed, as well as some adverse side effects and possible contraindications.

Logothetis, M. (1993). Disease or development: Women's perceptions of menopause and the need for hormone replacement therapy. In J. Callahan (Ed.), *Menopause: A midlife passage* (pp. 123–135). Bloomington: Indiana University Press.

The author presents qualitative data obtained from women who participated in a study of their use of hormone therapy. Quotations capture the richness of the women's skepticism about hormone therapy's effectiveness: "Why cause a bigger problem?" Current hormone users voiced concerns and reservations, including having "mixed feelings," worry about breast cancer; however, some women were firmly convinced of the value of hormone therapy. The voices of women in this study will sound familiar to many women who face a decision about taking hormone therapy.

Logothetis, M. (1991). Women's decisions about estrogen replacement therapy. *Western Journal of Nursing Research, 13*, 458–474.

The focus of the study was women's beliefs about menopause and their decision-making process regarding hormone therapy. When factors such as perceived levels of menopausal distress, susceptibility, seriousness, benefits, barriers, and philosophical orientation to menopause were controlled for in the sample, the investigator hypothesized that there would be significant differences between users and nonusers of hormone therapy. Women volunteers from a suburban community (252) between 40 and 60 years of age completed mailed questionnaires. Women who had bilateral oophorectomy were excluded from the study. This well-educated middle- to upper-income sample reported using hormones at rates resembling those found in other studies. More women who had hysterectomies (42%) were users than those who had not. The majority of women taking hormones for symptom relief

had done so for a short time, less than 2 years (75%). Only 10% mentioned prevention of heart disease or osteoporosis as a reason for using hormones. Scales used in the study reflected dimensions of the health belief model: susceptibility, seriousness, benefits, and barriers. Another scale measured philosophical orientation to menopause. Perceived benefits and barriers were most influential in differentiating women who used hormones from those who did not. Philosophical orientation to menopause also differentiated the two groups: women who used hormones had a view of menopause as a medical event rather than a developmental event. There was no difference between groups regarding seriousness of the consequences of menopause or susceptibility. These findings suggest that women's perceptions of benefits and risks associated with hormone therapy and barriers to its use, taken together with their philosophical orientation to menopause, are important in distinguishing those using hormone therapy from those who do not.

MacLennon, A., MacLennan, A., & Wilson, D. (1993). The prevalence of oestrogen replacement therapy in South Australia. *Maturitas, 16*, 175–183.

South Australian women (1047) over the age of 40 were interviewed regarding their use of hormone therapy. Although 13.6% were using estrogen therapy, 24% had used it at one time. The most prevalent use was among women aged 45 to 54 years. Hormone users were more likely than nonusers to have the following characteristics: (1) born in the United Kingdom or Ireland; (2) middle income earners; (3) intermediate education; (4) recent visits to a general practitioner; (5) in a current relationship; (6) previously had a hysterectomy; and (7) nonsmokers. Most women had used hormones for 1 to 5 years and a few for as long as 30 years. Past users had stopped using estrogen 6 months after first use, usually because of side effects. The most common reasons for estrogen use were post-hysterectomy treatment, symptom management, and reduction of the risk of osteoporosis. Only 4% of the women used estrogen to reduce the risk of heart attack or stroke. The current estrogen users were most aware of the short-term benefits.

MacPherson, K. (1993). The false promises of hormone replacement therapy and current dilemmas. In J. Callahan (Ed.), *Menopause: A midlife passage* (pp. 145–159). Bloomington: Indiana University Press.

The author reviews three false promises about the benefits of hormone therapy made to women by biomedical researchers, physicians, mass media, and pharmaceutical companies. These include the promise of eternal beauty and femininity (1966–1975), the promise of a safe, symptom-free menopause (1975–1981), and the promise of escape from chronic disease (1980 to present). MacPherson discusses the reasoning that was used to persuade women to use hormone therapy and concludes by questioning current efforts to use this therapy for the prevention of disease in healthy older women.

The following citations amplify some of MacPherson's analysis and may be useful for women and their health care providers in assessing their values about hormone therapy.

MacPherson, K. (1992). Cardiovascular disease in women and noncontraceptive use of hormones: A feminist analysis. *Advances in Nursing Science, 14*(4), 34–49.

Using a feminist lens, the author evaluates the use of hormone therapy as a measure to prevent cardiovascular disease.

MacPherson, K. (1981). Menopause as disease: The social construction of a metaphor. *Advances in Nursing Science, 3*(2), 95–114.

This historical analysis of how menopause was constructed as a disease addresses the changing perspective about menopause that predated and followed the introduction of hormone therapy.

MacPherson, K. (1985). Osteoporosis and menopause: A feminist analysis of the social construction of a syndrome. *Advances in Nursing Science, 7*(4), 11–22.

This article is a feminist analysis of use of hormone therapy to prevent osteoporosis.

Mansfield, P., & Voda, A. (1994). Hormone use among middle-aged women: Results of a three-year study. *Menopause, 1*, 99–108.

The investigators surveyed 291 perimenopausal women (35–55 years of age, mean age 46) over a 3-year period from across the United States using mailed questionnaire. The purpose of the study was to determine patterns of hormone use among perimenopausal women. Women were identified from the Tremin Trust Database and from alumnae listings from an eastern university. Most (75%) of the women were not using hormone replacement during the course of the study. The proportion of women using hormones rose from 9% to 21.6% over the 3-year study (1990–1992), with 1% stopping use each year. Women who used hormones were satisfied with the therapy. Their reasons for starting to take hormones included: menstrual cycle changes (29% to 41% over the three years), health provider recommendations (25% to 71%), hot flashes (16% to 71%), emotional changes (6% to 12%), appearance (0% to 12%), vaginal dryness (0% to 12%), and sleep problems (0% to 41%). Women who did not use hormones perceived no need (over 80% each year), did not like the idea of taking hormones (28%), and could not take hormones (as many as 16%). Six women who quit taking hormones did so because they did not perceive they needed them or because they experienced undesirable side effects. Although most women perceived no need to use hormones, they did experience changes that were related to menopause: a change in menstrual cycle (74%), emotional changes (33%), PMS (11%), sexual response changes (37%), body changes (61%), hot flashes (22%), and vaginal dryness (39%). Women who chose not to take hormones prescribed by their physician rejected the therapy because they did not perceive it was needed or did not like the idea of taking hormones. This survey provides an excellent review of predominantly Caucasian women's experiences with hormone therapy. Three explanations for discrepancy in physician enthusiasm and women's lack of enthusiasm for adopting hormone therapy included women's beliefs about menopause as a normal process, concern about side effects, and physician-patient relationships that did not include exchange of information that would help women make decisions about their care. These considerations should be helpful to health professionals as they determine appropriate ways to support women who face the decision to use hormone replacement.

National Women's Health Network. (1989). Taking hormones and women's health: Choices, risks, and benefits. Washington, DC: Author.

This review was conducted prior to the publication of more recent information about hormone therapy and the prevention of heart disease and osteoporosis. Written by a panel of scientists and women's health activists, this report provides comprehensive background information about use of hormone therapy and also outlines salient points that women should consider in making their decisions.

Office of Technology Assessment. (1992). The menopause, hormone therapy and women's health. Washington, DC: Author.

An extensive review of published works about the use of hormone therapy for menopause.

Rothert, M., Padoonu, G., Holmes-Rovner, M., Kroll, J., Talarczyk, G., Rovner, D., Schmitt, N., & Breer, L. (1994). Menopausal women as decision makers in health care. *Experimental Gerontology, 29*(3–4), 463–468.

Preliminary findings from a study testing an educational intervention to aid menopausal women in making decisions about HRT and self care suggest that women are impeded in their decision-making due to inadequate information about the possible costs and benefits of HRT for them and about self care measures to deal with menopause-related symptoms. Also women are not given opportunities to fully participate in decision-making with their health care providers.

Rothert, M., Rover, D., Holmen, M., Schmitt, N., Talarczyk, G., Knoll, J., & Gogate, J. (1990). Women's use of information regarding hormone replacement therapy. *Research in Nursing and Health, 13,* 355–366.

Women community volunteers 45 to 55 years of age (283), with an intact uterus, and not using hormone replacement completed 16 written case studies to identify their decision-making processes about cancer risk, osteoporosis risk, and the severity of hot flashes in their theoretical choice of hormone therapy. Women's policies about hormone therapy were influenced largely by a desire to relieve symptom distress associated with hot flashes and to a lesser extent a desire to reduce the risk of osteoporosis and/or a concern about the side effects of estrogen therapy. Women's responses to the case studies were sorted into groups. The largest group expressed a desire to reduce the incidence of hot flashes alone. The second group expressed the desire to control hot flashes and reduce the risk of osteoporosis. And the third group was concerned with hot flashes, osteoporosis, and also the side effects of estrogen/progestin therapy. These results emphasize the differences in women's concerns about using hormones and support the need to tailor counselling approaches to individual women's concerns.

Schmitt, N., Gogate, J., Rothert, M., Rovner, D., Holmes, M., Talarczyk, G., Given, B., & Kroll, J. (1991). Capturing and clustering women's judgment policies: The case of hormonal therapy for menopause. *Journal of*

Gerontology, Psychological Sciences, 46(3), 92–101.

Midlife women (275) recruited from churches and civic organizations, who had not had a hysterectomy and who were not using hormone therapy, rated 32 case studies to identify their policies about using estrogen or combined hormone therapy. Women's ratings sorted into four clusters:

1. Those who would take hormones if hot flashes were severe;

2. Those who would use hormones if hot flashes were severe, but would consider the risk of osteoporosis and cancer in making their decisions;

3. Those who were most influenced by the unpleasant effects of adding progestin to the hormone therapy; and

4. Those who considered health risks, particularly the risk of cancer.

Educational level, perceived stress, and attitudes toward menopause and use of medications differentiated the groups. Women in the second group had the most formal education, higher stress levels, and were more likely to use vitamins. Women in the third group (concerned about the negative effects of progestin use) had the most positive attitudes toward menopause. In all cases, prediction of willingness to take hormones was related to knowledge about menopause and its effect and the perception that hormone therapy would be helpful in symptom management. Women who expected menopause to be difficult were less likely to take hormone therapy. Comfort level was an important concern in women's choices. These results are informative about how women weigh risks and benefits, but they were derived from case studies and as such may not fully reflect women's real life decisions.

The Writing Group of the PEPI Trial (1995). Effects of estrogen or estrogen/progestin regimens on heart disease risk factors in postmenopausal women: The postmenopausal estrogen/progestin interventions (PEPI) trial. *Journal of the American Medical Association, 273*(3), 199–208.

The PEPI Trial results (Postmenopausal Estrogen/Progestin Interventions) have been eagerly awaited. This study was a 3 year multicenter randomized, double-blind, placebo-controlled trial that assessed pairwise differences between placebo, unopposed estrogen, and each of 3 different oral estrogen/progestin regimens on risk factors for heart disease in 875 healthy postmenopausal women aged 45 to 64. Heart disease risk factors were HDL, systolic blood pressure, serum insulin as a measure of carbohydrate metabolism, and fibrinogen to reflect coagulation. When each of the drug regimens were analyzed, HDL increased most with estrogen alone, but all the other regimens did significantly better than the placebo group, particularly the one that included cyclic micronized progesterone. All treatment regimens lowered LDL by about 10% over placebo. There were no changes in blood pressure, post oral glucose challenge insulin levels, and fibrinogen levels with any of the treatment regimens. However, there was a significant increase in 2 hour glucose levels compared with the placebo for all regimens containing a progestin. For the placebo group fibrinogen levels rose significantly compared with all active treatment regimens. There was no increase in breast cancer during the 3 years with any active treatment groups. Uterine cancer did increase significantly in women with a uterus treated with estrogen alone. Further study is needed to determine if the use of HRT will decrease cardiovascular disease in women and for how long women need to take HRT to obtain maximum benefit.

Utian, W., & Schiff, I. (1994). NAMS-Gallup survey on women's knowledge, information, sources, and attitudes to menopause and hormone replacement therapy. *Menopause 1*(1), 39–48.

Authors report the results of the North American Menopause Society's sponsored

Gallup poll of 833 women, age 45 to 60 years. The poll was conducted to identify women's attitudes and experience with menopause, and the various forms of hormone therapy they use. The sample included Black, Native American, and Asian American women, but the results were not broken down by ethnic groups. Although most women were aware that their bodies produce estrogen (83%), fewer women were aware that they also produced progesterone (46%) and androgen (20%). Most were aware that menopause was associated with a drop in estrogen, and fewer women were aware of the drop in progesterone. Although 84% of women who had seen a physician regarding their menopause reported their physician discussed hormone therapy with them, less than 2% indicated that the physician had discussed exercise, proper nutrition, medications, vitamins, calcium, hysterectomy, relaxation techniques, and vaginal creams. At the time of the survey, 34% of the women were taking hormone therapy, 8% had done so in the past, and 58% had never taken hormone therapy. Fifty-three percent of women who had a hysterectomy were taking hormone therapy, and of the women who had not had a hysterectomy 21% were taking hormone therapy. Of the women who had stopped taking hormone therapy, 34% had done so because of side effects, 18% because of their concern about cancer, especially breast cancer, 14% said the problem they used it for had resolved, and 11% did not need hormone therapy. In addition six percent stopped therapy due to cost and an additional 6% cited weight gain as reasons for discontinuing therapy. Fifteen percent of women indicated that they had been offered a prescription for hormones but that they refused or decided not to take it. These women indicated that side effects (35%) and concern about cancer (28%) were reasons they had not taken the medication. In addition a smaller percent said they did not want to take medication every day, did not think it was necessary, or it did not help. Women's concerns about weight gain, ability to tolerate the minimal symptoms and experiencing menstruation were disincentives. Although 41% thought menopause was the main reason for hormone therapy, 38% and 34% respectively said that prevention of osteoporosis and/or heart disease was the most important reason. About 30% indicated that using hormones would improve the quality of their lives. Although the results of this survey are informative about short term use of hormone therapy, more information is needed about women's decisions to use long-term hormone therapy.

Wren, B., Brown, L. (1991). Compliance with hormonal replacement therapy. *Maturitas, 13,* 17–21.

The investigators surveyed postmenopausal women (100) who were prescribed hormone therapy 12 months after their first visit. The purpose of the study was to identify how many women followed through with hormone replacement. Of the 79 women who returned questionnaires, 61% were taking hormone therapy, 27% had stopped, and 12% could not be determined. Major reasons for ceasing therapy were the return of menstrual bleeding, fear of developing cancer, and other long-term complications.

Chapter 2

Women's Sexuality

Linda A. Bernhard

Analyzing publications during any brief period, about *any* topic, can be misleading. However, this analysis of publications about women's sexuality exclusively during 1993 to mid-1994 demonstrates an unfortunate fact: little has changed. The majority of citations in this review concern women's sexuality with regard to illness or sexual dysfunction, and perpetuate a medical and/or male definition and control of women's sexuality. This is a book about women's *health*. Sexuality is a part of health; it is, of course, also influenced by illness, but much more than descriptions of sexual implications of illness is required for a comprehensive understanding of women's sexuality. Needed here are data adequate to represent how the diversity of women experience sexuality in the normalcy of their lives.

Just as it is difficult to define and describe health, it is difficult to define and describe sexuality. Most extant definitions of sexuality and women's sexuality are male-oriented, and both women and men have been well socialized to understand women's sexuality in that particular way, whether or not it is their experience. Two articles in this review (Daniluk, 1993; McCarthy, 1993) demonstrate that women define their sexuality from a male perspective.

Despite efforts of feminists and women's health activists to redefine sexuality in ways and language that are female-oriented, much of their work does not reach the majority of women. Furthermore, much feminist writing on sexuality is theoretical rather than descriptive. Some writers accomplish both goals, which is highly desirable. Ogden's book (1994), for example, is written for a general audience. The author has since appeared on popular television programs, making her book available to large audiences of women and men. In contrast, Holland and her colleagues published several research articles from their study of young women and AIDS prevention in England. Two articles were abstracted in the previous edition of this book. Their article in this review (Holland, Ramazanoglu, Sharpe, & Thomson, 1994) is more theoretical; they have moved their analysis to a higher level.

The articles in this review are limited in diversity. Although it is exciting to have two articles about women in Nigeria, there are no articles on African American, Hispanic, or Asian American women. The only article about lesbians studies them in comparison with heterosexual women. There are no articles on bisexuals or transsexuals. Capturing published articles on women's sexuality over one time period is just that. More representation, greater value attributed to it, and substantive discussion of all the diversity of women's sexuality are still to come as evidence that society truly values women and women's sexuality.

IMPLICATIONS

From a review of this body of literature related to women's sexuality, two questions emerge: (1) Is this information needed? and (2) How will this information benefit women? The first question, which calls into issue the motivations of the authors/researchers, is immediately answered with a message of academic freedom. Persons can study, theorize, and write about whatever they wish. Yet, ideally, persons interested in women's sexuality would be answering the second question affirmatively: their work would benefit women. The implications of the work in this review should benefit women in one or more of three classic areas: education, practice (or service), and research.

Education

The articles in this review provide data that can be incorporated in the education of health care professionals—physicians, nurses, and social workers and others. New and expanding research data should be reflected in what students are taught about women's sexuality.

The articles also have implications for the broader teaching of women's health and sexuality, for example, in women's studies or biology courses. Prinz and Caliendo (1988) described an academic course on women's sexuality in which the main goal was women-oriented redefinition of sexuality. In teaching their course, the authors sought to provide a space where women students could come together and reflect on their own sexuality in other-than-traditional ways. Women must reflect critically about what is known and not known with regard to women's sexuality, so that new ideas can emerge.

The article by Brock and Jennings (1993) has implications for sex education of young women. Because women were not taught positively about sexuality by their mothers, quality programs that give comprehensive sex education to women of all ages are needed.

Practice

Practice refers to service directly to clients—in this case, women. Providers include psychologists, alcohol and rehabilitation counselors, and other health professionals. Some writers (e.g., Andersen & Elliot, 1993) offer useful guides for assessment and intervention with women who have various health problems. Providers should consider incorporating these guides into their practice. Many specific findings, such as recognition that women with borderline personality may have a history of child sexual abuse, can be incorporated immediately into practice.

Practice, in the context of women's health and sexuality, can also mean activism. Several studies in this review demonstrate that women in laboratory settings have physiological arousal (i.e., lubrication) in response to "erotic films." Yet activists may wonder whether this finding is significant for women's sexuality. More concerned with issues of pornography and violence against women, activists may suggest that even the use of women in such research is abuse of women. Activists may practice in many different ways (e.g., writing letters to the editors of journals that publish these studies) to raise awareness and work for change concerning similar issues.

Research

The majority of articles in this review are reports of research; consequently, there are many implications for future research. Researchers in the area of women's sexuality should review all related literature to place studies in the context of what is already known. These articles indicate that some researchers have not done that. For example, numerous studies in this review, and others extant in a variety of disciplines, including medicine, nursing, psychology, and sociology, focus on the effects of hysterectomy and menopause on women's sexuality. The research published shows that the researchers themselves have not read studies in other disciplines.

Among the many reasons why researchers should read broadly, across disciplines, are: a need for critical reviews and/or meta-analyses of extant research on particular topics, such as the effects of diabetes on women's sexuality; avoidance of limitations that others recognized and of repetitive studies; identification of research tools/measures to use in further studies, so that results can be effectively compared; and, perhaps most important, identification of extant research that contributes toward pooled, comprehensive information about women's sexuality that will be useful to women first, and then to educators, practitioners, and other researchers.

More research must be conducted about women's sexuality. In topical areas where few studies have been published (e.g., urinary incontinence), more work should be done; in areas where there are many descriptive studies (e.g., hysterectomy), intervention studies should be initiated to determine whether women can be assisted with potential changes in their sexuality caused by health problems and/or treatments for those problems. Finally, there is great need for more research that allows women of all ages, races, sexual orientations, cultures, and abilities, to describe their own sexuality, in the hope of establishing definitions of women's sexuality that belong to women.

REFERENCES

Prinz, B., & Caliendo, C. L. (1988). Putting women first: The teaching of female sexuality. *Journal of Sex Education and Therapy, 14,* 17–22.

BOOKS

Lees, S. (1993). *Sugar and spice: Sexuality and adolescent girls.* New York: Penguin Books.

Interviews with British adolescent girls and boys form the basis of this book. The author is concerned that a sexual double standard still exists, and that young people continue to be socialized into it, especially through language. The issues of friendship, love and marriage, education and sex education, and violence are all interrogated for the impact they have on the development of sexuality in adolescent girls. Finally, the author discusses strategies of resistance that adolescent girls may learn, but worries that the use of these strategies may result in further violence by adolescent boys as they try to retain the status quo. Although the book is about British adolescents, and some of the language is not common to U.S. adolescents, the content is extremely applicable and can be used in a variety of contexts to discuss female sexuality.

McNeill, P., Freeman, B., & Newman, J. (Eds.). (1992). *Women talk sex.* London: Scarlet Press.

In the autobiographical writings of 20 women about their sexual histories, the women's individual voices and definitions of sexuality are heard and discussed; consequently, a great variety of topics are addressed. The women represent a diverse group by age, race, and sexual orientation. Their stories, told with frankness and thought, allow readers to add their own definitions and engage in discussion.

Ogden, G. (1994). *Women who love sex.* New York: Pocket Books.

Many women do love sex, but for different reasons and in many ways that are different from those men have traditionally prescribed for women. Women do define their own sexuality: that is the message of this book, written by a self-defined feminist sexologist and therapist. From talking with hundreds of women about their sex lives, the author created six composite characters who tell the stories of women who love sex. This book will be of interest to anyone interested in women's sexuality.

O'Sullivan, S., & Parmar, P. (1992). *Lesbians talk (safer) sex.* London: Scarlet Press.

This little book was written primarily for British lesbians. Controversy still exists about woman-to-woman sexual transmission of HIV, and the authors present information about both sides of the argument. Safer sex, they believe, can be discussed only in a context of open discussion about sexuality in general. The book presents clear and specific information about sexual activities and the risk of HIV. Numerous referral sources in Great Britain are presented.

Taylor, D., & Sumrall, A. C. (Eds.). (1993). *The time of our lives: Women write on sex after 40.* Freedom, CA: Crossing Press.

After the editors published *Women of the 14th Moon: Writings on Menopause,* they still had a large number of submissions that focused on sexuality, so they decided to edit another book. This collection includes 66 stories, poems, and essays written by midlife and older women about sexuality. The pieces are as diverse as their authors—fiction and nonfiction, heterosexual and lesbian, humorous and sad. The book is a delightful collection of women's

experiences, thoughts, and feelings about sexuality during the aging process.

ARTICLES

Andersen, B. L., & Elliot, M. L. (1993). Sexuality for women with cancer: Assessment, theory, and treatment. *Sexuality and Disability, 11*(1), 7–37.

The first part of this article is an excellent review of various kinds of cancer and their potential impact on women's sexuality. The second part presents a comprehensive framework for assessment and approaches to treatment of these problems. The authors have written an outstanding article that can be read and understood by health care providers, women with cancer, and the women's families.

Bellerose, S. B., & Binik, Y. M. (1993). Body image and sexuality in oophorectomized women. *Archives of Sexual Behavior, 22*(5), 435–459.

This study was undertaken to test hypotheses that women who have oophorectomies without hormone replacement have more mood, body image, and sexuality difficulties than women who do not undergo the procedure. Results showed negative effects of oophorectomy on sexual desire and subjective—but not physiological—arousal. There were no differences in mood, but body image differences were observed between the women who had had hysterectomy and the nonhysterectomized women. The authors urge health care providers to inform women, prior to hysterectomy and oophorectomy, that changes in desire and arousal could occur; this possibility often is not communicated.

Brock, L. J., & Jennings, G. H. (1993). Sexuality education: What daughters in their 30s wish their mothers had told them. *Family Relations, 42*(1), 61–65.

In this provocative study, women born between 1951 and 1960 were asked what they remembered their mothers had told them about sexuality and what they wished their mothers had told them. The women's mothers had told them very little, and what they were told was very negative. They wished for open, comfortable, positive discussions about both the physical and the emotional aspects of sexuality. Interestingly, the women consistently gave excuses for their mothers' incomplete discussions, but reported that they wanted to do better in the teaching of their own daughters. This study demonstrates that sexuality education by mothers of baby boomers was not adequate, and a cycle of inadequate education of another generation may well be repeated.

Clark, A., & Romm, J. (1993). Effect of urinary incontinence on sexual activity in women. *Journal of Reproductive Medicine, 38*(9), 679–683.

A survey (the tool is included in the article) of 32 women attending a urodynamics clinic shows the significant impact of three types of incontinence on these women's sexual activities, including all phases of the sexual response cycle. The authors suggest a model for intervention to assist women with these problems.

Cull, A., Cowie, V. J., Farquharson, D. I. M., Livingstone, J. R. B., Smart, G. E., & Elton, R. A. (1993). Early stage cervical cancer: Psychosocial and sexual outcomes of treatment. *British Journal of Cancer, 68*(6), 1216–1220.

British women who were 3 to 5 years post-treatment for stage IB cervical carcinoma completed a survey about their present health and sexuality status. Many complaints persisted, and only 40% of the sample had resumed their full pre-illness range of activities. About 75% of the women were sexually active; half of these reported deterioration in their sexual function. Women who had had radiation therapy were more likely than women who had had

surgery to report dyspareunia and loss of sexual pleasure, but there were no other differences in sexuality between treatment groups. The women reported difficulties in communication and lack of emotional support—though adequate practical help—from their partners. The authors note, with disappointment, the fairly negative outcomes for this group of women whose cancer is probably cured.

Daniluk, J. C. (1993). The meaning and experience of female sexuality. *Psychology of Women Quarterly, 17,* 53–69.

In this report of a group of 10 Canadian women, plus the researcher, each participant tells the story of her sexual and reproductive history. The group met for 2 ½ to 3 hours per week for 11 weeks. The themes generated from analysis of the tape-recorded sessions were: (1) the structural and institutional sources (medicine, religion, sexual violence, media) that the women believed had helped them to construct their sexuality, and (2) the events they pointed to as having defined their sexuality (sexual expression, reproduction, body image, intimate relationships). Although the author notes that both positive and negative themes emerged, the majority were negative, suggesting unpleasant life experiences of these women. No conclusion is drawn on whether they are typical.

Darling, C. A., & McKoy-Smith, Y. M. (1993). Understanding hysterectomies: Sexual satisfaction and quality of life. *Journal of Sex Research, 30*(4), 324–335.

The Family Stress Theory was used to test a causal model of sexual satisfaction and quality of life. Women who had had hysterectomies were compared with women who had not had hysterectomies. The model was better at predicting quality of life than sexual satisfaction. In women who had had hysterectomies, the strongest predictor of sexual satisfaction was physiological health; in women who had not had hysterectomies, the strongest predictor was psychological health. In both groups, fewer physiological or psychological stressors were predictive of higher sexual satisfaction. The results suggest a need for further research into both physiological and psychological stressors and their relationship to women's sexuality.

Davidson, J. K., Sr., & Darling, C. A. (1993). Masturbatory guilt and sexual responsiveness among post-college-age women: Sexual satisfaction revisited. *Journal of Sex and Marital Therapy, 19*(4), 289–300.

The source for this article is a massive survey of the sexual behavior of a nonrandom national sample of registered nurses, conducted by the authors. Survey results are compared with two perspectives on women's sexuality: (1) the sexual autonomy model of the 1970s and (2) the traditional "vaginal imperative." Eighty-nine percent of the women in the study reported masturbation, and 66% rarely or never felt guilty about it. The authors conclude that the remaining 34% have accepted the vaginal imperative.

Dennerstein, L., Gotts, G., Brown, J. B., Morse, C. A., Farley, T. M. M., & Pinol, A. (1994). The relationship between the menstrual cycle and female sexual interest in women with PMS complaints and volunteers. *Psychoneuroendocrinology, 19*(3), 293–304.

Participants in this research were Australian women with complaints of premenstrual syndrome, and healthy volunteers. Women were prospectively studied during two consecutive menstrual cycles. Results showed that sexual interest was significantly higher during the follicular and ovulatory phases of the menstrual cycle—the times of potentially greatest fertility. Feelings of well-being co-occurred with sexual interest. Results of this study can be used to educate women about pregnancy prevention or promotion, as well as about fostering sexual relationships.

Dunning, P. (1993). Sexuality and women with diabetes. *Patient Education and Counseling, 21*, 5–14.

The author reviews the literature on sexuality and diabetes, notes the conflicting results, and concludes that women with diabetes need counseling. Helpful approaches for providers who assess and counsel these women are described.

Gavaler, J. S., Rizzo, A., Rossaro, L., Van Thiel, D. H., Brezza, E., & Deal, S. R. (1993). Sexuality of alcoholic women with menstrual cycle function: Effects of duration of alcohol abstinence. *Alcoholism: Clinical and Experimental Research, 17*(4), 778–781.

Alcoholism results in sexual dysfunction in women, and improvement is reported following sobriety. This retrospective study, conducted with menstruating women in one treatment program in Italy, showed that sexual desire, arousal, and orgasmic ability improved dramatically within 6 months of sobriety. Other research with postmenopausal women showed a much longer time for return of sexual function. The authors note, appropriately, that because these findings may not be representative of the population of sober alcoholic women, more research is needed.

Helstrom, L., Lundberg, P. O., Sorbom, D., & Backstrom, T. (1993). Sexuality after hysterectomy: A factor analysis of women's sexual lives before and after subtotal hysterectomy. *Obstetrics and Gynecology, 81*(3), 357–362.

These authors conducted a prospective study to determine the effects of subtotal hysterectomy, which has become common in Scandinavia, on sexuality. Using statistical manipulations, they determined that five variables together—(1) frequency of desire, (2) coital frequency, (3) cyclicity of desire, (4) orgasm frequency, and (5) multiplicity of orgasm—were the most predictive of sexuality outcomes in these women. Overall, 50% of the women who underwent subtotal hysterectomy reported improved sexual functioning, 29% did not change, and 21% reported deterioration. The authors suggest preoperative counseling that deals with the five factors they identified.

Holland, J., Ramazanoglu, C., Sharpe, S., & Thomson, R. (1994). Power and desire: The embodiment of female sexuality. *Feminist Review, 46,* 21–38.

These authors, who interviewed 150 young (16–21 years) women in England, argue that the female material body cannot simply be dichotomized with the social meanings and management of the socially constructed feminine body. This inability to separate the physical from the social makes it extremely difficult for young women to negotiate heterosexual encounters and to practice safer sex. The young women with whom the authors talked tended most to disembody and detach themselves from their physical bodies; yet, the tension of their physical bodies and their social interactions with men require their ability to be in control of their bodies. Men continue to exercise power over women with regard to sexuality, as well as in other areas of life. The authors believe that embodiment of female sexuality is necessary, but not sufficient, to dismantle male power.

Hulter, B., & Lundberg, P. O. (1994). Sexual function in women with hypothalamo-pituitary disorders. *Archives of Sexual Behavior, 23*(2), 171–183.

These authors studied the impact of a variety of hypothalamo-pituitary disorders on the sexuality of 48 Swedish women, ages 17–57 (median = 42 years). For most of the women, symptoms of the disorder began at a young age, with menstrual difficulties. Forty-five of the women reported lack of sexual desire, lubrication and orgasmic difficulties, and other significant sexual problems. The authors speculate about the importance of normal androgen levels versus regular versus menstrual cycles as

causative of these problems, but more research is needed.

Hurlbert, D. F., & Apt, C. (1993). Female sexuality: A comparative study between women in homosexual and heterosexual relationships. *Journal of Sex and Marital Therapy, 19*(4), 315–327.

In this very quantitative study, partnered lesbians were compared with partnered heterosexual women on a number of sexuality variables. Lesbians reported greater interpersonal dependency, compatibility, and intimacy; heterosexual women reported greater fantasy, sexual assertiveness, desire, and more frequent sexual activity. No differences in sexual satisfaction or sexual narcissism were found between the groups, suggesting that measures of sexual desire and frequency of sex, often used in sex research, may be appropriate for heterosexual women but not for lesbians. The authors suggest the results reflect an essential femininity in lesbians.

Hurlbert, D. F., Apt, C., & Rabehl, S. M. (1993). Key variables to understanding female sexual satisfaction: An examination of women in nondistressed marriages. *Journal of Sex and Marital Therapy, 19*(2), 154–165.

Although this study is limited by its sample of military wives in first marriages, the results are quite interesting and support a female, rather than male, definition of sexuality. In far too much research, women's sexuality and sexual satisfaction have been determined only with the frequency of intercourse and number of orgasms, or, more recently, with the experience of desire and arousal. This study demonstrates that women's sexual satisfaction is also dependent on other variables: sexual assertiveness, sexual attitudes, and, especially, relationship closeness.

Hurlbert, D. F., Apt, C., & White, L. C. (1992). An empirical examination into the sexuality of women with borderline personality disorder. *Journal of Sex and Marital Therapy, 18*(3), 231–242.

Women are more likely than men to be diagnosed with borderline personality disorder. The behavior pattern of people with borderline is often chaotic and includes intense but stormy relationships. In an attempt to understand some of this pattern, the authors compared women with borderline personality with a matched group of women who did not have borderline personality, on a number of sexuality variables. Borderline women had significantly greater sexual assertiveness, erotophilia, sexual esteem, sexual preoccupation, sexual depression, sexual dissatisfaction, sexual boredom, and relationship problems, and were more likely to have extramarital affairs than nonborderline women. The most important explanation for these results was that the borderline women were more likely to have experienced child sexual abuse, and many of these behaviors have been documented as more prevalent in women who have experienced sexual abuse. Further research would be useful to test this hypothesis.

Koster, A., & Garde, K. (1993). Sexual desire and menopausal development: A prospective study of Danish women born in 1936. *Maturitas, 16*, 49–60.

This segment of a longitudinal study of a cohort of Danish women reports on their status at age 51. In this study, 75% of the women reported sexual desire and 70% said their desire had increased or not changed since age 40. The only predictor of decreased desire at age 51 was the women's anticipation, at age 40, of decreased sexuality as a result of menopause. The authors' conclusion is that hormones did not affect sexual desire. Whether this is finding is a result of culture requires more study.

Laan, E., Everaerd, W., Van Aanhold, M., & Rebel, M. (1993). Performance demand and sex-

ual arousal in women. *Behavioral Research and Therapy, 31*(1), 25–35.

Until this research in the Netherlands, performance demand was not studied in women. Forty-nine undergraduate psychology students participated in a laboratory setting. Results showed that performance demand (i.e., urging the women to become as sexually aroused as possible and to maintain that arousal as long as possible) did affect genital arousal, and the greatest effect was under the fantasy condition. Whether performance demand is important to women's sexuality, however, may be questionable.

Laan, E., Everaerd, W., van Bellen, G., & Hanewald, G. (1994). Women's sexual and emotional responses to male- and female-produced erotica. *Archives of Sexual Behavior, 23*(2), 153–169.

Current laboratory studies of women's sexual arousal include videos intended to stimulate. An issue in this type of research is the use of pornography, and women's responses to it. This study in the Netherlands was undertaken to determine whether "erotic films" made by a woman would be more arousing to women than traditional "erotic films" (made by men). Heterosexual participants were either undergraduate psychology students (who had a high refusal rate) or friends of the researchers. Women reported subjectively more arousal with the woman-made film, but vaginal vasocongestion did not differ between films. Implications about the validity of laboratory studies of women's sexuality, particularly arousal, should be addressed.

Lindgren, R., Berg, G., Hammar, M., & Zuccon, E. (1993). Hormonal replacement therapy and sexuality in a population of Swedish postmenopausal women. *Acta Obstetricia et Gynecological Scandinavica, 72*, 292–297.

Frequency of "sexual activities" was the only measure of sexuality in this large survey of Swedish women (1,867) from one city. Most women (61%) were sexually active, but more women on hormone replacement therapy than not on therapy were; however, only 10% of the women were using hormone replacement. The major reason for not having sex was not having a partner. Researchers questioned whether greater use of hormone replacement therapy would increase sexual activity among older women.

McCarthy, M. (1993). Sexual experiences of women with learning difficulties in long-stay hospitals. *Sexuality and Disability, 11*(4), 277–286.

This outstanding report concerns the sexuality of women who are developmentally disabled and live in institutional settings in Britain. The author has worked with these women (and men) for four years on a project to teach AIDS awareness and safer sex. The sexuality of these women is a result of male power. The women accept sex as something men do to women, and something for which women are paid (money or cigarettes). The payment is the only positive aspect of these women's sexuality. They do not masturbate, nor do they engage in sex with other women, even though they live in an institutional environment. The women do not know they have a clitoris, or what it is, nor are they aware that they could experience orgasms. Finally, these women do not understand that what they experience is unusual or abnormal; they have no concept that other women might enjoy sex. The author gives suggestions about how to change this situation for these special women.

Meyer-Bahlburg, H. F. L., Nostlinger, C., Exner, T. M., Ehrhardt, A. A., Gruen, R. S., Lorenz, G., Gorman, J. M., El-Sadr, W., & Sorrell, S. J. (1993). Sexual functioning in HIV+ and HIV− injected drug-using women. *Journal of Sex and Marital Therapy, 19*(1), 56–68.

Thirteen injected drug-using HIV+, mostly asymptomatic women were compared with 8 injected drug-using HIV− women with regard to their sexuality. Although the sample is quite small, the results suggest concern. Both groups had many sexual function problems, related to all phases of the sexual response cycle. There were few significant differences between the groups, but when problems were present, the HIV+ women were more affected. This article is part of a longitudinal study, and further reports will help us to understand some of the implications of HIV and AIDS for the sexuality of this unique group of women.

Omorodion, F. I. (1993). Sexual networking of market women in Benin City, Edo State, Nigeria. *Health Care for Women International, 14*(6), 561–571.

This research aimed to design culturally appropriate AIDS prevention programs for Nigerian market women, but the first step was to gather information about the women's sexual behaviors (i.e., networking). The 100 married women who participated in the face-to-face survey had multiple sexual partners, including strangers, before and during their marriages—primarily for economic reasons. These women are at great risk for AIDS and other sexually transmitted diseases (STDs), from their own and their partners' sexual networking (Nigeria is a polygamous society). The study documents new ideas about the sexual permissiveness of some African societies.

Orubuloye, I. O., Caldwell, J. C., & Caldwell, P. (1993). African women's control over their sexuality in an era of AIDS. *Social Science and Medicine, 37*(7), 859–872.

This article discusses the cultural traditions of African women's sexuality and reports on research, conducted in 1991, of Yoruba women in Nigeria. These women have the right to refuse sex, but only temporarily, e.g., postpartum or during treatment for their own or a partner's STD. Even though they may (and do) refuse sex, they risk having their man go to another wife or woman. Cultural traditions that support women's refusal of sex allow the women to return to their family of origin with full rights. Urban women seem to have greater flexibility than rural women. These women are at high risk of AIDS, especially since many cultural beliefs focus on the dangers and ineffectiveness of using condoms.

Puretz, S. L., & Haas, A. (1993). Sexual desire and responsiveness following hysterectomy and menopause. *Journal of Women and Aging, 5*(2), 3–15.

The authors compared three measures of sexuality—(1) vaginal lubrication, (2) sexual desire, and (3) sexual satisfaction—among premenopausal, postmenopausal, and hysterectomized women. An important difficulty with the research is that the menopausal status of the hysterectomized women is not clear. Women of the same age did not differ on these variables, and levels of these variables decreased with increasing age. When age was not controlled, menopausal and hysterectomized women had lower scores on these measures of sexuality than did premenopausal women.

Rabinowitz, B. (Ed.) (1994). Breast care: Reconstructing the body, mind, and soul. *Innovations in Oncology Nursing, 10*(2), 29–51.

This entire issue—four short articles and a tear-out patient information sheet—will be useful to both providers and consumers who are concerned about sexuality in women with breast cancer. The articles include an overview of issues related to sexuality and breast cancer, patient perspectives, nurse perspectives, resources, and ways to assist women in coping with the problems of this disease.

Rosen, R. C., Taylor, J. F., Leiblum, S. R., & Bachmann, G. A. (1993). Prevalence of sexual dysfunction in women: Results of a survey study of 329 women in an outpatient gyneco-

logical clinic. *Journal of Sex and Marital Therapy, 19*(3), 171–188.

A new measure of sexual functioning and satisfaction was mailed to a sample of women who attended a Women's Wellness Center. The majority of women were sexually interested and active; however, a substantial minority reported problems, including arousal and orgasmic difficulties, dyspareunia, and engaging in sex less frequently than desired. There was a consistent negative association between age and frequency of intercourse, fantasy, oral sex, and desire. The authors see a need for more treatment services for sexual difficulties, especially among aging women.

Roughan, P. A., Kaiser, F. E., & Morley, J. E. (1993). Sexuality and the older woman. *Clinics in Geriatric Medicine, 9*(1), 87–106.

Using a historical perspective, the authors present a comprehensive review of literature on sexuality and aging. The article gives useful information on many of today's issues for older women's sexuality.

Rudy, D. R., & Bush, I. M. (1993). Sexual dysfunction after hysterectomy. *Contemporary OB/GYN, 38*(3), 39–46.

This article, written by physicians and for physicians, discusses potential causes for sexual difficulties following hysterectomy. Many physicians do not acknowledge these potential problems, most of which are treatable with hormone replacement. The authors offer a good Checklist for Prehysterectomy Counseling, which may be of use to any woman considering a hysterectomy.

Sipski, M. L., & Alexander, C. J. (1993). Sexual activities, response and satisfaction in women pre- and post-spinal cord injury. *Archives of Physical Medicine and Rehabilitation, 74,* 1025–1029.

Perhaps because spinal cord injuries are much more common in men, little has been studied about women's experiences of spinal cord injuries and their effect on sexuality. This survey of 25 women with spinal cord injuries provides some beginning information; generally, women experienced less sexual satisfaction but no decrease in sexual desire following the injury. Only 11 women experienced orgasms post-injury. The authors compare their results to theoretical expectations of reflex and psychogenic lubrication, but note that far more research is needed to understand the sexuality of women with spinal cord injuries.

Virtanen, H., Makinen, J., Tenho, T., Kiilholma, P., Pitkanen, Y., & Hirvonen, T. (1993). Effects of abdominal hysterectomy on urinary and sexual symptoms. *British Journal of Urology, 72*(6), 868–872.

This prospective study shows positive outcomes following hysterectomy. Both urinary and sexual problems decreased following hysterectomy for benign causes. There was a significant decrease in dyspareunia, no change in frequency of orgasm, and a significant increase in libido. The authors attribute these changes in their surgical technique, but improvement in general health may be equally responsible.

White, M. J., Rintala, D. H., Hart, K. A., & Fuhrer, M. J. (1993). Sexual activities, concerns and interests of women with spinal cord injury living in the community. *American Journal of Physical Medicine and Rehabilitation, 72*(6), 372–378.

Forty women, randomly selected from a large database of persons with spinal cord in-

jury, participated in interviews conducted in the women's homes. Sex is not too important to these women: sex life was rated 10th, in both importance and satisfaction, on a list of 12 important life areas. Nonetheless, most women had had a sexual relationship since their injury. Length of time since injury seemed to be important. Longer times were associated with greater likelihood of having a sexual relationship, feelings of sexual attractiveness, and more interest in coping emotionally and helping a partner to cope emotionally with changes in sexual functioning. The study's results have important implications for patient education and counseling of women with spinal cord injuries.

Wincze, J. P., Albert, A., & Bansal, S. (1993). Sexual arousal in diabetic females: Physiological and self-report measures. *Archives of Sexual Behavior, 22*(6), 587–601.

Extending prior research on the sexuality of women with diabetes, these researchers used vaginal photoplethysmography to assess the sexual arousal of women with Type I diabetes. Seven white, middle-income women with well-controlled diabetes were compared with seven similar women who did not have diabetes. While viewing erotic and nonerotic videos, diabetic women had significantly less physiological arousal than nondiabetic women, although the subjective responses of all women were comparable. The authors suggest that the differential might be even greater in a study of women whose diabetes was less well-controlled.

Chapter 3

Health-Promoting Behaviors of African American Elderly Women

Doris Ballard-Ferguson

By 1999, nearly three of every five aged African Americans will be women. By the year 2030, people over age 65 will constitute an estimated 21% of the population, and people of color are the fastest growing aged population. Presently, African Americans make up approximately 12% of the population of the United States and have a short life expectancy. For example, the life expectancy of Anglo-American males is 71.1 years as opposed to 64.4 years for African American males, 78.5 for Anglo-American females, and 73 years for African American females (Hendricks & Hendricks, 1986). On the other hand, among people who reach the age of 85, no racial differences in life expectancy emerge. In fact, older African American males and females tend to live longer. Ethnic differences in health status have become a social policy focus. For example, "The Report of the Secretary's Task Force on Black and Minority Health" as well as the five broad national goals listed in *Promoting Health/Preventing Disease: Year 2000 Objectives for the Nation* (U.S. Department of Health and Human Services, 1986, 1989) clearly state that the health of African Americans is significantly worse than that of Anglo-Americans. Despite this disparity in health status, a paucity of research data exists on health, health behavior, and health promotion in the African American population.

Historically, minority research has focused on deficits rather than on strengths, and on majority–minority comparisons rather than on inter- and intraminority group differences (Anderson & Cohen, 1989; Gibson, 1989; Jackson, 1988). Research on the health of African Americans appears in clinical studies of disease process or studies that link global indicators such as sex, age, and socioeconomic status and utilization to health status (Jackson, 1988). However, we know little about the perceptions of health and health-promoting behaviors in ethnic and minority populations, and even less about health-promoting behaviors in elderly African American women. African Americans face a variety of health concerns as they grow older. The women experience different kinds of health issues than the men and tend to outlive males by six years. Consequently, African American women may use different behaviors in promoting their health. But, as demonstrated in the literature, researchers have yet to explore the health of older African American women. This overview begins by defining health and health-promoting behaviors, and then reviews crucial constructs germane to understanding and promoting healthy outcomes in older African American women.

DEFINITIONS OF HEALTH

In 1975, Illich posited that health was a personal task and successful health was the result of self-awareness, self-discipline, and inner resources. Individuals regulate their own daily rhythm to determine their health status. Health is the outcome of several choices and life-style decisions that are made within a social context. This holistic view of health is incongruent with a biomedical perspective of health.

According to the World Health Organization (WHO, 1947), health is defined as a state of complete physical, mental, and social well-being and not merely the absence of disease and infirmity. Health is considered to be multidimensional and is often identified as having four domains: (1) physical, (2) psychological, (3) social, and (4) spiritual. These domains refer, respectively, to the stability of biological processes, feelings of well-being, role and social functioning, and a feeling of inner peace.

African American elderly women define health as well-being or the ability to maintain stability in their lives and to function in their chosen roles (Ballard-Ferguson, 1991). According to African American elderly women, well-being is described by feelings, feeling good, and being happy. They specify that stability and functioning mean getting around and being able to go and do things in a manner they desire. In a study of health-promoting behaviors of African American elderly persons, Ballard-Ferguson (1991), found they defined health as follows:

> Health is the way you live, it's your drinks, activities and things like that that helps you to be healthy. Stay busy; think good instead of bad.

Health means a good life, able to go and do things that you want to do. Go and come as you want to.

Feel good . . . physically strong, able-bodied, free of—no, I don't think that. I started to say free of disease, but that ain't it . . . just a normal action of life, I say.

African American women define health as a way of living, a feeling of well-being, and engaging in activities of their choice. For Antonovsky (1987), a person moves toward health rather than away from disease. Health is a continuum rather than a dichotomy; therefore, as long as there is life, there is, in some measure, "health." This health-producing paradigm examines the origins of health as it overcomes "the inevitable stressor-rich environment" and reflects successful coping. Conceptually, this coping results in a sense of coherence, a pervasive and dynamic feeling of confidence that the stimulation received in the process of living is not only structured and predictable but also explicable; that resources are available to meet these stimuli; and that the demands from these stimuli are worthy of investment and engagement (Antonovsky, 1987). Consistent with this view, health is a lived experience.

According to Ballard-Ferguson (1991), older African American women's personal health practices are their means of promoting health. Consequently, they describe health-promoting behaviors as continuing activities that are integral parts of their life-style and enhance their health. Health-promoting behaviors are defined (or self-reported) self-care activities in which individuals engage in order to protect their health. With health as a way of life, activities older African American women find important in promoting health are diet, exercise, activity, rest and relaxation, and support. From this study, an acronym for these health-promoting behaviors was formed: DEARS. This acronym communicates the essential components of these women's preferred life-style, which operationalizes health-promoting behaviors through diet, exercise, activity, rest and relaxation, and support. These behaviors have empirical support in the literature for predicting health for the general population (Breslow & Enstrom, 1980; Kaplan, Seeman, Cohen, Knudsen, & Guralnik, 1987; Maloney, Fallon, & Whittenberg, 1984). Table 3.1 depicts the DEARS.

Diet

Older African American women believe that proper and adequate dietary intake promotes health. Very little is known about good nutrition for the older adult, but the African American elderly place extreme importance on diet. Their concept of diet includes preparation, timing, and intake of meals. The meal pattern they prefer is: two meals per day, from 9 to 9:30 A.M. and from

3 to 4 P.M. After 6 P.M. they eat only light snacks, such as milk, juices, or ice cream (Ballard-Ferguson, 1991).

Older African American women value and consistently practice these established dietary patterns and food choices. They need a balanced diet: essential amino acids, essential fatty acids, essential trace elements, vitamins, fiber, water, and enough calories for energy but not an excess that would lead to obesity. As guidelines, the 1989 Recommended Daily Allowances (RDAs) are not specific or sensitive for older adults. The RDAs list the amounts of 15 vitamins and minerals plus protein and calories estimated for both sexes throughout the life cycle. Specifically, the nutrients are protein, carbohydrates, fats, vitamin A, vitamin C, thiamin, riboflavin, niacin, calcium, and iron. Consumption of these nutrients will maintain good nutrition in almost all healthy persons in the United States under current living conditions. The RDAs afford a margin of safety above physiological requirements. Since 1943, a consensus group, without empirical evidence, has revised the RDAs every seven years. The RDAs collapse all people over age 51 and are based on data from younger groups, not the older population. Furthermore, they are based on a "healthy" state and do not allow for infections or other chronic illnesses.

Older African American women maintain nutritional health through a personal choice inherent in their life-style. Dietary counseling and education represent two major interventions needed to promote and maintain good dietary habits. Dietary counseling would help ensure that older African American females consume an adequate nutritional intake.

Exercise

Older African American women view physical activity as a survival need. Physical activity increases the likelihood of maintaining their current health status, by optimizing functional independence and enhancing their social and emotional well-being. Along with diet, an appropriate level of exercise is a significant health need. For these physically independent older women, walking provides the desired exercise benefits.

Exercise plays a key role in the consumption of body fat, reduction of blood pressure, reduction of blood sugar, and enhancement of musculoskeletal strength. It is important to assess, monitor, and facilitate walking as the exercise of choice for older African American women.

Activity

Activity involves the quality, not the quantity, of social activities and networks. For African American women, activity reflects their personal diversions and interests. Church activities are a valuable resource for active involvement, and most older African American women attend church frequently. As a result, they are involved with other people and groups and stay active through recreation and community activities. Older African American women wish to continue to be useful "when and as they chose." Assessing both the quality and quantity of activity from their perspective is necessary to their health.

Rest and Relaxation

Older African American women believe rest and relaxation rejuvenates them and helps them manage stress. They see pacing themselves as important to restoring physiological and psychic energies. They get enough sleep (six to eight hours per night). Reading (especially the Bible), napping (pull ups), and praying represent some of the ways older African American women achieve rest and relaxation and thereby increase their feelings of energy, vitality, and self-control. To promote rest and relaxation in older African American women, it is important to appreciate that spirituality plays an integral part in their everyday lives. Assessment of their rest and relaxation patterns should include: naps (frequency and length), methods of relaxation, and distribution of rest patterns throughout the day. Plans for decreased activity for rejuvenation should become a common practice for older African American women.

Support

Older African American women value meaningful relationships with friends and family as a way to maintain and promote their health. They use these relationships to prevent social isolation, to receive assistance with activities of daily living, and to have transportation. Older African American women have viable personal support networks that are not limited to kin relationships. They include friends, neighbors, and service providers. Sharing of food, of leisure time, and of shopping errands represents an area where support functions as health-promoting behavior. Because older African American women decide when and how often they will need this support, the intensity and frequency of support are based on their own perceived needs, not on the social network of family and friends or other support groups (or both). Consequently, it is important to assess the nature and extent of African American women's social networks, keeping in mind that these women structure the frequency and intensity of such support and may rely on friends, neighbors, social organizations, and others, for social connections rather than on immediate family members.

CHOICE, CONNECTEDNESS, AND CENTERING

The health-promoting behaviors of elderly African Americans can be further conceptualized as a philosophy of choice, connectedness, and centering.

Choice

Choice is the decision reached through the voluntary, purposive action of selecting from among favored alternatives. Choice is related to concepts of free will, decision making, and motivation. The choices and decisions thought necessary to facilitate health promotion and well-being are reflected in the acronym DEARS (see Table 3.1).

Other examples of choice are related to illness behavior and the use of home remedies. Many home remedies are not commonly thought of as home remedies. Some traditional choices have been replaced with over-the-counter drugstore products and with foodstuffs; for example: Anacin, aspercreme, and aspirin for pain and arthritis; Tylenol and Sleepytyme tea for sleep; Tums for indigestion; black draught and bran as laxatives; vitamin supplements for energy; and Sprite for gas.

Older African American women's concept of choice is again congruent with totality and the organismic philosophical position. The organismic approach posits that people act on their environment as active organisms. Although the organismic approach places primary importance on cognitive and/or affective processes as determiners of behavior, people act on their environment in a lawful and ordered way as determined by their thoughts and feelings.

When people initiate intentional behavior, they experience themselves as having originated the intention and the behavior. Personal causation then is

Table 3.1
DEARS: Health-Promoting Behaviors

Diet	Eat properly
	Two meals a day
	Vegetables, juices, water
Exercise	Walk daily
Activity	Self-care, hygiene, house chores
	Interactions with individuals or groups
Rest and relaxation	Naps, meditation, prayer, quiet time
Support	Social groups: family, friends

the initiation of behaviors intended to produce a change in the environment. The person is said to be the locus of causality and is intrinsically motivated (Deci & Ryan, 1985). Locus of causality is a motivation concept. Motivated behaviors are activities that people choose to do, in order to achieve some desired end-state. Intention must be present to have motivated behavior. Personal causality assumes intention to produce the observed effects. Intrinsically motivated behaviors are behaviors in which the rewards are internal to the person. The person engages in them to feel competent and self-determining. Extrinsic motivated behaviors are behaviors in which there is no apparent reward except the activity itself. People seem to engage in the activities for their own sake and not because they lead to an extrinsic reward. The activities are ends in themselves rather than means to an end. This definition also serves as an operational definition of intrinsic motivation. One can observe that there is no apparent reward and that the person is deriving enjoyment from the activity. (An activity that, regardless of its initiating motive, becomes intrinsically interesting was identified as functional autonomy by Allport (1968).) Competence refers to one's ability or capacity to deal effectively with one's surroundings. The behaviors lead to effective manipulation of the environment. Effectance motivation causes behaviors that allow a person to have feelings of efficacy. Therefore, intrinsic motivation to engage in behaviors allows a person to feel competence. The tendency toward self-determination is the essence of intrinsic motivation.

Connectedness

The second theme is connectedness, which is defined as being mutually supported. Found in the interdependent kin and non-kin relationships, connectedness is related to social networks. Connectedness was seen in the health-promoting behaviors described as activities of daily living and in the contact with individuals and social groups.

Centering

The third concept is centering—optimism based on spiritual faith that provides inner peace and is related to religious involvement. Older African American women are in touch with their inner selves regarding their health, as exhibited by thoughts of their well-being. Their inner peace and security are also reflected by their health-promoting behaviors of prayer, mediation, frequency of church attendance, and reference to their perception of health as a blessing. Centering is a key factor in influencing health. Centering is one's relationship with a higher power but is distinguished from religiosity in that the relationship gives identity, values, and meaning to life. Religiosity is a person's outward expression of meaning through activity and/or affiliation with a faith community. Centering may remain stable or increase despite a decrease in religiosity. When a person is centered, there is calmness amid confusion.

Some strengths that have enabled older African American women to survive mortality predictions are:

- accumulation of wisdom, knowledge, and common sense about life;
- creativity in doing much with little;
- ability to accept their own aging;
- sense of hope and optimism for a better day. (Dancy, 1977)

These strengths can be described as the concepts of centering, choice, and connectedness. These constructs are evident in older African American women's descriptions of strategies for implementing their health-promoting behaviors (DEARS). Choice, connectedness, and centering are mediating variables in psychological well-being (Ruffing-Rahal & Anderson, 1994). Elderly African American women's health behaviors are part of their life-style and their personal definition of health (Morse, 1987).

SUMMARY

African American elderly women define health as a functional, feeling state. People are healthy if they are feeling good and are able to function in their chosen roles. African American elderly women perform health behaviors that are incorporated within their life-style and do not always involve use of the health care system. This conclusion is consistent with the findings of Harris and Guten (1979) and reflects Dowie's (1975) thesis that health is produced by households. According to Dowie (1975), health is produced by combining various inputs such as diet, exercise, home conditions, and work conditions; utilization of health services is only one of many options in the production of health. Dowie (1975) held that the use of a medical paradigm to research health is inappropriate because it omits social, cultural, and psychological factors. Consequently, it is inadequate to use medically approved classifications of health behaviors such as having direct contact with health care professionals or compliance with health professionals' recommendation(s). Dowie believed there is a need to research health behaviors of the person and not the "patient."

Elderly African Americans define health as a feeling state and functional ability, a state of well-being. The value placed on well-being or on feeling good can have both positive and negative consequences in promoting the health of the elderly. The positive consequence is the quality-of-life value implied in the functional and structural integrity of their definition of health; that is, health requires physiological stability and emotional and environmental stability. The negative consequence of valuing "feeling good" as a definition of health is that, with the exception of arthritis, many chronic illnesses are asymptomatic and may have insidious onsets. "Feeling good" may be an intervening variable that deters people from seeking prompt medical care and, subsequently, delays recovery from illness (Leventhal & Prohaska, 1986).

On the other hand, the health-promoting behaviors of eating a proper diet, walking for exercise, being active, ensuring rest and relaxation, and having a support system are effective and positive behaviors to reinforce in the older—as well as the middle-aged—adult. According to Gibson and Jackson (1987), the older age group of African Americans is the most robust; therefore, we can intervene with middle-aged and younger African Americans by using some of the principles of health practiced by older African Americans.

In conclusion, to facilitate longevity and reduce the effects of chronic conditions, the long-term goal of health promotion must allow each individual to seek an independent and rewarding life. In particular, the well-being of African Americans should be supported by offering wellness programs that cover health information about diet, exercise, rest and relaxation, referral services for activities, and organized support through local black churches and/or community centers. The best health promotion efforts for older African Americans ensure dignity, equal opportunity to make choices, and reinforcement of the health-promoting processes that already exist. Health care providers and family members must facilitate African American elderly women's motivation and self-efficacy, at the same time understanding their desire and right to make their own decisions.

REFERENCES

Allport, G. W. (1968). *The person in psychology.* Boston: Beacon Press.

Anderson, N. B., & Cohen, H. J. (1989). Health status of aged minorities: Directions for clinical research. *Journal of Gerontology: Medical Sciences, 44,* M1–M2.

Antonovsky, A. (1987). *Unraveling the mystery of health: How people manage stress and stay well.* San Francisco: Jossey-Bass.

Ballard-Ferguson, D. E. (1991). Health-promoting behaviors of African Americans. Doctoral dissertation, University of Illinois at Chicago. *Dissertation Abstracts International,* 5712B.

Breslow, L., & Enstrom, J. E. (1980). Persistence of health habits and their relationship to mortality. *Preventive Medicine, 9,* 469–483.

Dancy, J. (1977). *The black elderly: A guide for practitioners.* Detroit: Wayne State University Institute of Gerontology.

Deci, E., & Ryan, R. M. (1985). *Intrinsic motivation and self-determination in human behavior.* New York: Plenum Press.

Dowie, J. (1975). The portfolio approach to health behavior. *Social Science and Medicine, 9,* 619–631.

Gibson, R. (1989). Minority aging research: Opportunity and challenge. *Journal of Gerontology: Social Sciences, 44,* S2–S3.

Gibson, R., & Jackson, J. S. (1987). The health, physical functioning, and informal supports of the black elderly. *Milbank Memorial Fund Quarterly, 65,* 421–452.

Harris, D. M., & Guten, S. (1979). Health-protective behavior: An exploratory study. *Journal of Health and Social Behavior, 20,* 17–29.

Hendricks, J., & Hendricks, C. D. (1986). *Aging in mass society: Myths and realities* (3rd ed.). Boston: Little, Brown.

Illich, I. (1976). *Medical nemeses: The expropriation of health.* New York: Bantam Books.

Jackson, J. S. (Ed.). (1988). *The black American elderly: Research on physical and psychosocial health.* New York: Springer.

Kaplan, G. A., Seeman, T. E., Cohen, R. D., Knudsen, L. T., & Guralnik, J. (1987). Mortality among the elderly in the Alameda County study: Behavioral and demographic risk factors. *American Journal of Public Health, 77,* 307–311.

Leventhal, E. A., & Prohaska, T. R. (1986). Age, symptom interpretation, and health behavior. *Journal of the American Geriatrics Society, 34,* 185–191.

Maloney, S., Fallon, B., & Whittenberg, C. (1984). *Aging and health promotion: Market research for public education* (executive summary). Washington, DC: U.S. Public Health Service, Office of Disease Prevention and Health Promotion.

Morse, J. (1987). The meaning of health in an inner city community. *Nursing Papers/Perspective in Nursing, 19*(2), 27–41.

Ruffing-Rahal, M. A., & Anderson, J. (1994). Factors associated with qualitative well-being. *Journal of Women and Aging, 6*(3), 3–18.

U.S. Department of Health and Human Services. (1986). The report of the Secretary's Task Force on Black and Minority Health. *Health status of minorities and low-income groups.* Washington, DC: U.S. Department of Health and Human Services.

U.S. Department of Health and Human Services. (1989). *Promoting health/Preventing disease: Year 2000 objectives for the nation.* Washington, DC: Author.

U.S. Public Health Service. (1986). *Health status of the disadvantaged: Chartbook 1986.* Washington, DC: Author.

World Health Organization, (1947). *Chronicle of WHO, 1*(1-2), New York: WHO.

Definitions of Health

Andersen, R. M., Mullner, R. M., & Cornelius, L. J. (1987). Black–white differences in health status: Methods or substance? In D. P. Willia & C. E. Driver (Eds.), *Currents of health policy: Impacts on black Americans (Part I)* (pp. 72–99). New Rochelle, NY: Milbank Quarterly, Cambridge University Press.

The authors evaluated the extent of the influence of measurement on the apparent differences in the health status of black and white Americans. The problems examined include measuring health status, sources of measurement error, problems with data collection methods, interpretation of those measures, and the types of measures used to represent health status. The health status of blacks is compared to whites using measures of death, disease, disability, discomfort, and dissatisfaction from recent national surveys. Findings shows that blacks generally have the greatest health deficits (based on objective observations) and the smallest differences on self-reports of illness conditions, symptoms, and restricted-activity days. Random errors in health status estimates and sampling biases tended to be greater for blacks. The investigators concluded that measured differences in the health status of blacks and whites often reflect differences in substance, but significant methodological problems tend to underestimate the problems experienced by blacks.

Anderson, N. B., & Cohen, H. J. (1989). Health status of aged minorities: Directions for clinical research. *Journal of Gerontology: Medical Sciences, 44,* M1–M2.

This editorial emphasizes that there has been a paucity of scientific attention to minority issues. The authors cite several reasons why biomedical research addressing minority issues is important: differential life expectancy, different physiologic characteristics, differential disease rates, and within-race disease variability rates. They report that, after a review of major geriatric and gerontologic journals, only 19 articles in the past 10 years could be considered biomedical research specifically focused on minority groups. The editorial concludes that research with minority populations that examines issues uniquely important to different racial groups should be made a priority. Research focused on both racial differences and within-race diversity has the potential to uncover clues to health and illness in minority populations.

Chatters, L. M. (1988). Subjective well-being evaluations among older black Americans. *Psychology and Aging, 3,* 184–190.

In this study, the relationship between subjective well-being (happiness) and social status, personal and economic resources, health, and stress factors was examined in 581 blacks aged 55 and older. Lower happiness ratings were associated with being younger, being widowed or separated from one's spouse, and having high levels of stress and low levels of health satisfaction. Health disability had a negative influence on happiness through its association with higher stress levels and reduced health satisfaction. In addition to the direct effects of age and of being widowed or separated, other social status and resource factors were important in predicting intermediate factors related to health status.

Duffy, M. E., & MacDonald, M. N. (1990). *Final report: Determinants of functional health of older men and women.* Washington, DC: AARP Andrus Foundation.

This study of 106 black women found that older persons define health differently than younger age groups. For older people, health takes on a more functional meaning that includes those activities needed to maintain independent life-styles. The authors conclude that professionals and laypersons alike need knowledge about what influences older persons' functional health, in order to dispel the prevailing myth that most older women are disease-ridden and severely limited by ill health, and to understand how to assist older black women in maintaining their functional independence and health throughout their senior years.

Edmonds, W. M. (1990). The health of the black aged female. In Z. Harel, E. A. McKinney, & W. Williams (Eds.), *Black aged* (pp. 205–220). London: Sage.

Health status is related to the coping style of older black women. The author suggests that the triple jeopardy that older black women face helps them develop strong coping skills, which, in turn, affect their perception of the world and their health. Historical social roles, economic inequities, and health beliefs also play a role. Consequently, the result is considerable variation in utilization of medical services by older black women. The article concludes with a call for sensitivity, on the part of policymakers, to these women's past.

Ferraro, K. F. (1980). Self-ratings of health among the old and the old-old. *Journal of Health and Social Behavior, 21,* 337–383.

Data from a stratified, multistage, clustered-design study were used to sample 3,402 individuals aged 65 and older from case rolls of the U.S. Bureau of the Census for self-ratings of health. Females constituted 63% of the sample. Of these elderly, 10% were African Americans. Self-ratings of health were measured with a question whether respondents would describe their health as excellent, good, fair, or poor. Objective measures of health status used were the number of illnesses or physiological disorders an individual reported from a checklist of 55 items and a disability scale. In the sample, 8.5% of the elderly rated their health as excellent, 29.4% as good, 37.4% as fair, and 24.7% as poor. From the results of the analysis, it is suggested that, although members of the old-old category (aged 75 and older), the group with a majority of African Americans, reported more health-related problems than the old (aged 65 to 74), they tended to be more positive in rating their own health.

Jackson, J. S. (Ed.). (1988). *The black American elderly: Research on physical and psychosocial health.* New York: Springer.

There are 19 conference papers in this collection covering the physical and psychological health of the African American elderly. Topics include: research on the demographic makeup of African American aging populations, cancer prevention and control, socioeconomic predictors of health in later years, and the nature of formal and informal social participation; basic differences between black and white elderly in the areas of social participation, nutrition, obesity and diabetes, hypertension, and dementing illnesses; the role of social factors in the subjective well-being of elderly African Americans, family and social supports, health-seeking behavior, health attitudes and health promotion/prevention, work, retirement, and disability; methological issues in survey research, case-control epidemiological research, and clinical trials.

Johnson, F., Cloyd, C., & Wer, J. A. (1982). Life satisfaction of poor urban black aged. *Advances in Nursing Science, 4*(3), 27–34.

This quantitive-descriptive study was designed to investigate differences between the life satisfaction of urban African American institutionalized and noninstitutionalized elderly and to identify probable causative factors. The study was conducted in a low-income high-rise apartment building for the aged and in several nursing homes in a midwestern metropolitan city. Participants included 22 institutionalized and 23 noninstitutionalized urban elderly subjects ranging in age from 65 to 92. Data were collected using the Mental Status Questionnaire, the Crichton Royal Behavioral Rating Scale, the life Satisfaction Index-Z Scale, and a Life Satisfaction Interview Schedule. The noninstitutionalized elderly exhibited higher life satisfaction resolution and fortitude, zest for life, congruence between described and achieved goals, and mood tone. Perceived health was an important determination of life satisfaction. Less support was established for education, income, occupation, political activity, personality variables, and religion as indicators for life satisfaction. Variables related to basic survival (living arrangements, support systems, and independence) emerged as significant correlates.

Health-Promoting Behaviors

Bailey, E. J. (1987). Sociocultural factors and health-care-seeking behavior among black Americans. *Journal of the National Medical Association, 79,* 389–392.

To study the health-care-seeking behavior of black Americans in the Detroit metropolitan area, the investigator analyzed 176 semistructured interviews and 27 life histories obtained from a variety of sources: clinic participants, community leaders, health care professionals, and nonclinic participants. The findings suggest black Americans follow a culturally specific health-care-seeking pattern that is significantly influenced by sociocultural factors. The health-care-seeking sequence is detailed in the following steps: illness appears; individual waits for a certain period; allows body to heal itself through prayer or traditional regimens; evaluates daily activities by reducing work or stress; seeks advice from a family member, church leader, or close friend; and, finally, attends health clinic or visits family physician. It is suggested that for intervention strategies to work, professionals need to (1) know what the people are thinking, (2) have a broad definition of health, and (3) realize the everlasting effects of discrimination.

Ballard-Ferguson, D. E. (1991). Health-promoting behaviors of African Americans. Doctoral dissertation, University of Illinois at Chicago. *Dissertation Abstracts International,* 5712B.

This cross-sectional study identifies and describes, from their perspective, the health-promoting experiences of elderly African Americans and the self-care activities in which they engage. A combination of qualitative and quantitative methodologies was used. Analysis of the interview data suggests that this group defines health as well-being and routinely practices health-promoting behaviors. The health-promoting behaviors they found efficacious were diet, exercise, activity, rest and relaxation, and support—categorized as DEARS. Additional analysis of the interview data revealed the themes of choice, connectedness, and centering as being central to health-promoting behaviors of African American elderly.

Bausell, R. B. (1986). Health-seeking behavior among the elderly. *The Gerontologist, 26,* 556–559.

This is a study of the degree of compliance among elderly, in comparison to adults between the ages of 18 and 64, with respect to 20 recommended health-seeking behaviors. One hundred and seventy-seven persons 65 years and older were interviewed by telephone and compared to 997 younger adults with respect to compliance with the recommended behaviors. The elderly reported greater compliance with these behaviors; the largest difference found between the two groups involved dietary behaviors (restricting salt, fat cholesterol, and sugar; consuming fiber, vitamins/minerals, and calcium). In addition to these dietary behaviors, the elderly were more likely (1) to have regular blood pressure checks, (2) to take steps to avoid home accidents, and (3) to neither smoke in bed nor live in a household in which someone else did. On the other hand, the elderly were significantly less likely to engage in regular strenuous exercise and to regularly visit a dentist, and they slept 7 to 8 hours per night. The investigator concluded that the elderly reported greater compliance with recommended health practices than the other age groups studied and this is an indication of a need for health promotion activities among persons 65 years of age and over.

Braithwaite, R. L., & Taylor, S. E. (Eds.). (1992). *Health issues in the black community.* San Francisco: Jossey-Bass.

This book covers a comprehensive examination of the health problems confronting the African American community. The strategies offered for providing improved health care and disease prevention to this population include formulating culturally sensitive health care policies and implementing self-determined strategic initiatives. Of particular relevance to the health of African American elderly women are the chapters on health status, health education, conceptual models for health promotion, health policies, and futuristic perspective.

Branch, L. G., & Jette, A. M. (1984). Personal health practices and mortality among the elderly. *American Journal of Public Health, 74,* 1126–1129.

The authors raise questions about the generalizability of past health practices and research to the elderly. Using data from the Massachusetts Health Care Panel Study, the investigators examined the association of physical activity, cigarette smoking, hours of sleep, alcohol consumption, and number of meals with five-year mortality rates. With the exception of elderly women's never having smoked, none of the personal health practices was related significantly to mortality among elderly men. The study services as a reminder that research on young and middle-aged populations frequently has limited generalizability among the aged population.

Harris, D. M., & Guten, S. (1979). Health-protective behavior: An exploratory study. *Journal of Health and Social Behavior, 20,* 17–29.

These investigators explored the concept of health-protective behaviors with 842 respondents. Of these randomly selected respondents, 25% were African Americans and 32% were 55 years or older. The findings confirm that most people perform some kind of health-protective behavior and that the most commonly performed activities do not involve use of the health care system. The most important health-protecting behaviors include nutrition (foods and eating conditions); sleep, rest and relaxation, and exercise; and physical activity and recreation. In this study, the respondents who rated their health as poor were older, poorer, less educated, and African American. However, these researchers concluded that health-protective behaviors did not markedly differ by health condition or by gender.

Maloney, S., Fallon, B., & Whittenberg, C. (1984). *Aging and health promotion: Market research for public education* (executive summary). Washington, DC: U.S. Public Health Service, Office of Disease Prevention and Health Promotion.

These authors point out that several life-styles could be referred to as health-seeking behaviors. These health-seeking behaviors are conceptualized as self-responsibility for health, nutrition, exercise, stress management, interpersonal relationships/support, spiritual growth and self-actualization, accident or injury prevention, safe/moderate use of medications and alcohol, self-care regimens for chronic illness, and accessing preventive health services. Subsequently, these life-styles are referred to as health promotion in the older adult.

Rakowski, W. (1988). Age cohorts and personal health behavior in adulthood. *Research on Aging, 10,* 3–35.

The focus of this study was an examination of nine personal health practices for predicting health-related behavior in adulthood. Using data from Wave 1 of the National Survey of Personal Health Practices and Consequences (N = 3,015), the investigator showed that education and gender were the most consistent predictors with each cohort. Additionally, functional health status, income, subjective health, perceived locus of control, a regular source of health care, and group participation were identified with some cohorts. All respondents were noninstitutionalized adults ranging in age from 20 to 64 with 38.7% of the sample female and 9.3% black.

Speake, D. L., Cowart, M. E., & Pellet, K. (1989). Health perceptions and life-styles of the elderly. *Research in Nursing and Health, 12,* 93–100.

This study examined the relationship of six aspects of a healthy life-style (nutrition, exercise, stress management, self-actualization, health responsibility, and interpersonal support) in the well elderly. The sample consisted of 297 volunteers who were recruited at health fairs, senior centers, and retirement groups in four counties in Northern Florida. Subject ages ranged from 55 to 93 (mean age = 71.9). Sixty percent were aged 70 and older. Seventy-one percent of the subjects were white and 29% were African Americans. Findings were that elderly subjects with an internal locus of control take more responsibility for engaging in health-promoting practices in later life.

Diet

Breslow, L., & Enstrom, J. E. (1980). Persistence of health habits and their relationship to mortality. *Preventive Medicine, 9,* 469–483.

In this 20-year longitudinal study, these investigators identified some social and behavioral factors associated with low mortality and morbidity. The health habits associated with low mortality and morbidity were eating a good breakfast and two other nutritious meals, exercising regularly and moderately, sleeping 7 or 8 hours each day, and not smoking or using alcohol. The investigators noted that older adults who had the same habits as the 35- to 44-year-olds were as healthy as middle-aged adults who practiced three or fewer of the habits.

Chen, P. N. (1980). Minority elderly: Continuity/discontinuity of life patterns in nutrition programs. *Journal of Nutrition for the Elderly, 1,* 65–75.

A study of the levels of participation by minority elderly (150 African Americans, Mexican Americans, and Chinese Americans) using the continuity/discontinuity theory. Independent variables examined were food patterns, health status, social interaction, and program activities. African American and Mexican American subjects preferred American food over ethnic food both at their present age and at age 40; Chinese Americans preferred ethnic foods at both ages. The elderly demonstrating high participation included those with continued good health as well as those whose health had declined, those who socialized outside the nutrition program, and those who showed a discontinuity of satisfaction with program activities. The author concluded that levels of participation were more related to social interaction, ordinary preferences for food, and activities that obscure ethnic influences than to ethnicity or continuity/discontinuity of satisfaction/dissatisfaction.

Sizer, F., & Whitney, E. (1994). Cultural cuisines: Do they support nutrition and health? In *Nutrition: Concepts and controversies* (6th ed., 59–69). New York: West Publishing.

The authors of this book chapter suggest that rural southern cuisine varies little between African Americans and people of European descent who suffer from heart disease, hypertension, obesity and diabetes, and illnesses associated with too much fat and salt in the diet. The authors recommend that the "trick" to choosing health-promoting rural southern food is to choose fruits and plain vegetables, and to avoid fatty, salty, fried foods.

Watson, W. H. (1988). *Nutrition among aging poor blacks: A discussion of selected socioeconomic and social psychological correlates.* Atlanta, GA: Atlanta University.

This study focuses on selected ethnic and socioeconomic correlates of nutrition among older blacks, with special reference to food preparation intake, and consequences for health. Findings show some evidence that race discrimination and economic poverty have a structural bearing on the nutrition and health of older blacks. This study gives special attention to nutrition education and social policy for the aged poor in the areas of health care and nutrition.

Exercise

Toliver, J. C., & Banks-Scott, P. M. (1992). Exercise: The outcomes of a program for elderly clients. *Journal of the Black Nurses Association.* Fall 2(1), 30–37.

The benefits of an exercise program for elderly African American females are identified in this study. Seven elderly African American

women, aged 60–79 years, volunteered to participate in a planned exercise program to increase their cardiorespiratory and muscular endurance, flexibility, balance, and muscular strength. The exercise program consisted of aerobic exercises, aerobic walking for cardiorespiratory endurance, range of motion for flexibility and dancing, yoga and hopping on one foot at a time for balance. Findings were that walking was the form of exercise preferred by the subjects and that the primary motivational outcomes for the exercise program were directly related to the elderly women's concern for increased cardiorespiratory endurance and flexibility. The researcher concluded that an exercise program for elderly African American women can aid in the development of new skills for self-health promotion and maintenance, thereby influencing their overall well-being.

Activity

Chin-Sang, V., & Allen, K. R. (1991). Leisure and the older black women. *Journal of Gerontological Nursing, 17*(1), 30–34.

The meaning of leisure in the lives of older African American women is described for 30 African American women born between 1896 and 1923 who participated in this qualitative study. All of the women were active members of Protestant churches and lived on fixed incomes. The most prevalent health problems among the women were hypertension, arthritis, and diabetes. Analysis of the verbatim transcripts revealed the themes of loneliness; church worship and duty; affiliative activities; and solitary activities. The findings further revealed that, even though the family circles of these women were narrowing, they sought and maintained extrafamilial connections. They have the ability to replace personal network losses with other significant relationships and activities. Further, elderly African American women rely on solitary activities to promote their spiritual and emotional health and they provide care for others by forming meaningful relationships in the community through affiliative groups at church and senior centers. The investigators recommend that leisure should be examined within the context of women's daily activities of self-care and the care of others; doing so will shed light on ways of helping older African American women maintain independence in the face of increasing loss.

Gaitz, C. M., & Scott, J. (1992). *Leisure activity, mental health, and ethnicity in middle age.* Houston: Texas Research Institutes of Mental Sciences.

A total of 1,441 adults living in Houston, Texas, were studied in an examination of leisure activity participation, mental health, and ethnicity. Approximately 240 individuals were chosen for each of the six age groups, with the two oldest groups ranging in age from 65 to 74 and 75 to 94. Participation in 17 leisure activities was tabulated in terms of active versus passive, social versus individual, and away-from-home versus homebound. The relationship between participation and mental health was considered, using indexes of self-satisfaction, ratings of happiness, and scores derived from a screening instrument that reflected anxiety and depression. Overall, frequency of participation in leisure activities was more important in enhancing mental health than the specific type of leisure activity involvement. The study concludes that varied leisure activity participation promotes positive mental health beyond the age of retirement.

Ruffing-Rahal, M. A. (1993). An ecological model of group well-being: Implications for health promotion with older women. *Health Care for Women International, 14,* 447–456.

In this study, qualitative methods were used to identify the properties of psychological well-being at the small-group level. Over a 20-month period, a core of 12–14 women participated in the research study. The majority were African American, widowed or divorced, and living alone in subsidized or rented housing. The women's mean age was 77 years. The findings reflected core themes of activity, affirmation, and synthesis. Activity refers to an individual's selection and structuring of a pattern of meaning-invested, daily activities, presuming the capability to successfully perform them and incorporate them as healthy life-style practices. Affirmation refers to the individuals' perception of a positive continuity in life-meaning over time, as expressed by such concepts as satisfaction, thankfulness, hopefulness, and religiosity. Synthesis is the individual's resolution of painful life experiences, assimilating them into a personal framework of identity and meaning. The investigator concludes that a framework for group well-being can be characterized as (1) group as ritual, (2) group as celebration, and (3) group as community.

Taylor, R. J. (1986). Religious participation among elderly blacks. *The Gerontologist, 26,* 630–636.

This study found that African American elderly display a high degree of religious involvement. They attend religious services on a frequent basis, are likely to be official members of a church or other place of worship, and describe themselves as being religious. Elderly women attend religious services more frequently, are more likely to be church members, and report a higher degree of religiosity than do elderly men. In comparison to married persons, divorced and widowed respondents attended religious services less frequently and reported lower levels of subjective religiosity. Divorced respondents were also less likely to be church members. Elderly African Americans who reside in rural areas were more involved in church activities than their urban counterparts. The author concluded that religion and the church are salient aspects of the lives of elderly African Americans.

Rest and Relaxation

Bearson, L. B., & Koenig, H. G. (1990). Religious cognitions and use of prayer in health and illness. *The Gerontologist, 30*(2), 249–253.

In this study, 40 adults aged 65 to 74 were asked about God's role in health and illness and about their use of prayer in response to recent physical symptoms. The sample consisted of 20 men and 20 women, with a mean age of 71. Twenty-one were African Americans. Findings showed that religious beliefs are intertwined with African Americans' belief about their health and physical symptoms. Many of these elderly subjects saw health and illness as being at least partly attributable to God and, to some extent, open to God's intervention. The authors concluded that such beliefs might impact on their health by causing them to delay reporting symptoms or resist complying with prescribed regimens. On the other hand, a more positive consequence could be that the subjects would find strength and motivation in compliance, reinforced by the sense that God is helping in the healing process. Therefore, the evidence suggests that health professionals should ask specific questions about religious beliefs so that knowledge of such beliefs can be used to tailor effective and sensitive health-promotion programs.

Haber, D. (1983). Yoga as a preventive health care program for white and black elders: An exploratory study. *International Journal of Aging and Human Development, 17,* 169–176.

Sixty-one elderly white volunteers and 45 elderly black low-income volunteers at two senior centers in Florida were randomly assigned to a yoga class or a control activity. Yoga classes were held once a week for 10 weeks at both sites, with daily homework assignments. The white participants, but not the black, significantly reduced their systolic blood pressure and improved self-assessed health status in comparison to the control group. The participants attended classes regularly, but the white elderly practiced an additional five times per week, while the black elderly practiced only one additional time per week. It was concluded that more frequent direct leadership may be needed with low-income, minority elders because they lack the orientation for personal control over future health events.

Hubbard, R. W. (1992). Stress, health, and the minority aged. In M. A. Wykle, E. Kahana, & J. Kowal (Eds.). *Stress and health among the elderly* (pp. 172–181). New York: Springer.

This author examines and challenges some of the current assumptions about ethnicity, stress, and health, and recommends reformulation of the research question. In a recent study conducted by this author, groups of alcoholic and nonalcoholic black elderly were studied using a perceived stress scale. All of the subjects were low-income inner-city elderly with one or more chronic illness. The items on the perceived stress scale measured failure to cope, such as the frequency of controlling anger, nervousness, and feelings of lack of control and of being overwhelmed. There were no differences between the alcoholic and nonalcoholic group, and individuals experiencing significant numbers of stressful conditions did not score high on perceived levels of stress because they were managing the conditions successfully. This study concludes that there is a lack of culturally appropriate measures for stress and subjective well-being for minority elderly and that using self-reports instead of demographics related to illness would identify resources used by minority elderly in defining, experiencing, and coping with stressors.

Support

Chatters, L. M., Taylor, R. J., & Jackson, J. S. (1985). Size and composition of the informal helper networks of elderly blacks. *Journal of Gerontology, 40,* 605–614.

The informal support networks of older African Americans were examined in this study, which focused on network size, composition, and characteristics. Taken from a national survey, the analysis was based on interviews with 581 African American elderly, aged 55 and older. Of this sample, 36%

responded that they had daily contact with nonhousehold family members. More than half of the sample could name three people who would offer them assistance in case of illness. Of the demographic factors studied, female sex, being married, and residence in the South significantly predicted larger network size. The presence of children was associated with larger helper network size. Most respondents had helper networks composed solely of immediate family members.

Dowd, J. J., & La Rossa, R. (1982). Primary group contact and elderly morale: An exchange/power analysis. *Sociology and Social Science Research, 66,* 184–197.

This study was an examination of the linkage between family interaction and morale, with particular emphasis on the potential impact of dependency as a contingent or qualifier variable. The hypotheses were that intervention with children will have a positive effect on morale only for subjects who are able to retain a sense of autonomy and control in their lives and that the morale of dependent elderly would be negatively affected by visiting family. The sample consisted of 920 residents in the Atlanta, Georgia, area, aged 50 to 80. Of this sample, 20% were African Americans. Dependency was measured by self-assessment of health; morale was measured by a modified version of the Philadelphia Geriatric Center Morale Scale. Race, income, sex, and age were used as control variables. The researchers concluded that frequency of contact with children was not significantly associated with morale. Those who reported seeing any of their children on a yearly basis had the highest morale.

Choice, Centering, and Connectedness

Gibson, R. (1989). Minority aging research: Opportunity and challenge. *Journal of Gerontology: Social Sciences, 44,* S2–S3.

The author of this article discusses reasons for improving the quality and increasing the quantity of minority aging research. Extant theoretical formulations and methological problems are addressed, as are strategies for developing a core body of knowledge.

Gibson, R., & Jackson, J. S. (1990). The black American oldest old. In R. Suzman, D. Willis, & K. Manton (Eds.), *The oldest old* (pp. 421–453). New York: Oxford University Press.

The authors state that the purpose of this chapter is to describe the health, functioning, and informal supports of the black oldest old and to recommend new directions for research on this population. The data for the analysis were drawn from two national probability samples, the National Survey of Black Americans and the Three-Generation Black Family Study. The health and functioning of the black oldest old (individuals 80 and over) are compared to the black young (aged 65 to 74) and old-old (aged 75 to 79). The article adds to what is already known about the healthy, functioning and social support of older community-dwelling blacks by examining differences in health and functioning and the association with differences in informal support.

Gibson, R., & Jackson, J. S. (1987). The health, physical functioning, and informal supports of the black elderly. *The Milbank Memorial Fund Quarterly, 65,* 421–452.

A subsample of the two national probability samples, the National Survey of Black Americans and the Three-Generation Black Family Study was selected for a study of the noninstitutionalized African American aged 65 to 101. The determinants of effective functioning are identified.

Harwood, A. (Ed.). (1981). *Ethnicity and medical care.* Cambridge, MA: Harvard University Press.

This author defines ethnicity and places it on an ideological and behavioral continuum.

Ethnicity defines groups of people on the basis of both common origins and shared symbols and standards for behaviors as these groups interact with a larger social system. The degree to which an individual adheres to ethnic standards of health behavior is related to the amount and kind of exposure to which he or she has been acculturated to more pervasive American norms of health behavior. A number of specific determinants of this acculturation are enumerated: (1) a relatively high level of formal education; (2) greater generational removal from immigrant status; (3) a low degree of encapsulation within an ethnic and family social network; (4) experience with medical services that incorporate patient education and personalized care into treatment; (5) previous experience with particular diseases in the immediate family; (6) immigration to this country at an early age; (7) urban, as opposed to rural, origin; and (8) limited migration back and forth to the mother country. The author suggests that the behavioral and ideological ethnicity that influences adherence to medical regimens consists of ethnic concepts of disease and illness, folk and popular traditions of health care, problems of language and translation, dietary practices, interactional norms, and the role of the family in compliance with long-term treatment. Because of any or all of these factors, individuals may not discontinue home remedies or cures prescribed by alternative healers. Consequently, it is recommended that health care professionals change the delivery system so that clinicians are able to spend time in applying ideas and contributing to the delivery of maximally efficient and beneficial service to members of ethnic groups.

Hopper, S. V. (1993). The influence of ethnicity on the health of older women. *Clinics in Geriatric Medicine: Care of the older women, 9*(1), 231–253.

This author profiles African Americans, Hispanic Americans, Asian Americans, and American Indian women, describing how ethnicity takes on a special meaning in late life. The interaction of ethnicity, cohort experience, risk factors, gender differences in health behavior and access to health care within each of these ethnic groups is examined.

Jackson, J. J. (1988). Aging black women and public policies. *Black Scholar, 19*, 31–42.

In this paper, the accuracy of characterizations of elderly African American women is evaluated and major issues related to the social, economic, and health conditions of their lives are identified. The author suggests that the literature and the media treat African American women as a homogeneous group and focus on their negative aspects, and that this perpetuates stereotypes and inaccurately links African Americans to other minorities with different cultural values and socioeconomic status. Demographic data are presented on the social well-being of older African American women, including their education, marital status, living arrangements, social contacts, housing, transportation, and safety. Data are also presented on the economic well-being of older African American women, including their income, retirement, employment, and the future of Social Security and Medicare. The health status of elderly African American women and issues that should be considered in data collection are identified.

Taylor, R. J. (1980). The impact of federal health care policy on the elderly poor: The special case of the black elderly. In Gerontological Society of America, *33rd Scientific Meeting of the Gerontological Society of America, Nov. 23, 1980, San Diego, CA.* (25). Washington, DC: Gerontological Society of America.

The focus of this study is the social and economic status of the African American elderly, their health status, rates of health service use, and the effect of Medicaid and Medicare on this group. African American elderly tend to rank lower than white elderly on social indicators of health status, that is, income, education, and housing. In addition, African American elderly tend to have lower health status than white elderly, as evidenced by several indicators (bed disability days, restricted activity days, and lower life expectancy). The data on use of health services indicate that African American elderly tend to use private physicians and hospitals less than do white elderly. This investigator concluded that Medicare and Medicaid do not adequately meet the needs of the African American elderly: they receive lower benefits per person enrolled. This investigator recommends, to promote full participation of African Americans in federal health care programs: (1) eliminate Medicare coinsurance payments; (2) alleviate nonfinancial barriers (transportation and discrimination) to medical care; and (3) emphasize preventive rather than institutional care.

Part II

Health Promotion and Maintenance

Chapter 4

Women, Diet, and Heart Disease

Amy Olson and Jackie Labat

Coronary heart disease (CHD), the leading cause of death in women, results in more deaths than all forms of cancer combined. Once considered a predominantly male disease, CHD is now recognized for the symptoms and death that occur in women 10 to 20 years later than in men. After menopause, the mortality rates in women increase, and deaths due to CHD actually exceed those for men (Amsterdam & Legato, 1993; National Cholesterol Education Program, 1993).

Many factors contribute to CHD; some are not modifiable, but many can be modified. This chapter focuses on diet-related variables that can alter blood lipids and, consequently, affect the potential risk of heart disease in women.

Among the dietary factors that may affect blood lipids are: alcohol, antioxidants, calories (particularly as they affect body weight and fat distribution), dietary cholesterol, the quality of fat in the diet (i.e., the amount of saturated, polyunsaturated, and monounsaturated fats, and/or trans fatty acids), and the total quantity of fat in the diet.

DIETARY VARIABLES AFFECTING BLOOD LIPID LEVELS

Alcohol

In France, death due to CHD is much less than would be expected, based on the saturated fat intake and serum cholesterol levels. The annual mortality rate due to CHD for women in Toulouse, France, is nearly 5 times lower than the annual rate for the women of Stanford, California; yet the average serum cholesterol level of French women is 9% higher than that of the women of Stanford (Renaud & de Lorgeril, 1992).

This French phenomenon is attributed to alcohol consumption. Alcohol increases high-density lipoproteins (HDLs), which are protective against heart disease, and alcohol may reduce the tendency to develop clots (Renaud & de Lorgeril, 1992). Alcoholic beverages, particularly red wine, may contain substances that act as antioxidants and prevent oxidation of blood lipids (Frankel, Kanner, German, Parks, & Kinsella, 1993). Oxidized lipids accelerate the process of plaque development (Steinberg, Parthasarathy, Carew, Khoo, & Witztum, 1989).

When large populations are studied, a strong relationship between alcohol intake and a reduced risk of heart disease is apparent (Garg, Wagener, & Madans, 1993; Linn et al., 1993; Meilahn et al., 1991). Women who consume 0.5 to 2 drinks per day have a 40% lower risk when compared to abstainers (Garg et al., 1993). Higher HDL levels appear to be associated with all types of alcoholic beverages—beer, wine, and liquor.

Higher HDL levels, however, do not account for all of the risk reduction. For example, HDL levels of the French women are not significantly higher than those of the California women. Red wine may be particularly protective because it contains antioxidant compounds, and wine is typically consumed slowly with a meal. Fats promote platelet aggregation (sticking together) and alcohol inhibits this clumping tendency. Therefore, alcohol may suppress or inhibit the clotting and thrombotic tendencies associated with higher levels of fat circulating in the blood (Renaud & de Lorgeril, 1992).

Antioxidants

The antioxidants include several vitamins, antioxidant enzymes, nonenzymatic scavengers, and minerals that act as activators (cofactors) for the antioxidant enzymes (Olson & Kobayashi, 1992). Most of the recent attention has gone to the antioxidant vitamins: vitamin E, vitamin C, and beta carotene. Antioxidants are believed to play a role in the prevention of cancer, cataracts, CHD, and, possibly, some neurological disorders. The primary function of antioxidants is to neutralize toxic compounds such as free radicals (molecules with an unpaired electron, which are very reactive). Free radicals are produced through normal metabolic processes involving oxygen and can trigger chain reactions that produce more free radicals. Under optimal conditions, enzymes and antioxidants break this chain reaction, limiting any damaging effect.

At the moment, antioxidants are a suggested but as yet unproven means to decrease the risk of cardiovascular disease. The existing data are strongest for vitamin E. Women who took vitamin E supplements of 100 to 250 IU (International Units) for more than 2 years demonstrated a substantial reduction in risk (Stampfer et al., 1993).

CALORIES, BODY WEIGHT, AND WAIST–HIP RATIO

Excess calories contribute to obesity, which has been identified as an independent risk factor for heart attack in women. Women who are 30% above ideal body weight are 3 times more likely to have a heart attack than lean women. Obese women who also have high serum cholesterol levels demonstrate 8 times the risk. It appears that the more severe the obesity, the greater the risk (Cole et al., 1992). For each pound gained above ideal weight, the death rate increases by 2% (Castelli, 1988). Obesity is also associated with lower HDL levels (Clifton & Nestel, 1992; Cole et al., 1992). Women with higher body weights have significantly lower HDLs compared to women with lower body weights (Meilahn et al., 1991).

The waist–hip ratio (WHR) reflects the distribution of fat and provides additional information regarding risk. A large WHR (the apple shape) is more characteristic of (but not limited to) men, and is associated with a higher risk than the pear shape (more characteristic of women) even when matched for body weight (Olson, 1993). Women with higher WHRs have significantly lower HDLs when compared to women with lower WHRs (Meilahn et al., 1991).

If excess weight is associated with lower HDLs, what is the effect of weight loss on blood lipids? Weight loss brings about a decrease in total serum cholesterol, a decrease in LDLs (low-density lipoproteins associated with the greatest risk of heart disease), a decrease in triglycerides, and an increase in HDLs (Dattilo & Kris-Etherton, 1992). However, weight regain or weight cycling causes greater risk than simply maintaining a higher body weight (Lissner et al., 1991).

DIETARY CHOLESTEROL

Of all the food components that affect health, Americans probably have heard the most about dietary cholesterol. Most consumers believe that the fastest way to develop heart disease is to eat eggs (a concentrated source of cholesterol). Early research identified the lipid deposits in blood vessels as cholesterol; consequently, dietary cholesterol was originally assumed to be responsible. However, later research revealed a complex relationship between diet and serum cholesterol levels: the latter are more affected by the quantity and type of fat in the diet than by the amount of dietary cholesterol. For example, when 3 eggs are eaten within a diet low in saturated fat (high in polyunsaturated fat), there is no effect on serum cholesterol; however, when eggs are eaten within a diet high in saturated fat (low in polyunsaturated fat), a significant increase in serum cholesterol is evident. With an increase in the total quantity of fat in the diet, an increase in serum cholesterol is observed (Grundy, Barrett-Connor, Rudel, Miettinen, & Spector, 1988; Hopkins, 1992).

FAT QUANTITY

Because a high intake of fat has been associated with many diseases, a reduction of dietary fat to the lowest practical level was assumed to be desirable. However, when women finally became the subjects of research, some unexpected results were observed. Decreasing the fat from 40% to 20% of the energy food intake yielded the anticipated decreases in total serum cholesterol and LDLs, but simultaneous decreases in HDLs and increases in serum triglycerides occurred. The overall result was *not* an improvement in the lipid profile for women (Brussard, Dallinga-Thie, Groot, & Katan, 1980; Cole et al., 1992; Jones, Judd, Taylor, Campbell, & Nair, 1987; Mensink & Katan, 1987). Low HDLs and high triglycerides are the major predictors of CHD risk in women, and adverse changes in these parameters actually overshadow any benefit of a lower total serum cholesterol and LDL (NIH Consensus Conference, 1993).

FAT QUALITY

In general, saturated fats raise serum cholesterol and polyunsaturated fats lower serum cholesterol. For every 1% increase in saturated fat, serum cholesterol increases approximately 2.7 mg/dL; in contrast, for every 1%

increase in polyunsaturated fat, a 1.4 mg/dL *reduction* in serum cholesterol is expected (Boyd et al., 1990; Cole et al., 1992).

Mediterranean diets, which are high in total fat intake (40% of calories), are associated with a surprisingly low incidence of CHD. The unique feature of these diets is their monounsaturated fat content. Diets high in monounsaturated fat (40.6% fat, olive oil) provide the same dramatic decreases in serum cholesterol as a low fat diet (22% fat). However, the low fat diet (high carbohydrate diet) also decreases HDLs and increases serum triglycerides (Mensink & Katan, 1987). The lipid lowering power of monounsaturated fat is evident without a decrease in the total quantity of fat and without adverse effects on HDLs. Monounsaturated fats do not lower HDLs even at high intakes (>12%) and may have the additional advantage of reducing oxidation of LDL particles. LDLs with high monounsaturated fatty acids are more resistant to oxidation than LDLs containing high polyunsaturated fat (McDonald, 1991).

The quantity of fat apparently is not as important as the type of fat. When fat quantity was reduced (37% to 30%) without a corresponding reduction in the saturated fat (i.e., only monounsaturated fat was reduced), no benefit in lipid profiles was observed (Barr et al., 1992; Masana, Camprubi, Sarda, Sola, & Turner, 1991).

Recent research has focused on the effects of specific fatty acids. Apparently, not all saturated fatty acids are equal in their influence on serum cholesterol. Myristic acid (C 14:0) is the most hypercholesterolemic, followed by palmitic acid (C 16:0), and lauric acid (C 12:0). Stearic acid (C 18:0), although saturated, is fairly neutral and is probably equal to oleic acid (C 18:1) in its effects relative to linoleic acid (C 18:2) (Kris-Etherton et al., 1988; Zock, de Vries, & Katan, 1994).

TRANS FATTY ACIDS

Unsaturated fatty acids have a characteristic geometry or shape, typically a *cis* configuration. When vegetable oils are partially hydrogenated, isomers (alternately shaped) fatty acids are formed, and a number of *trans* and unnatural *cis* isomers can result (Emken, 1984).

Consumer pressure to reduce the cholesterol and saturated fat content of commercial foods prompted the food industry to shift from the use of animal shortenings (which contain cholesterol and saturated fats) to vegetable oils (which do not contain cholesterol and are largely polyunsaturated). However, some food products and cooking methods (e.g., deep-fat frying) require fat in a semisolid form. Converting vegetable oils to semisolids can be accomplished through the process of hydrogenation, which changes some of the double bonds to single bonds, thereby improving the flavor and lengthening the fryer life of these fats. The more double bonds in the fat, the more easily it is oxidized and the faster it develops a rancid taste. The lengthened stability of partially hydrogenated fats has important economic implications for the food industry (Emken, 1984). The trans fatty acid content of commercial fats may vary from 0% for high-linoleic acid "diet" margarines to over 50% for certain frying fats (Katan & Mensink, 1992).

The major source of trans fatty acids is partially hydrogenated soybean oil in margarine and spreads, closely followed by industrial shortenings used in products such as cookies, crackers, mayonnaise, cakes, pies, rolls, candies, potato chips, roasted nuts, and many other snack and convenience foods (Hunter & Applewhite, 1991).

A recent assessment of trans fatty acid availability in U.S. diet estimates approximately 8.1 g/day/person, which is only slightly higher than the 1986 estimate of 7.6 g/day/person. The increase in trans fatty acid availability is attributed to the food industry's increased use of partially hydrogenated vegetable fats (and decreased use of animal fats) in snack and convenience items (Hunter & Applewhite, 1986, 1991). For example, the fat in McDonald's and Burger King's french fries is now 24% and 35% trans fatty acids respectively (Willett et al., 1993).

Because trans fatty acids are structurally different from natural dietary fats, a number of concerns have surfaced regarding how these altered fats are metabolized. Are trans fatty acids oxidized in the same way as other fatty acids? Do trans fatty acids accumulate in the body, increasing their potential risk over time? What specific changes are observed with increased levels of trans fatty acid intake?

Recent attention to the potential adverse effects of trans fatty acids was stimulated by a report, in 1990, that trans fatty acids adversely affected blood lipids. A diet high in trans fatty acids intake (11% of the daily energy) resulted in an increase in LDLs and a decrease in HDLs when compared to a diet high in monounsaturated fat (oleic acid). However, this level of trans fatty acids is approximately 4 times the estimated average American intake of trans fatty acids (Mensink & Katan, 1990). When a lower level ($\sim$ 8%) of trans fatty acids was used, a smaller increase in serum total cholesterol and LDLs was observed, and HDLs decreased slightly when compared to a diet high in polyunsaturated fat (linoleic acid) (Zock & Katan, 1992). Another change associated with elaidic acid, a trans fatty acid, is an increase in the levels of lipoprotein [a] [Lp[a]] (Nestel et al., 1992). Lp[a] is a genetic risk factor for premature CHD and is considered to be relatively resistant to change by low fat diets or lipid lowering medications (Scanu, 1992). The exact implication of this observation is not clear but warrants additional study.

IMPLICATIONS OF LITERATURE FOR EDUCATION, PRACTICE, AND RESEARCH

Education

The first step in education is to recognize the unique aspects of women and apply interventions specific to their needs and physiology. The levels of individual lipoproteins are different in women relative to men, and the predictive risks associated with the lipoprotein levels have different significance. Elevated serum total cholesterol is a known risk factor for men and women; however, in women, risk is not serious until serum cholesterol exceeds 264 mg/dL, whereas in men, significant risk is observed at 199 mg/dL (Cole et al., 1992). This observation can in part be explained by the fact that HDLs are 10 to 20 mg/dL higher in women than in men and stay relatively constant with age. LDLs are typically lower in women, which means that more of the serum cholesterol value is due to "good" cholesterol (i.e., HDLs); consequently, there is less risk. However, after menopause, LDLs increase and may exceed those observed in men, contributing to the increased risk observed postmenopause. In women, the strongest predictors of risk for CHD have been identified as: diabetes mellitus, HDLs below 45 mg/dL, serum total cholesterol–HDL ratio in excess of 5.5, and serum triglyceride levels greater than 150 mg/dL (Amsterdam & Legato, 1993; Bass, Newschaffer, Klag, & Bush, 1993; Castelli, 1988, 1990).

The newly revised National Cholesterol Education Program (NCEP, 1993) guidelines have largely been derived from data obtained from men and have limited sensitivity for women. The first problem is the recommendation to use serum total cholesterol as the initial screening tool. Total cholesterol is not a sensitive indicator of risk in women, as previously mentioned; HDLs would be a far better screening tool. A second problem is that the NCEP cutoff for HDL to identify individuals at risk, <35 mg/dL, is unreasonably low. Women with HDL levels > 35 but < 50 have demonstrated increased risk for CHD; 50 mg/dL as a cutoff would therefore be a more appropriate level for women. Finally, NCEP does not include a risk classification based on serum triglyceride levels, thus omitting another significant risk variable for women (Bass et al., 1993).

Some diet-related variables can significantly affect blood lipids in women and modify their risk of CHD. If HDL levels are raised by 10 mg/dL (from 40 to 50 mg/dL), the risk of CHD will drop by about one-third, according to the Framingham Heart Study. Women with a relatively low body mass index (BMI, an indicator of obesity) and low WHR, who don't smoke, who exercise to expend >2,000 Calories per week, and who have, on average, one alcoholic drink per day, will have HDL levels ~33 mg/dL higher than women with high BMI and WHR, who smoke >20 cigarettes per day, who don't drink, and who exercise to expend less than 500 Calories per week (Clifton & Nestel, 1992; Meilahn et al., 1991). This observation provides some optimism that the risk of CHD in women can be reduced through diet and life-style changes.

The following recommendations for diet take women's needs into account:

1. Consume at least 25% of your calories as fat in the diet. Diets containing <25% fat lower HDLs and increase triglycerides, which adversely affects risk in women. The current American Heart Association recommendation is to consume 30% "or less" fat, which unfortunately is frequently interpreted as "the lower your fat intake the better," a rule that is not true for women.

2. Consume a relatively equal mixture of fats—saturated, monounsaturated, and polyunsaturated—with an emphasis on monounsaturated fat. For example, cook with olive oil or canola oil.

3. Individuals who are at high risk for CHD should be aware of sources of trans fatty acids and avoid excessive consumption of foods containing partially hydrogenated vegetable oils. Trans fatty acids increase LDLs and decrease HDLs, potentially adding to the CHD risk in individuals with high blood lipids. The average woman who does not consume excessive quantities of convenience foods and commercial baked products and uses margarine or spreads in moderation does not need to be concerned about trans fatty acid intake.

4. If you consume alcohol, the key is consistent moderation. Individuals who drink 0.5 to 2 drinks per day may have higher HDLs. Avoid excessive alcohol consumption and occasional binge drinking; these behaviors have been clearly associated with adverse risk and other health problems. Women who are pregnant or at risk for breast cancer should not drink alcoholic beverages.

5. Antioxidants may be beneficial. Vitamin E appears to be effective at levels of 100–250 IU per day. This level of intake of vitamin E (α-tocopherol) cannot be realistically provided by food sources and therefore requires a supplement. The richest food sources of vitamin E are oils, seeds, and nuts. However, to obtain 100–250 IU of vitamin E (~67 to 168 mg) from safflower oil (a particularly rich source), ¾ cup to 2 cups of safflower oil would have to be consumed daily, for an intake of 1,541 to 3,854 calories! Incorporating this quantity of oil into foods would be challenging.

   Optimal doses for vitamin C and beta carotene for antioxidant activity have not been determined; however, research suggests that diets including daily menu items of fresh fruits and vegetables may provide sufficient quantities of these vitamins to derive beneficial results.

6. Aim for permanent weight loss. Women who lose weight may increase their HDLs and decrease triglyceride levels. However, because weight fluctuation or weight cycling is associated with increased risk, staying overweight may be safer than cycling your weight. Strive for a gradual weight loss accomplished by a moderate reduction in calories and an increase in exercise, and make these modifications as permanent behavior changes.

Practice

Several important observations must be remembered in practice:

1. Women are different from men;
2. Hypercholesterolemic individuals respond to diet more dramatically than do individuals with normal serum cholesterol;
3. Age exerts little effect in how women respond to diet;
4. Women demonstrate more dramatic changes in HDLs in response to diet than do men.

We currently label saturated fat as "bad" and polyunsaturated fat as "good." In reality, not all saturated fatty acids increase blood lipids, and some unsaturated fatty acids—trans fatty acids in particular—may have adverse effects. The effect of trans fatty acids appears to be similar to the effect of saturated fat, except that HDLs may also be lowered. Unfortunately, the new nutrition facts labels required by the Food and Drug Administration (FDA) do not specifically identify the trans fatty acid content of a product. The trans content is included in the polyunsaturated fat or monounsaturated fat values. For an individual who is at high risk for CHD, it is important to recognize the food sources of trans fatty acids and consume products that contain partially hydrogenated oils only in moderation.

Alcohol has been labeled one of the most efficient drugs for the prevention of CHD when consumed regularly and in moderation (1 to 2 drinks per day). The data on alcohol's effect on HDLs come largely from epidemiological studies, because of ethical problems with experimental designs that could precisely test cause-and-effect. In other words, we cannot predict the exact effect of a regular dose of alcohol on HDL; what we do know is that individuals who drink the most alcohol have the highest HDLs. Epidemiological studies fail to examine all the effects of alcohol; their focus is largely on HDLs. Heavier alcohol consumption (>3 drinks per day) is associated with many serious problems: cirrhosis, hemorrhagic stroke, hypertension, breast cancer, oral and esophageal cancer, and direct damage to the heart muscle itself (Linn et al., 1993). Binge drinking or heavy weekend drinking may result in a rebound effect of increased platelet aggregation increasing the risk of clot formation and sudden death (Renaud & de Lorgeril, 1992).

Many professionals are reluctant to recommend regular alcohol intake for protection against CHD, because of the potential risks associated with excessive alcohol consumption. Women who have significant risk factors for breast cancer (Longnecker, 1994) and women who are pregnant should avoid alcohol consumption completely. Alcohol consumption during pregnancy may cause damage to an unborn child, resulting in fetal alcohol syndrome.

Research

A number of important issues are being studied in current research. A large multicenter project funded by the National Heart, Lung, and Blood Institute is just beginning and will attempt to finally clarify much of the conflicting data regarding the effects of dietary fat on blood lipids. Failure to use similar control groups and extreme variations in experimental design have made a collective analysis of data from different researchers impossible. A major emphasis for the new project is the inclusion of sufficient women and minorities to extend the data to these understudied populations.

Two current studies, the Physicians' Health Study and the Women's Health Study, should help to fill the gaps in information regarding the effectiveness of antioxidants in preventing CHD. The Women's Health Study will involve 40,000 nurses and aims to determine the relative risks and benefits of beta carotene, vitamin E, and vitamin C (Kritchevsky, 1992).

Another goal of ongoing research is to determine how alcohol exerts its effect on HDLs. Alcohol stimulates synthesis of apoprotein A-1 (the major protein of HDLs) in cultured hepatocytes. If HDL production could be stimulated, we may in the future be able to increase HDLs to more protective levels without the potential adverse effects of alcohol (Staff, 1993). Research on the effects of specific fatty acids may ultimately direct the formulation of "designer fats." Natural products such as butter could be stripped of cholesterol and the proportions of fatty acids altered to reduce the hypercholesterolemic effects, thus avoiding unnatural products of hydrogenation. We may finally be able to have our butter and eat it too.

The bottom line is: more research is needed with women subjects. We are just beginning to recognize that women respond to diet differently. To protect their health and improve medical interventions, we must have data that are specific to women.

REFERENCES

Amsterdam, E. A., & Legato, M. J. (1993). What's unique about CHD in women? *Patient Care, 27,* 21–61.

Barr, S. L., Ramakrishnan, R., Johnson, C., Holleran, S., Dell, R. B., & Ginsberg, H. N. (1992). Reducing total dietary fat without reducing saturated fatty acids does not significantly lower total plasma cholesterol concentrations in normal males. *The American Journal of Clinical Nutrition, 55,* 675–681.

Bass, K. M., Newschaffer, C. J., Klag, M. J., & Bush, T. L. (1993). Plasma lipoprotein levels as predictors of cardiovascular death in women. *Archives of Internal Medicine, 153,* 2209–2216.

Boyd, N. F., Cousins, M., Beaton, M., Kriukov, V., Lockwood, G., & Tritchler, D. (1990). Quantitative changes in dietary fat intake and serum cholesterol in women: Results from a randomized, controlled trial. *The American Journal of Clinical Nutrition, 52,* 470–476.

Brussaard, J. H., Dallinga-Thie, G., Groot, P. H., & Katan, M. B. (1980). Effects of amount and type of dietary fat on serum lipids, lipoproteins and apolipoproteins in man. *Atherosclerosis, 36,* 515–527.

Castelli, W. P. (1988). Cardiovascular disease in women. *American Journal of Obstetrics and Gynecology, 158,* 1553–1560.

Castelli, W. P. (1990). Diet, smoking, and alcohol: Influence on coronary heart disease risk. *American Journal of Kidney Diseases, 16,* 41–46.

Clifton, P. M., & Nestel, P. J. (1992). Influence of gender, body mass index, and age on response of plasma lipids to dietary fat plus cholesterol. *Arteriosclerosis and Thrombosis, 12,* 955–962.

Cole, T. G., Bowen, P. E., Schmeisser, D., Prewitt, T. E., Aye, P., Langenberg, P., Dolecek, T. A., Brace, L. D., & Kamath, S. (1992). Differential reduction of plasma cholesterol by the American Heart Association Phase 3 Diet in moderately hypercholesterolemic, premenopausal women with different body mass indexes. *The American Journal of Clinical Nutrition, 55,* 385–394.

Dattilo, A. M., & Kris-Etherton, P. M. (1992). Effects of weight reduction on blood lipids and lipoproteins: A meta-analysis. *The American Journal of Clinical Nutrition, 56,* 320–328.

Emken, E. A. (1984). Nutrition and biochemistry of trans and positional fatty acid isomers in hydrogenated oils. *Annual Reviews of Nutrition, 4,* 339–376.

Frankel, E. N., Kanner, J., German, J. B., Parks, E., & Kinsella, J. E. (1993). Inhibition of oxidation of human low-density lipoprotein by phenolic substances in red wine. *The Lancet, 341,* 454–457.

Garg, R., Wagener, D. K., & Madans, J. H. (1993). Alcohol consumption and risk of ischemic heart disease in women. *Archives of Internal Medicine, 153,* 1211–1216.

Grundy, S. M., Barrett-Connor, E., Rudel, L. L., Miettinen, T., & Spector, A. A. (1988). Workshop on the impact of dietary cholesterol on plasma lipoproteins and atherogenesis. *Arteriosclerosis, 8,* 85–101.

Grundy, S. M., & Denke, M. A. (1990). Dietary influences on serum lipids and lipoproteins. *Journal of Lipid Research, 31,* 1149–1172.

Hopkins, P. N. (1992). Effects of dietary cholesterol on serum cholesterol: A meta-analysis and review. *The American Journal of Clinical Nutrition, 59,* 1050–1054.

Hudgins, L. C., Hirch, J., & Emken, E. A. (1991). Correlation of isometric fatty acids in human adipose tissue with clinical risk factors for cardiovascular disease. *The American Journal of Clinical Nutrition, 53,* 474–482.

Hunter, J. E., & Applewhite, T. H. (1986). Isomeric fatty acids in the U.S. diet: Levels and health perspectives. *The American Journal of Clinical Nutrition, 44,* 707–717.

Hunter, J. E., & Applewhite, T. H. (1991). Reassessment of trans fatty acid availability in the U.S. diet. *The American Journal of Clinical Nutrition, 54,* 363–369.

Jones, D. Y., Judd, J. T., Taylor, P. R., Campbell, W. S., & Nair, P. P. (1987). Influence of caloric contribution and saturation of dietary fat on plasma lipids on premenopausal women. *The American Journal of Clinical Nutrition, 45,* 1451–1456.

Katan, M. B., & Mensink, R. P. (1992). Isomeric fatty acids and serum lipoproteins. *Nutrition Reviews, 50,* 46–48.

Kris-Etherton, P. M., Krummel, D., Dreon, D., Mackey, S., Borchers, J., & Wood, P. D. (1988). The effect of diet on plasma lipids, lipoproteins, and coronary heart disease. *Journal of the American Dietetics Association, 88,* 1373–1397.

Kritchevsky, D. (1992). Antioxidant vitamins in the prevention of cardiovascular disease. *Nutrition Today, 27,* 30–33.

Linn, S., Carroll, M., Johnson, C., Fulwood, R., Kalsbeek, W., & Briefel, R. (1993). High-density lipoprotein cholesterol and alcohol consumption in U.S. white and black adults: Data from NHANES II. *American Journal of Public Health, 83,* 811–816.

Lissner, L., Odell, P. M., D'Agostino, R. B., Stokes III, J., Kreger, B. E., Belanger, A. J., & Brownell, K. D. (1991). Variability of body weight and health outcomes in the Framingham population. *New England Journal of Medicine, 324,* 1839–1844.

Longnecker, M. P. (1994). Alcoholic beverage consumption in relation to risk of breast cancer: Meta-analysis and review. *Cancer Causes and Control, 5,* 73–82.

Masana, L., Camprubi, M., Sarda, P., Sola, R., & Turner, P. R. (1991). The Mediterranean-type diet: Is there a need for further modification? *The American Journal of Clinical Nutrition, 53,* 886–889.

McDonald, B. E. (1991). Monounsaturated fatty acids and heart health. *Canadian Medical Association Journal, 145,* 473.

Meilahn, E. N., Kuller, L. H., Matthews, K. A., Wing, R. R., Caggiula, A. W., & Stein, E. A. (1991). Potential for increasing high-density lipoprotein cholesterol, subfractions HDL_2-C and HDL_3-C, and Apoprotein A-1 among middle-age women. *Preventive Medicine, 20,* 462–473.

Mensink, R. P., & Katan, M. B. (1987). Effect of monounsaturated fatty acids versus complex carbohydrates on high-density lipoproteins in healthy men and women. *The Lancet, 1,* 122–125.

Mensink, R. P., & Katan, M. B. (1989). Effect of a diet enriched with monounsaturated or polyunsaturated fatty acids on levels of low-density and high-density lipoprotein cholesterol in healthy women and men. *The New England Journal of Medicine, 321,* 436–441.

Mensink, R. P., & Katan, M. B. (1990). Effect of trans fatty acids on high-density and low-density lipoprotein cholesterol levels in healthy subjects. *The New England Journal of Medicine, 323,* 439–445.

National Cholesterol Education Program (NCEP). (1993). Summary of the Second Report. *Journal of the American Medical Association, 269,* 3015–3023.

Nestel, P., Noakes, M., Belling, B., McArthur, R., Clifton, P., Janus, E., & Abbey, M. (1992). Plasma lipoprotein lipid and Lp[a] changes with substitution of elaidic acid for oleic acid in the diet. *Journal of Lipid Research, 33,* 1029–1036.

NIH Consensus Conference. (1993). Triglyceride, high-density lipoprotein, and coronary heart disease. *Journal of the American Medical Association, 269,* 505–510.

Olson, A. (1993). Women and weight control. In B. J. McElmurry & R. S. Parker (Eds.), *Annual review of women's health* (pp. 199–242). New York: National League for Nursing Press.

Olson, J., & Kobayashi, S. (1992). Antioxidants in health and disease: Overview. *Proceedings of the Society for Experimental Biology and Medicine, 200,* 245–247.

Renaud, S., & de Lorgeril, M. (1992). Wine, alcohol, platelets, and the French paradox for coronary heart disease. *The Lancet, 339,* 1523–1526.

Scanu, A. M. (1992). Lipoprotein (a): A genetic risk factor for premature coronary heart disease. *Journal of the American Medical Association, 267,* 3326–3329.

Staff. (1990). Eicosanoid synthesis is unaffected by dietary trans fatty acids if sufficient linoleic acid is fed. *Nutrition Reviews, 48,* 185–196.

Staff. (1991). Trans fatty acids and serum cholesterol levels. *Nutrition Reviews, 49,* 57–60.

Staff. (1993). Ethanol stimulates Apo A-1 secretion in human hepatocytes: A possible mechanism underlying the cardioprotective effect of ethanol. *Nutrition Reviews, 51,* 151–152.

Stampfer, M. J., Hennekens, C. H., Manson, J. E., Colditz, G. A., Rosner, B., & Willett, W. C. (1993). Vitamin E consumption and the risk of coronary heart disease in women. *The New England Journal of Medicine, 328,* 1444–1449.

Steinberg, D., Parthasarathy, S., Carew, T. E., Khoo, J. C., & Witztum, J. L. (1989). Beyond cholesterol: Modifications of low-density lipoprotein that increase its atherogenicity. *The New England Journal of Medicine, 320,* 915–924.

Willett, W. C., Stampfer, M. J., Manson, J. E., Colditz, G. A., Speizer, F. E., Rosner, B. A., Sampson, L. A., & Hennekens, C. H. (1993). Intake of trans fatty acids and risk of coronary heart disease among women. *The Lancet, 341,* 581–585.

Zock, P. L., & Katan, M. B. (1992). Hydrogenation alternatives: Effects of trans fatty acids and stearic acid versus linoleic acid on serum lipids and lipoproteins in humans. *Journal of Lipid Research, 33,* 399–410.

Zock, P. L., de Vries, J. H. M., & Katan, M. B. (1994). Impact of myristic acid versus palmitic acid on serum lipid and lipoprotein levels in healthy women and men. *Arteriosclerosis and Thrombosis, 14,* 567–575.

Women and Coronary Heart Disease

Amsterdam, E. A., & Legato, M. J. (1993). What's unique about CHD in women? *Patient Care, 27,* 21–61.

Emphasizing the fact that more women than men die of coronary heart disease (CHD), this article focuses on the significance of different risk factors in women vs. men. CHD kills 250,000 women each year, accounting for one-third of all deaths in U.S. women. Although women are at greater risk for CHD after age 55, most risk factors for CHD are the same for men and women. The relative importance of each risk factor, however, is different. Having diabetes mellitus, high-density lipoprotein (HDL) cholesterol below 45 mg/dL and a total cholesterol–HDL ratio greater than 5.5 are the strongest predictors of cardiovascular mortality in women. An elevated level of triglycerides (>150 mg/dL) also significantly increases risk. Higher HDL levels premenopause may explain the lower risk associated with younger women when compared to younger men. Additional risk factors for women include hypertension, smoking, and inactivity. Obesity is not an independent risk factor but is associated with increased risk, especially in women who carry excess weight around the middle, giving them a high waist–hip ratio. Although postmenopausal women using estrogen may improve their lipid profiles, oral contraceptive users may adversely affect their lipid profiles. The article discusses the differences in diagnosis and treatment of CHD in women as compared to men.

Bass, K. M., Newschaffer, C. J., Klag, M. J., & Bush, T. L. (1993). Plasma lipoprotein levels as predictors of cardiovascular death in women. *Archives of Internal Medicine, 153,* 2209–2216.

In this excellent article, research data from 1,405 female participants, aged 50 to 69 years, from the Lipid Research Clinics' Follow-up Study, are utilized to evaluate associations between cardiovascular disease (CVD) death and total cholesterol (TC), high-density lipoprotein (HDL), low-density lipoprotein (LDL), and triglycerides (TG) in women. Average follow-up was 14 years. Relative risk (RR) for categories of lipoproteins was determined as well as age-adjusted CVD death rates. Based on age-adjusted CVD death rates, without considering HDLs, an elevated risk of CVD death was noted only in women whose TC was greater than 240 mg/dL. Women with low HDLs had almost a threefold increased risk of CVD death when compared to women with high HDLs. LDLs were a poor predictor of CVD mortality. Women with high levels of HDL had similar CVD mortality rates at all TC levels. Women with high TG levels and low HDLs had CVD death rates that were almost eight times those of women with low HDLs and normal TG levels. Using multivariate analysis and controlling for other lipid risk factors, HDL and TG levels continued to be independent predictors of CVD death. This study raises questions with regard to current lipid screening values from the National Education Program and their sensitivity to women.

Clifton, P. M., & Nestel, P. J. (1992). Influence of gender, body mass index, and age on response of plasma lipids to dietary fat plus cholesterol. *Arteriosclerosis and Thrombosis, 12,* 955–962.

This study is unique in that the effects of dietary fat on blood lipids were studied in both men and women. The influence of gender on plasma lipids is very clear, as are the differences due to age and body mass index. The 51 subjects were started on a low fat diet—25% fat and dietary cholesterol <250 mg/day—for 2 weeks. For the next 3 weeks, one of two different liquid supplements was added. One supplement provided 31 g of fat (56% saturated, 17% polyunsaturated) and 650 mg of cholesterol; the other supplement provided the same number of calories but no fat or cholesterol.

Age: Baseline data on older women (>50 years old) demonstrated higher TC (6.18 mg/dL) and LDLs (4.14 mg/dL) and similar HDLs (1.38 mg/dL), compared to younger women (<50 years old): TC 5.33 mg/dL, LDL 3.45 mg/dL, HDL 1.40 mg/dL. In response to the higher fat diet, older women demonstrated a lower percentage increase in TC and LDL, and a higher percentage increase in HDL; that is, older women demonstrated a lower TC–HDL ratio and a higher HDL–LDL ratio—a more favorable lipid profile compared to younger women, in response to a higher saturated fat diet. The opposite effect was observed in men: younger men demonstrated the better lipid profile in response to higher saturated fat.

Body mass index: Women with BMI >25 had markedly lower HDL cholesterol (HDL 1.28 mg/dL) compared to women with BMI <25 (HDL 1.54 mg/dL). LDL was not significantly different between these two groups of women; BMI <25, TC 5.75 mg/dL and LDL 3.73 mg/dL; BMI >25, TC 5.67 mg/dL, and LDL 3.77 mg/dL. TC was higher among the lower body weight women because of the higher HDL cholesterol. Men did not demonstrate a difference in HDL as a function of BMI. In women, in response to the higher fat diet, BMI did not influence TC or LDL; a greater increase was observed in HDL for the BMI >25 women.

Serum cholesterol levels: Women with higher baseline serum cholesterol levels demonstrated the most dramatic responses to the higher saturated fat diet. TC and HDL for women (TC >5.5 mmol/L) demonstrated double the percentage increase in response to fat. LDL levels also increased more markedly in the hypercholesterolemic group. This trend was also true for men: the hypercholesterolemic group demonstrated the most remarkable increases in response to the higher saturated fat intake, and the magnitude of increase was even greater among the men.

Cole, T. G., Bowen, P. E., Schmeisser, D., Prewitt, T. E., Aye, P., Langenberg, P., Dolecek, T. A., Brace, L. D., & Kamath, S. (1992). Differential reduction of plasma cholesterol by the American Heart Association Phase 3 Diet in moderately hypercholesterolemic, premenopausal women with different body mass indexes. *The American Journal of Clinical Nutrition, 55,* 385–394.

This exceptionally well controlled study examined the effectiveness of a low fat diet (American Heart Association Phase 3 Diet: 20% fat, P:S ratio between 1.1 and 1.5) in premenopausal women who had moderately elevated cholesterol [mean 211 mg/dL]. The women studied presented a wide range of BMI: 19.5 to 44. Serum cholesterol ranged from 4.58 mmol/L–8.12 mmol/L [177 mg/dL–315 mg/dL]. Following a 1-month baseline period of the average American diet (~ 40% fat, P:S 0.43, >400 mg cholesterol), the experimental (low fat) diet lasted 5 months, a relatively long period. Data are presented for 19 women. Subjects consumed 2 meals per day, on 6 days each week, at the laboratory dining room. The third daily meal and the remaining weekend meals were packed for consumption away from the research center.

The obese women had a smaller cholesterol-lowering response and a higher triglyceride-raising response to diet. Overall, a 6.7% decrease in total cholesterol, a 9% overall decrease in LDLs, and a 7.4% overall decrease in HDL were observed. However, a 10% drop in HDL cholesterol was demonstrated by the lean group, and smaller changes were observed in the higher BMI groups. The greatest change occurred in the HDL_2 subfraction. Some researchers have suggested that the HDL_2 subfraction is protective and the HDL_3 is more neutral in its effects. In this study, total and LDL cholesterol decreased, but a simultaneous decline in HDLs resulted in no improvement of the ratio in HDL–LDL. In other words, the low fat diet did not reduce the risk of CHD in these women, and it could be argued that the reduction in HDLs and corresponding increase in triglycerides actually posed a greater risk.

Emken, E. A. (1984). Nutrition and biochemistry of trans and positional fatty acid isomers in hydrogenated oils. *Annual Reviews of Nutrition, 4,* 339–376.

This thorough review provides a good background of the biochemistry of trans fatty acids. Included are: dietary sources of isomeric fatty acids; estimated intake; data from physiological and metabolic studies related to growth and cell function; effects of trans fatty acids on lipid-metabolizing enzymes, lipoproteins, and tissue lipids; and results from health-related nutrition studies. Much of the data presented and discussed is from animal research. Subsequent to this publication, numerous human studies have been reported; however, the author does an excellent job of assimilating the information then available.

Garg, R., Wagener, D. K., & Madans, J. H. (1993). Alcohol consumption and risk of ischemic heart disease in women. *Archives of Internal Medicine, 153,* 1211–1216.

National Health and Nutrition Examination Survey 1 (NHANES 1) studied a nationally representative sample of women over a period of 13 years. The study of alcohol consumption revealed that women reporting any amount of alcohol consumption demonstrated a 20% lower risk of heart disease. The risk reduction was greatest (~ 40%) for the group consuming between 0.5 and 2 drinks per day. Because the number of individuals consuming more than 2 drinks per day was small, no additional subdivisions were made; consequently, in the group with the highest alcohol consumption, individual consumption ranged from 2 to 17 drinks per day. The beneficial effect of alcohol on HDL levels appeared substantial, but the authors remind us of the increased risk of breast cancer with moderate alcohol consumption, and of cirrhosis, cardiomyopathy, and sudden death with excessive consumption. The authors stress that the mechanism responsible for alcohol's effect is not known, and further research is needed before recommendations regarding alcohol should be made to the public.

Hunter, J. E., & Applewhite, T. H. (1986). Isomeric fatty acids in the U.S. diet: Levels and health perspectives. *The American Journal of Clinical Nutrition, 44,* 707–717.

Consumer trends since 1960 have moved to reduce saturated and increase polyunsaturated fatty acids, as reflected in a shift from animal to vegetable sources of fat. Consumption of margarine and cooking oils has significantly increased; sales of butter and animal shortenings have declined. The process of forming margarine and shortening from vegetable oils involves hydrogenation and induces isomeric changes in some fatty acids, from the *cis* to the *trans* isomer. Consequently, the higher the intake of margarine and vegetable shortening, the higher the intake of trans fatty acids. Trans fatty acids naturally occur in milk, butter, and tallow as a result of biohydrogenation in ruminants; these sources contribute small amounts of trans fatty acids to the diet. The authors evaluate the available levels of trans fatty acids in the diet and estimate daily levels to be 7.6 g/person/day.

Hunter, J. E., & Applewhite, T. H. (1991). Reassessment of trans fatty acid availability in the U.S. diet. *The American Journal of Clinical Nutrition, 54,* 363–369.

In this update of their 1986 publication on the trans fatty acid content of the American diet, the authors estimate an average per-person availability. Household use and more detailed information regarding the trans fatty acid contribution of food service and industrial fats are included. The greatest sources of trans fatty acids are margarine and hydrogenated shortenings made from vegetable oils. Ruminant animal products—milk, butter, and tallow—continue to contribute only a small amount of trans fatty acids to the American diet.

In the 5 years between the two publications, a number of changes occurred in consumer consumption patterns and in the processes for manufacturing fats:

1. Household salad and cooking oils, which were partially hydrogenated and consequently a source of trans fatty acids, are now unhydrogenated (↓ trans fatty acids);

2. Use of household shortenings declined (↓ trans fatty acids);

3. Total use of margarine and spreads increased, but preference shifted to spreads and tub margarine, which are lower in trans content than stick margarine, resulting overall in a slightly lower intake of trans fatty acids (↓ trans fatty acids);

4. Manufacture of pourable dressings and some brands of mayonnaiselike products from unhydrogenated soybean oil is very small (no change in trans fatty acids);

5. Industrial fats (used in salted snacks, cookies, crackers, bread, cake, bakery products, and partially fried french fries) switched from tallow to hydrogenated oils in response to consumer pressure (↑ trans fatty acids).

When all these changes are collectively considered, the estimated availability of trans fatty acids is 8.11 g/day/person. The authors stress that research that attempts to estimate trans fatty acid availability or intake by examining only disappearance data will greatly overestimate actual use.

Jones, D. Y., Judd, J. T., Taylor, P. R., Campbell, W. S., & Nair, P. P. (1987). Influence of caloric contribution and saturation of dietary fat on plasma lipids of premenopausal women. *The American Journal of Clinical Nutrition, 45,* 1451–1456.

These investigators, interested in the relationship of plasma lipids to dietary fat intake in women, chose healthy premenopausal women as their subjects. The diets studied contributed either 40% or 20% of the energy intake as fat. In addition to the fat quantity difference, the effect of two P:S ratios (polyunsaturated fat to saturated fat intake) were examined (P:S 1.0 or 0.3) on both the low- and high-fat diets. Thirty-one women completed the study; following a one-menstrual-cycle baseline, the experimental diets each lasted 4 menstrual cycles. Subjects ate weekday morning and evening meals at the research dining facility, and a carryout lunch was provided. Weekend meals were prepackaged, making the same menus and foods available for home consumption. This research revealed that healthy young women who have low baseline TC (188 mg/dL) demonstrate only small changes in TC when comparing a high-fat to a low-fat diet. A significant decrease was seen in the HDL cholesterol at the low P:S ratio when women switched from a high-fat to a low-fat diet, and TG significantly increased (regardless of P:S ratio) on the low-fat diet.

Unlike many human studies, the dietary intake in this study was tightly controlled, and compliance and body weight changes were closely monitored. It might be anticipated, based on previous research with male subjects, that a low-fat diet [replacing fat with carbohydrate] would result in a significant drop in TC, and that a greater change would be observed with a high P:S ratio compared to a low P:S ratio. However, this study did not find statistically significant decreases in TC when the fat intake was decreased from 40% to 20% of the energy intake. Of greater concern was the decrease in HDL levels on the low-fat diet with a low P:S ratio; over half the decrease in TC in the low P:S group was attributable to the

decrease in HDL, which is actually increasing rather than reducing risk. The increased TG level (32% increase) associated with the low-fat diet is another potential concern for women because it is not clear whether this is a transient or a long-term effect.

Kris-Etherton, P. M. (1990). *Cardiovascular disease: Nutrition for prevention and treatment.* Chicago: American Dietetic Association: Sports and Cardiovascular Nutritionists.

Designed as a comprehensive reference for dietitians, this four-part book offers applications for other health professionals as well. The chapters in Part 1 review risk factors for coronary heart disease (CHD), lipoprotein metabolism, and the relationship between diet and CHD. Part 2 focuses on dietary treatment of CHD and discusses the full continuum of care, from assessment to treatment and prevention of CHD. Part 3 emphasizes treatment modalities other than diet, such as exercise and drug treatments. A chapter on behavior modification strategies is included. Part 4 provides an extensive listing of resources and organizations that can be useful for both patients and health professionals, and some assessment tools helpful to practitioners. This book does not provide much gender-specific information, but it is highly recommended for all health professionals as a resource on the prevention and treatment of CHD.

Linn, S., Carroll, M., Johnson, C., Fulwood, R., Kalsbeek, W., & Briefel, R. (1993). High-density lipoprotein cholesterol and alcohol consumption in U.S. white and black adults: Data from NHANES II. *American Journal of Public Health, 83,* 811–816.

The Second National Health and Nutrition Examination Survey (NHANES II) collected data on a probability sample of the noninstitutionalized U.S. population. This report provided results from 3,998 white men, 457 black men, 4,543 white women, and 576 black women. Analysis of the data revealed a positive effect associated with alcohol consumption on HDLs. This relationship was consistent for all types of alcoholic beverages—beer, wine, and liquor. Results were collected and separated by sex and race. Approximately 24% of all men, 40% of white women, and 46% of black women reported that they never consume alcohol. HDL levels among women ranged from 51.8 mg/dL (white women) and 54 mg/dL (black women) in the lowest quartile to 61 mg/dL for the highest quartile (all women). White women consistently demonstrated HDL levels at least 10 mg/dL above those of white men; black women also had levels higher than black men, but the difference was smaller. The levels of HDL were in all cases highest for the highest quartile of alcohol consumption, regardless of sex or race. The consumption of 1 gram of alcohol led to an increase of 0.87 mg/dL in mean HDL cholesterol level. However, the authors are quick to recognize that this analysis does not address the long-term effects of alcohol on HDL levels and caution that alcohol, particularly in high doses, has many adverse effects (association with stroke, cancer, and elevations in blood pressure) and should not be recommended to reduce risk of CHD.

Longnecker, M. P. (1994). Alcoholic beverage consumption in relation to risk of breast cancer: Meta-analysis and review. *Cancer Causes and Control, 5,* 73–82.

Some studies have observed an increased risk of breast cancer in women who consume alcohol; other studies have failed to observe this association. Poor self-reporting of actual alcohol consumption influences the slope of this dose–response relationship. This article provides an extensive review and reevaluation of the data available, in an attempt to explain the factors contributing to the variability in the results of different studies. From the meta-analysis, there seems strong evidence for a dose–response relationship between alcohol consumption and breast cancer. Studies that observed the strongest alcohol–breast cancer association were usually in countries with

high per-capita alcohol intake, raising a question of whether those women may have started consuming alcohol at a younger age. Studies with longer follow-up periods, such as the cohort studies, observed less strong associations between alcohol and breast cancer. An estimate that about 4% of all breast cancers in the United States are attributable to alcohol intake is based on current alcohol consumption rates by women. Variation among the studies is attributed to chance, bias among study results, publication bias, and effect modification. A risk–benefit analysis is suggested before any recommendations are offered on reduced alcohol consumption among those women who are light or moderate alcohol drinkers and who are not at risk for breast cancer.

Meilahn, E. N., Kuller, L. H., Matthews, K. A., Wing, R. R., Caggiula, A. W., & Stein, E. A. (1991). Potential for increasing high-density lipoprotein cholesterol, subfractions HDL_2-C and HDL_3-C, and Apoprotein A-1 among middle-age women. *Preventive Medicine, 20,* 462–473.

High-density lipoprotein levels have been determined to be one of the most effective predictors of risk of CHD in women. For women in the lowest quintile for HDL-C, the relative risk of CHD is three times higher than for those in the highest quintile. This study examined 429 women for an average of 36 months to analyze the determinants of HDL-C in women. The relative effects of age, BMI, waist–hip ratio, cigarette smoking, physical activity, and alcohol were considered. Body mass index (BMI) was divided into five categories, from BMI <22 to BMI >28.7. The lowest BMI group had a mean HDL of 63.4 mg/dL and the highest BMI, a mean of 48.4 mg/dL, or a decrease of 24% in HDL level at the highest BMI. Waist–hip ratios ranged from <0.71 to >0.825 and demonstrated decreasing HDL levels with increasing waist–hip ratios (from 64 mg/dL to 49.5 mg/dL, also a 24% decrease at the highest ratios). Smoking more than 20 cigarettes per day (compared to not smoking) resulted in a 6.7

mg/dL lower HDL-C. Women who did not drink alcohol averaged 55.4 mg/dL; women who drank >13.4 g/alcohol/day (approximately 1 drink) had HDL-C of 64.2 mg/dL.

The effects of increasing BMI (regression coefficient, −11.27) and waist–hip ratio (regression coefficient, −8.28) were greater than the effect of smoking >20 cigarettes per day (regression coefficient, −6.40). Drinking >13.4 g alcohol had a raising effect (regression coefficient, +6.59) as did physical exercise measured in calories expended per week. The regression coefficient of exercising at the level of >2000 calories per week was +0.82. For all parameters except alcohol, the effects on HDL were greater on the HDL_2 subfraction than on HDL_3.

Mensink, R. P., & Katan, M. B. (1989). Effect of a diet enriched with monounsaturated or polyunsaturated fatty acids on levels of low-density and high-density lipoprotein cholesterol in healthy women and men. *The New England Journal of Medicine, 321,* 436–441.

A control diet consisting of approximately 37% fat (19.3% saturated fat) was provided for 17 days; the study group was then divided and randomly assigned a diet providing either predominantly monounsaturated fat (15%) (mono diet) or predominantly polyunsaturated fat (12.7%) (poly diet). Total fat did not change from the control to the mono or poly diet; only proportions of saturated/monounsaturated/polyunsaturated fat were different. Changes in LDL cholesterol from the control period to the mono diet were similar for men and women (−17.7% and −18.1%, respectively) but men demonstrated a significantly greater drop in HDL cholesterol (−12.6% vs. +1.5%). The result was a more modest improvement in the HDL–LDL ratio of 6.3% for men compared to 21.2% for women. A similar pattern was observed with the poly diet: men demonstrated greater decreases than women, but less than were observed with the mono diet. HDL increased slightly for women on the poly diet; for men, HDL cholesterol decreased by 9%. A sex-specific effect on HDL cholesterol was demonstrated, and the authors stress the need for additional research studies of women. They conclude that both mono or poly fats will lower LDL and will have the same effect on HDL if polys are not provided in excessive amounts (>13%) of total energy intake.

Mensink, R. P., & Katan, M. B. (1990). Effect of trans fatty acids on high-density and low-density lipoprotein cholesterol levels in healthy subjects. *The New England Journal of Medicine, 323,* 439–445.

This article is largely responsible for the current focus on the health effects of trans fatty acids. The study, which included both men and women, examined the effects of three diets, each predominantly high in one of the following: oleic acid, trans fatty acids, or saturated fatty acids. The diets were assigned in random order. Dietary compliance was confirmed by determining fatty acid composition of erythrocyte membranes, which reflect dietary fatty acids. The results for women revealed that the 11% trans fatty acid diet increased TC by 10.4 mg/dL and LDL by 15 mg/dL, and decreased HDL by 7.0 mg/dL. This dramatic response should be evaluated while recognizing that the dietary intake of trans fatty acids provided was approximately 4 times the estimated average American intake. Nevertheless, these researchers revealed that previous studies, which measured only TC in response to trans fatty acids, may have missed the magnitude of the trans effect because the changes in LDL and HDL are not reflected in TC values.

MMWR. (1994). Daily dietary fat and total food energy intakes—Third National Health and Nutrition Examination Survey, Phase 1, 1988–91. *Morbidity and Mortality Weekly Report, 43,* 116–125.

Conducted by the Centers for Disease Control, the Third National Health and Nutrition Examination Survey (NHANES III) provides data to monitor changes in the nutritional, dietary, and health status of the U.S. population.

This report is one of the first releases of data from NHANES III, which was conducted from October 1988 to October 1991. In this survey, 17,467 people were interviewed and 14,801 completed a 24-hour dietary recall, using a computer-based automated dietary interview and coding system. Results indicated that the total food energy intakes (TFEI), for people 2 years of age or older, averaged 2,095 kilocalories. Thirty-four percent of their TFEI was from total dietary fat, and 12% from saturated fat. These numbers are decreased from the 1985 survey, when total fat intake was 36% of TFEI and saturated fat intake was 13%. The national health objective for the year 2000 is to reduce dietary fat to an average of 30% or less and saturated fat intake to less than 10% of calories in people 2 years of age or older.

Stampfer, M. J., Hennekens, C. H., Manson, J. E., Colditz, G. A., Rosner, B., & Willett, W. C. (1993). Vitamin E consumption and the risk of coronary heart disease in women. *The New England Journal of Medicine, 328,* 1444–1449.

The Nurses' Health Study, which included 87,245 female nurses aged 34 to 59 and originally screened as free of cardiovascular disease and cancer, involved follow-up for 8 years. Data were assessed for vitamin E intake and relative risk of CHD. Women in the highest quintile for vitamin E intake from dietary sources (median 208 IU), when compared with those in the lowest quintile (median 2.8 IU), had a relative risk (RR) of 0.95. Those who had consumed vitamin E supplements (>100 IU per day) for more than 2 years had a RR of coronary disease of 0.52. Interestingly, no further decrease in risk was observed with daily intakes higher than 100 IU per day. Users of vitamin E supplements had significantly greater risk reduction than multivitamin users (RR 0.57 vs. RR 0.92, respectively).

Willett, W. C., Stampfer, M. J., Manson, J. E., Colditz, G. A., Speizer, F. E., Rosner, B. A., Sampson, L. A., & Hennekens, C. H. (1993). Intake of trans fatty acids and risk of coronary heart disease among women. *The Lancet, 341,* 581–585.

This research focuses on women and examines the potential risk of coronary heart disease posed by trans fatty acid intake. The 85,095 subjects were part of the Nurses' Health Study. Food frequency questionnaires were used to collect dietary data and estimate trans fatty acid intake. The results were divided into quintiles of trans fatty acid intake. The lowest quintile consumed a mean of 2.4 g trans fatty acid per day, the highest, 5.7 g per day. Trans fatty acids were derived from animal sources (40%) and processed vegetable fats (60%). Relative risk (RR) was determined for the various intakes of trans fatty acids, and data were adjusted for age, smoking, hypertension, body mass index, alcohol intake, menopausal status, postmenopausal estrogen use, energy intake, family history of myocardial infarction, lipid intake, and use of multivitamins. The RR of CHD rose to 1.47 in the highest quintile, compared to 1.0 for the lowest quintile. The increased risk was entirely accounted for by the association of partially hydrogenated fats. Trans isomers from animal fats actually demonstrated a slight inverse association. Consumption of beef, pork, or lamb as a main dish was not significantly related to risk. Likewise, butter was not significantly associated with risk of CHD. In 1990, the fast food industry largely changed from beef tallow (3% to 5% trans isomers) to partially hydrogenated vegetable fats (~ 30% trans isomers). The four major categories of food related to risk in women were identified. All categories seemed to demonstrate a threshold; for example, margarine did not substantially increase risk until more than 4 teaspoons were consumed per day, and cookies substantially increased risk when the consumption increased to 1 per day. This research suggests that women with the highest intakes of trans fatty acids are at increased risk of coronary heart disease.

Zock, P. L., & Katan, M. B. (1992). Hydrogenation alternatives: Effects of trans fatty acids and stearic acid versus linoleic acid on serum lipids and lipoproteins in humans. *Journal of Lipid Research, 33,* 399–410.

This study repeats previous research with two primary differences: (1) the trans fatty acid intake was provided at a lower level of 8% of the total energy, and (2) the comparisons were made to diets high in linoleic acid and stearic acid. The results again demonstrated an increase in total and LDL-cholesterol (+5.4 mg/dL, + 8.9 mg/dL, respectively, in women), and a decrease of HDL-cholesterol (−3.9 mg/dL, in women) with trans fatty acid intake when compared to the linoleic acid diet. Both men and women were included in the study, but data were analyzed by gender. For most measurements, women's responses to dietary trans fatty acids were similar to the men's. The changes observed in blood lipids were essentially the same for both the trans fatty acid and the stearate diet. The magnitude of change seems small, but the authors provide the following statement of significance: for each 1% increase in energy intake as trans fatty acids, LDLs will increase by 1.2 mg/dL and HDLs will decrease by 0.6 mg/dL relative to oleic or linoleic acid. Consequently, if the current 3% to 4% of the diet which provides trans fatty acids were replaced with oleic or linoleic fatty acids, the LDLs would decrease by 4 mg/dL and HDLs would increase by 2 mg/dL. This change would potentially reduce risk of CHD by ~ 8%.

Zock, P. L., de Vries, J. H. M., & Katan, M. B. (1994). Impact of myristic acid versus palmitic acid on serum lipid and lipoprotein levels in healthy women and men. *Arteriosclerosis and Thrombosis, 14,* 567–575.

Previous research has demonstrated that, in men, the reduction of saturated fatty acids in the diet is more effective than limiting total fat quantity. Saturated fats composed of different chain lengths differ in their cholesterol-raising effect. Myristic and palmitic fatty acids, which collectively make up 25% to 30% of the fat in Western diets, were studied regarding their effects on serum lipoproteins compared to oleic acid. Each fatty acid was provided as 10% of the daily energy; lauric acid and trans fatty acid contents were kept constant. Myristic acid raised total cholesterol more than palmitic acid, but approximately one-half of the effect was due to HDLs. Both myristic and palmitic acids markedly raised LDLs. Men demonstrated greater increases in TC, HDL, and LDL in response to the myristic acid than did the women. A similar pattern was observed with palmitic acid, except that there was no appreciable change in HDLs for either sex, compared to the oleic acid diet.

Palmitic acid is less cholesterolemic than myristic acid; trans fatty acids have less effect than palmitic acid on total cholesterol but they lower HDLs in addition to raising LDL. Stearic acid produces a response similar to oleic acid, appearing nearly neutral with respect to lipoprotein cholesterol.

Part III

Delivery of Health Care to Women

Chapter 5

Care of Hospitalized Women

Patricia A. Geary

lthough women's health has received much attention in the media and legislation has been enacted to ensure greater attention to women in research, the acute care setting has not changed much for women. The situation is reminiscent of earlier times when women's health courses were not viewed as necessary because courses in health already existed. Yet, much of the content of these health courses was based on results of research using primarily male samples. Moreover, serious health-related concerns of women, such as breast cancer, have only recently been researched and adequately funded for large clinical trials. However, in acute care, despite the fact that women are hospitalized more frequently and longer than men for the same illnesses, care is still grounded in insufficient research on women.

In the previous annual review, three diseases were chosen for investigation: (1) breast cancer, (2) cardiac problems, and (3) lung cancer. Because breast cancer is largely a disease of women, it should reflect the most progress in acute care. Cardiac problems kill more women than cancer but frequently are not diagnosed in early stages. Diagnoses are generally made after the problems become more severe. Finally, the incidence of lung cancer is increasing in women. Analysis of the literature on these three diseases provides a snapshot of the progress made in acute care. Therefore, for this review, the three conditions that often result in women being hospitalized will be addressed as major categories. An effort was made to locate articles that specifically related to women's experiences with these diseases or that dealt specifically with the acute phases of the diseases.

Progress in attending to women's issues has been made in heart diseases. Studies uncovering women's experiences with cardiac problems are starting to emerge in the literature.

Apart from the investigation of specific diseases—their trajectory, experience, and best treatment in women—what general standards should be set for the care of women in acute settings? To begin addressing this critical question, a new category is added to this review of the literature: the nature of the acute care experience. Only a few articles in this category attend specifically to women.

SUMMARY

In a country where the majority of health care resources are consumed by the provision of acute care, the needs and issues of the majority of the population in that setting require greater attention. The situation in acute care parallels the issues and problems in childbearing that women have had to deal with for the past 25 years. Physiological and psychological differences in women impact on the constellation of symptoms they experience when ill. Although their response to treatment and their experience of the illness are known, this knowledge has not yet led to adequate action. Those differences are only superficially recognized, if at all, and are not used to plan and deliver care. In addition, women are not given sufficient power and control over health care decisions.

Knowledge is, after all, power. Because knowledge of the impact of gender differences on acute care is limited, women encounter serious barriers to the recognition and provision of competent care. Until both research and education begin to focus on the discovery of knowledge about women's physiological and psychological experience in acute illness, as well as on the dissemination of known information, women will not have the power and influence necessary to effect a change. When both women and men participate in research, and gender is not controlled as a variable, generalizations may disguise the real differences for women. Not only must the differences be identified, but knowledge must be sufficient to guide care and be used in providing care. In all the major categories reviewed for this chapter, with the exception of cardiac problems, the focus on women is minimal at best. The literature on lung cancer, which is steadily killing more women, directs little attention to women. Even with a rising incidence of breast cancer, a disease that almost totally involves women, treatments remain fundamentally the same. The one bright spot is King, Rowell, and Love's (1993) focus on choice for women, and these authors' recognition that the current choices are not optimal.

It is important to uncover new knowledge about the acute care of women; equally important, what is known must be shared with women as a routine part of their care. Women must be partners in decisions regarding their care, not simply recipients of preordained care. With ever-shortening hospital stays and the resultant acute nature of an illness during actual hospitalization, there is a danger that essential information they need to participate in their care will not be shared with women patients. Education demands space, time, and attention. When women are seriously ill and/or hospital staff are seriously overburdened, patient education is likely to be omitted.

It is critical that women attend carefully to health care policy. The current furor about the *cost* of health care is muting the real concerns about *quality*. Reduction in cost often means the excision of "extras" such as education and staffing adequate to provide patient teaching as well as technical care. Whether women can learn best about their illness prior to, during, or some time immediately after hospitalization must be the subject of careful research. Women need information, and it must be shared with them sometime during the illness event. Hospitalization can create an openness, a willingness to learn, an opportunity to screen for other conditions, and an atmosphere conducive to teaching about risk factors and prevention. Even among insured women, adequate primary care that provides such information may be nonexistent. In our current health care system, insurance often provides for only acute care. Women may not have access to primary care. Hence, an acute illness provides an opportunity to assess both the health of the woman patient and her knowledge about her health. For some women, acute illness may be their only opportunity to access the current knowledge, however limited, about women's health.

Acute care of women is the next frontier in women's health. Careful attention to education, research, and policy is critical. Both the women patients and the practitioners involved in their care must be educated to recognize the dearth of information available about women and demand the development of a knowledge base necessary to provide adequate care to women. Practitioners must be sensitized to the needs of women; they must begin to ask the clinical questions that will result in better care of women.

Research is necessary in almost every area of acute illness in women. Little is known about the illness experience of women, and without that knowledge, individuated care is impossible. We need investigations of individual disease states as well as the more general aspects of acute illness in order to recognize the differences between women and men.

There is a critical need to develop sound policies that address the requirements of acute care for women. Women must have access to primary care and knowledgeable primary care practitioners. We must ensure that the care health professionals render attends to the needs of individual women rather than settling for the provision of speedy and minimally safe technological care.

REFERENCES

Knobf, M. T., & Morra, M. E. (1993). Women and cancer. *Clinical Issues in Perinatal and Women's Health Nursing, 4*(2), 287–301.

McBride, A. B., & McBride, W. L. (1993). Women's health scholarship: From critique to assertion. *Journal of Women's Health, 2*(1), 43–47.

Norsigian, J. (1993). Women and national health care reform: A progressive feminist agenda. *Journal of Women's Health, 2*(1), 91–94.

Schaps, M. J., Linn, E. S., Wilbanks, G. D., & Wilbanks, E. R. (1993). Women-centered care: Implementing a philosophy. *Women's Health Issues, 3*(2), 52–54.

Telford, B. R., Stichler, J., Ivie, S. J., & Jellen, B. C. (1993). Model approaches to women's health centers. *Women's Health Issues, 3*(2), 55–62.

The Nature of Acute Care

[Author(s)] (1993). Acute care nursing: Self-test. *Nursing 93, 23*(4), 91–93.

This journal is read by many registered nurses in practice in acute care hospitals. The self-test is unsettling because it illustrates so well the situation of women hospitalized in acute care facilities today. Despite the importance of recognizing the particular needs of women, this test does not include any case studies in which women are patients. Instead, the patient presented is a male who requires acute care intervention. The test reinforces the stereotype of male health as the health standard and thus maintains the invisibility of women as consumers of acute care.

Cameron, B. L. (1993). The nature of comfort to hospitalized medical surgical patients. *Journal of Advanced Nursing, 18*(3), 424–436.

Using grounded theory methodology, the author interviewed ten hospitalized patients. Three to ten interviews with each patient were completed over a seven-month period. In addition, observational data were collected. Comfort, studied from the patients' viewpoint, was found to be an active process in which the patient, rather than waiting for comforting behavior, actively sought out comfort measures. Patients acted not only on their own behalf but also on behalf of others. Staff behavior was not necessarily comforting. Integrative balancing, the process of seeking comfort, occurred in three stages. A description of each stage is followed by a section on the implications for nursing practice.

This study presents a good case for comfort as an interactive process, but it does not explore whether there are any differences in comfort by gender. (Both genders were represented in the patient sample.) Current literature suggests that men and women may have different perceptions, yet the issue is not mentioned in this study. Although well-documented, the study includes few references after 1985. Current research is important in designing and interpreting a study of patient comfort. The almost exclusive reliance on early research may account for the investigator's lack of attention to gender. Further research is warranted to determine whether comfort-seeking behavior differs between men and women.

Holly, C. M. (1993). The ethical quandaries of acute care nursing practice. *Journal of Professional Nursing, 9*(2), 110–115.

This study of ethical dilemmas in acute care revealed three major themes: (1) exploitation, (2) exclusion, and (3) anguish. Data from interviews of 65 acute care nurses suggested that nurses perceive themselves and their patients to be powerless in high-technology settings. The author acknowledges that the nurses who participated were volunteers and therefore may have been seeking help with ethical issues—a potential sample bias; still, the themes themselves are chilling. The nurses see all of their patients as having little control over the decisions made in the acute care setting. It is suggested that ethical dilemmas in the increasingly high-tech, acute care setting merits considerable attention and more study.

Keane, A., & Richmond, T. (1993). Tertiary nurse practitioners. *Image, 23*(4), 281–284.

The authors describe the evolution of the tertiary nurse practitioner—a nurse with primary care skills who oversees hospitalized patients. Nurses in this role can contribute to improving the quality of care delivered to hospitalized patients. Not every specialty can be mentioned in an article of this type, but it is disheartening that no mention is made of the need for a specialist in women's health who can assist in fulfilling the unique needs of hospitalized women; or, at a minimum, the importance of developing a new role in which the nurse practitioner addresses the needs of women in acute care settings. The majority of nurses are women. They are a potential force for removing the invisibility of women's needs and developing the knowledge that will support the healing and cure of acutely ill women.

Kubsch, S. M., & Wichowski, H. C. (1992). Identification and validation of a new nursing diagnosis: Sick role conflict. *Nursing Diagnosis, 3*(4), 141–147.

A random sample of 99 adult patients was drawn from a pool of 380 hospitalized adults. The authors developed and tested a paper/pencil questionnaire for purposes of gathering data about the theoretical constructs underlying the nursing diagnosis: sick role conflict. The authors concluded that sick role conflict was likely to be experienced by the individual who filled multiple roles, was acutely ill, and received inadequate preparation prior to hospitalization. The researchers contend that the study provides sufficient empirical data to support the inclusion of sick role conflict as a valid nursing diagnosis. The researchers' approach to data analysis requires careful reading. The reliability of the instrument was tested in a split-half technique. However, how the items on the instrument were divided (e.g., first half/second half, odd-numbered half/even-numbered half) for comparison was not specified. The statistic provided is an r value, which suggests that the two halves were compared with one another without a comparison to the whole—an approach that would underestimate the reliability of the instrument. A second and perhaps more disturbing concern is the underlying philosophical question this study raises. Sick role is a sociological theory described by Parsons in the 1950s and 1960s. Parsons thought that, during illness, persons should take on the sick role in order to heal and become well. The authors do not question the underlying assumptions of this theory, nor do they adequately identify what behaviors they believe characterize the sick role or a sick role conflict. An examination of the 29 questions that comprise the instrument would help the reader to make that determination but this information is not provided. The degree to which any ill persons should abrogate their responsibility for themselves and assume a dependent role is questionable. Some literature suggests that a "feisty" patient, particularly a cancer patient, evidences a "healthier" response to illness. The possibility that nurses may be diagnosing and treating a sick role conflict and attempting to change that behavior without full knowledge of the philosophical and empirical underpinnings of the diagnosis is disturbing. It is particularly worrisome that women who generally have multiple roles may be the recipients of interventions aimed at making them more dependent, rather than stronger and more autonomous.

Larson, P. J., & Ferketich, S. L. (1993). Patients' satisfaction with nurses' caring during hospitalization . . . including commentary by Molzahn, A. E., with author response. (1993). *Western Journal of Nursing Research, 15*(6), 690–707.

This study represents both a step forward and a step backward. The nursing profession values caring as a central tenet of its practice. Patients need care in order to recover. The authors have developed a tool to measure patients' satisfaction with nurses' caring. In some institutions, patient satisfaction is measured by whether the food was delivered appropriately hot or chilled. The selection of the conditions, interaction with staff, and delivery of treatment that patients associate with caring is, therefore, important to the validity of any survey. The article describes a fourth phase in the development of the tool wherein the content is reformatted using a visual analog scale (a standard size line on which the person indicates the degree to which the item in question was experienced. An unsettling factor is an absence of discussion of gender differences or similarities in the responses to the tool. Caring and feeling cared for may have gender-specific as well as cross-gender components, but readers are left with no answer as to whether men and women differ in their perception of caring.

Looker, P. (1993). Women's health centers: History and evolution. *Women's Health Issues, 3*(2), 95–100.

This article should be on the reading list of anyone interested in the health and welfare of women. The author presents an excellent review of the reasons for the development of women's health centers, few of which are to benefit women. Generally, women's health centers and the recognized "women's" inpatient foci have merely relabeled gynecological services focused on the reproductive diseases of women. As long as that notion continues, women will not have adequate care that addresses their unique health care needs. Ten excellent hallmarks of women's centers are listed. If those qualities could be extended to the acute care of women, the quality of women's health care would markedly improve.

Mackenzie, J. (1993). Questioning the assumption that urinary catheterization is a pain-free event for women. *Journal of Clinical Nursing, 2*(2), 64–65.

For anyone wondering whether women are considered at all in the acute care setting, this article offers a ray of hope. Urinary catheterization may seem to be a small issue, but to any woman who has faced catheterization, it is not inconsequential. This is an example of the importance of critically examining commonly practiced nursing interventions in a woman-focused manner.

Swanson, K. M. (1993). Nursing as informed caring for the well being of others. *Image, 25*(4), 352–357.

This excellent review and analysis of caring makes the point that societal definitions may influence the perception of well being. What is not said is that caring and how caring is perceived may well be related to gender. It is important to identify and investigate those differences in order to deliver competent and compassionate care to acutely ill patients. This article makes an important contribution to the literature on caring.

Worthington, K. (1994). Workplace hazards: The effect on nurses as women. *American Nurse, 26*(2), 15.

The effects of the acute care environment on the woman caregiver, the nurse, are seldom investigated. This brief article, which highlights some of the effects of drugs and chemicals routinely used in the acute care of women, admonishes nurses to be concerned for their own safety. That these potential problems are becoming visible is a positive step. That the nurse must be concerned for her own safety, in the absence of standard protections offered in other industries, is a statement of how far acute care must progress to safeguard its employees.

THE SENTINEL DISEASES

Breast Cancer

Colditzs, G. A., Willett, W. C., Hunter, D. J., Stampfer, M. J., Manson, J. E., Hennekens, C. H., Rosner, B. A., & Speizer, F. E. (1993). Family history, age, and risk of breast cancer. *Journal of the American Medical Association, 270*(3), 338–343.

Twelve years' prospective data from the nurses' health study are analyzed by the authors to determine the risk of breast cancer in women whose mothers or sisters have had the disease. Compared to retrospective studies, this prospective study found a smaller rise of incidence of breast cancer within familial units than was previously identified. Family history accounts for only a small percentage (2.5%) of breast cancer cases—a comfort for women with a family history of breast cancer. However, if only 2.5% of the cases of breast cancer can be attributed to family history, the importance of further research about the explanation for breast cancer and how it might be prevented becomes all the more critical.

King, M., Rowell, S., & Love, S. M. (1993). Inherited breast and ovarian cancer: What are the risks? What are the choices? *Journal of the*

American Medical Association, 269(15), 1975–1980.

A relatively small percentage of breast and ovarian cancers are familial. This article discusses what is known about the risk of those cancers and the modification of that risk. The authors note that all breast cancer is genetic in the sense that cancer results from changes in DNA. Genetic research may ultimately lead to early treatment of noninherited cancers at the cellular level. The authors suggest that the rising incidence of breast cancer may be related to the doubling of the period of hormonal stimulation on dividing breast ductal cells, which results from early menarche and late childbearing. A measure of the sensitivity of these authors is their discussion of measures to safeguard women who are participants in these social changes. The risk associated with family history is illustrated through specific cases. Rather than discussing treatment of high-risk women, this article discusses choices available to women. The emphasis on choice is excellent. The authors recognize that none of the current options open to women is optimal. They suggest a registry to increase the collective information about the progression of breast and ovarian cancer in high-risk women, and they hold out hope that, eventually, cancerous cell changes will be identified early enough so that the abnormal cells can be removed by needle biopsy, a preferable alternative to surgery.

Cardiac Problems

Brenner, Z. B. (1993). Patients' learning priorities for reoperative coronary artery bypass surgery. *Journal of Cardiovascular Nursing, 7*(2), 1–12.

This excellent research report compares learning needs of patients facing initial surgery with those of patients having repeated coronary artery bypass surgery. Patients were given the same questionnaire while in the hospital and three months postoperation, and their responses were compared. The gender composition of the initial surgery group and the repeat surgery group was not comparable; however, this was not noted by the author. Some questionnaire items might have been answered differently by men and women. Although the author emphasizes the importance of education and individualized instruction, gender as one factor that may be important to individualized teaching is overlooked.

Crumlish, C. M. (1993). Coping and emotion in women undergoing cardiac surgery: A preliminary study. *MEDSURG Nursing, 2*(4), 283–334.

The authors present the results of a pilot study designed to examine the coping styles of 28 women undergoing cardiac surgery. The study was conducted using two valid and reliable instruments: one measures coping and the other, mood. Women's coping abilities were stable from the preoperative period through the postoperative period. Tension decreased from the preoperative period to the postoperative period, but fatigue increased significantly. To their credit, the authors note the limitations inherent in using these paper/pencil measures with women and the need for more research that employs an inductive approach to understanding women's surgical experiences. Women's coping styles must be identified and strengthened preoperatively. No mention is made of the findings related to fatigue. An increase in fatigue seems reasonable postoperatively, but, given the multiple role commitments of women and the likelihood of such role demands occurring in the age group studied, one wonders whether the postoperative experience of women is different from men.

Fitzsimmons, L., Verder, A., & Shively, M. (1993). Enhancing sleep following coronary artery bypass graft surgery. *Journal of Cardiovascular Nursing, 7*(2), 86–89.

Because acute care can mean acute sleep deprivation, this investigation of the use of white noise to enhance sleep in the postcardiac care unit is important. One-quarter of the participants in this well-designed study were women. No attempt is made to look at any differences between men and women, even descriptively. The authors do state that men and women may respond differently to measures to assist sleep; however, gender differences or similarities are not analyzed.

Hawthorne, M. H. (1993). Women recovering from coronary bypass surgery. *Scholarly Inquiry for Nursing Practice: An International Journal, 7*(4), 223–252.

The article and the two commentaries following it are valuable contributions to efforts aimed at improving the care of women in acute care settings. The author reports on interviews conducted with ten women, following cardiac surgery. The seven themes identified in analysis of the interviews reveal differences in the recovery process of women when compared to what is known about the same process in men. This study is important because it begins to describe the illness trajectory for women, thereby validating the importance of identifying nursing interventions that derive from research on women. Replication of this study, following a variety of surgical procedures, would be valuable for additional knowledge about the postoperative experience of women.

Holm, K., Penckofer, S., Keresztes, P., Biordi, D., & Chandler, P. (1993). Coronary artery disease in women: Assessment, diagnosis, intervention, and strategies for lifestyle change. *Clinical Issues in Perinatal and Women's Health Nursing, 4*(2), 272–285.

This article is an excellent overview of the risk factors for cardiac problems in women, difficulties with treatments, and ways to assist with life-style changes. Whether women are encountered in outpatient or inpatient settings, given the high annual death rate among women with cardiac problems, this article provides important information for nurses in practice. In imitation of women's health centers, the care of women in inpatient, acute settings should include an educational approach. A full assessment of women patients should take into account any factors that place them at high risk for particular diseases, and appropriate educational treatment. The authors include a section on why some women with cardiac problems experience poorer outcomes than others. These reasons should stimulate research on strategies to improve outcomes for women as well as foster vigilance in the assessment and care of women receiving acute treatment.

Hudson, G. R. (1993). Empathy and technology in the coronary care unit. *Intensive and Critical Care Nursing, 9*(1), 55–61.

This is a troubling article about the role of nurses in the critical care unit. The author describes a dichotomy in acute care, between caring and curing: the nurse is responsible for the "less valued" caring, and the physician is responsible for the curing. Caring and curing are portrayed as paralleling gender division, but both attributes have their place in the coronary care unit. The importance of caring is substantiated by the presence of death in the coronary care unit, and empathy is a necessity in dealing with dying patients. Yet, empathy is essential for any patients, particularly the women in critical care units. With so many factors stacked against women with coronary problems, empathy is critical to the discovery of effective nursing interventions. Patient needs should determine the necessary technological competence and empathy. The author concludes by noting that empathy can assist people in adjusting to the critical care technology, as well as in learning behaviors that will prevent repeated coronary incidents.

Penckofer, S., & Holm, K. (1993). Women and heart disease. *Nursing 93, 23*(6), 42–46.

Using three brief case histories, the authors review the risk for heart disease in women. The article offers an update for nurses on what is known about the risk factors for cardiac problems in women. Specific interventions are identified in each of the three case studies. Because this publication is often read by nurses who practice in acute care, the author sounds an alarm about potential cardiac risks in women patients. Content is presented in a straightforward manner and reflects recent research. The case histories are about women who have not yet developed acute illness; hence, the information is useful to anyone interested in knowing about cardiac risk factors in women.

Ridker, P. M., Hebert, P. R., Fuster, V., & Hennekens, C. H. (1993). Are both aspirin and heparin justified as adjuncts to thrombolytic therapy for acute myocardial infarction? *Lancet, 341,* 1574–1577.

One of the known problems with the "doctors' study" that identified aspirin as a preventive measure in cardiac disease was the fact that the sample was comprised of men exclusively. Although this review discusses studies that have a total of 62,000 participants, no mention is made of the effects of this therapy on women. Even more disheartening, the review does not mention the potential for differences between men and women. Instead, it begins with giving the aspirin dose for the "average man"!

Tucker, L. A. (1993). Post-pump delirium. *Intensive and Critical Care Nursing, 9*(4), 269–273.

Post-pump delirium, a postsurgical cognitive disturbance identified as a complication resulting from the cardiac bypass machine, affects a significant number of cardiac patients. This is an excellent overview of the causes of the problem and the potential actions the nurse can take to prevent this occurrence. Risk factors include: time on the bypass pump, age, drugs, and preoperative status, especially the degree of illness. No mention is made of the potential influence of gender in this condition, despite the author's stress on the importance of recognizing and intervening in possible predisposing factors. Because women undergoing cardiac surgery are often older people who are seriously ill, it is important to alert nurses to post-pump delirium as a potential risk for women. The author fails to identify the importance of investigating the incidence of this complication among women.

Valle, B. K., & Lemberg, L. (1992). A silent epidemic: Coronary disease in women. *Journal of Critical Care, 1*(1), 125–127.

The need to recognize the increasing incidence of cardiac problems in women is highlighted in this case study. Some of the risk factors that are particularly problematic in women, and the seriousness of cardiac problems in women patients are illustrated for the practicing nurse.

Lung Cancer

Potanovich, L. M. (1993). Lung cancer: Prevention and detection update. *Seminars in Oncology Nursing, 9*(3), 174–179.

The author presents a good overview of prevention and screening for lung cancer, and acknowledges that lung cancer deaths among women now surpass deaths from breast cancer. Tobacco companies' focus on selling tobacco

products to women is mentioned. At that point, however, the recognition of women stops. The information presented is good but not comprehensive. The author depicts solid progress in early detection and some implications for prevention, but ignores the possibility of gender differences or the need for research on women.

Schmitt, R. (1993). Quality of life issues in lung cancer. *Chest, 103*, 51–55.

Management of the side effects of treatment in cancer patients, as well as the symptoms of the disease process, is critical to maintaining a good quality of life. The author reviews the latest strategies for managing nausea and vomiting, weight loss and lack of appetite, increased blood calcium levels and pain. The information is excellent and up-to-date, but *gender blind.* The only specific mention of women is in a statement that anticipatory nausea and vomiting (prior to chemotherapy) occurs in "young, depressed, educated female patients who are usually of Latin American, Spanish or Jewish descent." This only mention of women has a negative tone, and little advice is given for preventing the occurrence of anticipatory nausea and vomiting in women or for supporting women patients who experience these side effects.

Part IV

Health and Work

Chapter 6

Occupational Issues in Women's Health

Susan Terry Misner
Jeanne Beauchamp Hewitt
Pamela Fox Levin

In recent years, political activity has focused on health care reform, changes in labor laws, and efforts to revise the Occupational Safety and Health Act (OSHA). Concurrently, there has been public dialogue about the potential benefits of restructuring workplace settings. This examination has considered the impact of family values on employee productivity and the impact of workplace values and policies on family life.

In the above context, the workplace issues that affect women's health demand a broad perspective. The lived experiences of women are not easily compartmentalized into work, home, and play. Research and social policies that address the complex nature of women's lives must include the relationship between work life and family life. To assist working women in managing their multiple roles, knowledge about methods to maintain and improve their health and productivity has become increasingly important to broad sectors of society. Figure 6.1 contains definitions of selected terms.

Attention to women's occupational health has increased because of the greater numbers of women in the work force. Women's employment rate was as high as 57.8% in 1992 and is projected to be 63% by the year 2005.

As of 1991, the employment rate for women with four or more years of college was close to twice that of women with less than high school education. In 1992, married women with children 6 to 13 years of age participated in the labor force at a rate of 74.9%. For married women with children under one year of age, the overall rate of employment was 56.7%. In the latter group, statistics showed some racial difference: 55.9% of married white women and 68.7% of married black women were employed. Compared to 6.4% of men, 5.9% of women held multiple paid jobs. Interestingly, more employed men reported flexibility in their work schedule than did working women: 13.2% versus 11.1%, respectively (U.S. Bureau of the Census, 1993).

Salary discrepancies continue: women earned a median weekly income of $381 in 1992, compared to $505 for men, and more women than men were paid at or below minimum hourly wage (U.S. Bureau of the Census, 1993). Salary discrepancy associated with gender continues to occur even in higher-income professions such as law (Hagan, 1990).

The social impact of women's participation in the labor force has been profound. Now, many women must balance work and home responsibilities that are influenced by socially prescribed, gender-based roles. The influence of gender on women's work, as well as gender domination within some occupational groups, is now being questioned, both for individual women workers and for traditionally female occupations (Dumais, 1992; Messing, Dumais, & Romito, 1993). Researchers contend that gender domination may retard women's advancement in their occupations (Baldwin, 1993; Meleis, Hall, & Stevens, 1994). Messing (1994) asserts that knowledge about the health of working women has been adversely affected by gender bias, which, in turn, has influenced the selection of research topics. Yet, Dumais (1992) suggests that women's increased participation in science has influenced research interests in the field of occupational health.

This chapter, together with the abstracts on specific occupational hazards, will review potential risks to working women's health, particularly risks to certain disenfranchised groups of women workers. The topics covered are: health, work, and gender; special female worker groups; multiple roles, motherhood, and employment; workplace hazards; and challenges for future research. The abstracts cover the content areas of pregnancy and work, physical hazards (ergonomics, noise, ionizing radiation and nonionizing radiation), thermal hazards, chemical hazards (heavy metals, pesticides, pharmaceuticals), biological hazards, psychological hazards, other hazards (dust, sick buildings, and work patterns), and special groups.

HEALTH, WORK, AND GENDER

The social trends of greater employment of women and changing gender roles necessitate the reframing of basic concepts, such as the nature of work and what constitutes the workplace (Glass, 1993). The definition of work usually is restricted to paid employment. However, the health risks of work should be examined not only in relation to exposure hazards, but also in relation to activities that use physiological or psychological energy. Using this perspective, the evaluation of health risks should include domestic work at home (Chamberlain, 1993). Evaluating health risks to women in this manner is important because of the added burden of women's work load at home (DeJoseph, 1993).

After examining the "gendered division of domestic labor" for families in five countries, Sanchez (1993) stated that "women and men may need to redefine societal meanings of public and private work before women's and men's material resources can be funneled toward nongendered sharing of activities" (p. 456). Gender bias and the devaluing of women's work are reflected in gender wage differentials. Several theoretical perspectives (e.g., economics, tokenism, social comparison, polarization, biology) have been used to explain the existence of sex-segregated work situations (Headapohl, 1993; Wharton, 1993). Regardless of these perspectives, the outcomes of gender discrimination are depressed wages, lowered feelings of self-worth, stifled creativity, and isolation from both coworkers and supervisors (Quinn & Woskie, 1990).

In 1986, Stellman stated that the "predominating feature of women's lives is role expansion together with clustering in underpaid undervalued jobs" (p. 2). In recent years, challenges to gender bias have been seen in traditionally male occupations, such as psychiatry and police service (Aguilar, 1994; Brown, 1994). Yet, problems persist for employed women in the areas of gender wage differentials, flexibility of work hours, nonwage compensation, and working conditions (Unger, 1993). Economic and social factors blur the relationship between women's work status and their health.

For some time, it has been suggested that many of the differences in health risks between men and women are primarily due to differential risks related to acquired roles (Verbrugge, 1985). Gender-based differentiation of work activities—whether paid or unpaid—would be expected to result in different and varying levels of exposure to risk for men and women. The preceding assertion is largely conjectural: the majority of occupational health studies have focused on men and male-dominated occupations. Headapohl (1993) has suggested that occupational health research should focus more often on the similarities between men and women. We propose that analytical and epidemiological studies (cohort and case-control) need to include sufficiently large samples of both men and women to compare risks at different levels of exposure. Furthermore, such studies need to include various exposures such as multiple roles, role strain, and toxic exposures in paid and unpaid work to clarify similarities and differences in risk between men and women.

Interest persists regarding the relationship between women's employment status and their health (Aston & Lavery, 1993; Doyal, 1990; Graetz, 1993). In a 15-year longitudinal study, Hibbard and Pope (1991) reported that employment for women may increase longevity. The health effects of part-time and interrupted work activities of women have been studied but remain unclear (Herold & Waldron, 1985; Hibbard & Pope, 1993). The beneficial effects of employment on women must be validated while accounting for the "healthy worker effect" (healthy workers select into the workplace and unhealthy workers select out of the workplace). (Dahl, 1993).

SPECIAL FEMALE WORKER GROUPS

Outside the United States, Canada, and Europe, women workers' health has remained largely unexplored. In international settings, resources for investigating occupational health concerns are limited. A worldwide survey conducted by the Global Environmental Epidemiology Network of the World Health Organization found little training available in occupational health (Phillip & Kjellstrom, 1994). Although the work activities of women vary between cultures, there is differentiation of labor activities by gender across cultures. In a survey of 56 countries, Jacobs and Lim (1992) found that women were more likely than men to work in gender-segregated occupations.

Researchers report problems in making cross-national comparisons of women's employment patterns (Figure 6.1). Windebank (1992) recommends that qualitative, as well as quantitative approaches be used to evaluate the influence of culture on women's labor participation. An ethnographic study of the work and health of women in an agrarian Egyptian hamlet illustrates the physical demands and hazards in women's work (Lane & Meleis, 1991). Yet, the work—housework, childcare, care of the sick, farming, animal husbandry, and sewing—is not recognized as work or included in government economic reports. This lack of recognition occurs despite the fact that the women's work makes a substantial contribution to the economic support of the family. The global status of women, particularly in developing countries, clearly warrants international attention to occupational risks for women.

Research on the health of women workers in the United States is making some progress. For example, in 1993, the National Cancer Institute, the Office of Women's Health, and other federal agencies sponsored an international conference on women's occupational cancer risks ("Second-Hand Leukemia," 1993). However, there are still large segments of women workers whose health has not been examined. These marginalized women include those in cottage industries, domestic work, prostitution, agriculture, and the garment industry. A number of recent articles reflect growing interest and concern about the occupational health and working conditions of female *maquiladora* workers (women working in transnationally owned plants on Mexican territory near the U.S. border) and

Figure 6.1 DEFINITIONS OF EPIDEMIOLOGICAL TERMS

Confidence Interval (CI)	The interval which includes the true population measure of effect with a stated level of confidence such as 95%.
Confounding	The inadvertent effect of another factor on the association between the exposure and outcome of interest; confounding can either mask a true association or produce a spurious association.
Odds Ratio (OR)	An estimate of the relative risk based on the odds of exposure for those who have the disease or conditions compared to the odds of exposure for those who do not have the disease or condition of interest.
Prevalence Rate	A proportion in which all individuals who have an existing or newly diagnosed disease or condition are compared to the base population of all individuals who are at risk for the disease or condition of interest.
Standardized Mortality Ratio (SMR)	A comparison of the observed number of deaths with an expected number of deaths that is derived from rates in a general population and which is multiplied by 100; SMRs are adjusted for one or more confounding factors such as age and time (calendar year).

Adapted from: Hennekens, C. H., & Buring, J. E. (1987). Epidemiology in Medicine, Boston: Little, Brown, & Co.

women in agriculture, especially migrant farm workers (Ahonen, Venalainen, Kononen, & Klen, 1990; Mobed, Gold, & Schenker, 1992; Moure-Eraso, Wilcox, Punnett, Copeland, & Levenstein, 1994). Farmworkers may sustain exposure to numerous hazards, particularly pesticides and fertilizers (Zahm & Blair, 1993).

In San Diego, California, researchers evaluated reproductive outcomes among clinic clients (Willis, de Peyster, Molgaard, Walker, & MacKendrick, 1993). These clients were primarily low-income Latina women, many of whom were recent immigrants from Mexico. Bicultural health care workers routinely asked the clients about occupational and environmental exposures to pesticides. Clients were tested to determine absorption of organophosphate pesticides. Occupational exposure to this pesticide class was not associated with spontaneous abortion, low birth weight, preterm delivery, or toxemia. Women farmers in Nebraska, however, who personally applied organophosphate pesticides, experienced a 4.5-fold elevated risk of non-Hodgkin's lymphoma (Zahm et al., 1993).

Among women garment workers, age- and smoking-adjusted bladder cancer risk has been linked both to working in the clothing industry and to employment as a tailor (Cordier et al., 1993). Although ergonomic risks to garment workers would be expected, because of the repetitive motions involved in cutting and sewing garments, little research has been done in this area.

No recent research could be found on hazards associated with cottage industries such as crafts or at-home office work. Cordier et al. (1993) examined women domestic workers' risk of bladder cancer, but no elevated risk for bladder cancer was detected for performing domestic work (industry) or being a maid (occupation).

The health risks of women engaged in prostitution are infrequently examined. Research that does examine the risks in prostitution often centers on the transmission of sexually transmitted diseases, particularly acquired immunodeficiency syndrome (AIDS). Yet, little research has been done in spite of obvious risks of exposure to stress and violence, as well as to sexually transmitted diseases. The clandestine nature of this industry may limit the systematic study of health risks for prostitutes.

Other working women of special interest include those with disabilities and older employed women. The employment opportunities for women with physical limitations should have increased as a result of the Americans with Disabilities Act of 1990 (ADA), but whether the quality of the jobs and the levels of compensation will reflect those of the general population is questionable. Unfortunately, the ADA does not affect preexisting-condition clauses in employers' health insurance policies, which may exclude comprehensive health coverage for disabled employees. Some disabled women may find it difficult to obtain health coverage because of their work status as part-time or temporary employees. Future research should explore the true impact of ADA on the health of working women who have disabilities (U.S. Equal Employment Opportunity Commission, 1991). Of particular interest is the health status of women with vocational impairments from posttraumatic stress disorder following violent acts (Murphy, 1994).

The aging of the work force has captured the attention of industrial planners (Annis, Case, Clauser, & Bradtmiller, 1991). Of importance to women workers are the effects of aging in combination with heat and cold exposure, ergonomic stress, and the potential effects of toxic exposures on cognitive abilities over the course of their work life (Dartigues et al., 1992; Garg, 1991; Pandolf, 1991; Young, 1991). Longitudinal studies are needed to follow women as they grow older and retire, become ill, or die.

An additional concern for women over 65 years of age is that their average pension income in 1992 was only $5,432, compared to $10,031 for men (U.S. Bureau of the Census, 1994). This discrepancy in pension income is related to salary as well as to women's part-time and temporary work status (Berg, 1994). In 1992, after a series of hearings that examined issues related to women and retirement, a report was issued from the Subcommittee on Retirement Income and Employment of the Select Committee on Aging for the U.S. House of Representatives. The report concludes that:

> . . . the promise of retirement security is a cruel illusion for millions of hard-working women. As a reward for raising our children and serving as caregivers for our elders, millions of today's working women will become destitute in old age . . . . (p. 23)

Other authors have reported on the effects of caregiving on women's social security benefits (Kingson & O'Grady-LeShane, 1993). These income issues have clear implications for the health of women who face poverty in their old age.

Using a life course approach, Moen, Robison, and Fields (1994), found that the changes in women's employment did not affect their caregiving roles. Women were likely to become caregivers whether they were employed or not, and women aged 55 to 64 years (36%) were more likely to become caregivers than those aged 35 to 44 years (24%). Along with age differences, gender differences in caregiving activities persisted. Allen (1994) studied a sample of 353 married people with cancer and found that husbands were less likely than wives to help their sick spouse with household tasks. For women who were very ill, nonspousal sources helped fill this gap, but this was not the case for women who were less ill.

MULTIPLE ROLES, MOTHERHOOD, AND EMPLOYMENT

Women in the so-called "sandwich generation" have multiple caregiving roles, and many researchers hypothesize about the potential health effects from the stress of role strain and role conflict. Rather than the mere number of roles, research results now indicate greater relevance for the perceived quality of the roles and the nature or degree of personal autonomy within those roles. Often the research on multiple roles is based on evaluation of the health effects of employment for mothers. However, one longitudinal investigation that linked census data with death registration for 4,667 English and Welsh women did not demonstrate any increased risk of death to women who combined employment with motherhood (Weatherall, Joshi, & Macran, 1994). The longitudinal analysis did not address the possible influence of natural selection of the worker group (healthy worker effect). Moreover, as Weatherall et al. (1994) pointed out, the failure to demonstrate the risk of an "early grave" for working mothers cannot be interpreted to mean that employed parents are free of stress.

More complex than the effects of combined employment and motherhood on women's physical health is the ongoing debate about the impact of multiple roles on women's psychological well-being. The division of labor within families is influenced by the complexities of women workers' social status and perceived gender roles. Investigations on the psychology of multiple roles include factors such as role demands and control, role density, role intensity, decision latitude and control, perceived job satisfaction, and perceived stress. Psychological outcomes are difficult to measure in a reliable and valid manner, particularly for large-scale longitudinal studies; yet such outcomes are essential to examine the effects of multiple factors on women's health. The research to date reflects a limited focus on white, middle-income women and on the role of mothers as compared to caregivers. There is a dearth of research on multiple roles and caregiving among women from a variety of socioeconomic and cultural backgrounds (Facione, 1994; Piechowski, 1992). One notable exception is Mui's (1992) research on black and white daughters caring for elderly parents. While "controlling for income and other differences, black women reported less caregiver role strain than did white women" (p. 209). The study results may reflect differences in coping or in interpretation of role strain.

A controversial area of research is the effect that maternal employment may have on children, husbands, and family dynamics. At least one group of authors suggests that the psychological impact of maternal employment on children may be measured by the use of retrospective reports from adult children about their parents' employment (Ayers, Cusack, & Crosby, 1993). These authors also considered the positive benefits for children from dual-career families, such as the possibility that the fathers would have more time to interact with their children. Research about the effects of maternal employment on children may be gender-biased; few studies examine the effects of fathers' employment on family members.

Another relevant area of research investigates the experiences of working mothers who breastfeed their infants. In 1987, Moore and Jansa reported that there was little evidence of workplace support for employees' breastfeeding. A position paper from the American Dietetic Association (1993) lists the lack of flexibility in the workplace as a barrier to successful breastfeeding. In one study, a large majority of the participating mothers (74%) who tried to express milk while at work experienced problems related to the workplace, especially the inaccessibility of a place to express and re-frigerate milk (Hills-Bonczyk, Avery, Savik, Potter, & Duckett, 1993).

Furman (1993) questioned the ethical values that lead to combining the employment of mothers with breastfeeding: "'Needing' two incomes is often a relative and not an absolute matter and has to do with life style" (p. 1). However, Wenk and Garrett (1992) found that a critical factor affecting maternal employment is the relative proportion of family income derived from the mother's salary. As the amount of real wages for men declines the importance of maternal income is likely to increase.

Another concern has been the transmission into breastmilk of toxic substances present in the workplace. Filkins and Kerr (1993) reviewed toxic exposures relevant to breastfeeding.

A substantial proportion of research continues to study the effects of employment during pregnancy on fetal and infant health outcomes and, to a lesser extent, on the health of women. Risk is associated with specific exposures that may occur in the workplace; however, very little evidence supports a conclusion that work during pregnancy, separate from hazardous exposures, incurs any risk to the mother, the pregnancy, or the long-term health of the child. Graham, Lessin, and Mirer (1993) discuss labor's perspective on reproductive hazards and offer guidelines for health-protective policy development. Protection of women's employment rights may require further legal strategies to assure that employers implement adequate environmental control measures (Clauss, Berzon, & Bertin, 1993).

WORKPLACE HAZARDS

Workplace hazards are a growing threat to women's health. There are still no conclusive data on the effects of nonionizing radiation from video display terminals (VDTs), but a growing body of research documents the musculoskeletal effects related to ergonomic factors associated with VDTs. Noise remains a concern; loud noise may cause hearing loss to the fetus during pregnancy (Niemtzow, 1993). Interest in thermal stresses is growing, in light of recent studies on the health effects of heat and cold for working women.

In recent reports, women exposed to benzene solvent had an increased incidence of soft tissue sarcoma. In the shoe manufacturing industry, which uses solvents such as toluene, methylethyl ketone, acetone, and hexane, increased mortality was observed for cancers of the larynx and lung, leukemias, and myelodysplastic syndromes. Women jewelry makers, who are exposed to solvents and heavy metals, have a significant excess proportion of deaths due to stomach cancer. In studies of adverse pregnancy outcomes, first trimester solvent exposures were implicated in a two- to fourfold increase in the risk of spontaneous abortions. Electronic components assemblers and production workers experienced a fivefold increased risk for low birth weight in infants.

Pesticide exposures among women farm workers has been associated with an increased risk of non-Hodgkin's lymphoma, leukemia, and myelodysplastic syndromes. Among nonsmoking women, pesticide exposure was associated with increased risk of lung cancer. Pesticide exposure has also been implicated in the development of aplastic anemia.

First trimester occupational exposure to antineoplastic (anticancer) drugs was associated with increased risk of ectopic pregnancy in health care workers (excluding physicians) and acute symptoms in pharmacy personnel (Valanis, Vollmer, Labuhn, & Glass, 1993). Ito and Koren (1993) conducted a risk assessment of health care workers' exposure to the antiviral drug, ribavirin. A teratogen, ribavirin is chemically similar to other antimetabolites that are used to treat cancer.

Although many women are exposed to biological hazards (e.g., human, animal, and plant products), few articles were found that used female samples or that analyzed findings by gender. However, research on hazards faced by health care workers is available and a large percentage of health care workers are women. A new worry for women employed in health care is latex allergy, which has emerged as a result of workers' wearing latex gloves to protect themselves from exposure to bloodborne disease, such as human immunodeficiency virus (HIV). Responses to latex allergens have ranged from skin irritations to life-threatening allergic reactions. Also, much has been reported about worker exposure to the biological hazards of HIV, hepatitis B virus, and tuberculosis. Although these hazards pose serious threats to women who work in the health care fields, enforcement of enacted standards continues to be an issue.

The principal psychological work hazards are stress and burnout. Evidence suggests that women often experience a spillover of home stress onto work; when resources are inadequate to meet home demands, work stress is amplified. Sources of stress for women include both personal and organizational factors. Data suggest that, in addition to gender differences in sources of occupational stress, sources of stress in women may differ across racial groups.

Dusts in the work environment may originate from biological, chemical, or physical agents. Dusts may also contribute to building-related illnesses such as sick building syndrome. Previous research has found that women report more symptoms associated with sick building syndrome than do men, yet when exposure levels of dusts and other air contaminants were analyzed by gender, no differences in frequency of symptoms between men and women were reported.

Women who rotate shifts or work during nondaylight hours are exposed to a combination of biological, psychological, and physical hazards. Findings indicate that there are gender-based differences in the quality and quantity of sleep in shift workers and that age has a mediating effect.

One of the most pervasive hazards that women face in the workplace and elsewhere is violence. Although domestic violence has been documented in many cultures (Fauveau & Blanchet, 1989; Heise, 1993; Lane & Meleis, 1991), workplace violence has been less well studied.

Heise (1993), citing the United Nations Commission on the Status of Women, noted that "violence against women [is] physical, sexual and psychological violence occurring in the family and in the community . . . [and includes] sexual harassment and intimidation at work, in educational institutions and elsewhere . . ." (p. 78). Fitzgerald (1993) reviewed the literature on sexual harassment at work. Studies on female homicide (Castillo & Jenkins, 1994) and sexual assault in the workplace (Alexander, Franklin, & Wolf, 1994) have furthered understanding of these forms of violence in the United States. In response to the high risk of violence toward health care and community-based service workers, the California Occupational Safety and Health Administration (1993) issued comprehensive guidelines for promoting the safety of these workers. Recommended measures included detailed recordkeeping and health surveillance.

Unfortunately, sexual harassment continues in the United States and is pervasive in some workplaces. Sexual harassment has been defined as "conduct of a sexual nature . . . unwelcome by the target . . . severe or pervasive enough to create a hostile or intimidating work environment" (Women Employed Institute, 1994, p. 2). The negative emotional consequences of sexual harassment can be devastating, and the experience of sexual harassment creates a career disaster for some women. They may face the necessity of leaving a job, lack of timely response to complaints by governmental agencies, and the stress and costs of legal courses of action. Jensvold (1993) provided insight about the potential damage from misinterpretation of psychiatric evaluations in the context of sexual harassment allegations. Another twist in the ongoing controversy transpired recently with regard to sex-based harassment (Mathewson, 1993). Sex-based harassment incorporates behavior that is unwanted but is not of a sexual nature, yet is directed at women. Recommendations for policy development to prevent and address harassment in the workplace include a clear statement that the policy applies to all employees, harassment is illegal, and it is the employer's responsibility to eliminate harassment.

CHALLENGES AND IMPLICATIONS FOR FUTURE RESEARCH

Consideration of sexual harassment as a workplace hazard is illustrative of some definitional issues in women's occupational health. Other concepts that require clarification include the definitions of work and the workplace.

As work takes place increasingly in home environments, the question "Where is the workplace?" refers to paid as well as unpaid work. Researchers should consider whether occupational risk associated with gender is a function of job characteristics. They might also test the relationship between multiple role stress and a high level of interpersonal conflict in the workplace.

Future studies must be designed to determine possible health effects when work tasks, such as some lifting or fine motor skills, are at the extreme limits of human ability for either sex. The extreme limits of human ability occur, for example, when only a few men and no women can perform a task or when only a few women and no men can perform a task. Researchers in the field of women's occupational health should use comprehensive approaches, such as the ecological model, to determine personal worker factors (tolerance for interpersonal conflict) and organizational factors (poor working conditions).

Because of the work status of many women, measurement of exposure to workplace hazards needs to be more specific. The use of job category as a measure of exposure may be inadequate. Instead of measuring the number of hours per day (or week) a woman is employed, the amount of time spent actually performing certain work tasks may be a better indicator of exposure levels.

A focus on pregnancy outcomes still dominates occupational health research. Thus, future research should examine a broader array of risks and place greater emphasis on impairment due to breast, lung, and other cancers; respiratory diseases; musculoskeletal disorders; and central and peripheral neurological impairment. The long latency period for some illnesses means that sufficient time must be allowed between the measurement of exposure and the outcomes that indicate adverse health affects. Sample size must be large, to provide analysis of research data that will detect true associations, particularly where adverse outcomes are rare. Equally important, future research must include a diverse sample of women workers, including women of different races, income levels, and age groups.

To advance knowledge about the effects of women's work on their health, new strategies must be created for the allocation of research funds. In determining current research priorities, policymakers rely on limited scientific data. Social factors limit the availability of data on workers' health, particularly for women. For example, work is gender-segregated across cultures. Based on beliefs about the nature of women's work, inappropriate assumptions may be made about the safety of female workers, or, in contrast, the danger of work to pregnant employees. Historically, women's work has been considered safe, but employment during pregnancy was thought to be dangerous. Yet, until recently, the topic of women's occupational health generated little research interest compared to the male workers' health. Assumptions about the nature of women's work influence research hypotheses and thereby affect the focus of data collection. For example, some work in largely female occupational groups may be classified as "light" when based on the weight of items that must be lifted, but the level of isometric muscle contraction involved in the work may nonetheless result in significant energy expenditure.

Consequently, biased assumptions about gender may influence definitions of work and reasonable work load and may result in inappropriate conclusions about the nature and safety of women's work. Little is known about the hazards specific to traditionally female worker groups or about women's capacity to do work that has been traditionally considered to be best performed by males. The lack of data reinforces existing assumptions and social norms about women and work, which in turn reinforces the low interest, priority, and funding devoted to research on issues in women's occupational health.

In summary, a circular pattern of social factors influences research on women's occupational health. Social norms often limit women to certain types of work activities. The work women do is frequently not valued, if compensated at all. When it is not valued, it may be considered to be easy and inherently safe. Further, if women's work is thought to be safe, policy-makers may deem it unnecessary to fund research on the risk of work to women, and we are denied the findings necessary to challenge the existing assumptions about women's occupational health risks.

Accountability is an issue for governmental agencies seeking to ensure gender equity. Gender equity requires an allocation of funding for women's health research, the inclusion of women workers in study samples, and the analysis of occupational health data by gender (Misner, Levin, & Hewitt, 1993). When allocating scarce resources for research, the methodological issues above apply to research designed to determine health risks and to intervention studies that evaluate the use of alternative substances and processes to reduce health risks. Further research is needed to improve the design and production of personal protective equipment, especially when protective equipment may become itself a hazard, as is the case with latex allergies (Levin, 1994).

CONCLUDING REMARKS

There is a growing interest in occupational issues in women's health. This area encompasses a range of women's activities, including both paid employment and at-home responsibilities. To address the concerns of working women will require serious review of and broad changes in social policies that affect crime, salary equity, availability of child care, and flexible workplace options. This social context, as well as workplace hazards, has meaning and relevance for research in women's occupational health.

REFERENCES

Aguilar, L. (1994, April 3). A milestone verdict with a cost. *The Washington Post,* p. B3.

Ahonen, E., Venalainen, J. M., Kononen, U., & Klen, T. (1990). The physical strain of dairy farming. *Ergonomics, 33,* 1549–1555.

Alexander, B. H., Franklin, G. M., & Wolf, M. E. (1994). The sexual assault of women at work in Washington State, 1980–1989. *American Journal of Public Health, 84,* 640–642.

Allen, S. M. (1994). Gender differences in spousal caregiving and unmet need for care. *Journal of Gerontology, 49,* S187–S195.

American Dietetic Association. (1993). Position of the American Dietetic Association: Promotion and support of breast-feeding. *Journal of the American Dietetic Association, 93,* 467–469.

Annis, J. F., Case, H. W., Clauser, C. E., & Bradtmiller, B. (1991). Anthropometry of an aging work force. *Experimental Aging Research, 17,* 157–176.

Aston, J., & Lavery, J. (1993). The health of women in paid employment: Effects of quality of work role, social support and cynicism on psychological and physical well-being. *Women and Health, 20*(3), 1–25.

Ayers, L., Cusack, M., & Crosby, F. (1993). Combining work and home. *Occupational Medicine: State of the Art Reviews, 8,* 821–831.

Baldwin, C. (1993). Gender domination in the work setting: Implications for dieticians. *Journal of the American Dietetic Association, 93,* 25–26.

Berg, O. (1994, May). *Olena Berg talking points for pensions not posies press conference.* Paper presented at the National Press Club, Washington, DC.

Brown, J. (1994, July). Gender equality in the police service. *Report of a seminar arranged by the Women's National Commission* (pp. 1–3). London: Women's National Commission.

California Occupational Safety and Health Administration. (1993). *Guidelines for security and safety of health care and community service workers.* Los Angeles: Author.

Castillo, D. N., & Jenkins, E. L. (1994). Industries and occupations at high risk for work-related homicide. *Journal of Occupational Medicine, 36,* 125–132.

Chamberlain, G. V. (1993). Work in pregnancy. *American Journal of Industrial Medicine, 23,* 559–575.

Clauss, C. A., Berzon, M., & Bertin, J. (1993). Litigating reproductive and developmental health in the aftermath of *UAW v. Johnson Controls. Environmental Health Perspectives Supplements, 101*(S2), 205–220.

Cordier, S., Clavel, J. C., Limasset, J. C., Boccon-Gibod, L., Le Moual, N., Manderear, L., & Hemon, D. (1993). Occupational risks of bladder cancer in France: A multicenter case control study. *International Journal of Epidemiology, 22*, 403–411.

Dahl, E. (1993). Social inequality in health: The role of the healthy worker effect. *Social Science and Medicine, 36*, 1077–1086.

Dartigues, J., Gagnon, M., Letenneur, L., Barberger-Gateau, P., Commenges, D., Evaldre, M., & Salamon, R. (1992). Principal lifetime occupation and cognitive impairment in a French elderly cohort (Paquid). *American Journal of Epidemiology, 135*, 981–988.

DeJoseph, J. F. (1993). Redefining women's work during pregnancy: Toward a more comprehensive approach. *Birth, 20*, 86–93.

Doyal, L. (1990). Health at home and in waged work: Part two. Waged work and women's well-being. *Women's Studies International Forum, 13*, 587–604.

Dumais, L. (1992). Impact of the participation of women in science: On rethinking the place of women, especially in occupational health. *Woman and Health, 18*(3), 11–25.

Facione, N. C. (1994). Role overload and health: The married mother in the waged labor force. *Health Care of Women International, 15*, 157–167.

Fauveau, V., & Blanchet, T. (1989). Deaths from injuries and induced abortion among rural Bangladeshi women. *Social Science and Medicine, 29*, 1121–1127.

Filkins, K., & Kerr, M. J. (1993). Occupational reproductive health risks. *Occupational Medicine: State of the Art Reviews, 8*, 733–754.

Fitzgerald, L. F. (1993). Sexual harassment: Violence against women in the work force. *American Psychologist, 48*, 1070–1076.

Furman, L. (1993). Breastfeeding and fulltime maternal employment: Does the baby lose out? *Journal of Human Lactation, 9*(1), 1–2.

Garg, A. (1991). Ergonomics and the older worker: An overview. *Experimental Aging Research, 17*, 143–155.

Glass, B. (1993). Where is the workplace and who is the practitioner? *Occupational Medicine, 43*, 7–8.

Graetz, B. (1993). Health consequences of employment and unemployment: Longitudinal evidence for young men and women. *Social Science and Medicine, 36,* 715–724.

Graham, T., Lessin, N., & Mirer, F. (1993). A labor perspective on workplace reproductive hazards: Past history, current concerns, and positive directions. *Environmental Health Perspectives Supplements, 101*(S2), 199–204.

Hagan, J. (1990). The gender stratification of income inequality among lawyers. *Social Forces, 68,* 835–855.

Headapohl, D. (1993). Sex, gender, biology, and work. *Occupational Medicine: State of the Art Reviews, 8,* 685–707.

Heise, L. (1993). Violence against women: The hidden health burden. *World Health Statistics Quarterly, 46*(1), 78–85.

Herold, J., & Waldron, I. (1985). Part-time employment and women's health. *Journal of Occupational Medicine, 27,* 405–412.

Hibbard, J. H., & Pope, C. R. (1991). Effect of domestic and occupational roles on morbidity and mortality. *Social Science and Medicine, 32,* 805–811.

Hibbard, J. H., & Pope, C. R. (1993). Health effects of discontinuities in female employment and marital status. *Social Science and Medicine, 36,* 1099–1104.

Hills-Bonczyk, S. G., Avery, M. D., Savik, K., Potter, S., & Duckett, L. J. (1993). Women's experiences with combining breast-feeding and employment. *Journal of Nurse-Midwifery, 38,* 257–266.

Ito, S., & Koren, G. (1993). Exposure of pregnant women to ribavirin-contaminated air: Risk assessment and recommendations. *Pediatric Infectious Disease Journal, 12,* 2–5.

Jacobs, J. A., & Lim, S. T. (1992). Trends in occupational and industrial sex segregation in 56 countries, 1960–1980. *Work and Occupations, 19,* 450–486.

Jensvold, M. F. (1993). Workplace sexual harassment: The use, misuse, and abuse of psychiatry. *Psychiatric Annals, 23,* 438–445.

Kingson, E. R., & O'Grady-LeShane, R. (1993). The effects of caregiving on women's social security benefits. *The Gerontologist, 33,* 230–239.

Lane, S. D., & Meleis, A. I. (1991). Roles, work, health perceptions and health resources of women: A study in an Egyptian Delta hamlet. *Social Science and Medicine, 33,* 1197–1208.

Levin, P. F. (1994). *Predictors of glove use by health care workers.* Unpublished doctoral dissertation, University of Illinois at Chicago.

Mathewson, M. (1993). Sex-based harassment: A new twist in discrimination law. *Illinois Bar Journal, 81,* 433, 399.

Meleis, A. I., Hall, J. M., & Stevens, P. E. (1994). Scholarly caring in doctoral nursing education: Promoting diversity and collaborative mentorship. *Image: The Journal of Nursing Scholarship, 26,* 177–180.

Messing, K. (1994). Danger: Women at work. *The Women's Review of Books, 11,* 11–13.

Messing, K., Dumais, L., & Romito, P. (1993). Prostitutes and chimney sweeps both have problems: Towards full integration of both sexes in the study of occupational health. *Social Science and Medicine, 36,* 47–55.

Misner, S. T., Levin, P. F., & Hewitt, J. B. (1993). Occupational issues in women's health. In B. J. McElmurry & R. S. Parker (Eds.), *Annual review of women's health* (pp. 31–65). New York: National League for Nursing Press.

Mobed, K., Gold, E. B., & Schenker, M. B. (1992). Occupational health problems among migrant and seasonal farm workers. *Western Journal of Medicine, 157,* 367–373.

Moen, P., Robison, J., & Fields, V. (1994). Women's work and caregiving roles: A life course approach. *Journal of Gerontology, 49,* S176–S186.

Moore, J. F., & Jansa, N. (1987). A survey of policies and practices in support of breastfeeding mothers in the workplace. *Birth, 14,* 191–195.

Moure-Eraso, R., Wilcox, M., Punnett, L., Copeland, L., & Levenstein, C. (1994). Back to the future: Sweatshop conditions on the Mexico–U.S. border. I. Community health impact of *maquiladora* industrial activity. *American Journal of Industrial Medicine, 25,* 311–324.

Mui, A. C. (1992). Caregiver strain among black and white daughter caregivers: A role theory perspective. *The Gerontologist, 32,* 203–212.

Murphy, P. (1994, Spring). *The edge of a large hole: Writings on the request for reasonable accommodation under the Americans with Disabilities Act of 1990.* (Available from the University of Illinois Center for Research on Women and Gender, 1640 Roosevelt Road, Room 207, Chicago, IL 60608.)

Niemtzow, R. C. (1993). Loud noise and pregnancy. *Military Medicine, 158,* 10–12.

Pandolf, K. B. (1991). Aging and heat tolerance at rest or during work. *Experimental Aging Research, 17,* 189–204.

Phillip, R., & Kjellstrom, T. (1994). Courses in environmental and occupational epidemiology. *World Health Forum, 15,* 43–47.

Piechowski, L. D. (1992). Mental health and women's multiple roles. *Families in Society: The Journal of Contemporary Human Services, 73*, 131–139.

Quinn, M. M., & Woskie, S. L. (1990). Women and work. In J. S. Felton (Ed.), *Occupational medical management: A guide to the organization and operation of in-plant occupational health services* (pp. 479–499). Boston: Little, Brown.

Sanchez, L. (1993). Women's power and the gendered division of domestic labor in the third world. *Gender & Society, 7*, 434–459.

Second-hand leukemia. (1993). *Science*, 987.

Select Committee on Aging. (1992). *How well do women fare under the nation's retirement policies?* (Comm. Pub. No. 102-879). Washington, DC: U.S. Government Printing Office.

Stellman, J. M. (1986). Editorial overview. *Women and Health, 2*(1), 27–47.

Unger, K. (1993). Working women: Economic and social considerations. *Occupational Medicine: State of the Art Reviews, 8*, 859–868.

U.S. Bureau of the Census. (1993). *Statistical abstract of the United States: 1993* (113th ed.). Washington, DC: Author.

U.S. Bureau of the Census. (1994). [Housing and Household Economic Statistics Division: Source of income in 1992—number with income and mean income in 1992 of persons 15 years old and over, by race, Hispanic origin, and sex.] Unpublished raw data.

U.S. Equal Employment Opportunity Commission. (1991). *The Americans with Disabilities Act: Your employment rights as an individual with a disability*. Washington, DC: Author.

Valanis, B. G., Vollmer, W. M., Labuhn, K. T., & Glass, A. G. (1993). Association of antineoplastic drug handling with acute adverse effects in pharmacy personnel. *American Journal of Hospital Pharmacy, 50*, 455–462.

Verbrugge, L. M. (1985). Gender and health: An update on hypothesis and evidence. *Journal of Health and Social Behavior, 26*, 156–182.

Weatherall, R., Joshi, H., & Macran, S. (1994). Double burden or double blessing? Employment, motherhood, and mortality in the longitudinal study of England and Wales. *Social Science and Medicine, 38*, 285–297.

Wenk, D., & Garrett, P. (1992). Having a baby: Some predictions of maternal employment around childbirth. *Gender & Society, 6*, 49–65.

Wharton, A. S. (1993). Women's and men's responses to sex-segregated work. *Occupational Medicine: State of the Art Reviews, 8*, 833–848.

Willis, W. O., de Peyster, A., Molgaard, C. A., Walker, C., MacKendrick, T. (1993). Pregnancy outcome among women exposed to pesticides through work or residence in an agricultural area. *Journal of Occupational Medicine, 35,* 943–949.

Windebank, J. (1992). Comparing women's employment patterns across the European Community: Issues of method and interpretation. *Women's Studies International Forum, 15,* 65–76.

Women Employed Institute. (1994). *Sexual harassment: The problem that isn't going away.* (Available from the Women Employed Institute, 22 West Monroe Street, Chicago, IL 60603.)

Young, A. J. (1991). Effects of aging on human cold tolerance. *Experimental Aging Research, 17,* 205–213.

Zahm, S. H., & Blair, A. (1993). Cancer among migrant and seasonal farmworkers: An epidemiologic review and research agenda. *American Journal of Industrial Medicine, 24,* 753–766.

Zahm, S. H., Weisenburger, D. D., Saal, R. C., Vaught, J. B., Babbitt, P. A., & Blair, A. (1993). The role of agricultural pesticide use in the development of non-Hodgkin's lymphoma in women. *Archives of Environmental Health, 48,* 353–358.

Pregnancy and Work

Chamberlain, C. V. (1993). Work in pregnancy. *American Journal of Industrial Medicine, 23,* 559–575.

Moss, N., & Carver, K. (1993). Pregnant women at work: Sociodemographic perspectives. *American Journal of Industrial Medicine, 23,* 541–557.

The above articles provide a timely update on the persistent debate about the effects of maternal work on pregnancy outcomes. In broadening the traditional concept of work related to pregnancy, Chamberlain has included domestic and leisure activities, as well as paid employment and has addressed the high stakes involved when recommendations are either overly cautious or insufficiently careful. Furthermore, the author discusses the serious ramifications from inaccurate research conclusions such as adverse fetal or maternal effects and adverse economic consequences when pregnant women are excluded from the work environment. The article also reviews chemical, biological, and physical hazards. The author chastises countries that fail to provide adequate social support in the form of paid maternal leave.

Moss and Carver evaluate sociodemographic, behavioral, and employment status on risk factors to low birth weight, using the 1988 National Maternal and Infant Health Survey. While controlling for a wide array of factors, the authors have found that maternal work during pregnancy is associated with decreased risk of low-birth-weight infants. The authors discuss trends in social economics, female work-force demographics, pregnancy outcomes among working and unemployed women, and social norms that affect the acceptability of being employed during pregnancy. Both of these articles conclude that women's employment during pregnancy is not associated with low birth weight (Chamberlain; Moss & Carver) or preterm delivery (Chamberlain). Based on these findings, future studies should measure stress; physical activity; occupational and environmental toxic exposures; and exposures to noise, heat, and vibration in women, as well as relevant paternal factors.

Physical Hazards

Ergonomics

Andersen, J. H., & Gaardboe, O. (1993). Prevalence of persistent neck and upper limb pain in a historical cohort of sewing machine operators. *American Journal of Industrial Medicine, 24*, 677–687.

Andersen, J. H., & Gaardboe, O. (1993). Musculoskeletal disorders of the neck and upper limb among sewing machine operators: A clinical investigation. *American Journal of Industrial Medicine, 24*, 689–700.

Jensen, B. R., Schibye, B., Sogaard, K., Simonsen, E. B., & Sjogaard, G. (1993). Shoulder muscle load and muscle fatigue among industrial sewing-machine operators. *European Journal of Applied Physiology, 67*, 467–475.

These articles address musculoskeletal problems of the upper arm regions in industrial sewing machine operators. The strain of piece sewing by garment workers has been an occupational health problem of women historically and has even been glamorized in the mass media. As an almost exclusively female occupation in most countries, piece sewing constitutes one of the greatest challenges to women's occupational health. Jensen et al. measured the shoulder muscle load and development of shoulder muscle fatigue during the work task performance of industrial sewing. A sample of 29 women was divided into two groups: (a) those with high frequency of shoulder/neck symptoms and (b) those with a lower frequency. Measurements included electromyelogram (EMG), muscle strength, anthropometry, and work station dimensions.

Workers who reported a greater frequency of symptoms were found to have significantly lower muscle strength ($p < .05$).

Andersen and Gaardboe conducted investigations on a historical cohort of garment industry workers in order to examine whether an exposure–response relationship exists between years of employment as a sewing machine operator and the prevalence of persistent neck and upper arm pain. A cohort of 424 garment industry workers was compared to 781 women from the general population. The sewing machine operators were divided into three groups according to their length of service: group I, 0–7 years (n=252); group II, 8–15 years (n=95); and group III, more than 15 years (n=77). The measure of exposure was years of employment. Based on the authors' professional experience, a classification system was developed for exposure groups according to current job status, identified by job title. Limitations of this method are the crude assessment of exposure level and the authors' failure to report interrater reliability for this process. A questionnaire was provided to each participant in the study, to determine self-reported levels of neck, shoulder, and arm pain. Multivariate logistic regression analysis was used to examine the effect of confounding variables: age, number of children, exercising, smoking, present exposure, and socioeconomic status. The risk for neck and shoulder pain increased for higher exposure groups and remained when adjusted for confounding factors. Those operators working for more than 8 years were likely to have cumulative shoulder and neck pain.

The clinical study by Andersen & Gaardboe evaluated 107 female sewing machine operators in an age-stratified sample and compared them with a group of auxiliary nurses and home helpers. Stratification for years of exposure was the same as for the prevalence study. The main clinical diagnosis groups were cervicobrachial fibromyalgia, cervical syndrome, and rotator cuff syndrome. These diagnoses were based on a comprehensive physical and psychological health examination. After adjustment for confounders, including present exposure, the relationship of years of exposure and clinical outcomes persisted. The authors state that the risk of 8 years or more of exposure demonstrated in the prevalence study was confirmed in this clinical analysis.

Conrad, J. C., Conrad, K. J., & Osborn, J. B. (1993). A short-term, three-year epidemiological study of median nerve sensitivity in practicing dental hygienists. *Journal of Dental Hygiene, 67,* 268–272.

Oberg, T., & Oberg, U. (1993). Musculoskeletal complaints in dental hygiene: A survey study from a Swedish county. *Journal of Dental Hygiene, 67,* 257–261.

Oberg, T. (1993). Ergonomic evaluation and construction of a reference workplace in dental hygiene: A case study. *Journal of Dental Hygiene, 67,* 262–267.

Injury related to repetitive motion continues to be costly to employers, in compensation and rehabilitation costs, and to employees, in lost income, pain, and disability. There has been concern that dental hygienists, a predominantly female occupational group, may have increased risk for cumulative trauma syndrome (CTS). As these articles point out, the potential risk of CTS for dental hygienists may be due to prolonged static work load that involves precise work and grasping of small diameter instruments.

Conrad, Conrad, and Osborn present a follow-up study of a cohort of 16 dental hygiene graduates who are working at least 32 hours per week. Using vibrometry, specifically to detect median nerve dysfunction, no statistically significant dysfunction was found after 3 years of practice in this cohort. However, although still within normal range, a statistically significant decrease ($p < .05$) in median nerve sensitivity (threshold shift) was detected. The authors caution that the usefulness of these data for predicting future development of CTS in this cohort is not known.

In their survey of 28 dental hygienists, Oberg and Oberg report a high percentage of neck, upper extremity, and back complaints,

which the hygienists considered to be primarily work-related. A predominance of complaints was related to right-sided musculoskeletal involvement. In a companion article, Oberg presents a case study on the development of a reference workplace designed for dental hygiene practice. This article illustrates a thorough and pragmatic approach to assessing and resolving ergonomic problems by modifying the work setting to fit the workers and work practice requirements. Workplace ergonomic analysis indicated a fixed working posture, with static load on the neck, shoulder, and arms without support rests for arms and hands. The author reports that the worksite modifications, such as an armrest for the dental operator's chair, were made at a cost of only a few hundred dollars (approximately $\frac{1}{10}$ the cost of a nonsurgical case of CTS). The worksite changes achieved a decrease in the reported shoulder complaints for the dental hygienist in the case study and generated considerable interest as a model across Sweden. This series of articles demonstrates a need for continued research on ergonomic factors in dental hygiene practice, including longitudinal investigation of nerve and muscle functioning; muscle load, fatigue, and pause patterns; and the effectiveness of work redesign in achieving a decrease in the development of CTS. The application of research in dental hygiene practice may serve as a model for addressing ergonomic problems in other female-dominated occupations.

Noise and Vibration

Green, M. S., Peled, I., Harari, G., Luz, J., Akselrod, S., Norymberg, M., & Melamed, S. (1991/1992). Association of silent ST-segment depression on one-hour ambulatory ECGs with exposure to industrial noise among blue-collar workers in Israel examined at different levels of ambient temperature—The Cordis study. *Public Health Reviews, 19,* 277–293.

This study is notable for its comparison of 1,845 men and 664 women factory workers. Using the electrocardiogram measure of silent ST-segment depression, the researchers evaluated the effects of industrial noise exposure

(>80 decibels) and cool ambient temperature. (Decibel, or dBA, is a measure of noise intensity. It is based on a logarithmic scale with modifications that approximate the human response to low frequencies of sound, including the range at which speech occurs.) Noise exposure was hypothesized to increase vasoconstriction and myocardial ischemia. Multiple logistical regression analysis was used to determine relative risk estimates adjusted for age, smoking, physical work, Quetelet's index of weight in kg/height in m^2, ventilation, and hearing loss. Among workers exposed to greater levels of noise exposure (80 dBA vs. 70 dBA), the prevalence of ST-segment depression was increased for men (RR=2.4; p=.01). For women, increased prevalence of ST-segment depression occurred at increasing noise exposure levels in association with lower ambient temperature. However, after adjustment for potential confounding variables, only ambient temperature remained significantly—but negatively—associated with ST-segment depression among women. At least among women, lower ambient temperatures "may accentuate the sensitivity of the coronary arteries to vasoconstriction resulting from noise" (p. 290). Therefore, the findings suggest gender differences for the myocardial effects of noise and ambient temperature.

Seidel, H. (1993). Selected health risks caused by long-term, whole body vibration. *American Journal of Industrial Medicine, 23,* 589–604.

This article presents an extensive review of the literature on the health risks of long-term exposure to whole body vibration (wbv). This hazard constitutes an important health risk for operators of motor vehicles and trams, mine workers, and both men and women workers in various other occupations. However, as the author points out, a limitation of the debate about health risks for women from wbv is the paucity of studies with female subjects. Of a substantial number of the studies reviewed, only one study was considered by the author to have presented reliable data on women. Sources used for this article included:

the literature collection of a research group studying the biological effect of vibration and noise in the Federal Institute for Occupational Health, Berlin; databases MEDLINE on CD-ROM 1989–1990 and OSHROM; and unpublished experimental data on the effects of vibration on the spine. A proposed classification system for vibrational disease, and noise as a confounding variable in the conduct of research on wbv are discussed. Of special interest is a section, "Health Risk to Female Reproductive Organs and Pregnancy." The author cautions that the quality of most of the studies reviewed for this section does not permit valid conclusions. Some of these studies examined age-related risks in occupational groups of women (seamstresses, stockweavers, etc.) Dependent variables included menstrual and gynecologic symptoms, pregnancy outcomes, and musculoskeletal effects. A review of animal studies suggests harmful fetal effects in animals; however, the applicability of these findings to humans is questioned. The author presents a technical and detailed discussion of the literature, denotes the limitations of the research to date, and suggests areas for future studies, including comparison of wbv effects in men and women.

Ionizing Radiation

Wingren, G., Hatscheck, T., & Axelson, O. (1993). Determinants of papillary cancer of the thyroid. *American Journal of Epidemiology, 138,* 482–491.

This case-control study used incident cases of thyroid cancer identified through the southeastern Swedish Cancer Registry. The researchers surveyed 205 female cases, 43 male cases, and 496 randomly selected population-based controls. Elevated but unstable odds ratios were identified for telephone operators (4.8), teachers (2.9), day nursery personnel, and women who worked with video display terminals (2.4) or unspecified chemicals (3.0). In women, diagnostic X-ray procedures in different anatomical regions (including dental X-rays) showed two- to threefold increased risks for papillary thyroid cancer. This study is important because thyroid cancer disproportionately affects women.

Nonionizing Radiation

Brandt, L. P. A., & Nielsen, C. V. (1992). Fecundity and the use of video display terminals. *Scandinavian Journal of Work and Environmental Health, 18,* 298–301.

The researchers conducted a case-control study of women members of the Danish clerical union. Birth register data from 1983 to 1985 were linked to the National Register of Inpatients to identify all women eligible for the study ($N = 24,352$). A 9.2% random sample was drawn ($n = 2,252$), of which 75.5% responded to a mail questionnaire. Analysis was restricted to employed women ($n = 1,365$). For this study, self-reported delayed pregnancy (≥ 7 months or ≥ 13 months) was used as the outcome measure. Risk factors for delayed pregnancy (≥ 7 months) were cigarette smoking (> 10/day; RR = 1.6), age 25–34 years (RR = 1.6), and age ≥ 35 years (RR = 3.9). Having at least one previous pregnancy protected against delayed time to pregnancy (RR = 0.6). Slightly stronger associations were found for these factors in relation to prolonged delayed pregnancy (≥ 13 months). Prolonged delayed pregnancy also was associated with working more than 20 hours per week with video display terminals (RR = 1.6; 95% CI = 1.1, 2.4). Considering the small to moderate effects detected in this study and the study design, these findings may be due to bias or uncontrolled confounding factors. Future research could address these limitations by using a cohort study design and reliably controlling for occupational and nonoccupational (including history of contraception use) exposures of the women, as well as paternal factors.

Evans, J. A., Savitz, D. A., Kanal, E., & Gillen, J. (1993). Infertility and pregnancy outcome among magnetic resonance imaging workers. *Journal of Occupational Medicine, 35,* 1191–1195.

The researchers conducted a cross-sectional survey of female magnetic resonance imaging (MRI) technologists and nurses employed in all NMR centers throughout the United States. In total, 1,915 females responded to the survey and provided data on 1,421 pregnancies, of which 20% qualified as exposed to MRI, a source of static electromagnetic radiation. Comparisons were made with pregnancies in which the women were either predominantly or solely homemakers or engaged in "other work." When compared to pregnancies that occurred when women did other work, risk ratios for MRI-exposed pregnancies were not elevated. When homemakers were used as the comparison group, the risk ratios were modestly elevated (50% to 70%) for infertility, prematurity, and low birth weight. The risk for fetal loss, however, was significantly elevated (RR = 3.2; 95% CI = 1.7, 6.0). The researchers attribute this finding to an unusually low rate of reported fetal loss (6%) among homemakers, which may represent underreporting. The authors assert that this is the first study of MRI workers and recommend further study of reproductive outcomes for a broader group of health care workers.

Thermal Hazards

Messing, K., Saurel-Cubizolles, M. J., Bourgine, M., & Kaminski, M. (1993). Factors associated with dysmenorrhea among workers in French poultry slaughterhouses and canneries. *Journal of Occupational Medicine, 35,* 493–500.

Women workers in the food industry are frequently exposed to static work load, repetitive tasks, and cold. Symptomatology for this worker group includes dysmenorrhea associated with cold exposure. This cross-sectional study evaluates the relationship between dysmenorrhea and occupational characteristics for 726 women in 17 poultry slaughterhouses and 6 cannery factories in France, where women comprise 15% of the food industry work force. A self-report questionnaire format was used to obtain data pertaining to working conditions and domestic work. Information on menstrual cycle, demographics, contraception use, smoking, and birth parity was also queried. The prevalence rate of pain before and/or during the menstrual period was 71%. Women reporting pain during the menses were more likely to have taken a sick leave during the previous year than those with no pain (p<.001). Environmental factors related to pain during (but not before) the menstrual cycle were: feeling cold and experiencing discomfort from draft, humidity (p<.001) and variable temperature (p<.039). Physical requirements of handling weights, exerted effort of either arm, and a lack of workstation adaptation were significantly associated with pain during menses (p≤.05). Other conditions, such as working on an assembly line and being unable to freely leave the workstation, were associated with dysmenorrhea either before or during menses (p<.05). The authors comment on the use of biologic indicators, such as the presence of pain, as a method to increase sensitivity in monitoring the effects of occupational exposures. The authors propose several biologically plausible mechanisms for dysmenorrhea to occur under cold stress conditions. Future studies should address the relationship between the effects of cold, physical work load, and ergonomics, and menstrual symptoms, and should examine the impact of improvement in work conditions on absenteeism and rates of sick leave.

Nag, A., & Nag, P. N. (1992). Heat stress of women during manipulative work. *American Industrial Hygiene Association Journal, 53,* 751–756.

This article describes a work simulation study on six healthy female tobacco-industry workers engaged in manual tobacco-processing activities. The authors investigated heat susceptibility of women under conditions of light work and heat. The effects of the women's heat susceptibility on their work output were studied, with heat exposure standards specific for women considered. While engaged in their usual manipulative work tasks, the women were exposed to a total of 9 different environmental conditions, combining 3 different temperatures and 3 humidity levels. Equivalent heat load was measured by using the effective temperature (ET) scale. Study measures included work output and physiologic data: skin and core body temperature, heart rate, oxygen uptake, and sweat loss. Participants also reported thermal comfort levels. The female subjects lived in a very hot climate where summer temperatures usually ranged from 38° to 45°C. They experienced (a) a statistically significant rise in core body temperature and oxygen uptake, and (b) perceptions of extremely hot conditions, particularly when the effective temperature rose above 31.6°C. At temperature levels of 31.6°C or greater, as core temperature rose and cardiovascular workload increased, sweating decreased significantly. Lowered sweat loss decreased the women's ability to regulate body temperature and endure hot humid conditions. Work productivity under these controlled experimental conditions decreased precipitously, particularly with increased duration (2–3 hours) of work. This study makes a significant contribution to the understanding of women's response to heat stress.

Chemical Hazards

Solvents

Lindbohm, M.-L., Taskinen, H., Sallmen, M., & Hemminki, K. (1990). Spontaneous abortions among women exposed to organic solvents. *American Journal of Industrial Medicine, 17,* 449–463.

These authors evaluated spontaneous abortion risk associated with first-trimester exposure to various solvents. The overall risk of spontaneous abortion was elevated in relation to solvent exposure. The most notable increased risks were associated with high-level exposure to aliphatic hydrocarbons, in general, and to toluene, specifically in the shoe manufacturing industry. Workers involved in graphic arts, painting, or tetrachlorethylene processes in dry cleaning also experienced increased risk of spontaneous abortion. This study has several strengths: (a) the availability of ambient air monitoring and biological monitoring for some workers or workplaces; (b) a population-based (Finland) database for identifying spontaneous abortions; and (c) an adequate sample size to evaluate risk associated with specific solvents and occupations.

Serraino, D., Franceschi, S., La Vecchia, C., & Carbone, A. (1992). Occupation and soft-tissue sarcoma in northeastern Italy. *Cancer Causes and Control, 3*, 25–30.

The researchers conducted a case-control study of histologically confirmed soft-tissue sarcoma (STS) in men (*n* = 53) and women (*n* = 40), to examine risk factors for this rare cancer. They used controls (371 men and 350 women) drawn primarily from adults hospitalized for trauma and musculoskeletal disorders. The researchers noted that benzene or other solvent exposure was associated with an unstable twofold increased risk when duration of exposure exceeded 10 years. The most intriguing finding was that benzene/solvent exposure was associated with a higher risk of STS in women compared to men. Neither, occupations such as agricultural workers or various exposures (wood, dust, herbicides, and pesticides) were implicated in this study. A limitation of the study was that, because self-reported exposures were not validated, recall bias may have influenced the study findings. Follow-up studies are needed to determine whether benzene or other solvents may be etiological agents in the development of STS.

Walker, J. T., Bloom, T. F., Stern, F. B., Okun, A. H., Fingerhut, M. A., & Halperin, W. E. (1993). Mortality of workers employed in shoe manufacturing. *Scandinavian Journal of Work and Environmental Health, 19*, 89–95.

The National Institute of Occupational Safety and Health (NIOSH) conducted a historical cohort study of white men and women who worked in one of two U.S. shoe manufacturing sites between 1940 and 1979. At these sites, various solvents were used, including toluene, methyl ethyl ketone, acetone, and hexane. Follow-up occurred through December 31, 1982.

Information on smoking was not available, but effect of confounding on lung cancer mortality was estimated. Among women, mortality from cancer of the larynx (based on two cases) was elevated (standardized mortality ratio (SMR) = 334; 95% CI = 40, 1209). Cancer of the lung/trachea/bronchus also was elevated (SMR = 130, 95% CI = 89, 186). In contrast to the experience of men, women had a less-than-expected mortality rate for nonmalignant chronic lung diseases (SMR = 79), which suggests that smoking was not highly prevalent among women. The SMR for lung cancer, indirectly adjusted for smoking among women, was 124. In total, 15 cases of leukemia and aleukemia were observed. For women, based on 9 cases, the SMR for leukemia and aleukemia was 123 (95% CI = 56, 111). The authors concluded that "the mortality experience showed a slight statistically nonsignificant elevated SMR for leukemia only for the women. . . . Although our study had low statistical power and little detailed exposure data, it does not provide evidence for an association between toluene and leukemia" (p. 94). The authors' conclusion is somewhat misleading. A more accurate statement regarding the lack of association was that there was insufficient power to detect a small effect if one existed. Even if a significantly elevated leukemia mortality risk had been found, one cannot accurately separate out any one solvent, such as toluene, when multiple solvents were in common use. Overall, the study is a good example of a historical cohort study design, and the investigators are to be commended for presenting data separately for men and women.

Heavy Metals

Hayes, R. B., Dosemeci, M., Riscigno, M., & Blair, A. (1993). Cancer mortality among jewelry workers. *American Journal of Industrial Medicine, 24*, 743–751.

This proportionate mortality study identified jewelry workers in one of two ways: (a) death certificates for the years 1984–1989 in 24 states, where occupation was coded as jewelry maker for 919 men and 605 women; (b) a

New York jewelry makers' union's records for an additional 1,009 men who died between 1950 and 1980. Women had a statistically significant excess of cancer deaths (proportionate mortality ratio (PMR) = 1.24; 95% CI = 1.07, 1.42), as did union men (PMR = 1.17; 95% CI = 1.02, 1.33). The proportion of excess cancer deaths among women was attributed to colon cancer (proportionate cancer mortality ratio (PCMR) = 1.36; 95% CI = 0.92, 3.27), stomach cancer (PCMR = 2.50; 95% CI = 1.20, 4.61), and non-Hodgkin's lymphoma (PCMR = 1.34; 95% CI = 0.75, 2.21). These findings in women are congruent with excess esophageal and colon cancer in the entire sample and cancers of the blood and lymphatic systems in men, as well as with findings from other studies. Exposures to heavy metals and solvents may have accounted for these excesses. A PMR study such as this provides leads for analytical studies.

Pesticides

Brownson, R. C., Alavanja, M. C. R., & Chang, J. C. (1993). Occupational risk factors for lung cancer among nonsmoking women: A case-control study in Missouri (United States). *Cancer Causes and Control, 4,* 449–454.

White Missourian women who were diagnosed with lung cancer between 1986 and 1991 and who were either lifetime nonsmokers or ex-smokers (15 years or more) were eligible for the study. Of 650 eligible cases 30–84 years old, 294 nonsmokers and 135 ex-smokers completed in-person interviews. Population-based controls were identified through Missouri driver's license files for women age 64 or younger. For women age 65 or older, controls were drawn from Medicare files. Of 1,527 eligible controls, 1,021 completed in-person interviews. Risk estimates were adjusted for age and history of other lung diseases. A statistically significant increased risk of lung cancer was observed for all women employed in the dry cleaning industry who were nonsmokers or who had quit smoking, and for nonsmokers only. Significantly increased lung cancer risk was also detected for exposure to asbestos among all women, but not for lifetime nonsmokers. Pesticide exposure, however, was associated with a statistically elevated lung cancer risk for all women, as well as for nonsmoking women only. When the researchers examined elevated lung cancer risks in relation to duration of exposure, they found evidence of a dose-response for women employed in the dry cleaning industry and women exposed to asbestos and pesticides. This study is noteworthy for its examination of occupational lung cancer risks in women and its control for the effect of smoking. The findings implicate pesticides and, potentially, solvents (in dry cleaning) as pulmonary carcinogens in women workers.

Fleming, L. E., & Timmeny, W. (1993). Aplastic anemia and pesticides: An etiologic association? *Journal of Occupational Medicine, 35,* 1106–1116.

The authors provide an integrated research review of pesticide-associated aplastic anemia incidence and mortality rates, and case reports/case series published in the literature over a 30-year period. Crude incidence rates ranged between 1.5 and 20.5 per million; age-adjusted mortality rates ranged between 3.0 and 9 per million. In all, 280 cases were found in the published literature. Data on age, gender, and latency were reported in 90 cases. Based on these cases, the median age was 28; the gender ratio (male:female) was close to 2:1; and mean latency was 5 months. The majority (62%) of cases, including in children, were occupational. However, a substantial proportion were also associated with the use of the chlorinated hydrocarbon, lindane (brand name Qwell), for treating lice infestations. Various pesticide classes (e.g., chlorinated hydrocarbons, organophosphates, carbamates, herbicides, heavy metals (arsenic), fumigants, and mixtures) were implicated in the etiology of aplastic anemia. The authors suggest that the most highly exposed populations may be migrant workers and workers in developing countries. This integrated review is an important contribution to the understanding of the role of pesticides in the development of aplastic anemia. Lindane has been taken off the market in the United States, but clinicians should be aware that other pesticides used to treat lice may also involve risk. Because aplastic anemia is rare, case reports and case series may be the only media for evaluating the role of pesticides in the etiology of aplastic anemia.

Zahm, S. H., Weisenburger, D. D., Saal, R. C., Vaught, J. B., Babbitt, P. A., & Blair, A. (1993). The role of agricultural pesticide use in the development of non-Hodgkin's lymphoma in women. *Archives of Environmental Health, 48,* 353–358.

In eastern Nebraska over a 36-month period (1983–1986), the researchers identified 206 cases of non-Hodgkin's lymphoma (NHL) among white women 21 years of age or older. For each case, 3 population-based controls were matched on race, gender, and age. In all, 184 cases and 707 controls participated in telephone interviews. A small but unstable risk of NHL was associated with the use of chlorinated hydrocarbon insecticides on farms. Personally handling organophosphate insecticides was associated with a 4.5-fold increased risk of NHL. Although based on small numbers, elevated risks of NHL were associated with personally applying chlorinated hydrocarbon insecticides on dairy cows or other animals. Risk of NHL was also elevated, although not statistically significant, when: (a) carbamates had been applied to crops; (b) chlorinated hydrocarbons had been applied to nondairy animals or farm buildings and noncrop areas; (c) organophosphates had been applied to nondairy animals or farm buildings and noncrop areas; or (d) unspecified insecticides had been applied to nondairy animals. It was uncommon for women to use protective equipment or for them to change out of their work clothes right after working with pesticides. Despite the large-scale case-control study, relatively few women had direct (personally applied) or indirect (use of pesticides on the farm) exposure to these agents, which limited

examination of the effect of specific pesticides. These findings, however, suggest that organophosphates may be associated with increased risk of NHL in women. Future studies should take into account the use of pesticides in the home and garden; involvement in transportation, storage, and mixing of pesticides; laundering of pesticide-contaminated clothing; and levels of pesticide residue in foods and water sources.

Pharmaceuticals

Ito, S., & Koren, G. (1993). Exposure of pregnant women to ribavirin-contaminated air: Risk assessment and recommendations. *Pediatric Infectious Disease Journal, 12,* 2–5.

The authors performed a risk assessment of occupational exposure to the antiviral drug, ribavirin, based on published toxicological, pharmacological, and occupational exposure data. Ribavirin is a known animal teratogen. Using a conservative safety factor of 1000, the authors estimate the safe level of systemic absorption of ribavirin in pregnant workers to be 0.135 μg/kg/day. A safety factor of 1000 was used to estimate the risk of biological absorption and to make the following recommendations. When the drug is administered in aerosolized form to patients on ventilators, resulting in air concentration of 1.5 to 4.7 μg/m³, a pregnant woman could work in excess of 10 hours/day. When ribavirin is administered in a ventilated room via an oxygen hood with operable scavenging equipment, resulting in air concentration of 7 to 15 μg/m³, pregnant workers could be in the room more than 3 hours/day. In reported research, when ribavirin was administered via an oxygen hood with operable scavenging equipment but inoperable ventilation, the room air concentrations were 286 and 189 μg/m³. Under these circumstances, the authors estimate that a pregnant worker's permissible exposure time per day would be less than 15 minutes. The authors conclude that ". . . , as used clinically, ribavirin exposure is either above or not far below the permissible exposure limit" and that their recommendations ". . . provide a tentative guideline for inhalational exposures of pregnant women to ribavirin" (p. 3). The authors point out that further pharmacokinetic research is needed on bioavailability of ribavirin when administered to the same individuals by inhalation and intravenously. In addition, more industrial hygiene studies are warranted to better characterize the airborne concentration of ribavirin when administered using various safety and drug administration procedures and equipment. This initial risk assessment and the resulting recommendations provide some basis to guide policy-making in clinical agencies. However, further research, including follow-up studies of exposed health care workers and their offspring, are urgently needed to more definitively guide policy-making and practice.

Saurel-Cubizolles, M. J., Job-Spira, N., & Estryn-Behar, M. (1993). Ectopic pregnancy and occupational exposure to antineoplastic drugs. *Lancet, 341,* 1169–1171.

This report on risk of ectopic pregnancy is based on a study designed to evaluate a variety of health outcomes in women (excluding physicians) who worked in one of 18 hospital operating rooms in Paris. During 1987–1988, all hospital staff were interviewed, using a standard format, prior to their annual employee health examination. The interview included questions on first-trimester exposure to anesthetic gases, formaldehyde solution (formol), antineoplastic drugs, and radiation. Personnel records were used to determine whether a woman worked in the operating room at any time during a pregnancy. All operating room personnel (exposed group) were included in the study, in order to examine the potential health effects of anesthetic gases. Non-operating room personnel were matched to exposed women on hospital, gender, occupation, age, and length of employment. A total of 734 pregnancies met the study criteria. In the unmatched analyses, the researchers found no increased risk of ectopic pregnancy associated with working in the operating room when the risk estimate was adjusted for exposure to

antineoplastic drugs, pregnancy number (1–2, 3, 4, or more), history of spontaneous abortion, and cigarette smoking. However, in the maximum-likelihood adjusted analyses, these researchers detected a statistically significant increased risk of ectopic pregnancy associated with first-trimester exposure to antineoplastic drugs. In the conditional logistic regression analyses, which retain the matching factors while controlling for extraneous variables, the crude odds ratio for antineoplastic drug exposure was 10.0. The researchers suggest that reporting bias may have been a factor, but the lack of any previous studies associating antineoplastic drug exposure with risk of ectopic pregnancy and the broad-based focus of this study argue against reporting bias, as does the lack of association between working in the operating room and risk of ectopic pregnancy. Although smoking was controlled for in this analysis, data on history of pelvic inflammatory disease were not available. Notwithstanding its limitations, this study provides a very useful lead for future research in that some, but not all, studies have reported increased risk of spontaneous abortion and congenital malformations associated with occupational exposure to antineoplastic drugs during pregnancy.

Biological Hazards

Bubak, M. E., Reed, C. E., Fransway, A. F., Yunginger, J. W., Jones, R. T., Carlson, C. A., & Hunt, L. W. (1992). Allergic reactions to latex among health-care workers. *Mayo Clinic Proceedings, 67,* 1075–1079.

Gloves are frequently worn in health care settings to prevent exposure to bloodborne and other diseases. These gloves are predominantly made of latex products. Recently, frequent and intensive exposure to latex products has been linked to a greater incidence of latex allergy among health care, public safety, and emergency response workers. In the late 1970s, latex allergies were first noted in children and adults undergoing surgical and medical procedures involving equipment that contained latex. Allergic reactions to latex have ranged from localized skin responses and asthma to life-threatening anaphylaxis. Changes in the manufacturing process of latex have been cited as a factor in the increased incidence of latex reactions. To meet the rapidly multiplied demand for latex gloves, manufacturers shortened the storage time for the unprocessed latex and stopped steam sterilization, thereby increasing the amount of latex proteins, the source of allergens. Rubber industry workers, patients with mengiomyelocele, and health care/public safety/emergency response workers have been identified as high-risk groups for IgE-mediated latex allergy. The authors describe the signs and symptoms of latex allergy in 45 female and 4 male workers employed in a large health care setting. The reported symptoms included contact dermatitis, itchy-watery eyes, sneezing, nasal congestion, dyspnea, chest tightness, and hives. A history of atopy was shared by 65% of the workers; symptoms included allergic rhinitis, asthma, and eczema. Three-quarters of the workers wore gloves frequently throughout the day. Skin-prick testing revealed that most of the workers exhibited an allergic response to latex. None of the workers reacted to cornstarch, which is used to powder the inside of latex gloves and was once considered the only source of worker irritations. Interestingly, washing the gloves diminished the allergic response. (However, other research indicates that washing latex gloves increases permeability and thereby provides less protection.) Additional results from the skin-prick testing revealed that over half of the workers had increased latex-specific IgE antibodies. Health care workers with a positive skin test to latex, a history of atopy, and symptoms of latex sensitivity need to be carefully counseled regarding work and personal exposures to latex products. Precautionary avoidance of latex products may be indicated. Simply switching to powder-free gloves, changing the brand of gloves, or using "hypoallergenic" latex gloves is not sufficient; powder is not the culprit, and all latex gloves contain some level of the offending allergens. Nonlatex gloves are an alternative; however, fit is problematic and there is some concern regarding the extent of protection.

Some women with latex allergies may not be able to safely work in an environment where latex is used. Latex allergies are an emerging concern, and continued research is needed to determine their prevalence and to develop alternatives to latex products. A national policy is needed to impose strict manufacturing standards on latex production.

Marcus, R., Culver, D. H., Bell, D. M., Srivastava, P. U., Mendelson, M. H., Zalenski, R. J., Farber, B., Fligner, D., Hassett, J., Quinn, T. C., Schable, C. A., Sloan, E. P., Tsui, P., & Kelen, G. D. (1993). Risk of human immunodeficiency virus infection among emergency department workers. *American Journal of Medicine, 94,* 363–370.

The Occupational Safety and Health Administration (OSHA) estimates that 4.9 million health care workers, many of whom are women, are at risk for exposure to bloodborne diseases, such as human immunodeficiency virus (HIV) and hepatitis B virus. In an effort to reduce or eliminate this health risk, OSHA enacted a standard requiring, among other precautions, that gloves be worn whenever there is a potential for blood contact with a patient. Sadly, many health care agencies protested OSHA's standard, stating that the cost of glove use far outweighed the benefit to workers' health in areas known to have low prevalence of HIV. These agencies contended that wearing gloves only with high-risk patients was adequate protection for the workers. As these authors systematically point out, a selective use of gloves places health care workers at great risk. In this study, health care workers were observed for their frequency of glove use and contact with patients' blood. In addition, the authors determined the percentage of HIV-infected patients whose infection status was unknown to the health care workers. The authors used three pairs of inner city and suburban emergency departments across the United States, in areas with high prevalence of HIV. HIV infections were unknown to health care workers from 40% to 91% of the time; the number of unknown HIV infections was generally highest in the suburban areas. Gloves were worn more often in the emergency departments with the highest HIV seroprevalence rate; glove use ranged from 62% to 98% of the time. Those not wearing gloves were almost 9 times more likely to come in contact with a patient's blood. The authors estimate that health care workers' current level of glove use lowers their risk of contact with HIV-infected blood by 64%. If gloves were worn at all times, this risk would be lowered by an additional 15%. Because all patients with bloodborne diseases cannot be identified prior to contact, OSHA's standard must be followed and enforced, even in areas of low HIV seroprevalence rate.

Psychological Hazards

Kandolin, I. (1993). Burnout of female and male nurses in shift work. *Ergonomics, 36,* 141–147.

Stechmiller, J. K., & Yarandi, H. N. (1993). Predictors of burnout in critical care nurses. *Heart and Lung, 13,* 534–541.

Wright, T. F., Blache, C. F., Ralph, J., & Luterman, A. (1993). Hardiness, stress, and burnout among intensive care nurses. *Journal of Burn Care and Rehabilitation, 14,* 376–381.

This series of studies examines the determinants of burnout in nurses. Burnout, a "severe state of psychological fatigue" (Kandolin, p. 141), is a consequence of prolonged stress. In the Kandolin study, three components of burnout—(1) emotional fatigue, (2) depersonalizing others, and (3) loss of work enjoyment—were investigated in male and female nurses who worked rotating shifts. Kandolin found gender differences in the effects of shift work on burnout. For women, shift rotation and work milieu were associated with burnout. For men, only work milieu was a factor in burnout. Specifically, women who worked all three shifts enjoyed their work less and reported more symptoms related to stress.

Stechmiller et al. investigated similar determinants of burnout in 300 female critical care nurses who worked in 9 hospitals. Only

emotional exhaustion was explained by this model ($R^2 = 0.34$); job satisfaction, commitment to career, and dealing with others at work defined emotional exhaustion. Other factors, which included situational variables, workload issues, and health symptoms, contributed to burnout in this group of nurses.

Wright et al. investigated the effect of hardiness on stress and burnout in a small sample of critical care nurses ($n = 31$). Hardiness was defined in this study as the nurses' level of commitment, their value of challenge, and their degree of personal control. Measurement issues with the hardiness tool, as well as the small sample size, limit the interpretation of this study's findings. In general, nurses who were hardiest experienced less burnout and nurses who reported less stress were less likely to experience burnout. Personal hardiness contributes to the understanding of stress and burnout and warrants further investigation. Overall, this series of studies indicates that stress and burnout have a strong perceptual component, but organizational and structural factors are important contributors. To develop intervention programs that may alleviate worker stress and burnout, future research should use: variables that have been identified as contributing to stress and burnout, consistent definitions, and stronger study designs.

Kushnir, T., & Kasan, R. (1993). Major sources of stress among women managers, clerical workers, and working single mothers: Demands vs. resources. *Public Health Reviews, 20,* 215–229.

In this review of the literature on gender and occupational role stressors (77 references in all), the authors point out that theoretical models developed to explain stress in men should not automatically be applied to women. The authors' model proposes that stress occurs when high occupational and home demands are coupled with inadequate personal, social, or organizational resources. For women, the dual demand of work and home may intensify occupational stress. In addition, women's health is affected by lack of status and power, and other workplace stressors. Accordingly, the authors discuss three high-risk groups of women workers for whom work or home demands are high and resources are often inadequate: single mothers, managers, and clerical workers. The authors' organizational framework for review of the literature on stress in working women may be useful for future research.

Snapp, M. B. (1992). Occupational stress, social support, and depression among black and white professional-managerial women. *Women & Health, 18,* 41–79.

Snapp used the Michigan Model of job stress to study the effects of race, class background, supervisory status, and parental/marital status on career support, job stress, and depression in an existing sample of 200 professional and managerial women. The author proposes that social–career support has a direct effect on job stress and mental health. In intensive interviews, participants were asked questions related to: (a) general depression; (b) friend, family, and coworker support (social support); and (c) work load, unfair or impersonal treatment, and any interpersonal conflicts (occupational stress). Social support was not predictive of depression independent of work stress. Black women received more support from their families; white women reported more support from coworkers. Interpersonal conflict (trouble with a boss or subordinates) significantly predicted depression in all of the women. In other words, support from family, friends, and coworkers did not buffer the impact of stress on mental health—an important finding, because interpersonal conflict has not usually been included in studies of occupational stress. Women value interpersonal relationships more than men do, so the lack of a measure of interpersonal conflict reflects a gender bias in previous research. This article provides a rich foundation for future studies. Stress reduction programs should address both gender and cultural diversity issues that may impact on perceived stress. The reader must be cautious, however, about generalizing these results. Because of the sample size, the study lacked sufficient power to detect all possible associations among the variables. Different study designs are needed to determine the causal role these variables play in women's occupational stress.

Other Hazards

Dusts

Greer, J. R., Abbey, D. E., & Burchette, R. J. (1993). Asthma-related occupational and ambient air pollutants in nonsmokers. *Journal of Occupational Medicine, 35,* 909–915.

Recently, exposure to second-hand smoke at the workplace has been identified as a hazard. This community-based research, a continuation of a 1977 study, examines second-hand smoke exposure in nonsmoking Californians. In 1987, the participants (females = 2,272; males = 1,305) were asked about their exposure to ozone, second-hand smoke at work or at home, and occupational exposure to 21 substances (e.g., dusts, vapors) known to produce symptoms related to asthma. A total of 78 respondents (females = 51) did not have asthma in 1977 and were diagnosed with definite asthma in 1987. No significant association was found between occupational dust or vapor exposure and the diagnosis of adult onset asthma for either gender. However, the authors advise that the study lacked sufficient power to detect an association with dusts and vapors because of the limited number of exposures. Ozone was a predictor of asthma in men but not in women. The men in the sample spent significantly more time outdoors during high-ozone periods than did the women. One of the special features of this study was the inclusion of tobacco smoke exposure while at work. The authors report that environmental tobacco smoke was the best predictor of whether this sample would develop asthma. However, the increase in risk associated with this workplace exposure was relatively small (relative risk = 1.45, 95% CI = 1.21, 1.80). As these researchers point out, exposure to environmental tobacco smoke is readily preventable, and this study supports the need for smoke-free workplaces.

Zuskin, E., Kanceljak, B., Schachter, E. N., Witek, T. J., Maayani, S., Goswami, S., Marom, Z., & Rienzi, N. (1992). Immunological findings in hemp workers. *Environmental Research, 59,* 350–361.

Hemp dust produces an asthma-like disease referred to as byssinosis, which can become debilitating. How dusts cause acute and chronic respiratory diseases like byssinosis is still unknown. Because byssinosis is similar to asthma, several studies have explored whether this disease may be induced by an allergic response to the bacteria and fungi found in hemp. If there is a strong association between allergic response to hemp dust and chronic respiratory disease, then it may be possible to detect the byssinosis early, prior to changes in lung functions. Zuskin and colleagues compared 42 women who, as employees in a Croatian hemp mill, had been exposed to hemp dust for an average of 16 years, with 49 women employed in a bottling factory. The two groups of women were similar in age and smoking history. All of the women were given skin-prick tests to determine allergic response to hemp dust, bacteria, and mold. Chronic respiratory symptoms were chronicled, as were acute symptoms such as cough, chest tightness, and headache. The hemp workers (35.7%) had more positive allergic responses to hemp dust than did the comparison group (5.0%) and reported a significantly greater prevalence of chronic respiratory symptoms in 6 out of 9 situations. Hemp workers who produced a positive allergic response generally reported a greater number of chronic respiratory symptoms (5 out of 9 symptoms). However, there was no association between allergic response and acute respiratory symptoms. Although this study was conducted on a site that experienced higher than permissible levels of hemp dust, the findings should be of interest to women employed in

the textile industry. The association of byssinosis with an allergic response may open the way for earlier detection of the disease.

Sick Building Syndrome

Chang, C. C., Ruhl, R. A., Halpern, G. M., & Gershwin, M. E. (1993). The sick building syndrome. I. Definition and epidemiological considerations. *Journal of Asthma, 30,* 285–295.

This review article (51 references in all) presents the state of the science related to sick building syndrome and building-related illness. Definitions are provided for this set of syndromes/illnesses which have been frequently reported but have proven difficult to objectively document. The authors point out that, although definitions exist in the literature, they are vague and are inconsistently used by researchers. Imprecise definitions coupled with a lack of confirmatory objective data have been obstacles to summarizing what is known about sick building syndrome. Of note in the studies reviewed by the authors, when gender was analyzed along with levels of exposure to contaminants, there was no difference in reported symptoms by gender. This is important information on women's occupational health, because many men and women perform different functions within an office and may be exposed to different contaminants or chemicals. In previous research, when females generally reported more symptoms than did men, a frequent conclusion was that simply being female was a contributing factor to the sick building syndrome. Future research, which should analyze exposure data by gender, should be directed toward: (a) identifying work-related versus non-work-related symptoms, (b) developing objective methods to measure symptoms, and (c) determining what agents are the cause of sick building syndrome.

McDonald, J. C., Armstrong, B., Benard, J., Cherry, N. M., & Farant, J. P. (1993). Sick building syndrome in a Canadian office complex. *Archives of Environmental Health, 48,* 298–304.

This study investigated an office building with a 6-year history of complaints related to sick building syndrome. The authors explored how health and environmental complaints were linked with work location and personal characteristics such as age, gender, and pregnancy outcome. To ensure a large enough sample to detect adverse pregnancy outcomes, current female employees aged 25 to 34 were identified as the "special female" sample and were oversampled ($n = 556$). The remaining sample—976 females and 324 males—consisted of a random selection of current and former employees. Half of the women worked in clerical positions and the remainder worked in professional/managerial positions. Only 11% of the men worked in clerical positions. The participants were surveyed regarding environmental working conditions, health complaints (including pregnancy outcome), and work space configuration (e.g., open, cubicle). Ventilation rates and supply of outdoor air were assessed for each floor. Additional environmental measures included temperature, relative humidity, and levels of air contaminants for each floor and each work area. When compared to a community-wide sample, frequency of poor pregnancy outcomes was no different. As assumed, symptoms related to sick building syndrome—nasal and throat irritation, headaches, drowsiness, and eye irritation—were frequently reported, as were stress-related symptoms such as exhaustion and sleepiness. Within the special female sample, the authors reported an association between the type of work location and health complaints. Women who worked in cubicles reported more frequent symptoms than those who worked in closed or open office spaces. However, only digestive, stress, and general complaints were significantly different ($p = 0.001$ to 0.03) between the work locations. Employees who had no health complaints also differed by work location ($p = .04$): women who worked in open and closed office spaces had fewer health complaints than did those working in cubicles. Outdoor air supply varied significantly when there was a combination of open and closed office spaces. Adequate ventilation occurred only when the work area was mainly open or mainly closed. Although limited because of questions concerning recall bias, this study supports the view that air supply must be tested in each work location because different office designs within a building may hamper adequate air circulation.

Work Patterns

Nakatani, C., Nozomi, S., Matsui, M., Matsunami, M., & Kumashiro, M. (1993). Menstrual cycle effects on a VDT-based simulation task: Cognitive indices and subjective ratings. *Ergonomics, 36*, 331–339.

In the past, concerns have been raised about women's capacity for work-task performance during the menstrual cycle, and research results have been inconsistent about the menstrual cycle's effects on women's functioning. This research examines the menstrual cycle (premenstrual, menstrual, and postmenstrual) for its effects on video display terminal (VDT) task performance. The sample consisted of 10 paid female volunteers who met the following criteria: had no amenorrhea in the previous 3 months, took no hormonal medications, were not pregnant, and did not smoke. Methods included the use of the Quidel Ovulation Luteinizing Hormone (LH) test to determine LH surge as an indicator of ovulation. Subjects entered their menstrual cycle data in a diary. Following a two-day practice session, task assessment was determined through a pattern-matching task performed on a VDT. The level of decision-making confidence was recorded by the subjects. Reaction time, target aiming accuracy, menstrual distress (via a menstrual distress questionnaire or MDQ), and fatigue (via an Inventory for Subjective Symptoms of Fatigue) were measured, and electroencephalogram, electrocardiogram, and visual accommodation technology was employed. Menstrual cycles averaged 32.9 days. Using repeated "multiple analysis of variance (MANOVA)" (p. 335), no significant changes among the phases were reported for correct response reaction time or for accuracy of the target-aiming task. The authors concluded that menstrual cycle phases did not affect VDT task performance in this small sample group. Limitations of the study include the sample size and only a 70% accuracy following the initial training sessions. The authors' discussion of their research reflects the complexities involved in assessing health effects and psychomotor skill performance during the menstrual cycle. Future research in this area is warranted, but larger sample sizes are needed to overcome the large intra- and interindividual variation.

Oginska, H., Pokorski, J., & Oginski, A. (1993). Gender, aging, and shift work intolerance. *Ergonomics, 36,* 161–168.

Tepas, D. I., Duchon, J. C., & Gersten, A. H. (1993). Shift work and the older worker. *Experimental Aging Research, 19,* 295–320.

Work occurs during daylight hours for most employees. However, in industrialized countries, work occurs regularly during nondaylight hours for approximately 15% to 30% of employees. Many women work nondaylight hours because of child care arrangements, lack of job seniority, or the need for the additional income offered in shift differentials. These two articles address an important question related to shift work and aging: Since aging affects men and women differently, is there an interaction between age/gender/work shift schedules and sleep/nap patterns? Tepas and colleagues surveyed 2,690 workers (28% female) aged 18 to 59 who were either employed in industrial plants or were members of labor unions. Overall, women averaged significantly less sleep than did their male counterparts (419.3 and 431.6 minutes, respectively), whether working in day, evening, or night shifts. However, gender differences disappeared after age 49. Night shift workers slept less than workers on other shifts, and both women and men lost sleep with advancing age. Women on the night shift slept as much as one hour less than their male counterparts and did not make up the sleep difference with naps. There was no significant gender difference in nap lengths. The authors posit that social demands, circadian effects, and environmental conditions may account for the night shift workers' fewer hours of sleep. For women, changes in sleep pattern may be due to child-rearing needs and family burdens.

The research conducted by Oginska and colleagues supports and extends the Tepas et al. study. Using equal numbers of men and women (n = 166), crane operators in a Polish steel plant were studied for the effects of shift intolerance. As in the Tepas et al. study, Oginska et al. found that the women working the evening or night shifts slept less than the men on those shifts did. There was also a difference in the quality of the workers' sleep. Women reported not only more difficulty in falling asleep but also more frequently awakening and overall poor quality of sleep. The authors used appropriate caution in interpreting their findings. There was no assumption that women are less tolerant of shift work; however, the extra burden of home responsibilities may prevent women, more than men, from resting while at home. The authors conclude that women's second job (home and family), not physiological variations, account for the differences between men and women in quantity and quality of sleep.

Special Groups

Decoufle, P., Murphy, C. C., Drews, C. D., & Yeargin-Allsopp, M. (1993). Mental retardation in ten-year-old children in relation to their mothers' employment during pregnancy. *American Journal of Industrial Medicine, 24,* 567–586.

Eskenazi, B., Guendelman, S., & Elkin, E. P. (1993). A preliminary study of reproductive outcomes of female *maquiladora* workers in Tijuana, Mexico. *American Journal of Industrial Medicine, 24,* 667–676.

Guendelman, S., & Silberg, M. J. (1993). The health consequences of *maquilador* work: Women on the U.S.–Mexican border. *American Journal of Public Health, 83,* 37–44.

These articles are of interest because of their mutual focus on women in the garment industry. There has been controversy regarding the health effects of work exposures for women in this industry, particularly effects related to working conditions and work situations for which few regulatory mechanisms exist. Recently, the adequacy of working conditions has been questioned in the rapidly expanding manufacturing sector along the U.S.–Mexican border, in Mexican territory. In these *maquiladoras*, or assembly plants, over 60% of which are staffed by women, work tasks are highly repetitive with few microbreaks. Other work-related hazards in *maquiladoras* include noise, poor ventilation, and possible toxic exposures. In the survey conducted by Guendelman and Silberg, of the 480 women in the sample, 121 were garment workers. The study compared the garment workers to service workers, as well as to women who have never worked outside the home. Health outcome measures used by Guendelman and Silberg were functional impediments, depression, nervousness, and a sense of control. This study did not demonstrate an occupational health burden for garment workers. In fact, some of the data suggested that a "healthy worker effect" may be operative for *maquiladoras*, possibly due to access to health care. However, this possibility would need cautious interpretation.

Eskenazi et al.'s analysis of reproductive outcomes for this same survey sample found no significant variance in rate of fetal loss by occupational groups. However, garment workers were more likely to give birth to infants whose weight averaged 653 grams less than infants of service workers.

Decoufle et al., in a case control study, examined a little-researched area, the long-term effect of maternal occupation on cognitive abilities in children. Data for cases were based on the Metropolitan Atlanta Developmental Disability Study. Control children were selected from the population of 10-year-olds who were born to residents of Atlanta and who were attending public school in the study area. Interviews conducted with the children's natural mothers included an extensive two-part occupational history. Birth records were also reviewed, and the complete selection process resulted in 352 case children and 408 control children. The covariates of race, education of the mother, and birth order of the child were incorporated into the multiple regression models. Results of the association between mental retardation in 10-year-old children of textile or apparel manufacturing workers and children of all other women demonstrated a high prevalence in the blue-collar workers. However, because exposures to hazardous materials or work conditions for the sample group were not known, the potential relationship between maternal exposure to hazards in the textile industry and long-term cognitive abilities of the fetus remains unclear. Findings from this case control study need to be confirmed or refuted using either case control or prospective study designs.

Headapohl, D. M. (Ed.). (1993). Women workers. *Occupational Medicine: State of the Art Reviews*, 8(4).

This journal issue, which is devoted to women's occupational health and women in the workplace, represents a significant resource for information. Some specific articles, cited in the introduction to this chapter, focus on gender and work, reproductive health risks for women workers, and economic issues that affect working women. Other contributions deal with depression, women and agriculture, and workplace ergonomics. The collection provides an extensive review of research and some reports of original research. Although the issue does not attempt to comprehensively address some specific types of exposure effects for women, such as those from heat and cold, the articles convey a broad and thoughtful perspective on health and social issues affecting working women.

Lyons, T. J. (1992). Women in the fast jet cockpit: Aeromedical considerations. *Aviation, Space, and Environmental Medicine, 63,* 809–818.

This review article is remarkable for its extensive consideration of the physical, physiologic, and medical aspects of gender in the aviation industry. Noting the long history of women as pilots, in both military and civilian aviation, the author reviews literature on the following topics: ergonomics factors; responses to acceleration, hypoxia, temperature, and radiation; gender issues of possible inflight medical incapacitation; and potential adverse effects of flight on pregnancy. Design issues, such as parachutes and ejection seats for female aviators, are discussed. The author sees a possible need for alterations of pilot helmets for women while under +G acceleration. Concerns regarding the adequacy of muscle strength and tolerance to acceleration force are reviewed. Reports cited reflect inconsistent findings about gender differences in body fat distribution and the association of body fat to tolerance of thermal stress. The author states that "concern that the aviation environment may differentially cause disease in women has focused on three areas: (1) cancer caused by radiation exposure; (2) menstrual irregularities; and (3) psychiatric illness" (p. 814). Each of these specific areas is discussed, as is the controversy about the potential effects of pregnancy on the female pilots' ability to perform, and the effects of aviation on the fetus. Based on review of the available data, the author suggests that fitness for aviation might be based on body size, strength, and general physical fitness rather than any consideration related to gender. Throughout this discussion, the author focuses on the need for further attention to gender considerations in flight research, and for adaptation of aviation equipment to accommodate a broader spectrum of physical requirements, without regard to gender. After acknowledging that gender differences that affect the capacity for work performance may have potential policy implications in workplace settings, the author addresses physiologic gender difference by suggesting a redesign of aviation equipment and the work setting of pilots.

Part V

Reproductive Health

Chapter 7

Childbearing

Marie Hastings-Tolsma
Patricia A. Geary

There continues to be an explosion of knowledge related to childbearing. The voluminous literature generated from 1992 to 1994 highlights this fact. This chapter examines some of the more pivotal literature influencing the health and care of childbearing women.

Over twenty years ago, Ehrenreich and English (1973) remarked that the medical system was strategic for women, serving as both the means for safe childbearing and a source for oppression. That is no less true today. Examination of the literature published over the past two years demonstrates the wondrous technological and scientific advances that ensure a safe childbearing experience. Improved fetal and maternal outcomes are evidence of the success that is possible.

It is also obvious that the childbearing period creates an enormous vulnerability and pregnancy holds potential danger and risk. Some of the most challenging dilemmas facing our health care system concern this vulnerability (Lessick, Woodring, Naber, & Halstead, 1992). There is the desire for support and care that show sensitivity to birth as a woman's unique experience. Recognition of childbearing as a natural, normative process is important if a woman is to shape the birth experience she desires. Childbearing women, as well as professionals delivering health care services, share a common goal: healthy outcomes for mothers and babies. Those caring for pregnant women are reminded of the primacy of the experience, their privileged position within that experience, and their responsibility to protect pregnant women in their birthing journey.

Within the current literature, certain lacunae still exist. Research that examines various aspects of the childbearing experience within diverse ethnic and cultural groups is limited. Childbearing experiences for minority women produce a special vulnerability by virtue of the status superimposed on gender. In addition, the primary research emphasis noted across studies involves methods that are largely reductionistic in nature. We are undoubtedly losing rich descriptions of the experiences of childbearing women when we limit the way we ask questions. Finally, theories useful in predicting and describing childbearing experiences have been generally lacking. Failure to detail how our research findings relate to theory is short-sighted and limits the value of findings (Meleis, 1991). Theory that guides research and is refined by new data will yield meaningful knowledge about the childbearing process.

The available literature was organized to highlight work deemed particularly valuable in shaping the delivery of care to childbearing women, affording them greater participation in making decisions regarding potential outcomes. Articles were selected that might positively or negatively affect the childbearing experience. Both types of articles have the potential to substantially shape the nature of the care delivered to pregnant women. Finally, the categories used in the 1989–1992 review—issues in childbearing; women with special needs; pregnancy, health, and illness; teen pregnancy; intrapartum; after birth; cesarean section; and breastfeeding—were again chosen to organize the present review. It is hoped that those groupings will be useful for comparative purposes. In some areas, relatively few articles have been identified. Those given here reflect the nature and extent of findings available during the period of review.

Implications

Control over the childbearing process continues to be a central issue, and fundamental change in maternity care continues to be elusive. Issues of power and finances remain key factors in the type of care rendered to childbearing women.

Reviews of issues in childbearing focus on the increased application of high technology. Who delivers that technology, and the associated care, and where that care is given, are the central aspects to be decided. National attention to the containment of health care costs may well be the major determinant in future decisions. This possibility is most clearly noted by Ewigman et al., who demonstrated that routine ultrasonography in low-risk pregnancies is unnecessary. Similarly, the work by Hueston and Rudy adds support to the growing body of literature documenting the role of the midwife in providing quality, cost-effective care. These reports should give impetus to change in current care approaches. The needs of the childbearing woman must be met in a way that does not reduce the experience of child-birth while moving toward quality health care delivery.

Women with special needs are increasingly opting to experience pregnancy. Improved technology and specialized treatment strategies have contributed to their ability to bear children. Care will require increased sensitivity and knowledge on the part of providers. The inherent high-risk status of these women demands communication of current knowledge regarding the hazards for fetus and self when pregnancy is undertaken. Women need accurate, up-to-date information in making a decision that has such long-term consequences. We must remain vigilant in providing support for women who need additional assistance to realize childbearing.

The section on pregnancy, health, and illness addresses literature affecting both high- and low-risk women. A recurring theme is the influence of technology in health and illness. Technology should not overshadow the experience for women. Literature in this area also reflects the impact of communicable diseases on women during the vulnerable childbearing period. Larger societal concerns regarding escalating rates of HIV infections, among other health threats, take on additional meaning when the fetus is involved. Expanded research is needed so that effective programs and interventions can be initiated.

Teen pregnancy continues to be an enormous social problem: the rate has risen since 1987. This trend, experts say, parallels a rise in suicides and homicides among young people (Klerman, 1993). These facts are reflected in the literature that focuses on implementing services individualized to specific populations. Many remedial programs have failed to demonstrate significant impact. Review in this area reflects the consensus that adolescent pregnancy is rooted deeply in American society, will be difficult to change, and will require multiple intervention strategies.

The literature surrounding the intrapartum demonstrates women's desire to experience birth in an undisturbed, natural fashion. Fear and anxiety surrounding the safety of the unborn child frequently overshadow that central desire, as clearly noted by McKay and Smith and by Gupton and Heaman. The parturient needs to experience control while having the opportunity to access technology and medical intervention if necessary. Meeting the needs of women during birth, in a way that creates a safe personal experience, may well require that the birth process occur in different settings. Cost issues, consumer dissatisfaction, and research generated by providers whose philosophy views women as central to maternity care (such as nurse midwives), may well serve as the impetus for significant change.

Experiences of women after birth are often reflective of a health care system that is fundamentally inconsistent and fragmented. Effort is being directed at smoothing transitions and at fostering relationships and competencies in role functioning during a time of enormous change. There is a need for renewed emphasis on assisting parents to develop competence in caregiving, and on encouraging them to make the decisions that will measurably alter later outcomes. Drosten-Brooks's article on kangaroo care is a poignant example of an intervention that is amassing growing empirical support. The impact of implementing such change, however, may well be more difficult for health care providers than for parents, who are eager to assume participation in the perinatal experience. For professionals, such change requires a fundamental change in philosophy.

Cesarean section rates remain alarmingly high. In one estimate, approximately half of all Cesarean sections performed in the United States are medically unnecessary (Shearer, 1993). Much attention has been given to strategies that will eliminate medically unnecessary operative deliveries. Unfortunately, despite irrefutable empirical evidence, the most powerful key to creating the change will likely be medical cost containment requirements.

The concluding section examines the literature related to breastfeeding. A clear body of knowledge exists regarding the superior benefits of breastfeeding. Reducing barriers to the initiation and duration of breastfeeding continues to dominate the work in this area. In the face of overwhelming evidence, innovative strategies need to be undertaken to promote and sustain breastfeeding efforts. Breastfeeding rates are declining dramatically among all U.S. population groups; the steepest decline is among the disadvantaged (Raisler, 1993). National and institutional policies that clearly support breastfeeding are needed and may go a long way to support this effort.

The implications, for education, practice, and research, of the existing literature on childbearing are clear and pressing. Changes must be considered within the context of calls for medical cost containment and a need for health care delivery system reform (O'Connor, 1994). Reprioritization of needs and services is required. The decisions will not be easy or comfortable, despite the nobility of the cause (Grad, 1993). The literature, however, should serve as a powerful force for achieving healthy, safe childbearing experiences shaped by the needs of women. We have gained enormous knowledge about what women desire in their birthing journey and what is necessary to achieve positive outcomes. But, as Goethe once remarked, "Knowing is not enough; we must apply. Willing is not enough; we must do."

REFERENCES

Ehrenreich, B., & English, D. (1973). *Complaints and disorders.* Old Westbury, NY: Feminist Press.

Grad, R. K. (1993). Why do I have to work so hard? *American Journal of Maternal Child Nursing, 18,* 9.

Klerman, L. V. (1993). Adolescent pregnancy and parenting: Controversies of the past and lessons for the future.

Lessick, M., Woodring, B. C., Naber, S., & Halstead, L. (1992). Vulnerability: A conceptual model applied to perinatal and neonatal nursing. *Journal of Perinatal and Neonatal Nursing, 6,* 1–14.

Meleis, A. I. (1991). *Theoretical nursing: Development and Progress* (2nd ed.). Philadelphia: Lippincott.

O'Connor, K. S. (1994). In an environment of health care reform. *American Journal of Maternal Child Nursing, 19,* 65–68.

Raisler, J. (1993). Promoting breastfeeding among vulnerable mothers. *Journal of Nurse-Midwifery, 38,* 1–4.

Shearer, E. L. (1993). Cesarean section: Medical benefits and costs. *Social Science Medicine, 37,* 1223–1231.

Issues in Childbearing

Ewigman, B. C., Crane, J. P., Frigoletto, F. D., et al. (1993). Effect of prenatal ultrasound screening on perinatal outcome. *New England Journal of Medicine, 329,* 821–827.

A randomized, multicenter study of more than 15,000 pregnant women at low risk for adverse pregnancy outcomes was designed to test the hypothesis that routine ultrasound screening on two occasions would reduce perinatal morbidity and mortality. The researchers also examined maternal management and outcomes. Women were assigned to one of two groups: ultrasound screening (N = 7,812) or the control group (N = 7,718). The mean numbers of sonograms obtained per patient were 2.2 and 0.6 in the ultrasound and control groups respectively. The findings demonstrated that overall rates of perinatal outcomes were virtually identical between groups, and that routine ultrasonography did not significantly increase diagnostic accuracy for fetal anomalies. Because routine ultrasonography in low-risk pregnancies does not improve perinatal outcomes and is not cost-effective, the revision of current practice patterns would result in significant savings.

Hueston, W. J., & Factors Affecting Cesarean Section Study Group. (1994). Obstetric referral in family practice. *The Journal of Family Practice, 38*(4), 368–372.

This is a retrospective review of deliveries from five medical centers over a 2-year period. A total of 2,568 women began their prenatal care with family physicians. Of this group, 167 were referred to an obstetric group, prior to the initiation of labor, for risk factors (e.g., uterine scar) and obstetrical problems (e.g., malpresentation). This referral group was more likely to lack private insurance but otherwise was similar in age, race, and parity. At the start of labor, 2,648 women were initially managed by family physicians. Cross-over arrangements between providers and the admission of patients without prenatal care resulted in the number of patients cared for in labor exceeding the number whose prenatal care had begun with family physicians. Of this later group, 249 were referred to obstetricians during labor. The late referral group had a higher parity and a higher rate of previous cesarean section and preeclampsia, and were less likely to be cigarette smokers than those not transferred. These results demonstrated that family physician referrals to obstetricians were relatively low and were generally made when specialist skills in performing cesarean sections were needed. Of the high-risk conditions identified, only preeclampsia was associated with an increase in the use of referral either before or during labor. Based on the findings, the authors suggest that referral bias is not a major source of differences in the populations cared for by family physicians and obstetricians. This conclusion is important in evaluating outcomes and making decisions regarding the choice of medical care provider.

Hueston, W. J., & Rudy, M. (1993). A comparison of labor and delivery management between nurse midwives and family physicians. *The Journal of Family Practice, 37*(5), 449–453.

The availability and cost effectiveness of health care providers are a special concern in rural areas. Practice associations between family physicians and nurse midwives offer a means to increase the availability of maternity care. This study examined the prenatal, labor, and delivery care of patients in a rural area who were cared for by a co-practice of nurse midwives and family physicians. Data were collected through a retrospective chart review of 913 randomly selected charts. The study was part of a larger multisite study conducted from 1990 through 1991. Few differences in the management of labor or delivery were noted between nurse midwives and family physicians. However, it was consistently found that family physicians were more likely than midwives to perform an episiotomy during delivery. In addition, nurse midwives were more likely to achieve a vaginal delivery in managing primiparous women in labor. These differing clinical management patterns between specialties and providers have been noted in earlier research and contribute to the varied cost of care and use of available technology. Findings from this study further validate the cost effectiveness of nurse midwives and affirm the importance of nurse midwives in providing maternity care.

McGregor, L. A. (1994). Short, shorter, shortest: Improving the hospital stay for mothers and newborns. *American Journal of Maternal Child Nursing, 19,* 91–96.

Health care delivery efforts to contain medical costs have changed the length of hospital stay. The author of this article describes one hospital's maternity service changes as dictated by insurance companies for the care of mothers and their infants in the postpartum period. Staff at the facility used the concept of "critical pathways" to develop patient outcomes and identify tasks to accomplish prior to discharge. Such changes require a reexamination of priorities and subsequent patient education. The author stresses the importance of education for women during the prenatal period. Dissatisfaction with care was expressed by consumers unaware of changes in the length of stay and the subsequent quick pace following delivery. Streamlining of care at one facility met with success because of collaborative efforts of providers and the design of a hospital maternity program that encourages the mother to determine the care and teaching she needs.

Pridham, K. F. (1993). Anticipatory guidance of parents of new infants: Potential contribution of the internal working model construct. *Image: The Journal of Nursing Scholarship, 25,* 49–56.

Anticipatory guidance is a clinical strategy for preparing parents of new infants to manage competently the expected daily events and developmental phenomena. However, there has been little study of the concept and its utility in clinical practice. This author offers a conceptual clarification of anticipatory guidance and the potential from theory development useful in guiding practice. Work of this nature contributes to substantive research in the area of childbearing health.

Roberts, C. L., Algert, C. S., & March, L. M. (1994). Delayed childbearing—are there any risks? *The Medical Journal of Australia, 160*, 539–544.

The research findings on the effect of delayed childbearing on pregnancy outcomes among primiparous women have shown conflicting results. In this study of an Australian population of 7,092 primiparous women aged 20 years or older, the researchers found that women 35 years of age and older were at no major risk for nongenetic adverse pregnancy outcomes, although there was an increased risk for antepartal hemorrhage, 33–36-week preterm delivery, and breech presentation. In addition, women over 35 were substantially more likely to have an induced labor and/or operative delivery. Findings from this study cannot be generalized as participants were largely white, married, of high socioeconomic status, and covered by private insurance. However, the trend in delaying childbearing continues for U.S. women. Findings from this report provide additional information for women about the potential risks—and benefits—of delayed childbearing.

Schenker, J. G., & Yossef, E. (1994). Complications of assisted reproductive techniques. *Fertility and Sterility, 61*, 411–419.

Assisted reproductive techniques have become well-accepted methods for the treatment of infertility. Complications have been noted with ovulation induction and the extracorporeal methods that are used for in vitro fertilization—embryo transfer (IVF-ET), gamete intrafallopian transfer (GIFT), and zygote intrafallopian transfer (ZIFT). In addition, pregnancies resulting from assisted reproduction are more complicated, as evidenced by reports of higher rates of ectopic, heterotopic, and multifetal pregnancies, as well as abortions and preterm deliveries. Following a review of the literature of the past 30 years, the authors note that assisted reproductive techniques should be carefully considered in light of the potential for serious complications. In addition, social controversy continues to surround the costs associated with

treatment of infertility, and a continued emphasis on cost containment in health care is likely to prevent broader access to infertility treatment technologies. The article is well documented and places infertility treatment in a larger perspective.

Summers, L., & Price, R. A. (1993). Preconception care. *Journal of Nurse-Midwifery, 38*, 188–198.

In 1990, the United States Public Health Service published *Healthy People 2000: National Health Promotion and Disease Prevention Objectives.* The targeted objective is preconception care designed to reduce the risk of poor pregnancy outcomes. This article carefully details effective preconception health counseling and advises on how to create a positive environment for conception. The authors have considerable experience teaching preconception classes and they include assessment criteria that are particularly valuable. They recommend that the preconception period be used as a time to "shop around" for a pregnancy care provider—a concept that is new to many women. The implementation of other recommendations will necessitate rethinking of routinely scheduled prenatal visits. Access to providers for the promotion of childbearing health is not yet designed for health promotion. Preconception visits, as well as frequent visits earlier in the prenatal period, may be important in achieving healthier mother–baby outcomes.

Stainton, M. C. (1994). Supporting family functioning during a high-risk pregnancy. *American Journal of Maternal Child Nursing, 19*, 24–28.

The family is often peripheral in the treatment of high-risk pregnancies. The author describes the complexities of the high-risk pregnancy and the dissonance it may create between the pregnant woman and her family. Examples underscore the role of the woman in the "kinship link and [as] the bearer and creator of history in the family." The experience of a high-risk pregnancy often separates the pregnant woman from many areas of family functioning. Because families experience stress during a high-risk pregnancy, activities that are appropriate for creating a nurse–patient partnership and for assisting the pregnant woman to maintain a sense of control are emphasized.

Women with Special Needs

Butz, A. M., Hutton, N., Joyner, M., Vogelhut, J., Greenberg-Friedman, D., Schreibeis, D., & Anderson, J. R. (1993). HIV-infected women and infants. *Journal of Nurse-Midwifery, 38,* 103–109.

Shannon, M. (1994). Clinical issues and therapeutic interventions in the care of pregnant women infected with the human immunodeficiency virus. *Journal of Perinatal and Neonatal Nursing, 7,* 13–30.

HIV infections in women are on the rise. Most women at risk for HIV infection are socially and economically disadvantaged, and minorities are disproportionately represented. Most cases of AIDS in women occur during the childbearing years, and HIV infection may first be diagnosed when a perinatally infected child is born or becomes ill. Early diagnosis is important in enhancing survival time and symptom-free intervals. However, women who are HIV-positive are often from a social milieu that prevents appropriate utilization of health care. Butz and colleagues studied 90 HIV-seropositive, indigent urban women for nearly three years. The purpose was to examine social and health characteristics associated with adequate use of and adherence to health care in HIV-infected women and their infants. The authors give suggestions for fostering awareness among HIV-positive women of their need to seek health care.

Shannon provides perinatal health nurse clinicians with an overview of the epidemiology and clinical manifestations of HIV infection in pregnant women. Therapeutic modalities and psychological aspects related to the care of childbearing women with HIV infection are included. A clear discussion of perinatal transmission is valuable.

Clark, S. L., & National Asthma Education Program Working Group on Asthma and Pregnancy, National Institutes of Health, National Heart, Lung, and Blood Institute. (1993). Asthma in pregnancy. *Obstetrics and Gynecology, 82,* 1036–1040.

As many as 4% of pregnancies are known to be complicated by bronchial asthma; the actual prevalence may be even higher. This report stresses that undertreatment of pregnant asthmatics remains a major problem in the management of asthma during pregnancy. Undertreatment is due, at least in part, to unfounded fears of adverse pharmacologic effects on the developing fetus. The pathogenesis of asthma is reviewed, as are its effects on pregnancy. Treatment strategies are discussed in relation to pregnancy. Recent findings suggest that asthma involves chronic airway inflammation in bronchial hyperreactivity and exacerbations of reversible airway obstruction. Control of inflammation should minimize or eliminate acute exacerbations, dramatically decreasing related morbidity and mortality. Available literature suggests that poor asthma control in pregnancy is the most influential factor in developing adverse effects. The article does not address the pregnant woman's subjective response to varied treatment approaches.

Collins, B. A., McCoy, S. A., Sale, S., & Weber, S. E. (1994). Descriptions of comfort by substance-using and nonusing postpartum women. *Journal of Obstetric, Gynecologic, and Neonatal Nursing, 23,* 293–300.

Matti, L. K., & Caspersen, V. M. (1993). Prevalence of drug use among pregnant women in a rural area. *Journal of Obstetric, Gynecologic, and Neonatal Nursing, 22,* 510–514.

Starn, J., Patterson, K., Bemis, G., Castro, O., & Bemis, P. (1993). Can we encourage pregnant substance abusers to seek prenatal care? *American Journal of Maternal Child Nursing, 18,* 148–152.

Sullivan, J., Boudreaux, M., & Keller, P. (1993). Can we help the substance abusing mother and infant? *American Journal of Maternal Child Nursing, 18,* 153–157.

Illegal drug use in the United States has risen dramatically and exacts an enormous social toll. Use of illicit drugs during pregnancy is particularly worrisome because of the effect on both mother and fetus.

Collins, McCoy, Sale, and Weber studied a convenience sample of 36 postpartum women to compare definitions of comfort held by substance users and nonusers. Groups were matched according to age, race, type of delivery, and parity. A qualitative design was used, and data analysis revealed three categories of themes common in both groups of participants. Findings supported the idea that comfort is more than the absence of pain and offered an interesting clarification of the concept of comfort among childbearing women.

Matti and Caspersen report on the prevalence of alcohol and illegal drug use among pregnant women in a rural area. A convenience sample of 202 pregnant women who were enrolling in prenatal care were screened for substance use by obtaining a urine sample. Participants ranged in age from 16 to 41 years. Most were married and privately insured. A 3.9% prevalence level of alcohol and illegal drug use was revealed—less than that reported for urban populations (11%). Because urine testing does not determine amount and frequency of drug use, caution is advised in interpreting the findings.

Starn and colleagues describe the Drug Identification, Screening and Counseling (DISC) project in Hawaii. This innovative program represents coordination of public and private health and social services for perinatal substance abusers.

Sullivan, Boudreaux, and Keller detail the development of the Perinatal Substance Abuse Intervention and Prevention Program. The program addresses identification and intervention strategies for cocaine-abusing women and their newborns in the acute care setting. Collaboration with other community programs and resources involved in substance abuse treatment is described.

Isaacs, J. D., Magann, E. F., Martin, R. W., Chauhan, S. P., & Morrison, J. C. (1994). Obstetric challenges of massive obesity complicating pregnancy. *Journal of Perinatology, 14,* 10–14.

This retrospective case control study examined the effects of massive maternal obesity on medical complications, mode of delivery, postpartum complications, and hospital confinement. When matched with leaner women, the obese women had a greater incidence of chronic hypertension and diabetes, were more likely to have a cesarean section, and were more likely to develop endometritis postoperatively. Postpartum confinement was significantly longer for the obese group. The findings are important for obese women contemplating pregnancy.

Kendrick, J. M. (1994). Fetal and uterine response during maternal surgery. *American Journal of Maternal Child Nursing, 19,* 165–170.

The purpose of this study was to assess and describe fetal heart rate (FHR) changes and uterine activity occurring during maternal surgery at 20 to 40 weeks' gestation. In addition, birth weights were examined in relation to surgery, as was the value of fetal monitoring during the operative procedure. The researchers used a convenience sample of 10 pregnant women who ranged in age from 19 to 36 years. Gestational age ranged from 20 to 36.5 weeks. Length of surgery ranged from 15 minutes to 3 hours and 50 minutes. Results of the study demonstrated significant uterine activity in half of the women patients; three required tocolysis. There were no preterm deliveries among the participants. FHR variability was decreased from baseline in all the women; the most dramatic decrease was noted in women undergoing general anesthesia. The mean birthweight was 7.2 pounds; recorded weights were comparable to weights of the mothers' older children. All mothers reported feeling more secure, knowing that fetal monitoring would be conducted during surgery; their greatest fear concerning surgery was the possibility of fetal loss. The researcher noted that perinatal nurses belong in the operating room when surgery is performed on the pregnant woman. The documented changes in uterine activity and FHR during maternal surgery underscore the need for skilled perinatal nursing specialists. Replication of the study is necessary, as is examination of the effect of differing anesthetic agents. When surgical intervention is warranted during pregnancy, crucial decisions need to be made because surgery presents a greater risk for the fetus than for the mother.

King, M. C., Torres, S., Campbell, D., Ryan, J., Sheridan, D., Ulrich, Y., & McKenna, L. S. (1993). Violence and abuse of women: A perinatal health care issue. *Clinical Issues in Perinatal and Women's Health Nursing, 4,* 163–172.

The authors provide an excellent discussion of the perinatal health issue of abuse directed at pregnant women by their partners. Their discussion includes the incidence and severity of violence during the particularly vulnerable period of pregnancy. Using a framework of advocacy and empowerment, strategies for primary prevention are described within a cultural context.

Martin, P. J., & Millac, P. A. (1993). Pregnancy, epilepsy, management and outcome: A 10-year perspective. *Seizure, 2,* 277–280.

This report is a description of the management and outcome of 348 pregnancies in 207 women with epilepsy, over a 10-year period. The researchers indicate that the outcomes were successful in 88% of the pregnancies. Analysis of data did not reveal a reduction in congenital malformation, spontaneous abortion, or low-birthweight infants. Monotherapy in anticonvulsant use is recommended during pregnancy. Findings from this research are valuable in making management decisions with pregnant epileptic women.

Petri, M. (1994). Systemic lupus erythematosus and pregnancy. *Rheumatology Diseases Clinics of North America, 20,* 87–118.

Women with systemic lupus erythematosus can generally achieve a successful pregnancy. However, fetal (fetal loss, preterm birth) and maternal (lupus flares, worsening of renal function) morbidity remain significant problems. This article describes predictors of fetal loss and preterm delivery, as well as current management strategies for pregnant women with lupus. The high-risk nature of the illness requires careful monitoring of the women and a clear discussion with them of treatment risks relative to the progression of the disease.

Verdru, P., Theys, P., D'Hooghe, M. B., & Carton, H. (1994). Pregnancy and multiple sclerosis: The influence on long-term disability. *Clinical Neurology and Neurosurgery, 96,* 38–41.

The effect of pregnancy on women with multiple sclerosis was investigated to determine whether pregnancy after the onset of the disease influences long-term disability. Patients who had at least one pregnancy after onset were wheelchair-dependent after 18.6 years. Wheelchair dependence for those who did not experience pregnancy after diagnosis occurred after 12.5 years. The researchers report that this difference is statistically significant after correction for age at onset of disease. Results of this study are limited; however, findings are important for counseling women with multiple sclerosis who are making a decision regarding the risk of pregnancy. Additional research is needed to understand the qualitative impact of pregnancy on women with this disease.

Wasser, A. M., Killoran, C. L., & Bansen, S. S. (1993). Pregnancy and disability. *Clinical Issues in Perinatal and Women's Health Nursing, 4,* 328–337.

The topic of this article is timely because increasing numbers of women with disabilities are electing to bear children. The authors discuss issues related to pregnancy in the presence of a disability and give examples relative to clinical practice. It is important that health care providers become familiar with this area.

Pregnancy, Health, and Illness

Baumann, P., & McFarlin, B. (1994). Prenatal diagnosis. *Journal of Nurse-Midwifery, 39,* 35S–50S.

This is an excellent review of the risks and benefits of prenatal diagnostic testing procedures, as well as those conditions calling for prenatal diagnosis. The information is important for childbearing women as they make decisions that will ensure healthy outcomes.

Bustan, M. N., & Coker, A. L. (1994). Maternal attitude toward pregnancy and the risk of neonatal death. *American Journal of Public Health, 84,* 411–414.

Fertility control options have been reduced over the past decade because of political and legal challenges. Not surprisingly, this trend has corresponded with increased numbers of women reporting unwanted pregnancies. The consequences of unwanted childbearing have not been studied well in U.S. populations. Using a longitudinal design, this investigation examined the association between attitude toward pregnancy and perinatal mortality. The sample (N = 8,823) was married, pregnant women. When questioned during the first trimester, approximately 14% (N = 1,274) of the women reported that their pregnancy was unwanted. Results demonstrated that having an unwanted pregnancy increased the risk of neonatal mortality. This investigation is the only known report of attitude assessment early in the pregnancy as compared to subsequent pregnancy outcomes. Delivery of an unwanted infant is a public health issue that implies potentially devastating outcomes.

Crawford, N. G., & Pruss, A. M. (1993). Preventing neonatal hepatitis B infection during the perinatal period. *Journal of Obstetric, Gynecologic, and Neonatal Nursing, 22,* 491–497.

Hepatitis B virus (HBV) infection is a growing problem. Many individuals acutely infected with HBV become chronically infected. Approximately 40% of chronic carriers become infected through perinatal transmission. The authors explore the epidemiology of HBV infection, the use of hepatitis B immune globulin and hepatitis B vaccines, and current recommendations for eliminating transmission of HBV during the perinatal period. An understanding of the information presented is crucial in developing strategies to reduce transmission of HBV.

Fox, H. E., & Badalian, S. S. (1993). Fetal movement in response to vibroacoustic stimulation: A review. *Obstetrical and Gynecological Survey, 48,* 707–712.

Fetal surveillance techniques are directed at the prevention or detection of perinatal mortality and morbidity. The vibroacoustic stimulation test (VAST), which evokes fetal movement, involves sound and vibration and originates in the extrauterine environment. The technique involves placement of an electric artificial larynx on the maternal abdomen to deliver the stimulus. The noncompromised mature fetus demonstrates an accelerated heart rate in response to the stimulation. Research is also under way to examine the usefulness of delivering the stimulus, then asking the mother whether she perceives fetal movement immediately afterward. Perception of fetal movement by the mother would constitute a positive response. The authors reviewed current research and literature about fetal movement in response to VAST. Currently,

VAST is used to reduce the duration of the nonstress test, and it has been shown to reduce the frequency of the equivocal nonstress test. Research has shown a clear association between use of the VAST and favorable neonatal outcomes, and VAST is inexpensive and easily obtainable. Additional research with large, heterogeneous clinical populations is necessary before the usefulness of VAST can be determined.

Freda, M. C., Mikhail, M., Mazloom, E., Polizzotto, R., Damus, K., & Merkatz, I. (1993). Fetal movement counting: Which method? *American Journal of Maternal Child Nursing, 18*, 314–321.

Fetal movement is highly individual for each fetus; however, it has been found that fetal movement is influenced by gestational age. The largest number of movements are experienced between 29 and 38 weeks' gestation. Movement decreases after that time period. This article describes a study of healthy pregnant women between 28 and 32 weeks' gestation. Participants were randomly assigned to one of two groups who had to count fetal movements daily, using one of two methods. Most of the women were black or Hispanic, under 25 years of age, and unmarried. About half of the women in each group were nulliparous. There were no significant differences between groups in compliance with performing fetal movement counts. Based on the findings, either method would be useful in counting fetal movement. Further study is warranted: fetal movement counting is an inexpensive, noninvasive method of enhancing well-being.

Higgins, P., Murray, M. L., & Williams, E. M. (1994). Self-esteem, social support, and satisfaction differences in women with adequate and inadequate prenatal care. *Birth, 21*, 26–33.

This descriptive study was designed to examine levels of self-esteem, social support, and satisfaction with prenatal care in a group of low-risk postpartal women (N = 193) who received adequate and inadequate care. Significant differences were found among participants in level of education, income, insurance, and ethnicity. Women who were most likely to seek prenatal care were high school graduates and those with greater incomes. In addition, significant differences were found in self-esteem, social support, and satisfaction of the two groups. Strategies designed to enhance self-esteem and social support for pregnant women at risk for receiving inadequate prenatal care are needed. Findings point to important areas in need of continued study. The qualitative study of prenatal care experiences should also be pursued to gain a greater understanding of individual expectations and needs.

Hines, T., & Jones, M. B. (1994). Can aspirin prevent and treat pre-eclampsia? *American Journal of Maternal Child Nursing, 19*, 258–263.

Pre-eclampsia is a major cause of maternal and neonatal morbidity and mortality. The etiology is still not understood and treatment is largely symptomatic. This article presents an excellent overview of the pathophysiology of pre-eclampsia and the role of low-dose aspirin as a therapeutic intervention. Studies examining the effects of aspirin in the prevention of pre-eclampsia are detailed.

King, T. (1994). Clinical management of premature rupture of membranes. *Journal of Nurse-Midwifery, 39*, 81S–89S.

Marshall, V. A. (1993). Management of premature rupture of membranes at or near term. *Journal of Nurse-Midwifery, 38*, 140–145.

Premature rupture of membranes (PROM) occurs in 5%–10% of all pregnancies. Most of the time, it occurs in term gestations. When it occurs during the preterm, it presents an even greater risk: efforts must be made to mitigate the adverse effects of prematurity. King describes the controversy in clinical management. Recommendations are made for treatment based on current research findings.

Marshall recommends that conservative management be initiated when PROM occurs at or near term. Her recommendations are based on a retrospective review of 909 charts. Conservative management was found to be safe for mother and infant and to be cost-effective.

Kinsella, S. M., & Lohman, G. (1994). Supine hypotensive syndrome. *Obstetrics and Gynecology, 83,* 774–786.

This article, an overview of the research of supine hypotensive syndrome, discusses onset, possibility of advance detection, and clinical presentation. It notes an incidence of about 8%, with as many as 60% of pregnant women experiencing supine symptoms some time during pregnancy. Analysis of approximately 100 reports suggests that supine hypotensive syndrome manifests on a spectrum of severity and is generally noted in late pregnancy. Presence of the syndrome generally compels the pregnant woman to change position. Inferior vena cava compression is the major determinant in the development of the syndrome; onset usually occurs 3–10 minutes after supine positioning. Symptoms range from restlessness to feelings of impending death. Fetal movements may cease. The authors note that women who develop symptoms of the syndrome will spontaneously move and "instinctively" avoid the position thereafter; they may either "resist attempts to make them lie supine, or acquiesce against their own judgment." Given the continued popularity of supine positioning for convenience of the provider, this work makes a compelling case for a change in practice.

May, K. A. (1994). Impact of maternal activity restriction for preterm labor on the expectant father. *Journal of Obstetric, Gynecologic, and Neonatal Nursing, 23*(3), 246–251.

This investigator interviewed 30 men whose partners experienced an activity-restricted pregnancy for preterm labor. The study involved two phases. In the first phase, 15 fathers were recruited within 2–3 weeks of the prescribed activity restriction. The fathers and their partners were interviewed twice during the activity restriction period and once after birth. Interviews, largely conducted in the home, focused on individual experiences of activity restriction, and conclusions about its effects on the fathers and the family. In the second phase, an additional 30 men whose partners had experienced an activity-restricted pregnancy within the previous 2 years were involved in a focus group interview. Five major themes were found on analysis: (1) little assistance from health professionals, (2) isolation, (3) shock and worry, (4) stress related to "doing it all," and (5) challenge in maintaining a close and satisfying relationship with their partner. Study participants were largely middle-class white men, and findings can only be viewed as preliminary. This study suggests that activity restriction in preterm labor holds emotional distress for these fathers and disruption for the family unit. These findings are in conflict with the general belief that activity restriction in pregnancy is relatively cheap and without significant hazard. Preterm labor is an enormous problem with a potentially devastating outcome. Health professionals need to recognize that, at least for some families, significant stress may compound the experience and impact the outcome.

Mercer, R. R., Feketich, S. L., & DeJoseph, J. F. (1993). Predictors of partner relationships during pregnancy and infancy. *Research in Nursing and Health, 16,* 45–56.

The authors examined the partner relationship of 218 women experiencing low-risk pregnancy and their partners (N = 147), as well as 153 high-risk, hospitalized pregnant women and their partners (N = 75). The purpose was to assess the partner relationships from pregnancy through 8 months after birth, recognizing that the birth of an infant alters family structure and function. The finding that there was an overall decline in partner relationship from pregnancy to 8 months was consistent with other literature. The researchers found no difference in partner relationships between high- and low-risk mothers. However, low-risk fathers reported better partner relationships than the high-risk fathers, except at the testing that occurred at 1 month. Partner relationships for all groups were higher during pregnancy and at birth than at 4 and 8 months after birth. Particularly interesting predictors were the gender differences. The men's readiness for the pregnancy predicted their satisfaction with the partner relationship during the pregnancy—underscoring the importance of both partners' being involved in planning a pregnancy. This study is particularly interesting because it is the first reported longitudinal study of the relationship among parents experiencing a high-risk pregnancy. It is an important area in anticipatory care of the developing family.

Newman, V., Fullerton, J. T., & Anderson, P. O. (1993). Clinical advances in the management of severe nausea and vomiting during pregnancy. *Journal of Obstetric, Gynecologic, and Neonatal Nursing, 22,* 483–490.

Nausea and vomiting are common complaints in early pregnancy. While bothersome, they are generally self-limiting. Severe and persistent vomiting, however, may produce serious compromise for the pregnant woman. This well-documented article discusses clinical management in a stepwise approach. Implications for treatment in both the outpatient and inpatient settings are discussed. The information presented should be of interest to all who work with women in the prenatal period.

Surratt, N. (1993). Severe pre-eclampsia: Implications for critical-care obstetric nursing. *Journal of Obstetric, Gynecologic, and Neonatal Nursing, 22,* 500–507.

Pre-eclampsia is a multisystem disease that accounts for significant perinatal morbidity and mortality. This article presents a review of the etiology, pathophysiology, and information crucial in conducting advanced assessment and nursing intervention. An understanding of the complexities of care required

for these patients is important in preventing maternal end-organ damage and neonatal complications. Current technologic adjuncts useful in precise assessment of select patients with severe pre-eclampsia are discussed. The article makes an important contribution to understanding the physiologic alterations in the critically ill pre-eclamptic patient.

Teen Pregnancy

Holden, G. W., Nelson, P. B., Velasquez, J., & Ritchie, K. L. (1993). Cognitive, psychosocial, and reported sexual behavior differences between pregnant and nonpregnant adolescents. *Adolescence, 28,* 557–572.

This multivariate research was designed to assess differences in pregnant (n = 69) and nonpregnant (n = 58) adolescents on variables from three domains: (1) cognitive, (2) psychosocial, and (3) reported sexual behavior. Pregnant teens were more likely to be doing poorly in school and were less likely to be using contraceptives. Pregnant teens were also more likely to have a relative or friend who was an adolescent mother and they tended to expect child-rearing to be easier than did their nonpregnant counterparts. The study is a valuable beginning for understanding the complex factors that influence the occurrence of teen pregnancy. Findings should be useful in developing a profile of teens who are at risk for pregnancy.

Julnes, G., Konefal, M., Pindur, W., & Kin, P. (1994). Community-based perinatal care for disadvantaged adolescents: Evaluation of the resource mothers program. *Journal of Community Health, 19*(1), 41–53.

An effort to improve perinatal health and birth outcomes for disadvantaged teens led to the development of the Resource Mothers Program (RMP). Numerous health services and programs are available to pregnant teens, but there has been limited success in decreasing the pregnancy rate. A more traditional approach is the clinic-based program built around multidisciplinary teams of health professionals. This study examined an alternative approach utilizing trained mothers and paraprofessionals from the immediate community. These individuals were similar to the teens in race and socioeconomic status and helped to recruit teens into the program. Their support for high-risk pregnant teens encouraged healthy behaviors and early intervention. In comparison to a more traditional clinic-based multidisciplinary health team, the RMP reached a higher percentage of pregnant adolescents characterized by young maternal age, black race, residence in targeted neighborhoods with low income levels, less than a high school education, and no prior pregnancies. RMP participants demonstrated improved adequacy of prenatal care, and birth outcomes were comparable to those in the more traditional program. These findings are particularly important in recognizing the rate of teen pregnancy and the scope of problems it presents. If cheaper, more (or equally) effective, programs can be developed to complement or expand existing services, it would seem important to explore this option. Perinatal health of high-risk pregnant teens may well be improved through innovative programming, such as lay home visiting. In coordination with existing services, this approach may serve the adolescent woman who is socially, economically, and educationally disadvantaged.

Jaskiewicz, J. A., & McAnarney, E. R. (1994). Pregnancy during adolescence. *Pediatric Review*, 15, 32–38.

This article presents a practical approach to care of the pregnant adolescent. Emphasis is placed on prevention strategies that are useful in decreasing the incidence of teen pregnancies. Health care providers, and others concerned with health care for this high-risk group, will find this article valuable.

Klerman, L. V. (1993). Adolescent pregnancy and parenting: Controversies of the past and lessons for the future. *Journal of Adolescent Health*, 14, 553–561.

The author challenges nine commonly held beliefs about adolescent pregnancy, based on an overview of recent research findings. The nine beliefs discussed are: (1) that nothing can reduce the rate of adolescent pregnancy; (2) that pregnant adolescents experience poor pregnancy outcomes; (3) that adolescent mothers do not complete their high school education; (4) that pregnant adolescents have large families; (5) that adolescent mothers remain on welfare for long periods; (6) that pregnancy in adolescence is a mistake and, given a chance to overcome the immediate problems associated with it, young mothers can go on to lead normal lives; (7) that welfare causes adolescent pregnancy and parenting; (8) that adolescent mothers are poor parents; and (9) that service programs can have a significant impact on adolescent pregnancy and parenting. Suggestions are made for achieving progress in the prevention and amelioration of problems experienced by pregnant adolescents.

Intrapartum

Biancuzzo, M. (1993). Six myths of maternal posture during labor. *American Journal of Maternal Child Nursing*, 18, 264–269.

Attention continues to be directed at the posture of women during labor. Several myths about positioning in labor are dispelled. Suggestions are made for assessing and intervening with the parturient as labor progresses. The information presented is described in relation to current literature findings. The discussion is particularly easy to read and is peppered with clinical examples and suggestions for fostering labor progression through position change.

Bivins, H. A., Newman, R. B., Fyfe, D. A., Campbell, B. A., & Stramm, S. L. (1993). Randomized trial of oral indomethacin and terbutaline sulfate for the long-term suppression of preterm labor. *American Journal of Obstetrics and Gynecology*, 169, 1065–1069.

Preterm labor is a major cause of neonatal morbidity and mortality, especially at the earlier gestational ages. Prevention is the goal, but health care providers must decide the most effective management once preterm labor has begun. This prospective study examined the efficacy and safety of two of the most common long-term tocolytic agents used in the treatment of preterm labor, terbutaline sulfate and oral indomethacin. Despite current use, terbutaline sulfate has been associated with undesirable and potentially life-threatening side effects for the mother. Use of indomethacin has been associated with adverse fetal effects. The researchers studied 65 women with singleton pregnancies between 26 and 32 weeks' gestation who were diagnosed with preterm labor. Patients were randomized to receive one of the two treatment protocols and were assessed weekly. The data suggest that both agents are effective tocolytics before 34 weeks' gestation. However, major fetal effects (oliguria and constriction of the ductus arteriosus) were noted with indomethacin use. The high incidence found in this investigation led to early termination of the study. The findings must be interpreted cautiously because of the small sample size. In addition, the incidence of fetal side effects and the necessity of monitoring for such adversity when indomethacin is administered may add significantly to the cost of management.

Cosner, K. R., & deJong, E. (1993). Physiologic second-stage labor. *American Journal of Maternal Child Nursing, 18,* 38–43.

Traditional management of second-stage labor generally includes coaching the mother to bear down in a prescribed manner with each contraction. A recent proliferation of research and literature recognizes second-stage labor as a normal physiologic event. A new definition of second-stage labor is emerging, based on the principle that the stage is a normal physiologic event that generally progresses to normal delivery without intervention. Rather than the provider's determining when pushing should be started, among other activities, it relies on cues from the parturient to manage care. Physiologic management of second-stage labor should be discussed with women prior to the labor experience. This article does much to further physiologic second-stage management

as the standard of care. Such reform may increase parturients' trust and participation in the normal processes of labor.

Golay, J., Vedam, S., & Sorger, L. (1993). The squatting position for the second stage of labor: Effects on labor and on maternal and fetal well-being. *Birth, 20,* 73–78.

This study examined the effects of maternal squatting during second-stage labor. The researchers evaluated the effect of squatting on the evolution and progress of labor and on maternal and fetal well-being. Research participants were 200 randomly selected women who were divided into two groups: those who squatted and those in a semirecumbent position. Women who squatted had a shorter second-stage labor and required significantly less labor stimulation by oxytocin. There was also a trend toward fewer mechanically assisted deliveries in the group of women who squatted. Findings reinforce the need to alter positioning in labor.

Gupton, A., & Heaman, M. (1994). Learning needs of hospitalized women at risk for preterm birth. *Applied Nursing Research, 7,* 118–124.

Preterm deliveries represent 8% to 10% of all births, yet account for over 60% of perinatal morbidity and mortality. Recent technological advances have not significantly decreased the incidence of preterm birth. Hospitalization is necessitated for many of these women. The purpose of this descriptive study was to identify the priority learning needs of hospitalized women at risk of preterm birth. Research participants were 24 pregnant women who had been hospitalized and were considered high-risk for preterm birth. The majority of participants were white, married, and high school-educated. The mean gestational age was 31.3 weeks. When respondents rated 18 teaching topics, those identified as most important were the consequences of prematurity and subsequent problems for the newborn. Study findings suggest that priority learning needs of these women need to be addressed early.

Ludka, L. M., & Roberts, C. C. (1993). Eating and drinking in labor. *Journal of Nurse-Midwifery, 38,* 199–207.

This excellent article questions the routine practice of denying food and fluids to women in labor. The authors' interesting historical overview clarifies how the practice of fasting in labor was established in the United States. From a review of the literature, the authors conclude that restrictive policies are based on tradition rather than on current scientific research. Recommendation is made that women be given the choice to eat and drink in normal labor. This article should be required reading for health professionals.

McKay, S., & Smith, S. Y. (1993). "What are they talking about? Is something wrong?" Information sharing during the second stage of labor. *Birth, 20,* 142–147.

This impressive report examines information sharing during labor. Twenty postpartal women were shown videotapes of their second-stage labors and were simultaneously interviewed. An analysis of themes found that many women wanted additional communication during the second stage. Most wanted more information that would alleviate their unvoiced fears about the baby's health. Caregivers and women agreed about what information laboring women require and how it should be given. However, caregivers' perceptions of the quality of their information giving were more positive than mothers' perceptions. The sample was small, but interesting areas are suggested for the clinician to consider, and areas in need of additional research are identified.

The National Institute of Child Health and Human Development Network of Maternal--Fetal Medicine Units. (1994). A clinical trial of induction of labor versus expectant management in postterm pregnancy. *American Journal of Obstetrics and Gynecology, 170,* 716–723.

Postterm pregnancy extends beyond 42 weeks of gestation. When the pregnancy is uncomplicated, management is controversial. This study examined the two most commonly used management strategies: (1) expectant management, where the pregnancy is allowed to progress to 42 weeks and beyond with labor induced only if the cervix is favorable, or if fetal compromise occurs; and (2) immediate induction, where labor is aggressively induced at 42 weeks or earlier, with cervical ripening agents used, as well as oxytocin and amniotomy, if necessary. Four hundred forty patients with uncomplicated pregnancies at 41 weeks' gestation were randomized to one of the two treatment groups. Results of the investigation demonstrated that there were no differences in maternal or perinatal outcome when an uncomplicated postterm pregnancy was managed either expectantly or by immediate induction of labor. The study also evaluated the efficacy of using prostaglandin E_2 gel for cervical ripening. Results indicate that a single intracervical administration of prostaglandin E_2 gel is more effective than placebo gel in initiating persistent contractions in nulliparous patients only. Application of the cervical ripening agent did not reduce the cesarean section rate or the induction–delivery interval. In summary, neither management approach demonstrated significant differences in perinatal morbidity or mortality. This is important information for the decision regarding management of postterm pregnancies, which account for approximately 10% of all deliveries.

Schorn, M. N., McAllister, J. L., & Blanco, J. D. (1993). Water immersion and the effect on labor. *Journal of Nurse-Midwifery, 38,* 336–342.

This was a prospective, randomized study of 93 pregnant women who were using water immersion for relaxation during labor. All patients were between 36 and 41 weeks' gestation, without complications, and in active labor (4–7 cm dilation) with intact membranes and a normal fetal heart rate pattern. Patients were assigned to either the warm water immersion (tub) during labor, or to the group not able to use the tub. All other pain relief measures were available to both groups. It was found that use of the tub did not alter the rate of cervical dilation, change the contraction pattern, change the length of labor, or alter the use of analgesia. While the study did not find that use of the tub helped labor to progress more quickly, there was no evidence of increased morbidity. Consumer groups have facilitated an increased request for tubs during labor. Findings from this investigation are reassuring in light of the growing popularity of the intervention.

Wheeler, D. G. (1994). Preterm birth prevention. *Journal of Nurse Midwifery, 39,* 66S–80S.

The author discusses the importance of preventing preterm birth and reviews relevant anatomy and physiology, as well as the etiology, risk factors and risk scoring, and diagnosis and management of preterm labor. A program of prevention is detailed, based on a comprehensive review of the existing literature.

After Birth

Drosten-Brooks, F. (1993). Kangaroo care: Skin-to-skin contact in the NICU. *American Journal of Maternal Child Nursing, 18,* 250–253.

Strategies for establishing a relationship between the infant cared for in the Neonatal Intensive Care Unit (NICU) and the parents are increasingly recognized as critical in preventing later care problems. The period of hospitalization in the NICU is known to be particularly vulnerable. Kangaroo care, suggested as one easy, cost-effective intervention, has been documented to include decreased oxygen requirements, longer quiet sleep periods, and shortened hospitalization. The article summarizes the available literature and makes suggestions for implementing the technique in

clinical practice, where applicable. Nurses are among the gatekeepers in special care units. The article highlights how health care providers can improve the NICU environment, fostering involvement and capability in caring for the infant. Technology in caring for critically ill neonates has grown exponentially. Appropriate implementation of kangaroo care for eligible infants and interested parents may be a tool in developing competent parents. Kangaroo care has the potential to allow parents greater control over the perinatal experience.

Dunn, P. A., York, R., Cheek, T. G., & Yeboah, K. (1993). Maternal hypothermia: Implications for obstetric nurses. *Journal of Obstetric, Gynecologic, and Neonatal Nursing, 23,* 238–242.

Hypothermia is a common intraoperative complication that may occur in obstetric patients. Obstetric patients are at increased risk of hypothermia because of vasodilation from pregnancy, administration of anesthetics and other medications, and inherent blood loss with rapid fluid replacement. Hypothermia in postpartum women may have potentially life-threatening sequelae. This article provides a succinct overview of the physiology of hypothermia, potential complications, and the nursing care needed to prevent multisystem problems. Early recognition and treatment may serve to prevent dangerous complications, hastening recovery for the postpartum mother. The information in this article is important in providing a safe recovery after birth. Astute observation by the provider has the potential to eliminate the need for more intrusive intervention.

Ferketich, S. L., & Mercer, R. T. (1994). Predictors of paternal role competence by risk status. *Nursing Research, 43,* 80–85.

Mercer, R. T., & Ferketich, S. L. (1994). Predictors of maternal role competence by risk status. *Nursing Research, 43,* 38–43.

Transition into the role of father or mother creates much uncertainty. New behaviors and competencies are requisite, and the extent to which parents achieve role competence is important in the development and health of the family.

The researchers examined role competence for mothers and for fathers. Mothers and fathers were categorized and grouped by whether the pregnancy had been low- or high-risk. High-risk pregnant women were hospitalized. Differences were examined over time for the two groups of fathers, as well as the two groups of mothers. Data were collected in the early postpartal period, and again at 1, 4, and 8 months postpartum. No difference in paternal or maternal role competence was found between groups. Anxiety was the major predictor of paternal role competence when the partner experienced a high-risk pregnancy; a sense of mastery and depression were the major predictors for the low-risk pregnancy group. The researchers concluded that the increased stress of a high-risk pregnancy did not seem to be a detriment in the fathers' achievement of role competence. Maternal role competence increased at 4 and 8 months over earlier levels. Self-esteem and mastery were reported as consistent predictors of maternal competence for both groups of women. Fetal attachment was a predictor of competence among the group of high-risk mothers only.

Overall, findings from the two investigations indicate that men and women experience a somewhat similar but still different trajectory in role attainment. Different variables are important to men in developing role competence when the partner is hospitalized with a high-risk pregnancy. Anxiety served as a major predictor for this group of men. How that anxiety is addressed may be important in examining the nature of the support these men are able to give their partners. In contrast, findings suggest that interventions aimed at fostering maternal self-esteem and mastery are important for women to achieve role attainment.

Norwood, S. L. (1994). First steps: Participants and outcomes of a maternity support services program. *Journal of Obstetric, Gynecologic, and Neonatal Nursing, 23,* 467–474.

The characteristics and pregnancy outcomes in a maternity support program are described for 220 postpartum patients. Only patients who received Medicaid were eligible for participation in the study. All participants had delivered within an 8-week period. Data were gathered from mothers who participated in the support program, as well as from those who did not. Results demonstrated that fewer nonparticipants quit smoking during pregnancy, but there were no other significant differences in this study sample. The researcher notes that social support programs and maternity support programs need to be carefully evaluated. If adequate medical care is available in the community, additional supportive services may not be necessary.

Symanski, M. E. (1992). Maternal–infant bonding: Practice issues for the 1990s. *Journal of Nurse-Midwifery, 37,* 67S–73S.

This article provides an excellent overview of the topic of maternal–infant bonding. The theoretical issues and the research that exists in this area are thoroughly reviewed. Specific recommendations for applying research findings to practice are offered. The article does not address bonding and attachment as they relate to adoptive mothers, but it does cover application of findings throughout the childbearing phases, as well as with high-risk women. Although findings in this area must be interpreted with caution, the author skillfully extracts significant empirical findings. The article is "must" reading for clinicians working to promote parent–child relationships.

Cesarean Section

Fawcett, J., Tulman, L., & Spedden, J. P. (1994). Responses to vaginal birth after cesarean section. *Journal of Obstetric, Gynecologic, and Neonatal Nursing, 23*(3), 253–259.

This study examined women's responses to vaginal birth after cesarean (VBAC) delivery, which is advocated as a means of reducing the accelerating cesarean birthrate. Findings consistently report that women, in general, find the vaginal birth more positive, and vaginal delivery generally holds fewer medical risks. Women need information and support regarding not only the safest mode of birth but the mode that affords them both physical and psychological benefit. They report comparative needs with both types of delivery. The safety of VBAC has been documented, and this work details the potential psychological benefit of the experience.

Flamm, B. L., Goings, J. R., Liu, Y., & Wolde-Tsadik, G. (1994). Elective repeat cesarean delivery versus trial of labor: A prospective multicenter study. *Obstetrics and Gynecology, 83*, 927–932.

This study of the outcomes of patients who attempted a trial of labor and those who underwent elective repeat cesarean delivery is particularly impressive because of the sample size (N = 7,229). Seventy percent (n = 5,022) of the women underwent a trial of labor, and the remainder (n = 2,207) had elective repeat cesarean delivery. Seventy-five percent of those undergoing a trial of labor went on to deliver vaginally; the risk of uterine rupture was less than 1%. The impressive results add to the existing literature in support of vaginal birth after a cesarean delivery. Findings in t his area should be reassuring to women considering vaginal birth following an operative delivery.

Breastfeeding

Crowell, M. K., Hill, P. D., & Humenick, S. S. (1994). Relationship between obstetric analgesia and time of effective breastfeeding. *Journal of Nurse-Midwifery, 39*, 150–155.

This study addressed the relationship of maternal analgesia and breastfeeding. Research participants consisted of 48 breastfeeding mothers who had delivered their first or second child vaginally, were 19 years of age or older, and had delivered a healthy, single, term infant at 37 or more weeks of gestation, weighing at least 2500 g at birth. All mothers received a local and/or pudendal anesthetic at delivery. One group (n = 22) received no medication during labor; the other group (n = 26) received butorphanol or nalbuphine. Results indicated that maternal labor analgesia can affect the infant's ability to breastfeed and may delay establishment of effective feeding by several hours. Findings from this convenience sample cannot be generalized, but it provides additional evidence for the growing body of knowledge supporting little or no medication and early initiation of breastfeeding.

Hill, P. D., & Aldag, J. C. (1993). Insufficient milk supply among black and white breastfeeding mothers. *Research in Nursing and Health, 16*, 203–211.

Women who choose to breastfeed tend to be older, of white ethnicity, well-educated, and more affluent. The superiority of breastfeeding has been well-documented. However, breastfeeding trends in differing populations, and ethnic differences in the initiation and duration of breastfeeding, have been less well documented. Because mothers report insufficient milk supply (IMS) as a reason for early termination of breastfeeding, this study investigated black (n = 42) and white (n = 148) breastfeeding women's incidence of IMS. This retrospective survey was conducted at 17 WIC agencies in a midwestern state. All research participants gave birth to a single infant. All had infants between 8.1 and 14 weeks of age, but were not necessarily breastfeeding, when they completed the questionnaires for the study. About half of both black and white mothers had no prior breastfeeding experience. This investigation found that the prevalence of IMS was similar for both groups of conveniently se-lected women. Black mothers started and stopped breastfeeding sooner, and those moth-ers with IMS were found to have fed less fre-quently and for shorter periods. Results of this investigation cannot be generalized. However, the differences suggest that black mothers may be receiving less support for breastfeeding from professionals. Increased attention to black women may assist in increasing the rate and duration of breastfeeding. The phenomenon of IMS is widespread and does not appear to be limited to any particular ethnic group. Atten-tion to women who are at risk for IMS may positively influence breastfeeding experiences for women.

Chapter 8

Contraceptive Options

Theresa Lawlor McDonald
Susan R. Johnson

T he status of a country's women is a major factor in the political and economic decisions the country makes about family planning programs. The single most important factor associated with the use of birth control methods around the world is the educational attainment of women. The more educated they are, the more women seek to limit the number of children they have and thereby improve their families' quality of life (Diczfalusy, 1993). Reproductive health goals are designed to improve the quality of life by:

- reducing maternal, infant, and child illness and death;
- remedying the unmet needs for family planning;
- counteracting the scarcity of family planning services and methods;
- reducing the number of persons with sexually transmitted diseases (Diczfalusy, 1993).

Pregnancies that are too early, too close, too late, or too frequent are more likely to result in health hazards for the woman and her child (Fathalla, 1993). The World Health Organization (WHO) estimates that during the last 10 years of this century, about 7 million women will die in childbirth. The majority of these deaths will occur in developing countries and could be prevented through basic health care, family planning, and pre-natal care. Ideally, a month's supply of contraceptives should not cost more than 2 hours' wages each month or 1% of the monthly family income (Dicz-falusy, 1993).

The WHO has pointed out the vast inequalities among countries' repro-ductive health expenditures. The United States spends $400 per person each year on health care; the poorest countries spend less than $5 per per-son each year. Government officials often cite a lack of money for repro-ductive services when, in fact, priorities on how funds are to be allocated are at issue. In 1986, $800 billion was spent on defense worldwide. Prepar-ing for the use of force and aggression, rather than improving citizens' quality of life, has been the priority of most world leaders. A recent com-parison of money spent on the military as opposed to education and health care showed that military expenditures were 55% of the amount spent on education and health care costs in industrialized countries, 104% in devel-oping countries, and 92% in the least developed countries (Diczfalusy, 1993).

Barriers to a rapid increase in contraceptive use are lack of (or absence of) money, community support, women's education and development, easy access, and quality of services. Additional barriers are present in cultures heavily influenced by religious and political views that are restrictive to-ward women (Diczfalusy, 1993).

Many men, in a variety of cultures around the world, are a negative po-litical force controlling contraceptive use inside and outside the home (Sai, 1993). A common cause is fear of a change in the domestic power balance when women's energies are not consumed by childcare and housework. In-side the home, men may discourage or limit their partner's contraceptive use or refuse to use condoms. Outside the home, men control most of the political and social organizations that regulate contraceptive distribution and use (Sai, 1993).

Besides economic, social, cultural, and political issues, there is the problem of population growth. In 1798, Thomas Robert Malthus wrote that an unchecked population increases in a geometric ratio, while food increases in an arithmetic ratio. At that time, factors limiting population growth were war, starvation, and disease; currently, these limiting factors have less effect. The world population has increased from 1 billion in the 19th century to 5.5 billion. Since 1900, there have been more than 200 wars with casualties of almost 90 million deaths—an insignificant num-ber compared to population growth. The projection of all deaths from AIDS (Acquired Immune Deficiency Syndrome) in the last 10 years of this century is equal to only one month's world population growth. Many peo-ple believe industrial and economic growth will absorb the negative ef-fects of population growth. They emphasize that growth *rates*, in contrast to absolute *numbers*, have been declining significantly since the early

1980s. Others who think population growth is a serious problem point out that the absolute numbers will continue to rise for at least another century, and the total may then overwhelm the food supply. The latter view is finding more support among those concerned about the ecosystem and environmental issues. However, demographic projections do not necessarily determine our destiny; they may change because of increasing deaths as noted above or by decreasing births through contraceptive use (Diczfalusy, 1993).

The articles reviewed in this chapter cover the following areas:

• cultural, social, religious, economic, and political issues;
• sexual behaviors, especially in teens;
• education of health consumers and professionals on old and new contraceptives;
• women with risk factors for contraceptives;
• the new oral contraceptives;
• new barriers: the female condom and a different sponge;
• postabortal contraception;
• birth control methods of the future.

Realizing that lines of distinction between contraception and early abortion are becoming less clear, we have included articles on emergency contraception, abortifacent medications, and menstrual extraction.

An article on nonsurgical female sterilization with quinacrine pellets is listed in the references section. The pellets are placed into the tubes of the uterus (womb). This causes scarring of the tubes so that the egg from the ovary cannot implant on the wall of the uterus, thus preventing pregnancy. The article was not reviewed because approval by the Food and Drug Administration (FDA) is unlikely in the near future.

A New View of a Woman's Body (Federation of Feminist Women's Health Centers, 1991) has good information on natural birth control methods and female barriers, with excellent illustrations by Suzann Gage. Her drawings of fertile preovulatory mucus and nonfertile mucus are especially interesting. Unfortunately, the information is out-of-date on the more effective birth control methods: oral contraceptives (OCs) and intrauterine devices (IUDs). These methods are presented in a more negative light than is warranted. Low-dose pills have some benefits and far fewer side effects than the higher-dose pills of the past. The types of IUDs in the book are no longer available in the United States, where women are currently limited to two choices in IUDs. The Paragard 380A IUD (approved by the FDA in 1988) can be left in place for 8 years. The Progestasert IUD, with slow release of progesterone, must be replaced annually.

One of the most important articles reviewed is by Westhoff, Marks, and Rosenfield (1993). It describes a study of training for medical residents in obstetrics and gynecology (OB/Gyn). The residents reported that the majority of their contraceptive training was in oral contraceptives and sterilization. No wonder these methods are the two most commonly used in the United States! Physicians tend to encourage use of the methods they know best.

Residents reported little training in family planning settings, and few residents had any training in abortion techniques (Westhoff et al., 1983). The lack of physicians well trained in performing abortions is a serious concern for those in the family planning field and a significant barrier to overcome in attaining woman's reproductive rights.

IMPLICATIONS FOR TEACHING, RESEARCH, CLINICAL PRACTICE, AND HEALTH POLICY

The articles and books described provide many considerations in the areas of contraception and pregnancy termination for those who use or deliver women's health services.

Anastasi's article on the female condom will help clinicians with their education efforts on contraception and sexually transmitted disease (STD).

Longitudinal studies are needed to determine the long-term effectiveness of the female condom for both contraceptive and STD protection. Current effectiveness rates for the female condom are based on a study conducted over a 6-month period. Use of barrier methods generally improves over time, thus increasing the method's effectiveness.

More education and follow-up are needed to promote the use of the Reality female condom. Women should be shown the device and given the opportunity to hold it in their hand and ask questions. The following points are important for women to know:

- The penis should be guided into the condom.
- Positions may be important.

This type of female condom may be more likely to be displaced when the woman is on top during intercourse or especially with penetration from behind. These risks should be emphasized during counseling and client education on birth control methods.

In addition to describing first sexual encounters, Bouris's book *The First Time* addresses women's fear and dislike of pelvic exams. Clinicians must demonstrate sensitivity and patience with female patients. The author highlights the importance of sexuality education for both male and female children, including the emotional and the physical aspects of sexual encounters.

Bouris's research is an important first step, but more studies are needed to determine whether negative sexual experiences are as common as this study indicates. The response rate from 1,000 mailed questionnaires was only 15% and it is possible that women with negative experiences were more likely to respond.

Braverman and Strasburger, in the article on adolescent sexuality, indicate that practitioners would be wise to train peer educators and then act as consultants to the teen educators. Information should include ways to express sexual feelings without having intercourse and/or risking pregnancy. Research into this area might be more productive if teens are involved in collecting, processing, and interpreting information about sexuality and contraception. This participatory approach increases the likelihood that the knowledge gained will be communicated by teens to their peer groups.

Chalker and Downer (1992) indicate that, because of the conservative but politically vocal antichoice minority, women's groups, once again, may need to know how to do menstrual extractions. Women's groups were very important in the women's health movement in the 1970s and they could be again. This is a time in history when there should be even more involvement from health professionals in the dissemination of health information. Much pertinent research comes out of women's sharing of information with each other.

There are still many contraceptive barriers in the developed world. Teens and older women have specific contraceptive needs. Research is necessary to identify and address the unique contraceptive needs of these two groups.

Teen pregnancies are a critical women's health concern. In clinical practice, health professionals can be alert for "the teachable moment" with children, parents, or families. School nurses might become more involved in classes on sex education, family living, values clarification, assertiveness training, and decision making. Research is needed to clarify the reasons couples, especially teens, do not use contraceptives and to evaluate interventions that promote contraceptive use. For instance, has a buddy system been initiated? (Girls and women regularly call female friends, and boys and men who call male friends to remind them to use contraception.) The buddy system is being tried with breast and testicular self-exam; research is needed to determine how effective this approach might be in increasing contraceptive use.

Many risk factors that women may have or may develop can complicate contraceptive choice. Systemic lupus erythematosus and sickle cell disease are examples. Women afflicted with these diseases should be involved in the contraception decision because only they can balance the risk of the contraceptive against the risk of pregnancy.

Much research has already been done to identify risk factors for the various contraceptive methods, but research must be continuous as methods are redesigned and new contraceptive methods are developed.

Behavioral disorders create a variety of challenging problems involving contraception. Compliance and side effects are difficult to evaluate in women with behavioral disorders—for example, depressed women who are subject to mood changes. In cases where OCs, IUDs, and injectables are used, clinicians should emphasize the need to use one method for contraception and another method (condoms and/or spermicides) for protection against sexually transmitted disease. An important but difficult area of research is the use of contraception and STD protection among the frequently "lost to follow-up" street people.

Speroff and DeCharney's (1993) article comparing the three new progestins to oral contraceptives previously on the market may be of interest to clinicians and some clients. Most clients are primarily interested in effectiveness and side effects such as bleeding, missed periods, weight gain, and acne. The authors discuss these side effects as well as other physiologic changes. Because many of the studies reviewed were small, larger clinical trials are needed. It would be helpful if new studies could replicate some of the previous methodology so that meaningful comparisons can be made.

Emergency contraception is an exceedingly important option that should be available to all women. However, women should be informed that there are potential complications regardless of whether they choose the older method of taking larger doses of oral contraceptives, or postcoital insertion of an IUD, or the newer oral emergency contraceptives. Ectopic pregnancy (in a uterine tube instead of in the uterus) has been reported following treatment with larger doses of OCs. Clients should be informed of this risk. A history of blood clots is a contraindication for this method. If an IUD is inserted, clients should be informed about the risk of pelvic inflammatory disease (PID). IUDs are contraindicated if there is a history of ectopic pregnancy or PID. Further clinical trials are needed to evaluate the effectiveness of the newer approaches to emergency contraception such as progestins, RU 486, and danazol.

Contraceptive vaccines and melatonin are still in the early stages of research. This area is wide open for clinical research on effectiveness, side effects, and complications.

Oddens (1993) and Sai (1993) address the cost of contraceptives relative to availability and choice. Oddens' conclusion that cost does not seem to have much effect on women's choice of birth control method is surprising. Considering these findings, practitioners and researchers need to evaluate the basis on which women make their contraceptive choices.

Sai (1993) discusses a variety of factors that affect a woman's ability to obtain the contraceptive of her choice. It is important for clinics that provide contraceptives to consider not only the cost of the product, but the cost of delivery to the consumer: the expense of frequent return visits, travel costs, waiting time, and time lost from work.

The article by Westhoff, Marks, and Rosenfield (1993) on the training of obstetrical and gynecological (OB/Gyn) residents is disturbing. An adequate clinical experience for OB/Gyn residents cannot be left to optional, elective, or moonlighting opportunities. The limitations on education and on the availability of contraceptives are serious problems now, but the lack of physicians trained in pregnancy termination may become critical over time. Early-trimester abortion services are currently provided in some areas by nurse practitioners and physician assistants with physician backup. This increases the availability of services. However, second-trimester abortions and complications from first-trimester abortions often require the direct care of a physician. Research is needed to evaluate the quality of training and of the abortion services delivered by nonphysician health professionals. If future gynecologists are to provide the family planning options that women want and need, specific competency goals must be established in OB/Gyn resident training.

It is vital that political activity be initiated to create change in federal, state, and local government health care practices that discriminate against women. These practices are guided by national health care policies that provide inadequate funding of family planning clinics and restrictive laws concerning pregnancy termination. We need the energy of a revitalized women's movement to bring about these changes. Improving the status of women will directly increase the well-being of the family. At present, many social, religious, and political leaders of both conservative and liberal backgrounds agree that the deterioration of the family unit is a major cause of the rising crime and violence in our country. The status of women has a direct effect on the family unit. Unfortunately, as Daley and Gold (1993) point out, the current level of public funding for contraception and abortion presents a rather dismal picture of current and future health care.

Our national and international policies have both a direct and an indirect effect on women and their families in many other countries as well as our own. Our position as one of the more influential world leaders increases the importance of making changes in restrictive policies toward women. We need people who are willing to become politically active in demanding that all women have access to the contraceptive of their choice, with abortion as a backup if their contraceptive fails.

REFERENCES

Diczfalusy, E. (1993). Contraceptive prevalence, reproductive health and our common future. *Obstetrical & Gynecological Survey, 48*(5), 321–332.

Fathalla, M. (1993). Contraception and women's health. *British Medical Bulletin, 49*(1), 245–251.

Federation of Feminist Women's Health Centers. (1991). *A new view of a woman's body*. West Hollywood, CA: Feminist Health Press.

Mishell, D. (1993). Vaginal contraceptive rings. *Annals of Medicine, 25,* 191–197.

Anastasi, J. (1993, June). What to tell patients about the female condom. *Nursing 93,* 71–73.

This short article provides helpful information for education about use of the female condom for contraception and sexually transmitted disease (STD) protection. The current effectiveness rate of female condoms for birth control is based on the initial 6 months of use. This would most likely inflate the failure rate: other female barriers also have higher failure rates during the first few months of use, when couples are learning a new contraceptive method. Studies that evaluate female condom use over an extended period of time are needed to determine the effectiveness of this method both as a contraceptive and for protection against STDs.

Bouris, K. (1993). *The first time.* Berkeley, CA: Conari Press.

This is an important book for individuals involved in women's health care. It contains many descriptions, in women's own words, of first sexual encounters. The descriptions were collected by the researcher from 150 responses to 1,000 questionnaires given or mailed to women in a variety of settings. The questionnaires went to women's shelters, support groups, professional associations, clubs, colleges, special-interest-group mailing lists, friends, and professional contacts. The author also interviewed women who felt more comfortable speaking than writing; this group ranged from homeless women to busy working mothers.

Women respondents related some positive experiences but the majority reported that their first sexual experience was negative—humiliating, shameful, painful—even when it was not legal rape. This research may be biased in that women with negative reactions may be more likely to respond than would those who had had positive experiences.

Braverman, P., & Strasburger, V. (1993, December). Contraception. *Clinical Pediatrics, Adolescent Sexuality Part 2,* 725–734.

The United States has the highest rate of teen pregnancy in the Western world. One half of adolescents in the United States are sexually active by age 17. Although the rate of sexual activity is lower than the rest of the world, US teens are less likely to use contraception. One reason, the authors state, is that information on contraceptives is more difficult for teenagers to obtain in the United States. Sexuality education is not available in many elementary and junior high schools, where a high number of students are already sexually active. This information is not communicated in most homes, and teenagers are often afraid, for several reasons, to go to their family physician—if they have one. Many teens fear that their parents might find out or that the staff may be judgmental. Others cannot afford to pay for office visits. The result is that the average time between first intercourse and a visit to a health care facility is 1 year, and this visit is often made to rule out pregnancy. Unfortunately, half of adolescent pregnancies occur in the first 6 months after first intercourse and 20% occur in the first month.

Many teens in this report said practitioners should initiate a discussion on the subject of contraceptives because students were too shy to ask. Others do not know where to get contraceptives, cannot get to a clinic, or fear the pelvic exam. Fear is especially widespread among those who have been abused, and the experience of previous pelvic exams does not decrease this fear.

Most gynecologists, two-thirds of general practitioners, and one-third of pediatricians are willing to provide contraceptive services to a 15-year-old. However, one-fifth of gynecologists, two-fifths of general practitioners, and two-thirds of pediatricians would require parental consent. This may explain why many teens are reluctant to seek the more effective prescriptive contraceptive methods.

An understanding of adolescent development is important for health care practitioners who deliver services to this population. There are two very important considerations. First, adolescents are progressing from concrete to abstract thinking. Individuals who cannot think abstractly cannot adequately solve complex problems or comprehend the consequences of their actions. Some adolescents believe they are invulnerable to harm. Adolescents who acknowledge their sexuality and the risks associated with sexual activity and who are willing to tell others they use contraceptives are at less risk for unwanted pregnancies and STDs. In addition, those who seek out family planning and make their own appointments are less likely to engage in unsafe sex practices.

Second, peer influence is often more important than that of adults. Peer educators are especially helpful in teaching content on sexuality. Peers are also a source of support. The authors state that teenage males are more likely to use condoms if they have peer support.

Chalker, R., & Downer, C. (1992). *A Woman's Book of Choices*. New York: Four Walls Eight Windows.

A Woman's Book of Choices addresses the option of abortion when contraceptives fail. It contains a wonderful account of the women's health movement during the early 1970s.

Subjects covered are the women's self-health movement, menstrual extractions by women's groups, and the start-up and control of abortion clinics by women. There are drawings of the Del-Em menstrual extraction kit and information on prostaglandins and abortifacient herbs. The authors also list dangerous folk remedies that are ineffective.

The book contains a chapter on RU-486 (mifepristone), a drug that acts against progesterone (the hormone that maintains pregnancy). To be effective, RU-486 must be taken within seven to nine weeks after the last menstrual period, and it is more effective when a prostaglandin is used concurrently. Because of increased risk of heart attack and stroke, the drug is contraindicated in women ages 35 and over who smoke.

There is a very good chapter on abortion complications, but emergency contraception is not adequately addressed. The authors provide an extensive list of women's clinics in the United States although some information may be out-of-date. For example, both the Iowa abortion clinic addresses are incorrect.

Women who lived through the feminist revolution of the 1960s and 1970s might enjoy this revisit to the past, and young women may be interested in their "herstory."

Coley, K. (1993). Contraception: What pharmacists should tell their patients. *American Pharmacy*, NS33(9), 55–64.

We appear to be moving toward a fuller use of pharmacists' knowledge & skills. Much of the education of pharmacists has been underutilized for many years. This article is an excellent general refresher course on the menstrual cycle and contraceptives.

Comp, P., & Zacur, H. (1993). Contraceptive choices in women with coagulation disorders. *American Journal of Obstetrics & Gynecology*, 168(6), Part 2, 1990–1993.

This article reviews blood clot formation and the diseases or other conditions (such as surgery) that increase risk of blood clots. The importance of ruling out risk factors when choosing contraceptives is emphasized. The authors point out that the effectiveness of oral contraceptives (OCs) may make them a good choice for contraception among women taking anticoagulants. These women need effective contraception because of the increased risk of (1) birth defects from taking anticoagulants, and (2) bleeding into the abdomen at ovulation while on anticoagulants. Practitioners should pass on this information to clients when obtaining informed consent. Because of the seriousness of coagulation disorders, this condition has generated much research activity over the past 30 years.

Daley, D., & Gold, R. (1993). Public funding for contraceptive, sterilization and abortion services, Fiscal Year 1992. *Family Planning Perspectives, 25*(6), 244–251.

This study reports that total public expenditures for contraceptive services have decreased by 27% since 1980 and that Medicaid has replaced Title X as the primary source of funding for contraceptive services. Federal funds are provided through four major sources:

1. Title X (Public Health Service Act): Family Planning
2. Title V (Social Security Act): Maternal and child health block grant
3. Title XIX: Medicaid
4. Title XX: Social Services block grant

The Department of Health and Human Services (DHHS) distributes Title V and Title XX grants to public and private agencies through its 10 regional offices. Title V and Title XX block grants go to state government agencies, and they determine what, if any, funding goes to family planning. With Title V programs, the state must match $4 of federal funds with $3 of state funds. Title XX, which needs no matching funds, is distributed by state social services agencies.

Title XIX (Medicaid) uses both federal and state funds in providing medical care to low-income people. Medicaid is an entitlement program in which the amount of funding is determined by reimbursement for services, not by set congressional appropriations.

Title X is the only federal program in which the primary purpose is providing family planning services. The diminished role of Title X is significant to family planning services because, unlike Medicaid, which pays for direct patient care services, Title X provides money for creating or expanding clinic sites.

In 1977, the Hyde Amendment nearly eliminated use of federal funds for abortions. The majority of abortions for poor women are now performed in the 13 states on the east and west coasts that have continued to fund abortions for the poor. The lack of adequate funding creates a severe limitation on women's access to health care.

Drife, J. (1993). Contraceptive problems in the developed world. *British Medical Bulletin, 49*(1), 17–26.

"Many countries developed in economic terms have underdeveloped contraceptive services," states this author. Surveys indicate that 50% of the pregnancies in Great Britain and the United States are unplanned. High abortion rates are a byproduct of inadequate planning and lack of contraceptive availability. The unavailability of contraceptives is especially significant for young women in the United States. Countries with open attitudes toward sexuality have lower rates of teenage pregnancy. The Netherlands promotes public matter-of-fact discussion of sex in both the public arena and within the family. The U.S. capitalizes on sex in advertising but strongly discourages sex education in schools. The U.S. abortion rate is 28 (per 1,000 women ages 15 to 44); in the Netherlands, the rate is only 5.6. Reducing the number of unplanned pregnancies in the United States will result in fewer abortions.

Ford, N., & Mathie, E. (1993). The acceptability and experience of the female condom, Femidom, among family planning clinic attenders. *The British Journal of Family Planning,* *19,* 187–192.

This study of the Femidom female condom was conducted in the United Kingdom. Femidom, renamed for sale abroad, is the Reality female condom produced in the United States. This research is important for its insights, from the users' perspective, on the advantages and disadvantages of the female condom. The information is also helpful for counseling clients.

Of the 142 users who returned the questionnaire after first use, 67 continued to use the condom for three months. One-third of the sample were health professionals—a fact that could bias the study results: some health professionals have negative attitudes toward the female barrier contraceptives, cervical caps and diaphragms. Their negativism may be due in part to the lower use effectiveness rates of the cap and diaphragm and to unfamiliarity with these methods. All couples in the study were using, and continued to use, a nonbarrier contraceptive method in addition to the female condom. This concomitant use was required because acceptance of the condom, not its effectiveness, was being tested. Questionnaires were completed upon admission to the study, after the first, fifth, and tenth uses, and after 3 months of use.

Many people, seeing the condom for the first time, commented on its appearance and large size. Initially, there was some difficulty with insertion, but on the tenth use 70% reported that it was easy to insert (compared with 25% on first use). Some important advantages of the female condom are:

- Contraceptive effectiveness
- Protection, controlled by women, against pregnancy and STDs.

The following reasons were given for discontinuing use:

- Discomfort to either partner
- Difficult to use (including insertion)
- Negative affect on sex life (less enjoyable or spontaneous)
- Male partner resistance
- Preference for the method previously used
- Noise during use.

Discomfort originated from the rings or from insufficient lubrication. However, many women complained that the condom was so slippery that insertion was difficult.

Resistance by the male partner was a reason given for discontinuation throughout the study. The report after first use indicated one-fourth of women had trouble getting their partner to agree to use the Femidom. Partner resistance rose to 30% on tenth use. These results indicate a need to make the condom attractive to men as well as women. A few women were embarrassed by the outer ring of the condom hanging out. One woman said, "it rustled as I walked."

The significant problems with Femidom were:

- The penis entering outside the outer ring
- The outer ring being pushed inside
- The condom slipping out
- Leakage of sperm from the condom either inside or outside the vagina.

Despite the problems with the female condom, it is another option that allows women to protect themselves against pregnancy and sexually transmitted diseases.

Fraser, I. (1993). Contraceptive choice for women with "risk factors." *Drug Safety, 8*(4), 271–279.

Counseling an individual or couple on contraceptive methods needs to take into account the risk to the woman of an unplanned pregnancy. This article is a thorough review of the medical risks, side effects, and complications associated with contraceptive methods, and should be useful to practitioners when helping clients select a method and educating them on proper usage.

Hale, R., Char, D., Nagy, K., & Stockert, N. (1993). Seventeen-year review of sexual and contraceptive behavior on a college campus. *American Journal of Obstetrics & Gynecology, 168*(6), Part 1, 1833–1838.

This survey of students at the University of Hawaii was compared to similar studies done in 1974 and 1979. Of the 1,921 questionnaires mailed, 40% were returned. Compared with data from 1974 and 1979, more students had intercourse at a younger age with slightly less use of contraception.

Additional questions were asked about onset of sexual activity, number of sexual partners, type of contraceptives used and consistency of use, sexually transmitted diseases, the impact of AIDS on condom use, and sexual assault or abuse. Approximately one-fourth of women reported being forced to have sexual intercourse.

This study suggests that many young people are at risk for pregnancy and STDs, including AIDS.

Hankoff, L., & Darney, P. (1993). Contraceptive choices for behaviorally disordered women. *American Journal of Obstetrics & Gynecology, 168*(6), Part 2, 1986–1989.

Depression, anxiety, and thought disorganization often make contraceptive choices more difficult. The choice becomes more complicated when, as often occurs in behavioral disorders, the afflicted women also abuse drugs. Protection from sexually transmitted disease is another important consideration. Psychiatric clinicians often forget or ignore clients' birth control needs. Because these women often are already compromised in their ability to cope, pregnancy and motherhood may exacerbate their behavioral disorder. Informed consent may be difficult to obtain because of these women's diminished ability to understand the risks, benefits, and alternatives of contraceptives.

Women who take phenthiazines or tricylic antidepressants may have elevated prolactin levels leading to breast discharge, lack of ovulation, and no menstrual periods. Women taking anticonvulsants may need higher doses (50 micrograms) of estrogen.

Heath, C. (1993). Helping patients choose appropriate contraception. *American Family Physician, 48*(6), 1115–1124.

For busy practitioners, this article is a good review of birth control methods. Several tables give concise information on topics such as contraceptive effectiveness, episodic and continual methods with contraindications, advantages and disadvantages, comparative costs of methods, and suggested follow-up schedules for different methods. Some of the tables might be shared with clients during contraceptive education.

Howard, R., Lissis, C., & Tuck, S. (1993, June 26). Contraceptives, counseling, and pregnancy in women with sickle cell disease. *British Medical Journal, 306*, 1735–1737.

Pregnancy can be a serious situation for women with sickle cell disease. Medical staff frequently advise against pregnancy, but the advice is frequently ignored. In this study of 156 sexually active women ages 17–53, 67 (45%) had taken oral contraceptives (OCs) at some time and 19% had used an intrauterine device (IUD). Most authors report that the IUD is safe in women with sickle cell disease. Of the 67 women who used OCs, four reported an increase in sickle cell crises and two women had thrombophlebitis (blood clot in the leg). The exact dose of oral contraceptives was not known; assuming clinic policy was followed, the dosage was low. Thirty women in the study (20%) used progesterone pills, and 26 women (17%) used injectable progestogens; neither group had serious side effects.

The high rate of pregnancy in this study (64%) suggests that use of contraceptives is far from adequate. However, a weakness in this study is the lack of a control group to assess rates of unplanned pregnancy in the general population. The authors offer only a statement that a previous report suggests the rate is around 32%.

Practitioners must balance the risks of contraceptive use against both the risks of serious complications from contraceptive use and the risks from pregnancy. In the absence of specific data to the contrary, the authors suggest that all methods of contraception must be considered with caution. Research is needed on the impact of modern methods of contraception on sickle cell disease.

Julkunen, H., Kaaja, R., & Friman, C. (1993). Contraceptive practice in women with systemic lupus erythematosus. *British Journal of Rheumatology, 32*(3), 227–230.

Women with systemic lupus erythematosus (SLE), a disease of the immune system in which the body damages its own tissues, including blood vessels, are less likely to use contraception than healthy women. In addition, they tend to use safer but less effective birth control—probably on the advice of doctors regarding the side effects and complications of oral contraceptives (OCs) and intrauterine devices (IUDs) in women with SLE. Vessel damage increases the risk of heart attacks and thrombophlebitis, and infection is more likely because of the compromise to the immune system. Case reports and one retrospective study indicate that OCs make SLE worse, but this information is based on the older, higher-dose pills. New low-dose OCs and the progesterone-releasing IUD have fewer side effects and, in the future, may be used more often by women with SLE.

Women in general need to know about the decreased risk of side effects in current OCs and IUDs. This area warrants future research.

Lahteenmaki, P. (1993). Postabortal contraception. *Annals of Medicine, 25,* 185–189.

Return of fertility may be rapid after a first-trimester abortion. The first ovulation may occur in two weeks, and 50% of women have ovulated within three weeks postabortion. Estrogen and progesterone levels drop within a few days; however, human chorionic gonadatropin is present an average of 38 days later, and may be present until after the first postabortal menstrual period.

All of the most effective methods of contraception—IUD insertion, implants, injectables, and oral contraceptives—may be used immediately after the abortion procedure. These authors warn that some methods could mask or even cause complications. For example, the IUD introduces a slight increased risk of perforation, infection, expulsion, and prolonged postabortal bleeding. The authors also state that hypercoagulability may occur with oral contraceptive use. Because hypercoagulability may persist one to two weeks after the abortion procedure, clinicians should consider delaying the start of oral contraceptives until 1 week after the abortion procedure. Concern about hypercoagulability needs to be balanced against the need for immediate contraception. Research studies should be done to determine whether this slight risk of hypercoagulability is clinically significant and, if it is, to identify where the risk of hypercoagulability stops so that the safe use of oral contraceptives may be started as soon as possible.

Lincoln, D. (1993). Contraception for the year 2020. *British Medical Bulletin, 49*(1), 222–236.

Those who enjoy biochemistry might find this technical article easy to read. Others may wish to confine themselves to the abstract. Three new methods of contraception are described:

1. A follicle-stimulating hormone (FSH) antagonist that will prevent ovulation;

2. A human chorionic gonadatropin (hCG) antagonist that would cause deterioration of

the corpus luteum (egg sac in the ovary) to bring on menses;

3. A binding protein to inactivate lutinizing hormone (LH) and hCG (currently administered as a vaccine).

Antibody titers from the vaccine are lasting approximately 6 months. Another potential vaccine may be developed from the peptides (amino acids) of the zona pellucida (egg) and sperm. The author states that it is easier to intercept a small transient signal than to neutralize a hormone present throughout the menstrual cycle, and this technique may be safer for women.

Administration of peptides is difficult. They cannot be taken orally because of enzyme breakdown. Other possible routes are nasal spray, vaginal ring, and injection. Vaccination and gene therapy may provide the right dose to the right place at the right time. Peptides that regulate the reproductive cycle can be made antigenic (capable of stimulating antibodies) through the immune system. Antibodies inactivate antigens and can interrupt the reproductive cycle. However, there is a risk that the autoantibodies may damage cells that generate the antigen. Reversibility depends on a decline in the antibody titer which may be unpredictable and long-term.

A product with an interrupted signal could offer control and reversibility. Every 28 days, the foreign material could be activated to prevent pregnancy or activated to assist pregnancy. This is an idea with potential.

Oddens, B. (1993). Evaluation of the effect of contraceptive prices on demand in eight Western European countries. *Advances in Contraception, 9,* 1–11.

This study has surprising results. Although various national reimbursement policies have created wide differences in individual costs for contraception among European countries, contraceptive choices were *not* related to national reimbursement programs.

Either there were errors in the study or important factors other than cost entered into the choice of contraceptives. Annual costs were calculated per method, and the type of provider was noted. In calculating annual expenditure, it was assumed that couples would use one method through their fertile years, although most couples use several methods. It is not known how this factor might affect the results. More information is needed about factors that influence women's contraceptive choices.

Psychoyos, A., Creatsas, G., Hassan, E., Georgoulias, V., & Gravanis, A. (1993). Spermicidal and antiviral properties of cholic acid: Contraceptive efficacy of a new vaginal sponge (Protectaid) containing sodium cholate. *Human Reproduction, 8*(6), 866–869.

This is a report of a study of 20 women who used a new spermicidal sponge for one year. The effectiveness was 100%. The main spermicidal ingredient was cholic acid (sodium cholate), which is known to have strong spermicidal and antiviral properties. In addition, it contained low concentrations (0.5%) of nonoxynol-9 (a spermicide) and benzalkonium chloride (a germicide). Cholic acid is a natural substance that is present in high concentrations in uterine fluids during the last part of the menstrual cycle.

The sponge is inserted within 12 hours preceding sexual intercourse and is left in place for 4 to 6 hours after the last act of intercourse. Studies with rats showed no signs of vaginal irritation, unlike the Today contraceptive sponge, which produced vaginal irritation that resolved after 72 hours. The antiviral properties of cholic acid may help prevent the spread of the human immunodeficiency virus that can cause AIDS. The sponge has not been approved for use in the United States because of the limited research. Before approval will be considered, larger clinical research studies are needed on the side effects and effectiveness of this new contraceptive method.

Sai, F. (1993). Political and economic factors influencing contraceptive uptake. *British Medical Bulletin, 49*(1), 200–209.

This author discusses the ways traditional and moralistic groups can restrict availability of contraceptives. Traditionalists fear the freedom contraceptive choices give to women. Politics influences family planning policies and population, overtly or covertly, and may also influence social policies that affect availability and use. Governments wishing to increase birthrates may restrict the availability of contraceptives and, at the same time, increase payments for expectant mothers, provide state-supported care of children, and give a monthly allowance to parents. National or local governments that wish to "ethnically cleanse" a population may coerce people into limiting their family size. The U.S. "Mexico City Policy" of not funding any organization that promotes abortion has had a significant impact on family planning programs (regardless of whether they used U.S. money).

Another important factor affecting the availability of contraceptives is their cost. When considering contraceptive costs, one must include the cost of the product, the cost of delivery to the consumer, and ancillary costs such as travel and waiting time. When planning delivery of health services, total costs to the consumer often are not given equal consideration alongside the convenience of the clinic staff who provide the services. Frequently, consumers are expected to take time from work (which may mean loss of pay), or to wait for long periods of time in order to access services during clinic hours.

In addition to costs, contraceptive use is affected by the education of women and their perception of children as either an economic asset or an expense. Where children contribute to family income, family size tends to be larger. If children are perceived as an expense, as occurs when providing them with educational and social opportunities, family size tends to be smaller.

Schenker, J., & Rabenou, V. (1993). Family planning: Cultural and religious perspectives. *Human Reproduction, 8*(6), 969–976.

For those interested in a history of birth control methods from ancient to modern times or in the influence of major religions on contraceptive use, this article is recommended. Contraception educators may find it helpful in understanding culturally and religiously diverse populations. Investigating cultural or religious differences through a case study methodology is a valuable form of explanatory research.

Silman, R. (1993). Melatonin: A contraceptive for the nineties. *European Journal of Obstetrics & Gynecology & Reproductive Biology, 49*, 3–9.

Is it an evolutionary phenomenon or does the presence of artificial light cause human beings to be fertile throughout all four seasons (unlike many animals, which spend more time in darkness during the winter)? This article explores this question.

The pineal gland transforms nervous input (light/dark) from the optic nerve into the hormonal output (melatonin) that controls reproduction. Light stimulates the hypothalamic gonadatropin-releasing hormone (GnRH) pulse generator. The pulse generator activates the pituitary gland. The pituitary gland stimulates the ovary through the pituitary hormones—follicle-stimulating hormone (FSH) and lutinizing hormone (LH).

Darkness prolongs nighttime release of melatonin from the pineal gland, which elevates melatonin levels. Levels above 500 picomoles per liter (pmol/1) inactivate the hypothalamic GnRH pulse generator, thus interfering with ovulation in females. Melatonin levels are higher in children than in adults, which is why the reproductive cycle does not operate in children.

For melatonin to be used as birth control, the problem of maintaining the concentration above 500 pmol/1 for 12 to 14 hours at night must be solved. A dose of 75 milligrams has been shown to inhibit release of gonadotrophins for more than 12 hours. In the Netherlands, melatonin is currently in phase III clinical trials as a contraceptive. Side effects of this method are not covered in this article.

Speroff, L., DeCherney, A., & The Advisory Board for the New Progestins. (1993). Evaluation of a new generation of oral contraceptives. *Obstetrics & Gynecology, 81*(6), 1034–1047.

Data for this article were collected and analyzed from approximately 100 published reports on phasic and fixed-dose pills, dating back to 1980. The authors examined effectiveness, breakthrough bleeding and missed menses, androgenicity, and coagulation, carbohydrate, and lipid metabolism. They concluded that the new formulations—desogstrel, gestodene, and norgestimate—were similar to each other and to other low-dose pills. The new pills appeared to have fewer androgenic effects and to have less effect on carbohydrate and lipoprotein metabolism. Cycle control was similar to other low-dose pills. There were minor changes in coagulation-promoting and antithrombotic factors. Because of the small sample size and methodologic differences between studies, it is not possible to determine clinical relevance. For those who are wondering about the differences between the new OCs and the older pills, this article offers a wealth of information.

Sulak, P., & Haney, A. (1993). Unwanted pregnancies: Understanding contraceptive use and benefits in adolescents and older women. *American Journal of Obstetrics & Gynecology, 168*(6), Part 2, 2042–2048.

The highest percentages of unintended pregnancies and the largest increases in birthrates reported in the United States in recent years were in adolescents and in women older than 35. In 1989, the Centers for Disease Control (CDC) reported that very young adolescents averaged almost one abortion for every live birth. Women more than 40 years old averaged one abortion for every two live births.

Already a higher-risk group, teenagers had significantly more high-risk second-trimester abortions. Informing teens of the benefits of different contraceptive methods may encourage their usage. Moreover, older women need information about gynecologic problems they have or may experience. As problems occur, they need contraceptives responsive to their changing needs.

Van Look, P., & von Hertzen, H. (1993). Emergency contraception. *British Medical Bulletin, 49*(1), 158–170.

Family planning programs must make emergency contraception available to more women. Widespread access to emergency contraception is overdue: the technology to make these methods has been known for 30 years.

Emergency contraception (also called "the morning-after pill" and postcoital contraception) is a one-time procedure used after intercourse to prevent pregnancy. It can be used up to 10 to 14 days after unprotected intercourse that takes place near ovulation. This makes the term "morning-after pill" incorrect and confusing.

Combined estrogen/progestin pills (Ovral) can be used by women. Two pills are taken 12 hours apart (a total of 4 pills in a 12-hour span).

Another form of emergency contraception is the copper IUD. It may be inserted before implantation, up to 5 to 6 days after ovulation.

Newer approaches are progestin-only pills (2 doses of 0.75 mg taken 12 hours apart), danazol (2 or 3 doses of 400 mg each at 12-hour intervals), and mifepristone (RU-486). Women tend to use progestin and danazol, which have fewer side effects, more than Ovral. The side effects of danazol are also shorter and milder.

Westhoff, C., Marks, F., & Rosenfield, A. (1993). Residency training in contraception, sterilization, and abortion. *Obstetrics & Gynecology, 81*(2), 331–314.

Information on the training of OB/Gyn residents was collected by questionnaire from residency program directors and from chief residents in most of the programs. Residents and program directors reported similar didactic experiences but residents reported less experience than did their program directors.

The Council on Residency Education in OB/Gyn has educational objectives that describe the knowledge and skills residents must have. These objectives state that residents should be able to "educate the patient, and prescribe, fit or insert the form of contraceptive selected." They should also be able to carry out sterilization and first- and second-trimester abortion procedures. The last objective is weakened by an alternative objective of being able to "arrange contact with a facility or personnel" who can provide such care. Only 13% of OB/Gyn residency programs had a family planning rotation and 46% of chief residents spent no time in a family planning clinic setting during their 4 years of residency. Thirty-four percent of the programs have an abortion service but only 20% of residents spend any time there. Oral contraceptives and tubal ligations were the only methods most residents had substantial experience with in their clinical rotations. Gynecologists who are familiar only with OCs and tubal ligations are unlikely to recommend other methods to their patients.

Part VI

Physical Diseases and Health Problems

Chapter 9

Women's Cardiovascular Health

Karyn Holm, PhD, RN, FAAN
Sue Penckofer, PhD, RN

There has been increased emphasis on the cardiovascular health of women since the publication of the previous review (Holm & Penck-ofer, 1993). First, under a federal mandate, research must include women and minorities or, if not, give good cause for their exclusion (Marshall, 1994). Second, research funding initiatives, both federal and nonfederal, have been and are currently directed toward women. A good example is the call for applications from the National Institute of Aging and the National Institute for Nursing Research (NIH Guide for Grants and Contracts, 1993) to conduct studies that examine women's transition into menopause and related outcomes. With the onset of menopause, the incidence of coronary and vascular disease increases. Third, because the diagnosis and treatment of women have been shown to be biased (Steingart et al., 1991), efforts are under way in most major healthcare institutions across the country to prevent this bias from recurring. Recently, investigators identified that, rather than sex bias, the problem is the fact that women have a lower rate of positive exercise tests and, hence, a lower rate of referral for cardiac catheterization (Mark, Shaw, DeLong, Califf, & Pryor, 1994).

Contemporary thinking suggests that the risk factors for coronary disease are similar for men and women. Factors that cannot be modified include gender (women at older years); age (rates increase with advancing age); family history (positive family history increases risk); and race (black men and women are at greater risk). Modifiable risk factors are hypertension (risk increases with increased blood pressure); cigarette smoking (rates are higher in women); hyperlipidemia (women seem more susceptible); obesity (women are more susceptible in their later years); physical inactivity (for both genders at all ages); diabetes (seems more important in women); and menopause (heart disease rates in women escalate after menopause). Changes in women's life-style are needed if their risk of cardiovascular disease is going to be reduced.

Since the mid- to late 1980s, when the American Heart Association and the National Institutes of Health identified coronary heart disease (CHD) in women as a priority, interest has escalated. Across the nation, conferences that address the issues and research designed to determine whether women have a different experience than men are now commonplace. With the push for cost containment in health care and the fact that women are living longer than men, coronary disease in women is an important health issue if women's later years are to be healthy years. The timing could not be better. Considerable gains have been made in recognizing the importance of the cardiovascular health of women. We cannot afford to lose the momentum.

IMPLICATIONS FOR EDUCATION, PRACTICE, AND RESEARCH

The need for studies of coronary risk and coronary disease in women continues. Since the 1980s, researchers have attended more to the study of women or at least have recognized the need to include women in their samples. Even the popular press reinforces what some researchers now claim. In a recent article in *Atlantic Monthly,* a male physician (Kadar, 1994) stressed that there is no bias in the diagnosis and treatment of women because women seek medical care more frequently than men do and, therefore, have more access to all available treatments. Yet, the time it takes for women to be diagnosed remains a critical concern. Consider the "yentyl syndrome," having to prove that you are a man before you can be treated like one (Healy, 1991). This phenomenon may be somewhat alleviated if women choose a female health care provider (Lurie et al., 1993) who will inherently be more understanding and attentive to their clinical presentation. It has also been repeatedly demonstrated that women are older and have more advanced symptoms and more comorbidity when they receive an initial diagnosis of coronary disease, which typically takes the form of angina. On the real issue—whether these older women are getting the same treatment as younger men—there is insufficient evidence to date.

Much more interest surrounds hormone therapy, particularly combination therapy. Guidelines for prescribing therapy are increasingly common in the literature. However, unlike the late 1980s and early 1990s, health care providers are now more likely to stress that each woman's health history must be considered before hormone therapy is initiated (Holm & Penckofer, in press). Studies of alternatives to hormone therapy, such as exercise, vitamins, and diet are now in order to determine whether these simple life-style changes are equally effective.

Race, socioeconomic status, and education all continue to be factors in coronary risk. Higher education and socioeconomic status are associated with lower risk for disease. Because women of color continue to have higher risk for coronary disease, efforts toward prevention should be aimed at nonwhite women. For all women, two important risk factors—obesity (defined as 30% above normal body weight for height) and inactivity—are more prevalent than ever before and deserve the same attention that has been directed at the reduction of smoking.

Implications for Education

Helping students to understand the issues surrounding heart disease in women is an imperative and a challenge. Undergraduate and graduate clinical courses need to address differences between risk factors and symptoms in men and women. For example, women have a tendency to gain weight around menopause, and increased body weight and inactivity often occur together; these facts should be included in any discussion of coronary risk factors in women. Another consideration is that, in most texts, the descriptions of angina are based on research and clinical experiences with men, who were long thought to be "typical" heart patients. Students should be taught to listen carefully to women when they report symptoms that may seem atypical, because they may signal the presence of ischemia or infarction. Because of the increasing awareness of bias in the diagnosis and treatment of women, students must be made aware of the possibility that health care providers may either underestimate or overestimate coronary disease in women. Further, because menopause, when viewed as a risk factor for heart disease, is modified by hormone therapy, the implications of hormone therapy for each individual woman must be considered. Discussions of benefits and risks of hormone replacement are necessary to ensure that students have the most current information needed to individualize therapy. More time must be spent considering the impact of race, socioeconomic status, and education on coronary risk. To be effective in caring for female patients, future nurses should be appraised of how these variables influence their own perceptions of female patients, the access these women will have to the health care system, and the resources available to support life-style changes.

Implications for Practice

The fact that women with coronary disease tend to be older and have more coexisting disease, such as arthritis and bone loss, should be considered when formulating plans of care. Because many of these women are post-menopausal, they are likely to have outlived their spouses, another key consideration during the rehabilitation phase of recovery.

In acute care, nurses can determine how congruent the symptoms are with the outcomes of diagnostic tests, and compare women's recovery from myocardial infarction or coronary artery bypass surgery with that of men. With decreased lengths of stay in acute care, the coordination with ambulatory services and home care must begin upon admission, to ensure follow-up after hospitalization. For those in primary care, there is an opportunity to help women implement life-style changes that are tailored to their risk-factor profiles. Helping women take an active role in their health care requires careful assessment of their personal and family histories, with particular attention to prior attempts at life-style changes. Clinicians who encourage women to ask questions about their health conditions, the treatment options, and the potential risks and benefits of different therapies recognize the importance of women becoming informed consumers of health care. Information should be delivered in manageable doses and tailored to each individual's educational level. Follow-up and patient education are essential to support women in their attempts at life-style changes. Written information, videotapes, and audiotapes are useful adjuncts to verbal instruction.

Implications for Research

The role of the researcher is to seek answers to questions that further our knowledge of heart disease in women. To this end, researchers who are partners with clinicians in designing and implementing studies are more likely to identify gaps in our current knowledge base and also address clinically meaningful questions. The experience of women in seeking diagnosis and treatment must be further delineated in an effort to improve access to and utilization of health care services. To determine whether life-style changes in younger women decrease the incidence of heart disease, future studies should explore prevention strategies in infants, school-age children, and young women.

Partnerships between clinical and basic science researchers would be useful to delineate the mechanisms underlying clinical and epidemiological observations. For example, even though we have observed that replacing estrogen at menopause cuts the risk of heart disease in half, we still don't understand how this occurs. In the absence of menstruation, is iron retained, and is iron really the culprit? Or age? Because of a growing conviction that estrogen therapy will prevent coronary disease in women, there is a need to follow up on women who take hormones, to determine whether their risk profile improves over time.

Clinical observations should be linked to physiological processes. For example, have we actually identified the precise cellular mechanisms that support the current status of estrogen as the vehicle to prevent heart disease in women? Probably not. If these mechanisms, as defined, have a true impact on disease rates, then we must determine the most therapeutic length of time women should take hormones.

One step in the right direction is the recently initiated 10-year study of hormone therapy and diet in women, funded by the National Institutes of Health. Yet, this is far from sufficient. The National Institute for Nursing Research, the National Institute on Aging, and the Heart, Lung and Blood Institute can have a significant impact on our knowledge of women and heart disease. Funding is needed to conduct ongoing longitudinal studies of women. The more knowledge we gain, the greater the likelihood that interventions will be found to prevent the serious and often devastating consequences of heart disease.

REFERENCES

Healy, B. (1991). The yentl syndrome. *New England Journal of Medicine, 325*(4), 274–276.

Holm, K., & Penckofer, S. (1993). Women's cardiovascular health. In B. McElmurry & R. Parker (Eds.), *Annual Review of Women's Health* (pp. 289–310). New York: National League for Nursing Press.

Holm, K., & Penckofer, S. (in press). What women should know about hormone therapy. *American Journal of Nursing.*

Kader, A. (1994, August). The sex bias myth in medicine. *The Atlantic Monthly,* 66–70.

Lurie, M. D., Slater, J., McGovern, P., Ekstrum, J., Quam, L., & Margolis, K. (1993). Preventive care for women: Does the sex of the physician matter? *New England Journal of Medicine, 329*(7), 478–482.

Mark, D. B., Shaw, L. K., DeLong, E. R., Califf, R. M., & Pryor, D. B. (1994). Absence of sex bias in the referral of patients for cardiac catherization. *New England Journal of Medicine, 330* (16), 1101–1106.

Marshall, E. (1994). New law brings affirmative action to clinical research. *Science, 263*(4), 602.

NIH Guide for Grants and Contracts. (1993, September 3). Menopause and health in aging women. *NIH Guide, 22* (32), 6–8. Bethesda, MD: National Institutes of Health.

Steingart, R. M., Packer, M., Hamm, P., Coglianese, M. E., Gersh, B., Geltman, E. M., Sollano, J., Katz, S., Moye, L., Basta, L. L., Lewis, S. J., Gottlieb, S. S., Bernstein, V., McEwan, P., Jacobson, K., Brown, E. J., Kukin, M. L., Kantrowitz, N. E., Pfeffer, M. A., for the Survival and Ventricular Enlargement Investigators. (1991). Sex differences in the management of coronary artery disease. *New England Journal of Medicine, 325*(4), 226–230.

Demographics, Educational Level, Race, and Socioeconomic Status

Becker, L. B., Han, B. H., Meyer, P. M., Wright, F. A., Rhodes, K. V., Smith, D. W., Barrett, J., & the CPR Chicago Project. (1993). Racial differences in the incidence of cardiac arrest and subsequent survival. *New England Journal of Medicine, 329*(9), 600–606.

Data from all nontraumatic, out-of-hospital cardiac arrests in Chicago from January 1, 1987, through December 31, 1988, were analyzed. The population comprised 6,451 patients, of which 3,207 (50%) were white, 2,910 (45%) were black, and 334 (5%) were other races; 3,664 (57%) were men and 2,787 (43%) were women. The average age was 67.4 years, and the women were approximately 5 years older than the men. The incidence of cardiac arrest was significantly higher for blacks than for whites in all age groups. The higher survival rate noted for whites was similar among white men and white women. The association between race and survival remained, even when controlling for coronary risk factors.

Cooper, R. S., & Ford, E. (1992). Comparability of risk factors for coronary heart disease among blacks and whites in the NHANES-1

epidemiologic follow-up study. *Annals of Epidemiology, 2*(5), 637–645.

The true incidence of heart disease in blacks relative to whites, an issue that has been unclear for many years, is addressed in this analysis of 12,599 persons. Black men and women experienced higher age-adjusted mortality than their white counterparts. However, hospitalization rates for blacks were lower than for whites. The strength of coronary risk factors was similar for both races in all age groups; the exceptions were smoking and body mass index, which were stronger in white women.

Kannel, W. B., & Vokonas, P. S. (1992). Demographics of the prevalence, incidence, and management of coronary heart disease in the elderly and in women. *Annals of Epidemiology, 2*(1/2), 5–14.

It is projected that the U.S. population over 65 years will double to 60 million by 2030, and that nearly 70% of all deaths in people older than 75 will be attributable to coronary heart disease (CHD). With the significant increase in the female elderly population and the fact that women often do not experience coronary disease until well after menopause, the need to understand coronary disease in these groups is intensified. The most common manifestation of CHD in men is myocardial infarction, commonly called a heart attack; in women, it is angina pectoris, commonly called chest pain. The most important risk factors in both elderly men and women are hypertension and diabetes. Assessment of all coronary risk factors and interventions to modify risk are important. Serum lipids are usually more elevated in older women than in older men, which demonstrates the need for research directed at lowering lipids in women.

Kaplan, G. A., & Keil, J. E. (1993). Socioeconomic factors and cardiovascular disease: A review of the literature. *Circulation, 88*(4), 1973–1998.

The relationship between lower socioeconomic status (SES) and poor health has been observed for centuries. Today, this relationship holds true for cardiovascular disease: low SES may be important enough to be considered an independent risk factor associated with cardiovascular disease. Psychosocial factors such as social isolation, social support or lack of it, coping styles, job stress and strain, anger, and hostility may activate the relationship between SES and cardiovascular disease. Deaths from coronary disease are proportionately higher in lower SES groups—perhaps a result of their having more heart disease risk factors. Hypertension, smoking, obesity, and physical inactivity are more prevalent at lower SES levels. More information is needed, however, to determine the relationships among cholesterol, diabetes, and SES. Many people of low SES status, particularly the working poor who are without health insurance, do not have access to health care. Public education concerning the prevention of cardiovascular disease in lower SES groups is recommended.

Keil, J. E., Sutherland, S. E., Knapp, R. G., Lackland, D. T., Gazes, P. C., & Tyroler, H. A. (1993). Mortality rates and risk factors for coronary disease in black as compared with white men and women. *New England Journal of Medicine, 329*(2), 73–78.

In the 30-year follow-up of the Charleston Heart Study, estimates of mortality from coronary disease in men and women, both black and white, were calculated. Risk factors for coronary disease were similar in all four groups. Rates of death from coronary disease were somewhat lower among black men than white men but higher among black women than white women.

Luepker, R. V., Rosamond, W. D., Murphy, R., Sprafka, J. M., Folsom, A. R., McGovern, P. G., & Blackburn, H. (1993). Socioeconomic status and coronary heart disease risk factor trends: The Minnesota heart survey. *Circulation, 88* (part I), 2172–2179.

It has been repeatedly noted that affluence is associated with an increased risk of coronary heart disease (CHD). As a consequence, awareness of health risks may be on the increase, especially in higher socioeconomic groups; however, this does not seem to be true in lower socioeconomic groups. In this study, over time, blood cholesterol decreased for men and women and was inversely related to the women's level of education. For men, income was positively related to blood cholesterol: those with higher incomes had higher cholesterol. This pattern did not hold true in women. For both men and women, blood pressure was inversely related to education level. Cigarette smoking for both men and women decreased over time; the smoking levels among college graduates were ½ to ⅓ of those among less educated subjects. Body mass index increased over time for both men and women; the most educated had the lowest body mass. Higher income was associated with higher body mass for men and lower body mass for women. Leisure physical activity increased over time for both men and women; less affluent and less educated women increased their physical activity. Overall, coronary heart disease was strongly related to education in both men and women, but the relationship between income and coronary risk was not as strong.

Pappas, G., Queen, S., Hadden, W., & Fisher, G. (1993). The increasing disparity in mortality between socioeconomic groups in the United States, 1960 and 1986. *New England Journal of Medicine, 329*(2), 103–109.

Death rates in the United States have declined markedly over the years. However, poor people and poorly educated people still die at higher rates than others. Over the 26-year period studied (1960 to 1986), disparities in educational level increased for whites and blacks by over 20% in women and 100% in men.

Reynes, J. F., Lasater, T. M., Feldman, H., Assaf, A. R., & Carleton, R. A. (1993). Education and risk factors for coronary heart disease: Results from a New England community. *American Journal of Preventive Medicine, 9*(6), 365–371.

The relationship of education to coronary risk factors in both men and women over a 10-year period was studied in people aged 25 to 64 years. Those with less education had a greater body mass index (weight: height ratio), higher total cholesterol, and a lower high-density lipoprotein (HDL) level. In addition, among females, there was more hypertension, and more smoking was observed in both men and women. These results support the assertion that higher education facilitates positive attitudes toward a healthy life-style.

Wilson, P. W. F., & Evans, J. C. (1993). Coronary disease prediction. *American Journal of Hypertension, 6,* 309S–313S.

Using Framingham Heart Study (a population-based longitudinal community study initiated in 1948) data on risk factors for coronary disease, these researchers determined that, during 12 years of follow-up, the incidence of coronary disease among men was 5% at ages

30–39 and rose to 26% at ages 70–74. Among women, the incidence of coronary disease at ages 30–39 was 1% and rose to 20% at ages 70–74. Although arterial blood pressure, diabetes, and smoking are major risk factors for both coronary and cerebrovascular disease, the double threat is not true for other risk factors. For example, elevated blood lipids are much more closely associated with coronary disease, and atrial fibrillation and heart valve abnormalities are more closely related to cerebrovascular disease.

Prognosis

Eaker, E. D., Chesebro, J. H., Sacks, F. M., Wenger, N. K., Whisnant, J. P., & Winston, M. (1993). Cardiovascular disease in women. *Circulation, 88*(4) Part 1, 1999–2009.

In this discussion of cardiovascular disease in women, risk factors, prevention/diagnosis, treatment, prognosis, and rehabilitation are highlighted. Occurrence of strokes in postmenopausal women is reviewed, as is peripheral vascular disease. The authors' suggestions for improving the cardiovascular health of women are important: public education; education of health care providers; and more intensive research on how to change unhealthy behaviors in women, the effects of risk modification, and case histories of women who survive heart attack, stroke, coronary bypass surgery, or angioplasty.

Murabito, J. M., Evans, J. C., Larson, M. G., & Levy, D. (1993). Prognosis after the onset of coronary heart disease: An investigation of differences in outcome between the sexes according to initial coronary disease presentation. *Circulation, 88*(6), 2548–2555.

All participants in the Framingham Heart Study who had clinically apparent coronary disease from 1951–1986 were evaluated. Of the 5,144 subjects, 1,569 (895 men, 674 women) developed new coronary heart disease over the years studied. The mean age of onset was 63 years in the men and 67 years in the women.

Myocardial infarction was the most common presentation in men, and angina was most common in women. Men and women showed differences in risk profiles. For example, diabetes was most prevalent in women who experienced a myocardial infarction or coronary death. Further, women presenting with angina or unrecognized myocardial infarction had more favorable risk factor profiles than women with other coronary disease presentations. Women with angina were younger, had lower cholesterol levels, and were less likely to smoke.

Wenger, N. K., Speroff, L., & Packard, B. (1993). Cardiovascular health and disease in women. *New England Journal of Medicine, 329*(4), 247–256.

These authors summarize the recommendations of participants attending an invitational conference sponsored by the National Heart, Lung and Blood Institute in January 1992. Among the clinical practice recommendations were: differential diagnosis of chest pain to rule out cardiac origin, and exercise electrocardiograms for women who present with a history of angina. Basic guidelines for hormone therapy are given, but the reader is alerted that knowledge is still limited about the effects of hormones, specifically combination therapy. An important addition to the literature is the discussion of heart disease in the childbearing years, an emerging but frequently ignored health concern in younger women.

Risk Factors: Family History

Marenberg, M. E., Risch, N., Berkman, L. F., Floderus, B., & de Faire, U. (1994). Genetic susceptibility to death from coronary heart disease in a study of twins. *New England Journal of Medicine, 330*(15), 1041–1046.

The major finding of this study is that death from heart disease is influenced by genetic factors in both men and women. Another major implication is that this genetic effect decreases at older ages. However, the genetic mechanisms that make people susceptible to heart disease remain unknown. It is important to identify both men and women who have a family history of heart disease. The influences of heredity cannot be changed, but modifiable risk factors can be addressed.

Risk Factors: Smoking

Freund, K. M., Belanger, A. J., D'Agostino, R. B., & Kannel, W. B. (1993). The health risks of smoking. The Framingham study: 34 years of follow-up. *Annals of Epidemiology, 3*(4), 417–424.

Follow-up of the Framingham cohort at 34 years revealed that cigarette smoking was significantly related to coronary heart disease in men aged 45 to 64 years, but not in women and older men. The sample included 1,916 men and 2,587 women. *The number of years smoking per person was higher for men by 50%.* Fewer women were smokers and those who did smoke, smoked less. Other findings included the fact that the relationship between cigarette smoking and death from all causes was strong. For example, death rates for moderate smokers were 40%–80% higher than those for nonsmokers. These data reinforce the claims of negative effects of smoking.

Kawachi, I., Colditz, G. A., Stampfer, M. J., Willet, W. C., Manson, J. E., Rosner, B., Speizer, F. E., & Hennekens, C. H. (1994). Smoking cessation and time course of decreased risks of coronary heart disease in middle-aged women. *Archives of Internal Medicine, 154,* 169–175.

Twelve years' follow-up data from the Nurses Health Study were used to assess the influence of the elapsed time since quitting smoking on coronary heart disease incidence and mortality in middle-aged women. Smoking status comparisons were as follows: current smokers (1976 = 33.2%; 1986 = 22.1%); never smoked (1976 = 43.3%; 1986 = 42.6%); and former smokers (1976 = 23.5%; 1986 = 35.3%). During the 12 years studied, 970 cases of definite and probable coronary heart disease occurred (701 nonfatal myocardial infarction and 269 fatal myocardial infarction). Higher rates of coronary disease were found in current smokers as compared to women who had never smoked. Risk increased sharply with the number of cigarettes: women who smoked 45 or more cigarettes daily had 10 times the risk of those who did not. Even smoking fewer than 5 cigarettes a day doubled the risk. The risk among former smokers was higher than among those who never smoked, but not as high as among current smokers.

Nelson, D. E., Giovino, G. A., Emont, S. L., Brackbill, R., Cameron, L. L., Peddicord, J., & Mowery, P. D. (1994). Trends in cigarette smoking among U.S. physicians and nurses. *Journal of the American Medical Association, 271*(16), 1273–1275.

The models for positive health behavior are traditionally physicians and nurses. Prevalence of smoking among these two groups was examined. Compared to data from 1974, 1976, and 1977, data from 1990 and 1991 demonstrated that cigarette smoking declined from 18.8% to 3.3% among physicians and from 31.7% to 18.3% among nurses. Prevalence of quitting smoking also declined. Trend analysis indicated an average decline of 1.15 percentage points per year for physicians and 0.88 percentage points for nurses. The most marked changes were for physicians. Nurses, predominantly women, lagged behind.

Risk Factors: Cholesterol

Barrett-Connor, E. (1992). Hypercholesterolemia predicts early death from coronary heart disease in elderly men but not women: The Rancho Bernardo Study. *Annals of Epidemiology, 2*(1/2), 77–83.

To determine whether the relationship between cholesterol level and risk of coronary disease in elderly men and women was similar to that found in middle-aged men, 761 males and 938 females aged 65–89 years (part of the Rancho Bernardo cohort) were studied between 1984 and 1987. Compared to men, the women had higher mean levels of total cholesterol, low-density lipoprotein (LDL) cholesterol, and high-density lipoprotein (HDL) cholesterol. Triglycerides were similar in both genders. Men had twice the coronary heart disease mortality rate. A total plasma cholesterol of 5.17 mm/L or greater was associated with increased risk of fatal coronary disease in the men but not in the women.

Criqui, M. H., Heiss, G., Cohn, R., Cowan, L. D., Suchindran, C. M., Bangdiwala, S., Kritchevsky, S., Jacobs, D. R., O'Grady, H. K., & Davis, C. E. (1993). Plasma triglyceride level and mortality from coronary heart disease. *New England Journal of Medicine, 328*(17), 1220–1225.

To address the question of whether plasma triglyceride level is an independent predictor for coronary mortality, triglyceride levels from men (n = 4,129) and women (n = 3,376) enrolled in the Lipid Research Clinics Follow-up Study were analyzed. Rates of coronary disease increased with triglyceride level. There also were gender differences. In men, there was not a clear relationship between triglyceride level and death from coronary disease except at the highest triglyceride levels. In women, the increase in risk began at moderate triglyceride levels, and the relationship continued to hold true at the highest triglyceride levels.

Risk Factors: Alcohol

Gaziano, J. M., Buring, J. E., Breslow, J. L., Goldhaber, S. Z., Rosner, B., VanDenburgh, M., Willett, W., & Hennekens, C. H. (1993). Moderate alcohol intake, increased levels of high-density lipoprotein and its subfractions, and decreased risk of myocardial infarction. *New England Journal of Medicine, 329*(25), 1829–1834.

An inverse relationship was noted between moderate (one or more drinks daily, but fewer than three) alcohol consumption and risk of myocardial infarction. The sample of 340 patients included both men and women. Another noteworthy finding was that alcohol consumption was associated with increases in HDL subfractions 2 and 3. This supports the theory that the positive influence of alcohol on risk of myocardial infarction is related to an increase in HDL subfractions.

Risk Factors: Diabetes

Barakat, H. A., Mooney, N., O'Brien, K., Long, S., Khazani, P. G., Pories, W., & Caro, J. F. (1993). Coronary heart disease risk factors in morbidly obese women with normal glucose tolerance. *Diabetes Care, 16*(1), 144–149.

It has been hypothesized that obese subjects are hyperinsulinemic and that this condition may be caused by increased resistance of their tissues to insulin activity. In this study, obese subjects (greater than 35 kg/m2) had a lower insulin sensitivity index (ISI) than those who were not obese. In addition, at a threshold weight of 31 kg/m2, ISI may be associated with cardiovascular risk. Beyond this weight, ISI does not change significantly and therefore cardiovascular risk may not change substantially.

Risk Factors: Obesity

Alexander, J. K. (1993, July/August). Obesity and the heart. *Heart Disease and Stroke,* 317–321.

Changes occur in the heart as a result of excessive body weight. Even after making adjustments for age and blood pressure, obesity is strongly related to increased thickness of the walls of the left ventricle, resulting in volume and pressure overloads as well as congestion in the pulmonary circulation. If these detrimental effects are to be avoided, weight reduction measures should be encouraged in obese women who are greater than 30% above normal weight.

Beard, C. M., Orencia, A., Kottke, T., & Ballard, D. J. (1992). Body mass index and the initial manifestation of coronary heart disease in women aged 40–59 years. *International Journal of Epidemiology, 21*(4), 656–664.

There are potential problems in diagnosing coronary heart disease in obese women. Obese women often are labeled by physicians as having angina, and a positive association of obesity and coronary heart disease may be made because of physicians' expectations. This study addressed whether obese women who were diagnosed with coronary heart disease actually had the disease. Cases included all female residents of Rochester, Minnesota, who were 40–59 years old and whose initial manifestations of coronary disease were: unexpected sudden death (n = 18), myocardial infarction (n = 90), or angina (n = 133). There was no association between myocardial infarction or unexpected sudden death and body mass index. However, when considering angina alone and its relation to body mass, a significant association was noted. Further studies are needed to yield a precise definition of coronary disease measures and avoid misdiagnosis.

Risk Factors: Physical Activity

Anderson, L. B., & Haraldsdottir, J. (1993). Tracking of cardiovascular disease risk factors including maximal oxygen uptake and physical activity from late teenage to adulthood: An 8-year follow-up study. *Journal of Internal Medicine, 234,* 309–315.

Changes in coronary risk factors from adolescence to young adulthood, and how these changes related to alterations in life-style, were analyzed in 88 male and 115 female school children in Denmark. The increases in blood pressure, cholesterol, and body mass index were twice as large in the males. Triglycerides increased in the males but no changes were noted in the females. More males than females participated in sports activity; however, for both males and females, the average time spent in physical activity decreased over the 8-year follow-up period. Furthermore, over the 8 years, total coronary risk increased for males but did not increase for females.

Bovens, A. M., Van Baak, M. A., Vrencken, J. G., Wijnen, J. A., Saris, W. H., & Verstappen, F. T. (1993). Physical activity, fitness, and selected risk factors for CHD in active men and women. *Medicine in Science Sports Exercise, 25*(5), 572–576.

Volunteers (2,661 men and 1,257 women) over the age of 40 years participated in sports-medical examinations in the Netherlands. Men, who reported more hours of activity per week, had higher systolic and diastolic blood pressures, and more men currently smoked. The association between physical activity in leisure time and cardiovascular fitness was moderate in both genders, but the association between occupational activity and cardiovascular fitness was not significant in either men or women.

Eaton, C. B., Reynes, J., Assaf, A. R., Feldman, H., Lasater, T., & Carleton, R. A. (1993). Predicting physical activity change in men and women in two New England communities. *American Journal of Preventive Medicine, 9,* 209–219.

In 1986–1987 and in 1990–1991, participants (424 men and 657 women) were asked to report their level of physical activity. In addition, information on coronary risk factors was collected. Most of the men and women did not participate in regular activity (at least three times per week) at either baseline or at follow-up. In women, experience with exercise, being currently employed, and interaction with those who exercise were predictive of whether they maintained recently initiated physical activity.

Lakka, T. A., Venalainen, J. M., Rauramaa, R., Salonen, R., Tuomilehto, J., & Salonen, J. T. (1994). The relation of leisure-time physical activity and cardiorespiratory fitness to the risk of acute myocardial infarction in men. *New England Journal of Medicine, 330*(22), 1549–1554.

Although this was a study of men only, the protocol warrants replication in a sample of women. The primary finding was that higher levels of leisure physical activity and cardiorespiratory fitness are inversely related to risk of coronary heart disease. Measurements of physical activity included a detailed questionnaire and exercise testing. The average time for follow-up was 4.9 years. The subjects were normal healthy men who stated that they did not have heart disease or cancer.

Mittleman, M. A., Maclure, M., Tofler, G. H., Sherwood, J. B., Goldberg, R. J., Muller, J. E., for the Determinants of Myocardial Infarction Onset Study Investigators. (1993). Triggering of acute myocardial infarction by heavy physical exertion: Protection against triggering by regular exertion. *New England Journal of Medicine, 329*(23), 1677–1683.

Both men (n = 836) and women (n = 392) participated in this study. Over half of these individuals had engaged in heavy physical exertion within an hour before the onset of a myocardial infarction. Among their activities were: lifting and pushing, jogging and racquet sports, and mixed activities such as gardening and splitting wood. Symptoms began during the activity in 82% of the cases. The calculated risk for myocardial infarction was 5.9 times higher during heavy physical exertion than during light activity or no activity. Relative risk varied according to the patient's usual level of physical exertion: those who usually engaged in regular activity had lower risk than sedentary individuals. The primary implication of this study is that sedentary people, particularly those who are at risk for coronary heart disease, should not precipitously engage in heavy physical activity.

Psychosocial Factors

Berkman, L. F., Vaccarino, V., & Seeman, T. (1993). Gender differences in cardiovascular morbidity and mortality: The contribution of social networks and support. *Annals of Behavioral Medicine, 15*(2/3), 112–118.

This article discusses the effects of social networks and support on cardiovascular morbidity and mortality in men and women. Research indicates that, regardless of gender, not having emotional support is strongly related to higher mortality. Following myocardial infarction, 60% of men and 43% of women with no source of emotional support died within 6 months after hospitalization. Although differences between genders regarding psychosocial stress and cardiovascular disease need further study, the following should be considered: (1) premenopausal women react to psychosocial stressors differently than postmenopausal women because of hormonal differences; (2) women may "psychologically define events differently"; (3) given that women wait longer before seeking emergency assistance, lack of social support should be investigated as a possible reason; and (4) empirical studies are needed to determine whether social support influences the choice of treatment women receive.

Dimsdale, J. E. (1993). Coronary heart disease in women: Personality and stress-induced biological responses. *Annals of Behavioral Medicine, 15*(2/3), 119–123.

Most studies that examine reactivity to stress focus largely on men because of concern surrounding interference of hormonal variations in women's menstrual cycle. This article reviews reactivity differences and coronary-prone behavioral differences in men and women. The authors contend that blood pressure and heart rate reactivity are probably not influenced by changes in the menstrual cycle. In addition, few prospective studies have examined the cardiovascular consequences of Type A behavior and anger/hostility in women. Finally, although depression is seen more often in women than men, research examining its effect on the development of cardiovascular disease in women deserves further study.

Shumaker, S. A., & Czajkowski, S. M. (1993). A review of health-related quality-of-life and psychosocial factors in women with cardiovascular disease. *Annals of Behavioral Medicine, 15*(2/3), 149–155.

These authors offer a summary of research studies on health-related quality of life (HRQL) in women following coronary artery bypass graft (CABG) surgery; hypertension and myocardial infarction are addressed. Following CABG surgery, both men and women reported improved HRQL for up to 18 months. Gender differences in physical and emotional well-being reported after CABG may be evidence of preoperative conditions. Further investigation is needed in this area. HRQL in hypertense women is one area of cardiovascular research that has been extensively studied: findings indicate that pharmacologic agents have complex effects on HRQL, and behaviorally based interventions such as diet and weight loss may improve HRQL. Finally, there may be significant gender differences in the HRQL following myocardial infarction. Women seem to have longer recuperative periods and more mood disturbances than men after this event. Overall, additional research in this area is warranted.

Multiple Risk Factors

Hanson, M. J. S. (1994). Modifiable risk factors for coronary heart disease in women. *American Journal of Critical Care, 3*(3), 177–184.

In women, risk factors that are modifiable deserve attention because life-style changes can alter the degree of coronary risk. Elevated serum lipids, hypertension, smoking, oral contraceptives, obesity, menopause, diabetes, physical inactivity, and a range of socioeconomic and psychological factors are all identified as modifiable. Many of these risk factors are shared by men, but approaches to life-style modifications may have to be gender-specific. At least two factors are unique to women: (1) the use of oral contraceptives and (2) a lack of endogenous estrogen with menopause. Unlike the higher-dose contraceptives used in the

1960s, today's low-dose oral contraceptives are not considered a risk factor for coronary disease. Studies are needed of women who have taken low-dose oral contraceptives and have other risk factors. The use of hormone therapy at menopause also warrants further investigation, to avoid sweeping recommendations for use of this therapy as a preventive measure.

Prevalence of Adults with No Known Major Risk Factors for Coronary Heart Disease—Behavioral Risk Factor Surveillance System, 1992. (1994). *Morbidity and Mortality Weekly Report, 43*(4) 61–69.

For both men and women, the percentage of respondents with no known coronary risk factors was highest for 18–34-year-olds. For women, the percentage varied inversely with age; for men, the percentage was lowest for those in midlife (50–64 years). Overall, in 1992, only 18% of adults reported having no known risk factors for coronary heart disease. This supports the conclusion that, despite efforts to prevent and control coronary disease, many adults continue to be at high risk.

Diagnosis and Treatment

Hannan, E. L., Kiburn, H., Racz, M., Shields, E., & Chassin, M. R. (1994). Improving the outcomes of coronary artery bypass surgery in New York State. *Journal of the American Medical Association, 271*(10), 761–766.

The data for this study came from 30 New York hospitals where coronary artery bypass surgery was performed between 1989 and 1992. All hospitals reported their information voluntarily to the Cardiac Surgery Reporting System (CSRS). The entire process was designed to help hospitals improve their quality of care and provide consumers with information that would be helpful in selecting a surgeon and a hospital for coronary artery bypass surgery. The volume of surgery increased 30% over the four-year period. There was a reduction in mortality even though many of the patients had more severe coronary disease. Although separate statistics for men and women were not presented, it is commendable that women as well as men in New York are now provided with information as to where the greatest success in bypass surgery is realized. Other states should follow New York's lead.

Lincoff, A. M., Califf, R. M., Ellis, S. G., Sigmon, K. N., Lee, K. L., Leimberger, J. D., Topol, E. J., for the Thrombolysis and Angioplasty in Myocardial Infarction Study Group. (1993). Thrombolytic therapy for women with myocardial infarction: Is there a gender gap? *Journal of the American College of Cardiology, 22*(7), 1780–1787.

To determine whether gender influences the decision for thrombolytic therapy following myocardial infarction, 348 women were compared with 1,271 men who were part of the Thrombolysis and Angioplasty in Myocardial Infarction (TAMI) trials. Both groups were hospitalized within 6 hours of experiencing chest pain. Women were older (61 years) than men (55.3 years) and, following a myocardial infarction, had a higher incidence of major risk factors.

Mark, D. B., Shaw, L. K., DeLong, E. R., Califf, R. M., & Pryor, D. B. (1994). Absence of sex bias in the referral of patients for cardiac catheterization. *New England Journal of Medicine, 330*(16), 1101–1106.

Previous studies have shown that women are less often referred for further diagnostic studies related to coronary heart disease. To determine whether a sex-related bias remains, these investigators prospectively studied 410 symptomatic outpatients (280 men and 130 women) undergoing exercise testing for possible coronary disease. Overall, women were referred for cardiac catheterization significantly less often than men: 18% versus 27%. After accounting for pretest likelihood of coronary disease as judged by their physicians and the fact that women had a lower rate of positive exercise test results, sex was not an independent predictor for cardiac catheterization referral. However, it should be noted that physician rating is not without bias and can be influenced by predetermined expectations. Furthermore, it is well known that few women are able to exercise to their maximum, another bias. These factors must be considered when interpreting these results.

Sempos, C. T., Looker, A. C., Gillum, R. F., & Makuc, D. M. (1994). Body iron stores and the risk of coronary heart disease. *New England Journal of Medicine, 330*(16), 1119–1124.

The question addressed in this study is whether higher body iron stores increase the risk of coronary heart disease. To assess the impact of iron as measured by serum transferrin (serum iron concentration divided by total iron-binding capacity), 4,518 men and women were studied. Results indicated that the risk of coronary heart disease or myocardial infarction was not related to transferrin saturation in white men and women. Among white women, there was a significant inverse trend between mortality from all causes and transferrin saturation. These trends were not noted in black men and women. Thus, the results suggest an inverse relationship between serum transferrin and cardiovascular mortality.

White, H. D., Barbash, G. I., Modan, M., Simes, J., Diaz, R., Hampton, J. R., Heikkila, J., Kristinsson, A. K., Mouloupoulos, S., Paolasso, E. A. C., Van der Werf, T., Pehrsson, K., Sandoe, E., Wilcox, R. G., Verstraete, M., von der Lippe, B., Van de Werf, F., for the Investigators of the International Tissue Plasminogen Activator/Streptokinase Mortality Study. (1993). After correcting for worse baseline characteristics, women treated with thrombolytic therapy for acute myocardial infarction have the same mortality and morbidity as men except for a higher incidence of hemorrhagic stroke. *Circulation, 88* (part 1), 2097–2103.

Women develop coronary disease much later than men—specifically, at least a decade following menopause. Therefore, when women suffer a first myocardial infarction, their mortality and complication rates are usually much higher, primarily because of advanced age and more serious coronary disease. In this study, thrombolytic and antithrombotic therapy after acute myocardial infarction was compared in women and men. Patients in 13 countries were randomly assigned to receive either intravenous tissue plasminogen activator or streptokinase with or without subcutaneous heparin. There were 6,317 men and 1,944 women in the study sample. The women, who were older (67 versus 61 years), received treatment 18 minutes later, were more apt to have had a previous infarction and angina, were more likely to have hypertension and diabetes, and were sicker upon admission. Conversely, fewer women were smokers. Women had a higher hospital death rate—12% versus 7.2%. Women also had a significantly poorer 6-month survival rate. Yet, when adjustments were made for these characteristics, there were no differences in outcome for men and women treated with streptokinase or tissue plasminogen activator. Yet, women suffered more cerebral hemorrhage/stroke. It is not known why women are more susceptible to hemorrhagic stroke after thrombolytic therapy.

Hormonal and Reproductive Factors

Belchetz, P. E. (1994). Hormonal treatment of postmenopausal women. *New England Journal of Medicine, 330*(15), 1062–1071.

This author discusses the benefits (decreased risk of heart disease and prevention of osteoporosis) of hormone therapy and highlights studies that support these contentions. The risks of hormone therapy—specifically, endometrial cancer (estrogen alone) and breast cancer (estrogen alone and estrogen in combination with progesterone)—are presented, and the various hormone regimens are explained. The author stresses that none of the currently used approaches to hormone therapy has been able to recreate the premenopausal hormone environment. While not stated, premenopausal levels of estrogen might be considered as a guide to postmenopausal therapy.

Manolio, T. A., Furberg, C. D., Shemanski, L., Psaty, B. M., O'Leary, D. H., Tracy, R. P., Bush, T. L., for the CHS Collaborative Research Group. (1993). Associations of postmenopausal estrogen use with cardiovascular disease and its risk factors in older women. *Circulation, 88*(5) part 1, 2163–2171.

The Medicare eligibility lists of four U.S. communities were used to recruit women into this study. Present users of estrogen (n = 356) were those who recorded use in a medication inventory, regardless of past use. Past users (n = 784) were those who had once taken premarin or other estrogens for hot flashes or other symptoms of menopause but did not have a current prescription. Past and present estrogen use was associated with being younger and with prior hysterectomy. Median duration of use was 18 years for present users and 3 years for past users. Past and present use of estrogen was associated with obesity, higher levels of HDL and lower levels of LDL, cholesterol, fibrinogen, glucose, and insulin. Estrogen use was also related to lower levels of subclinical disease, which the investigators attributed to risk factor differences.

Nabulsi, A. A., Folsom, A. R., White, A., Patsch, W., Heiss, G., Wu, K. K., & Szklo, M., for the Atherosclerosis Risk in Communities Study Investigators. (1993). Association of hormone-replacement therapy with various cardiovascular risk factors in postmenopausal women. *New England Journal of Medicine, 328*(15), 1069–1075.

Using data from the Atherosclerosis Risk in Communities Study, 4,958 postmenopausal women were classified into four groups: (1) current users of estrogen alone; (2) current users of estrogen with progestin; (3) nonusers who had formerly used estrogen alone or estrogen in combination with progesterone, and

(4) nonusers who had never used the hormones. Associations between use of hormones and plasma lipids, serum glucose, serum insulin, and blood pressure were calculated. The majority of women had never used hormones (63%); 16% were former users. Current users comprised 21% of the sample; of these, 83% were using estrogen alone (primarily premarin) and 17% were using estrogen (again, primarily premarin) in combination with progesterone (provera). White women were more likely to be current users than black women. Current users of estrogen alone had significantly higher triglyceride levels than the women in the remaining three groups combined. They also had higher levels of HDL, apolipoprotein A-I, and serum cholesterol, and lower levels of LDL, apolipoprotein B, and lipoprotein (a). The values of these variables were similar for current users of estrogen and progesterone. Current users of estrogen alone or estrogen in combination with progesterone had significantly lower mean fasting concentrations of serum glucose and insulin than nonusers. There were no significant differences in blood pressure between the two user groups and nonusers. This study is important because it includes a group on combination therapy. Many of the associations between estrogen therapy and the variables in question were similar for women who use combination therapy.

Ness, R. B., Harris, T., Cobb, J., Flegal, K. M., Kelsey, J. L., Balanger, A., Stunkard, A. J., & D'Agostino, R. B. (1993). Number of pregnancies and the subsequent risk of cardiovascular disease. *New England Journal of Medicine, 328*(21), 1528–1533.

Women enrolled in either the Framingham Heart Study or the National Health and Nutrition Examination Survey (NHANES) were studied to determine whether relationships existed among reproductive history, morbidity, and mortality from cardiovascular disease in later life. Findings revealed that number of pregnancies was an important factor in cardiovascular morbidity and mortality, but higher morbidity and mortality rates were statistically significant only in women who had had six or more pregnanceis. Whether simply the number of pregnancies or other unidentified factors associated with pregnancy were significant requires further investigation.

Speroff, L., & Lobo, R. A. (1994, May/June). Postmenopausal hormone therapy and the cardiovascular system. *Heart Disease and Stroke,* 173–176.

Although more males than females continue to die from coronary heart disease, the problem in women cannot be ignored. Published studies on hormone therapy and cardiovascular disease in women are abundant. From a 1993 conference of international experts in women's health care, cardiovascular physiology, and epidemiology came these opinions: estrogen is beneficial in the primary prevention of heart disease; the benefits of estrogen far outweigh the risks in smoking and nonsmoking women; there are too few studies of the relationship between combined (estrogen and progesterone) hormone therapy and cardiovascular risk; and although life-style changes such as diet, exercise, and smoking cessation may have positive effects on cardiovascular risk at menopause, there is insufficient information comparing hormone therapy and life-style changes to say with any certainty that one is better than the other.

Subbiah, M. T. R., Kessel, B., Agrawal, M., Rajan, R., Abplanalp, W., & Rymaszewski, Z. (1993). Antioxidant potential of specific estrogens on lipid peroxidation. *The Journal of Clinical Endocrinology and Metabolism,* 77(4), 1095–1097.

Contemporary studies have linked the use of estrogen following menopause to a decreased risk of heart disease. Many kinds of estrogen preparations are used by postmenopausal women, but it is not known whether structural differences in the estrogen molecule interfere with or enhance cardioprotective effects. Estrogens do differ, and equine estrogen has the strongest antioxidant properties.

Wren, B. G. (1992). The effect of oestrogen on the female cardiovascular system. *The Medical Journal of Australia,* 157, 204–208.

After reviewing over 100 published papers representing a decade of research, the author concludes that published evidence supports the concept that oestrogen reduces the risk of atherosclerosis and myocardial infarction. The primary mechanism cited in these studies is the positive effect on the lipid profile: HDL increases and LDL cholesterol is lowered. Evidence is mounting that oestrogen also produces vasodilatation and improves blood flow.

Chapter 10

Sexually Transmitted Diseases

Catherine Ingram Fogel

S exually transmitted diseases (STDs) are infections spread from person to person during sexual contact. The STD problem is steadily growing: increased numbers of persons contract more severe infections every year (Aral & Holmes, 1991). Approximately 13 million Americans are newly infected with symptomatic STDs yearly (Hatcher et al., 1994). The cost of STDs exceeds $3.5 billion annually (DHHS, 1990), and the cost of pelvic inflammatory disease (PID) and PID-associated ectopic pregnancy and infertility exceeds $4.2 billion (Washington & Katz, 1991). Although deaths caused by STDs have declined in the past 40 years, they still account for almost one-third of reproductive mortality in the United States (Grimes, 1986). Women with sexually transmitted infections are found in every socioeconomic class, culture, ethnicity, and age group. All too often, frustration, anxiety, fear, shame, and guilt are characteristic of their experience with STDs.

Most STDs show a biological sexism (Hatcher et al., 1994). Although women account for only half of all sexually transmitted infections (STIs) each year (Donovan, 1993), they and their children suffer more frequent and severe long-term consequences than infected men do (DHHS, 1990; Donovan, 1993). The medical complications are exacerbated because many women infected with STIs have no symptoms and therefore may go untreated for long periods of time (Lesserman, 1993). Women are also more likely than men to acquire an STI from a single sexual encounter (Hatcher et al., 1994). In addition to HIV infection and subsequent acquired immunodeficiency syndrome

(AIDS), the most serious complications are PID, infertility, ectopic pregnancy, cervical cancer, chronic pelvic pain, fetal and infant death, preterm delivery, and mental retardation of offspring (DHHS, 1990; Fogel, 1995).

More than one million women per year experience an episode of PID, primarily as a consequence of an undetected STD (NIAID, 1992); about one in nine women aged 15–44 years is treated for PID during her reproductive years (Aral, Mosher, & Cates, 1991). If current trends continue, one-half of women aged 15 in 1970 will have had PID by the year 2000 (PHS, 1991). In addition, up to 150,000 women may become infertile, and 45,000 may experience a life-endangering ectopic pregnancy as a result of a previous STD infection (Donovan, 1993). About one-half of the more than 88,000 ectopic pregnancies occurring every year are caused by previous STD infections and complications (CDC, 1992). Nearly 5,000 women die every year of cervical cancer, which is strongly associated with several common strains of HPV (CDC, 1992). AIDS has become the fourth leading cause of death among U.S. women aged 25–44; in 1993, diagnosed cases attributed to heterosexual transmission exceeded those attributed to injection drug use (CDC, 1993a, 1993b). The most common STDs in women are Chlamydia trachomatis infections, human papillomavirus, gonorrhea, genital herpes, syphilis, and HIV infection.

The medically underserved (e.g., the poor; racial and ethnic minorities) experience higher rates of STDs and disability than the population as a whole (DHHS, 1990). Women are disproportionately represented among those living in poverty. As early as 1988, McBarnett noted that, because of increasing numbers of women who are poor, a convergence between class and gender has occurred that is unprecedented in America. Poor women, who have limited access to adequate health care services, are impacted more heavily by sexually transmitted infections and their associated complications.

Women of color also experience a greater burden of STDs. For example, between 1985 and 1990, the infectious syphilis rate increased 230% among black women whereas it rose only about 10% among white women (CDC, 1992). Approximately three-quarters of women diagnosed with AIDS since 1981 are black and Hispanic, even though they represent only about 20% of all U.S. women (CDC, 1992). The fact that minority women are more likely than white women to experience serious consequences from sexually transmitted infections reflects, at least in part, their lack of access to health care. For poor women, sexually transmitted infections, especially HIV/AIDS, are life-threatening conditions linked to factors such as poverty, racism, and sexism. Two-thirds of those infected with an STD each year in the United States are under 25 (DHHS, 1991). Thus, young minority women are at greater risk for the adverse consequences associated with STDs.

The relatively new discipline of women's health is undergoing a major shift in emphasis (Dan, 1994; McBride, 1993a), from a critique of patriarchal practices to an assertion of positive values (McBride, 1993b). Certain beliefs and assumptions undergirding women's health have been explicated (Cohen, Mitchell, Olesen, Olshansky, & Taylor, 1994; McBride, 1993a, 1993b):

- Women are not a monolithic group; their experiences differ by race, ethnic origin, class, and age (among other factors).
- Women are complex, perceptive, healthy individuals who experience their lives in varied ways and create their own meanings of their experiences.
- Women's health exists within a social/cultural/political context that includes racism, sexism, classism, and homophobia. Poverty, chemical dependency, powerlessness, and dependency are integral features of many women's lives and affect their health profoundly.

These beliefs and assumptions emphasize the complexity and interrelatedness of women's health care. The meaning of women's experiences as they live them is critical. Physical/health assessment and disease management remain important components of women's health care, but understanding women's subjective experiences within their social context is essential. In nursing practice and research with women experiencing sexually transmitted diseases, the important components are: prevention and self-care, the social/political/historical context within which women experience STDs, and women's relationships. We need a frame or lens through which to view women and STDs, and a guide for research that attends to gender, class, and race or ethnicity. Unfortunately, much of the published research does not address these issues; when it does, the focus is usually on HIV/AIDS research and not other STDs.

Much STD research and discourse considers women as vectors of transmission and focuses only on their reproductive capacities. Many practice articles also reflect this view. Promotion or improvement of the health of women has not been the central concern of researchers, and little attention has been paid to the context of women's lives, within which they contract and experience STIs. The few articles that addressed women's lived experiences with STIs focused on HIV infection. Attention to the lived experiences of women with HIV is essential, but the experiences of women with other STIs must not be ignored. Concern over HIV should not cause researchers to lose sight of the other STDs and their impact on women's lives.

A recommended approach would start with women's lived experiences with STIs and sexual protective practices. There is similar need for research that explores women's relationships and the effect that unequal power, control by a partner, and violence have in the transmission of STIs. Additional research in the area of sexual behavior and practices should use qualitative approaches that ask young women to describe how they negotiate sexual encounters and how they do or do not practice sexual protective behaviors. Studies must be conducted not just with college or childbearing women but with women of differing ages (adolescent, midlife, older), classes, and ethnicity.

The nursing profession has long recognized the importance of women's sexuality, yet there has been scant examination in the nursing literature of sexual behavior and activity in the female population. Given the wide range of sex-related issues that are of great social and public health concern today, data on women's sexual habits and behaviors are necessary for all nurses who care for women. In general, good information is available on patterns of adolescent sexuality, rates of intercourse in marriage, and reproductive behaviors of women. Unfortunately, the usefulness of the majority of surveys of sexual behavior in adults is limited because researchers sampled subpopulations such as college students, volunteers, or jail residents. Studies that used probability methods to obtain general population respondents often limited their measures of sexual behaviors. The types of instrumentation and methods used further limit the conclusions regarding sexual behavior. Knowledge of sexual behavior is necessary for planning and implementing interventions aimed at preventing sexually transmitted pathogens. A number of articles presenting data on sexual activity and behavior are therefore included in this review.

Although biological factors heighten a woman's chances of becoming infected if exposed to an STI, risk of infection is primarily affected by personal behavior. Some behaviors (e.g., substance abuse, multiple partners, trading sex for drugs) increase the likelihood of exposure to STDs; others (e.g., condom use) reduce the risk of infection. Personal attitudes, knowledge, psychological attributes, prior experience, sociodemographic factors, and habits can shape a person's decision to adopt disease protective behaviors. Attitudes are postulated to be important predictors of individual sexual disease protective behaviors (Ajzen & Fishbein, 1980), and attitudes are thought to reflect salient beliefs about the consequences of performing the sex act and evaluations of those consequences (Jemmott & Jemmott, 1991). Articles relating to sexual risk and sexually protective behaviors are reviewed.

Until recently, the primary sexual disease protective practice implemented by heterosexual couples was use of a male condom. In these couples, the effectiveness of condoms is likely to depend less on efficacy (in barring transmission per coital act) and more on acceptance by the male partner (Stein, 1990). In heterosexual encounters, men must comply with women's suggestion that they use a condom. A key problem with the use of the condom, from a woman's point of view, is that it calls on the woman to assert dominance in the sexual act—although, almost everywhere, dominance is not her traditional mode (Hatcher et al., 1994; Stein, 1990). Use of the male condom may often depend on power relations between the man and woman. Articles that explore women's control in sexual relations with partners are also included in this review.

In this chapter, nursing, medical, sociological, psychological, and public health articles published in late 1992 through mid-1994 are examined. The following guidelines were employed in their selection:

1. Does the article contribute to the reader's understanding of the effect of race, class, and gender on women with a sexually transmitted disease?

2. Does the article enrich the reader's understanding of prevention and self-care practices related to STDs? Topics included in this group are: women's sexual activities and practices, and STDs and women's relationships.

3. Does the article provide new information regarding a particular STD in terms of incidence, risk, and/or treatment?

4. Does the article add to information presented in previous volumes of this publication?

REFERENCES

Ajzen, I., & Fishbein, M. (1980). *Understanding attitudes and predicting social behavior.* Englewood Cliffs, NJ: Prentice-Hall.

Aral, S. O., & Holmes, K. K. (1991). Sexually transmitted diseases in the AIDS era. *Scientific American, 264*(2), 62–69.

Aral, S. O., Mosher, W. D., & Cates, W. (1991). Self-reported pelvic inflammatory disease in the United States, 1988. *Journal of the American Medical Association, 266,* 2570–2573.

CDC (Centers for Disease Control and Prevention). (1992). *Division of STD/HIV Prevention 1991 Annual Report.* Atlanta, GA: Author.

CDC. (1993a, August 6). Update: Barrier protection against HIV infection and other sexually transmitted diseases. *Morbidity and Mortality Weekly Report, 43,* 589–591.

CDC. (1993b, September 24). 1993 sexually transmitted diseases treatment guidelines. *Morbidity and Mortality Weekly Report, 42,* 1–102.

Cohen, S. M., Mitchell, E. O., Olesen, V., Olshansky, E., & Taylor, D. L. (1994). From female disease to women's health: New educational paradigms. In A. J. Dan (Ed.), *Reframing women's health* (pp. 56–66). Thousand Oaks, CA: Sage.

Dan, A. J. (1994). *Reframing women's health.* Thousand Oaks, CA: Sage.

DHHS (Department of Health and Human Services). (1990). *Health people 2000. National health promotion and disease prevention objectives.* Washington, DC: Author. DHHS Pub. No. (PHS) 91-50212.

DHHS. (1991). *Sexually transmitted disease surveillance, 1990.* Atlanta: Centers for Disease Control and Prevention/DHHS.

Donovan, P. (1993). *Testing positive: Sexually transmitted disease and the public health response.* New York: Alan Guttmacher Institute.

Fogel, C. I. (1995). Sexually transmitted diseases. In C. I. Fogel & N. F. Woods (Eds.), *Women's Health Care* (pp. 571–609). Thousand Oaks, CA: Sage.

Grimes, D. A. (1986). Deaths due to sexually transmitted diseases: The forgotten component of reproductive mortality. *Journal of the American Medical Association, 255*(13), 1727–1729.

Hatcher, R. A., Trussell, J., Stewart, F., Stewart, G. K., Kowal, D., Guest, F., Cotes, W. Jr., Policar, W. S. (1994). *Contraceptive technology* (16th ed.). New York: Irvington Publishers.

Jemmott, L. S., & Jemmott, J. B. (1991). Applying the theory of reasoned action to AIDS risk behavior: Condom use among black women. *Nursing Research, 40,* 228–234.

Lesserman, J. (1993). *In sickness, in health: The status of women's health in North Carolina.* Raleigh: NC Equity.

McBarnett, L. (1988). Women and poverty: The effects on reproductive status. In C. W. Perales & L. S. Young (Eds.), *Women, health, and poverty* (pp. 55–81). New York: Haworth Press.

McBride, A. B. (1993a). Preface. In B. J. McElmurry & R. S. Parker (Eds.), *Annual review of women's health* (pp. vii–viii). New York: National League for Nursing Press.

McBride, A. B. (1993b). From gynecology to gyn-ecology: Developing a practice–research agenda for women's health. *Health Care for Women's International, 14,* 316–325.

NIAID (National Institute for Allergies and Infectious Diseases). (1992). Pelvic inflammatory disease. *Factsheet.* Bethesda, Md: National Institutes of Health.

PHS (Public Health Service). (1991, November). Curbing the increase in rates of STDs. *Prevention Report.*

Stein, Z. (1990). HIV prevention: The need for methods women can use. *American Journal of Public Health, 80,* 460–462.

Washington, A. E., & Katz, P. (1991). Cost of and payment source for pelvic inflammatory disease. Trends and projections, 1985 through 2000. *Journal of the American Medical Association, 266,* 2565–2569.

Astemborski, J., Vlahov, D., Warren, D., Solomom, L., & Nelson, K. E. (1994). The trading of sex for drugs or money and HIV seropositivity among female intravenous drug users. *American Journal of Public Health, 84*(3), 382–387.

Until recently, intravenous drug use (IVDU) was the major mode of transmission of the human immunodeficiency virus (HIV) among women; however, recent studies documenting higher HIV seroincidence rates in female than in male intravenous drug users suggest that sexual transmission is more important for women. A national survey of female prostitutes found significantly higher rates of HIV among those who reported IVDU, suggesting that prostitution might be a means of buying or obtaining drugs. The purpose of this study was to identify whether trading sex for drugs or money was associated with HIV infection among intravenous drug-using women, independent of drug injection practices. Intravenous drug users were recruited by word of mouth from community agencies. Women were at least 18 years, had a history of injecting drugs within the previous 10 years, and had no history of AIDS-defining illness at the onset of the study. Women were asked about their drug injection behaviors and a 10-year sexual history gathered specific data such as total number of male sex partners, number of male IVDU partners, and number of males with whom sex was traded for money or drugs. In this study, nearly 40% of women reported exchanging sex for drugs or money at least once in the previous 10 years. Women were grouped as to the number of partners involved in their trading of sex for drugs or money: none, low (1–49), or high (50 or more). Low trading was not associated with seropositive HIV infection. HIV seropositivity rates were similar among low traders (23.7%) and nontraders (23.3%). High trading (as compared with no trading) was significantly associated with HIV seropositivity (47.6%) after adjusting for cocaine use, history of STDs, and duration of IVDU. An independent effect of frequent trading of sex for drugs or money is indicated. These findings contribute to the growing literature on risk factors for and sexual practices associated with HIV infection among women who use intravenous drugs, but many more questions must be asked. Detailed information on the frequency of condom use, types of prostitution and the sexual activities involved is needed. The data provide additional support for increased efforts to develop effective interventions for the vulnerable population.

Binson, D., Dolcini, M. M., Pollack, L. M., & Catania, J. A. Multiple sexual partners among young adults in high-risk cities. *Family Planning Perspectives, 25*(6), 268–272.

Dolcini, M. M., Catania, J. A., Coates, T. J., Stall, R., Hudes, E. S., Gagnon, J., & Pollack, L. M. (1993). Demographic characteristics of heterosexuals with multiple partners: The national AIDS behavioral study. *Family Planning Perspectives, 25*(5), 208–214.

The findings in these two articles, based on data from the National AIDS Behavioral Surveys, highlight sexual behaviors that place women at risk for acquiring STIs. The data were obtained from interviews with 10,630 persons aged 18–75, conducted between June 1990 and February 1991. The sample was composed of two overlapping samples: a national sample and a high-risk cities (cities with high prevalence of AIDS) sample. Focus groups were used to examine perceptions of survey procedures and comprehension of survey questions, and the procedures and instruments were changed to reflect the focus groups' results. A national pretest telephone survey was then done. Approximately 48% of both samples were women. Interviewing procedures were designed to ensure anonymity and privacy and to be sensitive to cultural and ethnic differences. Examples of the types of findings reported in these articles are: Women have been shown to be more likely than men to report having a risky partner (5.6% versus 0.5%), and almost 10% of women nationally reported more than one partner in the past year (20% reported more than one in the past 5 years).

Bradley-Springer, L. A. (1994). Reproductive decision making in the age of AIDS. *Image, The Journal of Nursing Scholarship, 26*(3), 241–246.

As the HIV epidemic infects increasing numbers of women and their children, nurses will be called on to assist women in making difficult reproductive decisions. This author uses four levels of analysis to explore current knowledge about reproduction in HIV-infected women: (1) societal, (2) organizational, (3) interpersonal, and (4) personal. The societal level focuses on institutional and social policies influenced by social resources, priorities, and policies. Illustrative concepts include sexism, stigma, lack of power, and drug use. At the societal level there are dicta that influence an HIV-infected woman's decision to avoid or delay pregnancy. This reflects the public health goal—to decrease infection rates—but does not address issues of relative risk assessment or loss of reproductive opportunity.

The organizational influences include rules, organizational policy, and community norms. Often, organizational policies encourage directive counseling; however, nondirective approaches are more effective. Further, organizational policy often dictates the extent of HIV testing of pregnant women. A number of studies addressing reproduction issues among individual women have found that knowledge of HIV status is not a major determinant in reproductive decisions. Rather, decisions are based on personal and cultural considerations. The author notes that reproductive decision making by HIV-infected women is a complex process and suggests that single-focus interventions may be counterproductive. She recommends interventions, nursing actions, and outcome criteria for all four levels.

CDC (Centers for Disease Control and Prevention). (1993). Sexually transmitted diseases treatment guidelines. *Morbidity and Mortality Weekly Report, 42* (RR-14). 1–102.

All nurses who care for women with STDs should be knowledgeable regarding current treatment recommendations. In 1993, CDC guidelines were developed based on the recommendations of experts. Included are new recommendations for single-dose oral therapy for gonnococcal infections, chlamydial infections, and chancroid; new regimens for the treatment of bacterial vaginosis; outpatient management of pelvic inflammatory disease; new patient-applied medication for treatment of genital warts; and a revised approach to management of sexual assault victims. New sections deal with subclinical human papillomavirus infections and cervical cancer screening for women who attend STD clinics or have a history of STDs. Also presented is more information on the management of asymptomatic HIV infection and vulvovaginal candidiasis, STDs in those coinfected with HIV, and STDs among infants, children, and pregnant women.

Gielen, A. C., Faden, R. R., O'Campo, P., Kass, N., & Anderson, J. (1994). Women's protective sexual behaviors: A test of the health belief model. *AIDS Education and Prevention, 6*(1), 1–11.

Using the health belief model as a framework, these authors examined the extent to which 567 pregnant poor women reported using protective sexual behaviors. Women were asked if they had used any of the following protective sexual behaviors because they were afraid of getting AIDS: had fewer partners, had sex less often, talked with a partner about AIDS, decided not to have sex with a partner because of fear that he might have the AIDS virus, used condoms during sexual intercourse, and carried condoms with them in case they might have sex. Women in this study perceived themselves to be moderately susceptible to AIDS; were well aware of the severity of this disease; felt that protecting themselves from AIDS was not that difficult; and felt that recommended sexual protective behaviors were highly effective in preventing AIDS. At the same time, three sexual protective practices were reported by fewer than half of the women: using or carrying condoms, talking with a partner about AIDS, and having fewer sex partners. Beliefs about personal susceptibility were consistently associated with use of protective sexual behaviors; thus, those women who perceived themselves as more susceptible were more likely to adopt protective practices. The fairly consistent relationship between perceived barriers (burdensome nature of protective behaviors) and protective behaviors suggests that women need less burdensome options such as the female condom and opportunities to discuss and practice negotiating the use of condoms. This study focused on HIV/AIDS concerns and protective sexual practices, but the findings are applicable to prevention of any STI.

Hinkle, Y. A., Johnson, E. H., Gilbert, D., Jackson, L., & Lollis, C. M. (1992). African American women who always use condoms: Attitudes, knowledge about AIDS, and sexual behavior. *Journal of Medical Women's Association, 47* (6), 230–237.

This study adds to the scant but growing body of knowledge regarding the attitudes and the beliefs African American women have about condom use. The authors examined the interrelationships among attitudes about condom use, knowledge about AIDS, sexual behavior, and drug use among 121 African American women who varied in their intentions to use condoms: 17% were steady users, 62% did not use condoms but had high intentions to do so, and 21% did not use condoms and had low intentions to do so. The women were young (average age, 21.6 years), single and never married (83.5%), and in the first three years of college (69.5%). The researchers state that three important findings emerged from their research. First, there was no significant relationship between AIDS knowledge and condom use. Women were knowledgeable but failed to take precautionary measures to prevent infection. The three groups did not differ in their overall knowledge about AIDS or their attitudes toward condom use for contraception. Second, a large percentage of steady users tested positive for HIV (10% as opposed to 0% or 1%). Third, women with low intentions to use condoms were the angriest about negotiating condom

use and held significantly more negative attitudes about the use of condoms than the women in the other group. Not only do these women not use condoms but they also report being angered when they are seen purchasing condoms. There were no differences among the groups in terms of drug use, previous treatment for STDs, or perceived risk for exposure to AIDS. The researchers note that this study is cross-sectional in design and that additional research is needed before any assumptions about causal relationships can be inferred.

Hobfall, S. E., Jackson, A. P., Lavin, J., Britton, P. J., & Shepard, J. B. (1993). Safer sex knowledge, behavior, and attitudes of inner-city women. *Health Psychology, 12*(6), 481–488.

Women attending an obstetrics clinic at a city medical center were recruited for a study aimed at defining the typical sexual practices of inner-city women. The purpose of the study was to establish prevention goals that were specific and appropriate for inner-city populations. Respondents were 280 single pregnant women who were predominantly white European Americans (44%) or African Americans (53%). Only 12% had ever been married, and 19% lived with a current partner. More than two-thirds had income of less than $10,000 annually, and 40% had not completed high school. Through questionnaires, data were collected on sexual activity, safe-sex behaviors and intentions, knowledge of HIV transfer and prevention, and perceived risk and risk behavior. In contrast to the stereotype of single pregnant women as a sexually active group, the women were not as sexually active as the researchers had anticipated. Despite some risky behaviors (lack of condom or of spermicide use), the women did not perceive themselves at risk for HIV transmission. In part, this lack of risk perception was based on their having a single sexual partner. Partners' current or past behavior was not viewed as placing them at risk: they believed that their partners were not infected. Yet, many were involved with men who had been in jail, who used IV drugs, or who had had sexual relationships with other women. The women acknowledged that women like themselves were at potential risk for AIDS, but they considered themselves to be exceptions. Their knowledge about prevention and transmission of HIV infection was limited. The authors point out that although attempting to alter the women's beliefs that monogamy placed one at low risk would seem at first glance to be an attractive first intervention, this could be dangerous. Challenging men's behavior might also challenge the underlying trust and integrity of the couple's relationship and could place the women at risk for violence. Instead, increasing the women's knowledge of HIV transmission and safer sex would prepare them to make better decisions, and improving their negotiating skills would enable them to present their views and persuade their partner(s) to use safe sex practices.

Leigh, B. C., Temple, M. T., & Trocki, K. F. (1993). The sexual behavior of U.S. adults: Results from a national survey. *American Journal of Public Health, 83*(10), 1400–1408.

This article presents data from a 1990 survey of a nationally representative sample of adults in the United States. The survey interview included detailed measures of different parameters of sexuality, including number of partners, condom use, and frequency of risky and safer sexual behaviors. Data on sexual activity patterns, condom use, and attitudes, beliefs, and subjective risk are reported. This article is a starting point for practitioners and researchers who want an overview of sexual behaviors in U.S. adults.

Murphy, P. A., & Jones, E. (1994). Use of oral metronidazole in pregnancy. *Journal of Nurse-Midwifery, 39*(4), 214–220.

Metronidazole is the recommended treatment for trichomoniasis and bacterial vaginosis in nonpregnant women. Because of questions regarding the potential embryotoxic and carcinogenic effects of this drug, clinicians have been reluctant to prescribe it during pregnancy.

This review summarizes evidence on risks and benefits of using metronidazole during pregnancy. The authors conclude that although there is evidence that antibiotic treatment for vaginitis will reduce the risk of preterm birth, there are few well-designed reports that confirm negative effects during pregnancy. There are no clear answers to the question of whether the benefits of oral metronidazole in pregnancy outweigh any potential risk. The authors recommend that decisions be individualized and based on perinatal risk profile, symptomatology, gestational age, patient preference and perception of risk, and availability of acceptable treatment alternatives.

Norr, K. F., McElmurry, B. J., Moeti, X., & Tiou, S. (1992). AIDS prevention for women: A community-based approach. *Nursing Outlook, 40*(6), 250–256.

Approaches to AIDS prevention have generally followed epidemiologic and medical models. From the perspective of women's AIDS prevention needs, there are several problems with the epidemiologic model. Targeting high-risk groups may have the unintended effect of supporting the stigmatization of AIDS sufferers and a view of AIDS as somebody else's problem. Focusing on high-risk groups may slow acceptance by the general public that behaviors, rather than social categories, place women at risk. The highest-risk groups are not necessarily the easiest groups to change.

There are problems associated with the medical model approach: a strong tendency to focus more on diagnosis and treatment than on prevention, and a focus on individuals that limits the model's effectiveness in AIDS prevention. The authors offer an approach to AIDS prevention that grew out of a project to promote health in low-income, inner-city communities in Chicago. Key elements of the program include: recognition of women as key health promoters for families and communities; acceptance of primary health care as a global strategy for providing minimum essential health care needs; recognition of interaction between health and social conditions, stressing self-care and community competency; and development of collaboration among health professionals, universities, and community workers. Using peer education/support groups led by trained community women and coordinated by a nurse, the model focuses on the supports needed to achieve lasting behavioral changes. These changes promote health while recognizing that achievement of health-promoting behavioral change is not solely a matter of education. The authors remind us that lasting change is only accomplished when individuals (1) recognize that their personal behaviors place them at risk, and (2) identify what they wish to change, what barriers exist, and what resources (internal and external) are available to them. The authors describe in detail how these principles are implemented to meet women's AIDS prevention needs. Readers interested in learning practical strategies are encouraged to read this article.

Nyamathi, A., Bennett, C., Leake, B., Lewis, C., & Flaskerud, J. (1993). AIDS-related knowledge, perceptions, and behaviors among impoverished minority women. *American Journal of Public Health, 83*(1), 65–71.

Women, particularly poor women of color, have become the fastest growing group likely to contract HIV/AIDS. Further, differences in AIDS knowledge and attitudes have been documented based on race, education, and place of birth. The majority of current educational programs designed to slow or prevent transmission of HIV infection are designed for gay and bisexual men. Providing education for poor women of color has been particularly difficult because of educational barriers and cultural insensitivity. Little research has focused on determining, on the basis of culture, the educational needs of impoverished minority women. In this study, 1,173 poor women of color (78% African American, 22% Latina) living in homeless shelters or enrolled in drug recovery programs were interviewed about their knowledge of AIDS, perceived risk of contracting AIDS, and sexually

risky behaviors over the previous 6 months. Assimilation into the U.S. culture was measured for the Latina women, but acculturation was not measured for the African American women, 97% of whom had been born in the United States. Women in this study were predominantly single, unemployed, and born in the United States. They ranged in age from 17 to 75. Overall, African American and Latina women were equally knowledgeable about AIDS symptomatology, the etiology of AIDS, and the behaviors known to decrease risk of HIV infection; however, misconceptions relating to HIV transmission via casual contact were prevalent. Unsafe behaviors were common, despite considerable variation between groups.

Low-acculturated Latinas reported low perceived risk and were least likely to engage in illegal drug use and sexual activity with multiple partners. Intravenous drug use was most prevalent among high-acculturated Latinas. Nonintravenous drug use and high-risk sexual activity were most prevalent among African American women. Compared to those who had no concern about contracting AIDS, women who perceived themselves to be at high risk were about 10 times as likely to have multiple partners and approximately 7 times as likely to use intravenous drugs. These findings raise further questions for investigation. Do issues of survival and lack of resources constitute barriers that override any potential impact of perceived risk among these women? Study findings strongly suggest the need for culturally sensitive programs that are not based on race alone but also on levels of acculturation. The researchers underscore the need for qualitative strategies such as focus groups and ethnographic observations. These methodologies will help us more fully appreciate the effects of drugs on sexual activity and foster the development of more effective intervention programs.

Pivnick, A. (1993). HIV infection and the meaning of condoms. *Culture, Medicine and Psychiatry, 17,* 431–453.

Health professionals frequently express disappointment about the nonuse of condoms by poor, urban sexual partners whose behaviors (or those of their partners) place them at risk for contracting STIs. Many health professionals base their health education efforts on a biomedical view of sexual behavior and sexual relationships that excludes consideration of social, cultural, and economic contexts and determinants of behaviors. This article is rich in information on the context within which condom use occurs for poor minority women. Described are activities and constructions of meaning associated with condom use among 126 drug-using African American and Latina women in methadone treatment. Statistics of condom use, marital status, and shared knowledge of HIV infection are also presented. Data were gathered over a two-year period through observation of members of a weekly support group for drug-using women in a methadone clinic. Questionnaires were used to obtain demographics, reproductive histories, drug use, and marital and residence histories. Qualitative data were derived from open-ended questions about the meanings associated with contraception, partners, HIV infection, and childbearing. Data sources were field notes, videotaped group sessions, and participant observations of informal gatherings. Meanings of condom use with long-term sexual partners included: loss of male protection; violation of constructions of intimacy; fidelity, conjugal bonding, and female identity; illness; and death. The author recommends that attempts to change condom use patterns must be based on increased vocational, educational, and social opportunities for women. STI prevention efforts would be enhanced if safer sex information interventions were based on the meaning that condom use have for women.

Schlicht, J. R. (1994). Treatment of bacterial vaginosis. *Annals of Pharmacotherapy, 28,* 483–487.

Bacterial vaginosis is the most commonly reported vaginal tract infection among women of childbearing age. Whether it is a sexually transmitted disease continues to be debated. Because it has been associated with serious health problems, such as development of preterm labor, pelvic inflammatory disease, and abnormal uterine bleeding, bacterial vaginosis can be very uncomfortable for symptomatic women and is difficult to cure. Complications of pregnancy, risk of treatment in pregnancy, method of transmission, and clinical trials of clindamycin cream or metronidazole gel are among the topics reviewed. The authors conclude that there is evidence for and against bacterial vaginosis being an STD and that potential complications such as preterm labor, delivery of a low-birthweight infant, and PID may warrant treatment of high-risk asymptomatic women, especially during pregnancy. Clindamycin vaginal cream 2% 5 gm qd for 7 days and metronidazole gel 0.75% 5 gms bid for 5 days provide safe, effective, but expensive alternatives to oral antibiotic regimens (metronidazole 500 mg po bid for 7 days or clindamycin 300 mg po bid for 7 days).

Seidman, S. N., & Reider, R. O. (1994). A review of sexual behavior in the United States. *American Journal of Psychiatry, 151*(3), 330–341.

Knowledge of the descriptive epidemiology of sexual behavior of women can enhance nursing practice with women in the areas of prevention of sexually transmitted diseases as well as general well-woman assessment and care. Using data from American surveys, the authors describe changing patterns of sexual behavior with age. Data on men and women provide a description of normative sexual behavior across the life cycle. The serious limitations of the selected studies are acknowledged. The Kinsey studies of sexual behavior in the human male and female are among the classic studies of sexual behavior that are reviewed.

Sheahan, S. L., Coons, S. J., Seabolt, J. P., Churchill, L., & Dale, T. (1994). Sexual behavior, communications, and chlamydial infections among college women. *Health Care for Women International, 15*, 275–286.

Sexual activity is an integral component of mate selection for many young women in the United States today. Thus, coping with sex-related problems becomes a significant task for college-age females. All too often, a young woman acquires a sexually transmitted infection because she does not practice safe sexual behavior, such as inquiring about a partner's sexual history. The researchers in this study (1) explored the sexual behavior patterns of a sample of college women; (2) discussed the women's communication with partners about prior sexual activity and STDs; and (3) determined the prevalence of chlamydial infections among the women. Recruited over a 4-month period were sexually active women over age 18 who came to a student health gynecology clinic with a condition necessitating a pelvic exam. The sample consisted of 146 sexually active students who had a new partner within the past 6 months, had a purulent or mucopurulent cervical exudate, cervical bleeding induced by swabbing, lack of contraception or use of nonbarrier method, and vaginal smear with 10 or more white blood cells/high-power field. In addition, a sexual risk history was obtained. In response, 38% of the women reported a history of 1 to 4 episodes of an STD, and 21% stated they had had 2 or more sexual partners within the past 6 months. Only 12% used condoms alone or in combination with another birth control method; 31% had discussed with their partner their own of their partner's sexual history. Ten percent of the women tested positive for C. trachomatis. The presence of a mucopurulent cervical discharge was the only factor found to be significantly associated with chlamydial infection. None of the sexual risk factors already noted was significantly related. Despite use of a convenience sample and possibility of provider bias in implementing screening inclusion criteria, the findings in this study support previous data on risk behaviors in young women in college.

Shervington, D. O. (1993). The acceptability of the female condom among low-income African American women. *Journal of the National Medical Association, 85*(5), 341–347.

Data from a premarketing study of the female condom, Reality, were used to assess knowledge, attitudes, and practices of low-income African American women. Three focus groups, each with 12 African American women, were used to explore the acceptability of the female condom. Discussions indicated that previously reported low-risk perceptions of HIV among African American women were true among these groups. The women included medical students, low- to middle-income high school graduates, and low-income women from a housing project health clinic. The medical students were highly informed about STDs, but the members of the other groups were generally misinformed about STDs, with the exception of HIV. All three groups reported that their male partners were resistant to condom use and that it was difficult to get their partners to use or even consider using condoms. Cultural norms of female submission and passivity in sexual negotiations were a major barrier to preventive actions among the women. For example, they felt that it would be very difficult to insist on condom use during sexual intercourse. They were enthusiastic about the female condom: they felt it would allow them control over safe sex practices without having to challenge the power of their male partners. The researcher offers some strategies for condom education, especially on use of the Reality condom: interactive small-group condom theme parties; availability of Reality in nontraditional markets such as beauty salons and nightclubs; and rap poetry such as "Ladies, protection is no longer random; for guess what, Reality is now your condom."

Stebleton, M. J., & Rothenberger, J. H. (1993). Truth or consequences: Dishonesty in dating and HIV/AIDS-related issues in a college-age population. *College Health, 42*, 51–54.

A major strategy in STD prevention has been to encourage couples to ask about their sexual partner's previous sexual history. Earlier research has suggested that large numbers of men and women lie to their new partners for the purpose of having sex. In other research, more than half of the students who had an STD reported having unprotected sexual intercourse while infected and, of these, 22% did not inform their sexual partner of their infected condition. This study explored the issue of dishonesty in dating among college students. In their survey of 171 undergraduates at a large university in the Midwest, the authors found significant attitudinal differences between male and female students. Of the students involved in monogamous relationships, 21% of women and 36% of men reported being sexually unfaithful to their current partner or to previous partners. More women than men asked partners about sexual histories prior to sexual activity, and more men than women admitted that they had lied to their sexual partner(s). A limitation of the findings is the study's lack of ethnicity information. Ethnicity questions were deliberately excluded so that individual responses could not be identified (minority enrollment is low at the study site university). Nevertheless, these findings, combined with earlier research, challenge the advisability of identifying as a component of STD prevention the questioning of partners regarding their previous sexual histories. If almost 50% of the partners can be expected to give dishonest responses, the usefulness of this strategy is limited. Educational programs should include data on the frequency of lying behaviors. The message of self-protection, with an emphasis on abstinence and consistent condom use, may then be more viable among college populations.

Stein, Z. (1993). HIV prevention: An update on the status of methods women can use. *American Journal of Public Health, 83*(10), 1379–1382.

In a follow-up to her 1990 article (Stein, 1990) calling for methods on which women might rely to protect themselves from heterosexual transmission of HIV, Stein assesses what has been learned since then and what is yet to be achieved. She notes that it is now accepted that sexually transmitted diseases other than HIV can enhance transmission of HIV. Two logical implications are the need for microbiocides and for greater emphasis on the use of barrier methods for prevention. What is currently known about chemical barriers such as nonoxynol-9 is reviewed including recent studies that suggest that low doses of this spermicide appear to provide protection. Important to note is the existence of individual local sensitivity to moderate to low doses. Factors that increase sensitivity include the vehicle, stage of a woman's menstrual cycle, presence of low grade infection, and a woman's age and nutritional status. The article also discusses the potential barrier methods such as the diaphragm, cervical cap, and female condom have for preventing HIV. She raises important questions that nurses are ideally suited to answer through well designed qualitative studies: Will women find the motivation, persistence, and resources to put a barrier in place prior to every sexual encounter? And if they do, which barrier will it be? Will partners notice the devices, and if so, will they accept or reject them? What is the role of partner negotiation and how is it achieved? Will adherence vary by culture, by training, or by context? What is the role of training and what are its essential components? Noting that we already have a battery of largely untried barrier methods, the author suggests that we must discover how to overcome behavioral obstacles to their use. Rather than speculate, we need to study unanticipated behavioral and gynecological consequences of their use.

Tichy, A. M., & Talashek, M. L. (1992). Older women: Sexually transmitted diseases and acquired immunodeficiency syndrome. *Nursing Clinics of North America, 27*(4), 937–949.

While STDs are found most often in young women (under age 25), older women (over age

50) have been diagnosed with STDs including HIV/AIDS. Reviewed in this article is information on STDs in women over 50. Specific information is described on sexual behavior in older women and the effects of aging on sexual response as well as societal views of sexuality in aging women. Primary and secondary prevention strategies are discussed and an attempt is made to identify points specific to older women. Much of the information presented in this review article is not new; what is new however is the acknowledgment that older women are at risk for contracting STDs. The article is important in that it focuses the attention of health professionals caring for older women on this largely ignored and often hidden problem.

Chapter 11

Women and AIDS/HIV

Donna Huddleston

In the United States, the paucity of HIV/AIDS studies for women underlines the importance of introducing a women's health perspective in the design of future studies. Internationally, the potentially relevant literature has focused on the transmission of HIV/AIDS in mother/infant pairs and in women labeled as prostitutes. Most of the remaining international studies examine transmission of HIV by women, and women's use of condoms.

Qualitative studies that explore women's experiences of HIV/AIDS were not found for this review. The lay literature has numerous studies of women's experiences but tends to sensationalize the emotional aspects of HIV/AIDS. Many researchers, in the United States and in other countries, have conducted studies to determine what behaviors and cognitions impede a woman from carrying condoms or initiating their use. Most studies warn that HIV transmission must be stopped but give little attention to promoting the health of women. In fact, the health of women has not been a primary concern of most researchers.

HIV/AIDS RESEARCH IN WOMEN: KEY ISSUES

Because of the complexities involved in designing comprehensive studies, several issues should be explored before conducting HIV/AIDS research, especially with women participants. First, a study should reflect a women's health perspective that looks toward improving or promoting women's well-being. This perspective should be evident in the design of the study, the development of informed consent among the women selected as participants, the methodology of the study, the analysis of the results, and the distribution of the findings to professional practitioners and to the general population of women. Too often, findings of current studies cannot be generalized beyond women labeled as prostitutes or are limited to small population segments identified with certain minority groups or with specific geographic locations.

A second issue in the design of HIV/AIDS studies of women is language. Poirer (1993) has pointed out that one's perspective in communication on topics related to HIV/AIDS can come from direct involvement or from evasion: with either choice, HIV/AIDS is still there. The language used to discuss sex and sexual matters differs from couple to couple, from household to household, and from group to group, and that variation further compounds the silence about HIV/AIDS. The silence surrounding AIDS in the United States is overwhelming, Poirer says, especially for African Americans and for residents of rural communities. That same silence about AIDS also extends to women.

To give readers a common vocabulary for purposes of this chapter, the terms and abbreviations specific to HIV/AIDS are provided in Table 11.1.

A third research issue is whether the questionnaires and instruments used to gather data about women and HIV/AIDS are valid and reliable. In most of the studies reviewed, reliability measures were given for ELISA and the Western Blot test. Frequently, these were the only reliability measures mentioned.

A fourth, international issue is hidden in many of the texts about women and HIV/AIDS: the young age of some women labeled as prostitutes. Review boards that approve HIV/AIDS studies need sensitivity to the ethical considerations that protect the inherent worth and dignity of women, especially in cultures where very young and even minor women are considered to have advantages as prostitutes. When a national government requests funding from an international body or invites researchers from abroad to conduct HIV/AIDS research, is there an intent to improve the status of these women's health, to link them with socioeconomic resources, or to encourage them to seek other work options? In some countries, widows have no other work options except prostitution and their vulnerability to AIDS is the only dimension that is examined.

**Table 11.1
Definitions/Abbreviations Specific to HIV/AIDS**

AIDS.	Acquired immune deficiency syndrome; for women, includes invasive cervical cancer (CDC, 1993e).
CD4 count.	CD4 T-lymphocyte counts, the best laboratory indication of clinical progression of HIV/AIDS. In a healthy person, the count is usually 800 to 1,200 per ml. A person with HIV/AIDS and a count > 500 generally has no symptoms. With a count of 200–500, a person is likely to develop symptoms; with a count < 200, the person has an increased risk for health problems.
Cervical ectopy.	A variation in the lining of the cervix; columnar epitheliam are found on the endocervix. Also called *erosion* or *eversion*.
*Elisa.	The enzyme immunosorbent assay (EIA). The test detects antibodies produced in response to HIV infection.
HIV-1.	Human immunodeficiency virus, the retrovirus that causes AIDS.
HIV-2 HTLV-11.	A human immunodeficiency virus that has an extremely low prevalence in the United States. Rather than routine testing, the CDC recommends testing for this virus only when high-risk factors are indicated or when there is a clear evidence of AIDS and an absence of a positive HIV-1.
Seroconversion.	A serum change from HIV-negative to HIV-positive, confirmed by the Western Blot test.
Vertical transmission.	Transfer of HIV from mother to child at birth or through breastfeeding.
Western Blot Test.	An antibody test that is more specific than ELISA. Differentiates between HIV antibodies and other antibodies that react to ELISA and indicate positive results.
ZVD, Retrovir R (Zidovudine).	An antiviral agent, formerly known as azidothymidine (AZT). Principal medication for HIV infection. Also used prophylactically during labor to prevent vertical transmission.

* Interpretive criteria are available from CDC at 1-800-458-5231.

A PROPOSED FRAMEWORK FOR HIV/AIDS RESEARCH

In the *Annual Review of Women's Health* (McElmurry & Parker, 1993), HIV/AIDS topics were a common thread in several chapters. Articles were abstracted for discussion of different aspects of women's health, but, as in this review, HIV/AIDS was seen as touching all parts of women's lives, from the bedroom to the workplace.

For this review, nursing, medical, sociology, psychology, public health, and women's studies journals were examined extensively for articles/studies published in 1993 and 1994 that pertained to women with HIV/AIDS and women's lived experiences of HIV/AIDS. The half-dozen articles dated prior to 1993 have not been previously reviewed in the *Annual Review of Women's Health*. Other articles/studies reviewed here examine some of women's behaviors and cognitions regarding HIV/AIDS.

What areas should researchers explore? A proposed framework for HIV/AIDS research is presented in Figure 11.1. The first sphere of activity is self-explanatory: information on AIDS precautions, symptoms, transmission, patient interaction, available treatment and support, and mortality must keep pace with or outdistance the spread of the disease.

The second sphere encompasses women's lived experiences of HIV/AIDS. Researchers' case studies and women's personal narratives tell how HIV/AIDS touches all parts of women's lives. Their lived experiences, which illustrate how HIV/AIDS has crept into the cultural, sexual, and socioeconomic aspects of daily living, are an excellent starting point for future action.

The proposed framework for HIV/AIDS research places self-care responses alongside women's lived experiences (see Figure 11.1). From these two sources can come relevant unification of the existing information about HIV/AIDS and practical guidance for future research. Self-care is a nursing framework communicated to patients through individual or group instruction. From the perspective of women patients, self-care encompasses women's behaviors and cognitions as they perceive HIV/AIDS and similar threats to their sexuality.

This review of the literature revealed that theoretical underpinnings for the HIV/AIDS research in women were lacking. It is imperative that we replace epidemiological models, which portray women as carriers of disease, with models grounded in theories that reflect women's experiences. In addition, the research should focus on the underlying effects of a universal health concern for women and its impact on their lives. At the University of Illinois College of Nursing, a substantial body of work has been assembled on women's self-care responses to real or perceived threats to their sexuality (e.g., Webster et al., 1986). Other past studies have examined

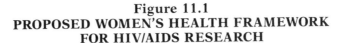

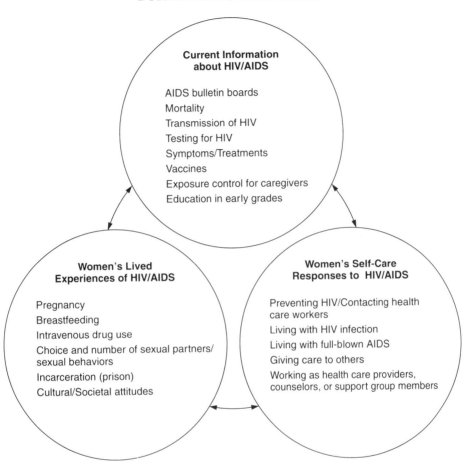

Figure 11.1
PROPOSED WOMEN'S HEALTH FRAMEWORK
FOR HIV/AIDS RESEARCH

threats to women's sexuality from mastectomy, premenstrual syndrome, and menopause.

Current Information About HIV/AIDS

AIDS Bulletin Boards.   Evidence suggests a strong and growing grassroots movement in the United States: individuals with HIV/AIDS are using electronic highways to communicate information about symptoms and treatments and to offer support to each other. Some women with HIV/AIDS are able to correspond on these electronic bulletin boards. Two popular AIDS support boards are found on Prodigy and America Online. These networks identify other bulletin boards and instruct the users in how to access them.

Mortality.   In 1994, AIDS was the fourth leading cause of death for women aged 25 to 44 in the United States. In nine major U.S. cities, AIDS was the primary cause of death for women in this age group (NIAID, 1994).

Transmission of HIV.   According to the Centers for Disease Control and Prevention (CDC) (1993a), HIV is primarily transmitted by sexual intercourse or by sharing needles with a HIV-infected person. Babies born to HIV-infected mothers may also become infected. Zidovudine is now being used to prevent HIV transmission from mother to infant (CDC, 1994). Because breast milk of HIV-positive mothers is a source of HIV transmission, researchers in other countries are studying the impact of breast feeding by HIV-infected women on child survival (Heymann, 1990). Researchers concur that HIV has a low infectious ability and that cofactors could ease transmission. Some of these cofactors are thought to be drugs, alcohol, and perhaps, geographical location.

Testing for HIV.   The CDC (1993d) reported that two tests are widely used to determine seroconversion after exposure to HIV: (1) ELISA and (2) the Western Blot (see Table 11.1). The CDC advises that ELISA results should never be used exclusively to report a positive final result. A positive ELISA should always be followed by a confirming Western Blot test. ELISA detects antibodies from other antibodies that could give a false positive. When administered together, the two tests are 99% accurate. The polymerase chain reaction (PCR) test for HIV seroconversion is experimental and is only used in research (CDC 1993c).

Symptoms/Treatments.   Little is known about women's HIV symptoms and less is known about treatments. In 1977, the U.S. Food and Drug Administration (FDA) barred women of childbearing age from early clinical trials, but this ruling has now been rescinded (Drug trial changes, 1993). The FDA cautions that frequent yeast infections could be an early sign of HIV in women (FDA warns, 1993). Invasive cervical cancer has been added to the list of diseases that are found in women with full-blown AIDS.

Vaccines.   A specific vaccine for HIV/AIDS has not been tested. However, over 20 vaccines are currently being considered for widespread testing. The article by Lurie et al. describes how these vaccines are categorized as either prophylactic or therapeutic.

Exposure Control for Caregivers.   As of November, 1993, only 39 health care workers in the United States had been documented as having seroconverted to HIV following occupational exposure (CDC, 1993b). Currently, the CDC does not recommend any established treatment or preventive measure for occupational exposure other than to report the injury to a personal physician or local health department.

OSHA regulations in some states require that exposure control supplies must be provided for employees of health care institutions. These same regulations do not apply to nonprofessional caregivers, who are most likely to be women. In the health care setting, the major risks of HIV transmission are blood contact due to percutaneous injuries, and, to a lesser extent, mucous membrane and skin contact (CDC, 1992; CDC, 1993e).

Education in Early Grades.   Sex education should begin with instruction in using a universal language for parts of the body and for body fluids. A fluids, common vocabulary would be useful to both health professionals and laypersons.

Women's Lived Experiences of HIV/AIDS

The articles reviewed for this chapter discuss women's lived experiences of HIV/AIDS. Topics covered include pregnancy, breastfeeding, intravenous drug use, choice and number of sexual partners/sexual behaviors, incarceration, and cultural/societal attitudes.

Pregnancy.   Pregnancy raises two issues pertaining to women's lived experiences: (1) HIV testing prior to pregnancy for high-risk mothers and infants and (2) vertical transmission of HIV from mother to infant during pregnancy or at delivery. It is critical to identify mothers and infants who are at risk and require further intervention.

Breastfeeding.   In the United States, breastfeeding is not as great a problem as it is in developing countries. American women have access to supplies of formula and to programs for women and infants that assist in preventing vertical transmission of HIV. In other world regions, particularly in developing countries, women have no access to such supplies and programs, and problems in providing women with health services will continue.

Intravenous Drug Use.   Hughes (1993) has noted that HIV transmission has been closely linked to alcohol and other drug (AOD) abuse. AOD abuse can impair immune responses and could possibly explain subsequent high infection rates in AOD abusers. Shields and White (1993) reported that drug dependency was a principal diagnosis in hospitalized HIV-infected women. Furthermore, cocaine users had more sexual partners and more STD diagnoses (NIAID, 1994).

Choice and Number of Sexual Partners/Sexual Behaviors.   Women live in varied cultural settings within the United States. The mores of each culture are reflected in women's choice and number of sexual partners, women's sexual behaviors, and women's beliefs about their partners' sexual behaviors. Women's sexual behaviors are in part governed by gender roles in a given cultural setting (Bernhard, 1993). Negotiating safe sex can be a primary concern for a woman socialized into a pattern of submissive behavior.

Incarceration.   Imprisonment is another concern for some women with HIV/AIDS. Studies of incarcerated women are needed to understand how to achieve health promotion and to identify the socioeconomic factors that hinder their health care.

Cultural/Societal Attitudes.   The research that has been published to date reflects a society that favors men and children over women and mothers. The stigma of STDs persists in our society. HIV/AIDS is seen by many as evidence of sin, and an underlying theme of our society is to equate sex with procreation or sin. In addition, a double standard is applied to women's behavior (Bernhard, 1993). Bernhard has posited that sexuality equals intimacy for many women. Thus, asking women, whether married or not, to carry condoms and negotiate safe sex and condom use threatens their sexuality by putting their relationships on the line. A woman is asked repeatedly, across her life cycle, to negotiate safe sex. In addition, condoms are not acceptable to many women because of reproductive issues and because they conflict with religious/cultural beliefs.

As we seek to change the behaviors of the population and to encourage women to take initiatives on their own behalf, it is helpful to examine the international studies of peer education and support for women's groups that have proven to be effective in changing behaviors.

Women's Self-Care Responses to HIV/AIDS

The self-care responses of women can be categorized by their awareness and/or acknowledgment of the risk of HIV/AIDS. Qualitative studies in this area would lead to instrument development and appropriate interventions to promote women's health and prevent the spread of HIV. Women's self-care responses can be categorized in at least 5 ways:

1. Preventing HIV/Contacting health care workers. An important self-care response is obtaining current, accurate, individualized health

information, testing, and support. The self-care responses would also include the behaviors and cognitions that women use to protect themselves from HIV infection.

2. Living with HIV infection. This category spans a woman's experiences from the time she is diagnosed as HIV positive until she has full-blown AIDS. Research would include: how the woman seeks treatment, her transmission concerns, and her breastfeeding and pregnancy decisions. What criteria do women apply when they must select health care institutions? What other agencies are needed to help meet their health and self-care needs, support their families, and access personal support, especially as the disease progresses?

3. Living with full-blown AIDS. Issues here include attainment of adequate health care, preparation for death and settlement of personal affairs, and arrangements for child care or surrogate parents for motherless children.

4. Giving care to others, usually family or friends. As caregivers, women act to prevent the spread of AIDS, promote their own health and that of others, and maintain confidentiality.

5. Working as health care providers. Key areas of concern are the hazards of occupational exposure and the quality of care provided for individual with HIV/AIDS.

REFERENCES

Bernhard, L. A. (1993) Women's sexuality. In B. J. McElmurry & R. S. Parker (Eds.), *Annual Review of Women's Health* (pp. 67–93). New York: National League for Nursing Press.

CDC (Centers for Disease Control and Prevention). (1992). Hospital infections program. CDC Doc. 370154. Atlanta: Author.

CDC. (1993a). AIDS information HIV transmission (pp. 1–2). CDC Doc. 320020. Atlanta: Author.

CDC. (1993b). Oral health program (pp. 1–2). CDC Doc. 231117. Atlanta: Author.

CDC. (1993c). AIDS information (p. 1). CDC Doc. 320320. Atlanta: Author.

CDC. (1993d). AIDS information evaluation of testing. CDC Doc. 320310. Atlanta: Author.

CDC. (1993e). Sexually transmitted diseases treatment guidelines. *Morbidity and Mortality Weekly Report, 42* (14), 10–19.

CDC. (1994). Zidovudine for the prevention of HIV transmission from mother to infant. *Morbidity and Mortality Weekly Report, 43* (16), 285–287.

Drug trial changes should open doors for HIV-positive women: U.S. Food and Drug Administration has rescinded its 1977 guidelines barring women of childbearing age from early clinical trials. (1993). *AIDS Alert, 8*(9), 129–131.

FDA warns frequent yeast infection could be early sign of HIV. (1993). *Public Health Reports, 108*(2), 259.

Heymann, S. J. (1990). Modeling the impact of breastfeeding by HIV-infected women on child survival. *American Journal of Public Health, 80*(11), 1305–1309.

Hughes, T. L. (1993). Research on alcohol and drug use among women: A review and update. In B. J. McElmurry & R. S. Parker (Eds.), *Annual Review of Women's Health* (pp. 243–285). New York: National League for Nursing Press.

McElmurry, B. J., & Parker, R. S. (Eds.). (1993). *Annual Review of Women's Health* (p. 1). New York: National League for Nursing Press.

NIAID (National Institute of Allergy and Infectious Disease). (1994). *Women and HIV infection* (pp. 1–7). Author.

Poirer, S. (1993). On writing AIDS: Introduction. In T. F. Murphy & S. Poirer (Eds.), *Writing AIDS* (pp. 1–8). New York: Columbia University Press.

Shields, A., & Whyte, B. (1993). Drug dependence: A leading diagnosis in hospitalized HIV-infected women. *Journal of Women's Health, 2*(1), 35–40.

Webster, D., Leslie, L., McElmurry, B. J., Dan, A., Biordi, D., Boyer, D., Swiden, S., Lipetz, M., & Newcomb, J. (1986). Concept paper: Nursing practice in women's health. *Nursing Research, 35* (3), 143.

American Health Consultants. (1993). Phlebotomy, IV manipulation pose most risk to nurses. *AIDS Alert, 89,* 26–27.

Although the discussion in this article is based on CDC-provided data, the authors emphasize important points for nurses about handling needles and IV paraphernalia. As of October 1991, 11 nurses had been occupationally intected with HIV; one nurse sustained two separate injuries. Seven of the injuries occurred during manipulation of an IV device. Of these 7, 3 occurred during manipulation of an IV device, 3 during cardiopulmonary resuscitation, and 1 when a patient suddenly moved. The injuries sustained by the nurses suggest that appropriate universal procedures and equipment for IV therapy should be developed to protect nurses in the same way that protocols have been developed for the safe use and disposal of needles and other sharps.

Andrews, S., Williams, A. B., & Neil, K. (1993). The mother–child relationship in the HIV-1 positive family. *Image: The Journal of Nursing Scholarship, 25*(3), 193–198.

At the Yale School of Nursing, preliminary data were analyzed from a qualitative study of the mother–child relationship for 80 women, 20 of whom were incarcerated. The women were HIV-1 seropositive and had completed one pregnancy while seropositive. Because the target enrollment for the study was 125 women, recruitment was ongoing. The purpose of the study was to examine the relationship among the amount of social support reported by the mother, her use of clinical services, and the clinical outcomes for the mother–child pair. Two interviews, at 4 months and at 6 months, were collected. The Norbeck Social Support Questionnaire and the Addiction Severity Instrument were administered. Reliability and validity of the instruments were not addressed. To gain a collective description of women's experience, the interview schedule administered to each woman had the following items:

1. Give three reasons why you remain as healthy as you are.

2. What are the reasons to tell someone you are HIV positive?

3. What are the reasons not to tell someone you are HIV positive?

4. What does support mean to you?

Data regarding CD+ cell counts and clinical status were also obtained. The mean age of the preliminary group was 30.3 years; 25% were white, 40% were African Americans, and 18% were Latinas; 51% of the women had not graduated from high school. The women were more likely to perceive their parent or their sex partners as supportive and reveal their serostatus.

Children were not always seen as supportive; some mothers feared that disclosing their HIV status to their child might lead to unwanted disclosure to neighbors, friends, and acquaintances. The mother–child relationship was perceived as burdensome by some mothers.

Asamoah-Adu, A., Weir, S., Pappoe, M., Kanlisi, N., Neequaye, A., & Lamptey, P. (1994). Evaluation of a targeted AIDS prevention intervention to increase condom use among prostitutes in Ghana. *AIDS, 8* (2), 239–246.

The use of condoms has been a global recommendation to reduce HIV transmission from women labeled as prostitutes. Family Health International (FHI) collaborated with the Ghana Medical School and the Ministry of Health to plan and implement a community-based condom program in 1988. The messages that the six peer educators delivered to the women were: (1) AIDS can kill you; (2) AIDS is spread by sex; (3) you can get AIDS even if your partner looks healthy; (4) be smart, use a condom every time you have sex; and (5) be prepared, carry condoms with you. In addition, women were provided with role playing situations that depicted methods to convince men to use condoms. In 1991, a larger group of women (n = 176) was recruited. Attrition hindered analyses of changes in condom use from the 1988 group to the 1991 group. The women who had received peer education and condoms reported increased use of condoms for 6 months following the intervention. If condoms are the answer, perhaps educational classes should be repeated on a regular basis. The researchers listed several reasons a woman might not use condoms. These are: (1) the client is a well known regular customer and looks healthy; (2) refusing sex is not an option: the money is needed for rent or food; (3) men ejaculate quicker without a condom; (4) the women lack peer social support; and (5) the women experience impaired judgment due to intoxication.

Carey, R. F., Herman, W. A., Retta, S. M., Rinaldi, J. E., Herman, B. A., & Athey, T. W. (1992). Effectiveness of latex condoms as a barrier to human immunodeficiency virus-sized particles under conditions of simulated use. *Sexually Transmitted Diseases, 4,* 230–234.

A question almost every woman has: How safe are condoms? The Food and Drug Administration's Division of Physical Sciences Center for Devices and Radiological Health tested 89 condoms in an in vitro system for viral particle leakage, using a suspension of fluorescence-labeled simulated HIV, 110-nm polystyrene microspheres. Leakage of HIV-sized particles was detectable in 29 of the 89 condoms tested (P < 0.03). The researchers concluded that the use of latex condoms substantially reduces, but does not eliminate, the risk of HIV transmission. For women, the length of exposure would be proportionate to the length of time they have contact with condoms filled with ejaculate. Thus, condoms decrease the length of exposure even with pinhole leakage.

Catania, J. A., Coates, T. J., Golden, E., Dolcini, M. M., Peterson, J., Kegeles, S., Siegel, D., & Fullilove, M. T. (1994). Correlates of condom use among black, Hispanic, and white heterosexuals in San Francisco: The AMEN longitudinal survey. *AIDS Education and Prevention,* 6(1), 12–26.

The AMEN Longitudinal Study, Center for AIDS Prevention Studies, University of California, San Francisco, is examining the distribution of HIV risk behaviors. In this part of the study, the condom use of 396 women and 320 men was correlated to socioeconomic aspects, sexual practices, and cognitions as well as to self-efficacy beliefs. Self-efficacy was defined as the belief that condoms provide an effective means of preventing HIV/STD transmission and the person's degree of confidence in his or her ability to use condoms. The mean age of the women was 30.5 years. Data were collected in two waves based on a lag model; condom use reported at Wave 2 was regressed on predictions assessed at Wave 1. People who used condoms

in their sexual encounters, relative to those who used them none/some of the time: (1) labeled their sexual behavior at high risk for HIV transmission; (2) reported sexual enjoyment when using condoms; (3) reported a history of behavioral commitment to condoms; (4) possessed better health-protective communication skills; (5) were single, divorced, or widowed rather than married; and (6) were more likely to be male than female.

Clemetson, D. B. A., Moss, G. B., Willerford, D. M., Hensel, M., Emonyi, W., Holmes, K., Plummer, F., Ndinya-Achoia, J., Roberts, P. L., Hillier, S., & Kreiss, J. K. (1992). Detection of HIV DNA in cervical and vaginal secretion: Prevalence and correlates among women in Nairobi, Kenya. *Journal of the American Medical Association, 269,* 2860–2865.

This study, conducted in Nairobi, found a relationship among 97 women's use of oral contraceptives, cervical ectopy and pregnancy, and the presence of HIV in cervical samples. HIV DNA was detected in 28 of 84 cervical samples and in 13 of 77 vaginal samples. The risk of HIV in the cervical samples increased as the areas of ectopy increased and slightly increased with the presence of cervical inflammation. The authors concluded that the presence of cervical inflammation, ectopy, and the use of oral contraceptives may increase the risk of HIV transmission from an HIV-infected woman to her sexual partners and infants. This study does not address women's risk of contracting HIV-1 when cervical ectopy is present.

Clerici, M., Levin, J. M., Kessler, H. A., Harris, A., Berzofsky, J. A., Landay, A. L., & Shearer, G. M. (1994). HIV-specific T-helper activity in seronegative health care worker exposed to contaminated blood. *Journal of the American Medical Association, 271*(1), 42–46.

The authors posited that the risk of HIV-1 transmission to health care workers from patients' blood or body fluids is low. For this study, 8 health care workers (6 men and 2 women) with high-risk occupational exposure to HIV-positive blood or body fluids were enrolled. A control group was composed of 9 women exposed to HIV-negative body fluids. Needlestick accounted for 7 of the exposures to HIV-1. Peripheral blood mononuclear cells (PBMCs) were tested in blind experiments. Polymerase chain reaction (PCR) analysis was done and reported elsewhere. The presence of the HIV antibody was measured with ELISA. The data showed an HIV-specific T-helper activated after exposure to HIV in 75% of the exposed health care workers. A significant difference in the response of the two groups was found ($P < .008$) using Fisher's exact two-tailed test. Thus, the health care workers' exposure to HIV-infected blood resulted in HIV inoculation without any evidence of seroconversion in the health care workers even after 64 weeks. The researchers also found that after aspiration of HIV-inflicted blood through a needle, HIV can be readily cultured for up to 24 hours from the residual blood contained in the needle.

Cohen, D. A., Clyde, D., Mackinnon, D., & Hahn, G. (1992). Condoms for men, not women: Results of brief promotion programs. *Sexually Transmitted Diseases, 5,* 245–251.

For some men, condoms decrease sensation during sex and interfere with spontaneity. The purpose of this study was to determine the contextual aspects of condom use in terms of social influences, community norms, and interpersonal communication skills. Data were collected from medical records (n = 609) and from a survey (n = 612) of five urban STD clinics in Los Angeles. Medical records were not available for 17% of the samples surveyed. Information on condom skills, social influences, and availability of condoms was collected after presentation of a brief intervention program that implemented three approaches:

1. Skills approach: a health educator explained condoms and demonstrated how to use them.

2. Social influence approach: a health educator emphasized: (a) condoms are becoming popular; (b) people who use condoms send a message that they care about themselves and are responsible persons; (c) condoms can be exciting—they can be fun in foreplay, they transmit body heat, and sex lasts longer; (d) role playing different strategies/approaches rehearses how to convince one's sexual partner to use condoms.

3. Businesses were recruited to provide free distribution of condoms when a person showed the appropriate card.

Among women, none of the intervention programs significantly changed the rate of return for STD reinfection (chi-square = 71, p = 0.07). Men had fewer STDs after the intervention. The change occurred even though, as the authors point out, men in other studies reported decreased sensation and spontaneity using condoms. The authors recommend that further research be conducted to identify behavior change mediators for women.

Connor, R. I., & Ho, D. D. (1994). Tenth anniversary perspective on AIDS: Transmission and pathogenesis of human immunodeficiency virus type 1. *AIDS Research and Human Retroviruses, 10* (4), 321–323.

Although not specific for women, this is an excellent review article from Aaron Diamond AIDS Research Center, New York University School of Medicine. The review covers transmission and pathogenesis of HIV/AIDS, including infection, disease progression, and long-term survivors. The review includes 22 references.

Del Mistro, A., Chotard, J., Hall, A. J., Fortuin, M., Whittle, H., De Rossi, A., & Chieco-Bianchi, L. (1994). HTLV-I/II seroprevalence in Gambia: A study of mother–child pairs. *AIDS Research and Human Retroviruses, 10*(5), 617–620.

The purpose of this study was to evaluate the vertical transmission of HIV from infected mothers to their children. ELISA and Western Blot tests were used to confirm seroconversion. Among the 909 mothers tested, 11 were seropositive. The median age of the mothers was 29. Researchers concluded that anti-HTLV-I antibodies decrease exponentially in the first 3–6 months of life and reach seronegativity at 6–9 months. Seroconversion occurred from 3–24 months after the disappearance of maternal antibodies. Breast milk of HIV-positive mothers is thought to be a principal route of vertical transmission. In Gambia, breastfeeding is universal for 18 months. The researchers proposed a 3-year follow-up program on the children born to HTLV-I infected mothers.

Ford, K., Rubenstein, S., & Norris, S. (1994). Sexual behavior and condom use among urban, low-income, African American and Hispanic youth. *AIDS Education and Prevention*, 6 (3), 219–229.

The purpose of this study was to determine levels of sexual activity, condom use, and reasons for condom use and nonuse in this population segment. Data were gathered from a household probability sample in Detroit, Michigan. The survey was conducted by the Survey Research Center of the Institute for Social Research of the University of Michigan. The data were collected from men and women aged 15–24. Over 95% of parents of persons contacted about the study agreed to let their children participate. A Spanish-language version of the questionnaire was developed for Hispanic respondents. Overall, 398 African American and 349 Hispanic females responded. The study found that a higher proportion of the Detroit African American women aged 15–19 had experienced intercourse than the national sample of women used as a control group, (p < .05). For the Hispanic group, the proportion (51.4%) was similar to the national sample. However, the Hispanic group was less likely to use any method of birth control (54% versus 39%) and less likely to have used condoms (42% versus 34%) than the national sample (p < .05). Only a small proportion of the women interviewed

reported a casual partner, compared to 44% of the African American men and 40% of the Hispanic men. This study indicates the need for planned interventions for inner-city women ages 15–24 and introduction of HIV/AIDS prevention information at a much earlier age. In addition, research that explores the differences between men and women regarding "casual sex" would be productive.

Gellert, G. A., Maxwell, R. M., Higgins, K. V., Pendergast, T., & Wilker, N. (1993). HIV infection in the women's jail, Orange County, California, 1985 to 1991. *American Journal of Public Health*, 83, (10), 1454–1456.

From 1985 to 1991, a total of 3,015 women incarcerated in Orange County Jail were tested for HIV antibody. Risk factors were determined for 59% of the women. These included IV drug use, multiple sex partners, high-risk partner, transfusion receipt, and contact with a person known to be HIV positive. Serum samples were analyzed by ELISA and Western Blot tests. Eighty-two women tested HIV positive, a ratio of 1.8 positive persons per 100 tests, or 2.7% of all women tested. The researchers recommended that efforts continue to be directed at drug treatment and AIDS prevention for incarcerated women. Furthermore, the researchers concluded that HIV prevention should focus on achieving voluntary behavior change and that voluntary rather than mandatory testing may be preferable because it fosters women's acceptance of risk reduction counseling.

Gielen, A. C., Faden, R. R., O'Campo, P., Kass, N., & Anderson, J. (1994). Women's protective sexual behaviors: A test of the health belief model. *AIDS Education and Prevention*, 6(1), 1–11.

The purpose of this study was to describe protective sexual behaviors to prevent HIV infection among women who were HIV negative or whose HIV status was unknown. The study was conducted at the Johns Hopkins obstetrical

(OB) clinic. A total of 573 women who were planning to receive their prenatal care at the clinic were recruited and enrolled in the study. (Six women who tested HIV positive were not included in the final sample size.) The participants were 90% African American; 50% had completed high school or more advanced education, 65% were age 24 or younger, and 73% were never married. The study participants were asked whether they had used the following protective sexual behaviors to prevent HIV infection: (1) had fewer sex partners (62.1%); (2) had sex less often (47½%); (3) talked with a partner about how AIDS might affect their sex life (71.9%); (4) decided not to have sex with someone because of fear of contracting the AIDS virus (46.8%); (5) used condoms when having sex (49.4%); and (6) carried condoms with them just in case they might have sex (48%). Pearson's correlation coefficients ranged from .16 to .41 for correlations among items. Carrying condoms was moderately correlated to using them ($r = .41$). Each protective behavior was analyzed separately. In addition, a health belief model was developed and tested.

Glick, M. E. (1994). Centers for AIDS research renewed, added. *NIAID AIDS Agenda*, Summer, 8.

The National Institute of Allergy and Infectious Disease (NIAID) awarded grants for three new and eight continuing centers for AIDS research at leading U.S. research institutions. These institutions and their research directors are:

1. Baylor College of Medicine, Janet Butel, Ph.D.
2. Medical College of Wisconsin, Jeffery A. Kelly, Ph.D. (in Milwaukee; supported by NIMIH)
3. Case Western Reserve University, Stuart LeGorici, Ph.D.
4. University of California at San Diego, Flosie Wong-Stool, Ph.D.
5. Aaron Diamond AIDS Research Center at New York University, David Ho, M.D.
6. Albert Einstein College of Medicine, Arye Rubinstein, M.D.
7. Dana-Farber Cancer Institute, Joseph Sodroski, M.D.
8. Duke University, Dani Bolognesi, Ph.D.
9. University of Alabama at Birmingham, Eric Hunter, Ph.D.
10. University of California at Los Angeles, Irvin S. Y. Chen, Ph.D.
11. University of California at San Francisco, Paul Volberding, M.D.
12 University of Washington at Seattle, King K. Holmes, M.D., Ph.D.

Heymann, S. J. (1990). Modeling the impact of breastfeeding by HIV-infected women on child survival. *American Journal of Public Health*, 80 (11), 1305–1309.

Vertical transmission of HIV may occur prenatally at or during birth, and postnatally by breastfeeding. Estimates were that 54% to 76% of infants are uninfected at birth.

Hutchison, M. K. (1993). HIV infection (letter). *Journal of Obstetrical, Gynecologic and Neonatal Nursing*, 22 (5), 400–401.

This letter made some excellent points regarding women's risk of HIV infection, and summarized some of the current literature (8 references) in this area. Three points made were extremely important. (1) Women distance themselves from shame by using a "them, not us" syndrome so that they will not be labeled "bad girls." The shame and stigma associated with AIDS, which often act as barriers to women's self-risk recognition, should be dispelled. (2) Women are often unaware of or uninformed about their partners' sexual history, and cultural norms about sexual communication and sex roles could interfere with women's abilities to question their partners. (3) Even when women recognize their sex partners as potential sources of HIV infection, poverty, economic dependence, threats of physical violence, and a desire to satisfy their sexual partners' needs could further inhibit negotiation for "safer sex."

Lurie, P., Makonnen, B., Chesney, M. A., Cooke, M., Fernandes, M. E. L., Hearst, N., Katongole-Mbidde, E., Koetsawang, S., Lindan, C. P., Mandel, J., Mhloyi, M., & Coates, T. J. (1994). Ethical, behavioral, and social aspects of HIV vaccine trials in developing countries. *Journal of the American Medical Association, 271* (4), 295–301.

The authors discuss the ethical issues of testing vaccines for HIV/AIDS in developing countries. Vaccines for HIV/AIDS were divided into two broad categories: (1) prophylactic vaccines and (2) therapeutic vaccines. Prophylactic vaccines prevent HIV infection. As of April 1993, there were 15 prophylactic vaccine candidates. The therapeutic vaccines prevent progression of HIV in those already infected; at least 10 of those vaccines have undergone evaluation.

McCray, E., Onorato, I. M., and the Field Services Branch. (1992). Sentinel surveillance of human immunodeficiency virus infection in sexually transmitted disease clinics in the United States. *Sexually Transmitted Diseases, 1,* 235–241.

In 1988, the Centers for Disease Control and Prevention (CDC) conducted a nationwide study in 37 metropolitan areas. A total of 176,439 sera from patients at STD clinics were analyzed for HIV. A median of 1,481 sera per clinic were tested. The sera were tested using enzyme immunoassay (EIA) and confirmed by Western Blot test. The median seroprevalence of HIV per clinic was 2.3%, with a range from 0% to 38.5%. HIV seroprevalence rates were highest in Miami, Florida, and San Juan, Puerto Rico. Both cities' rates were greater than 10%. Patients who did not report risk for HIV infection per patient record had a risk for HIV infection that was 1.0%, with a range of 0% to 10.7%. The median rates were 57% higher in men than in women (10.7%; $P < D.001$,

Wilcoxon Signed Rank Test). Gender rates in women and men who did not report risk for HIV were positively correlated with rates in male IV drug users in the same clinic, $r = 0.8$, $p = 0.001$ for women. The CDC cautions that the high level of HIV infection in IV drug users with STDs indicates a potentially explosive environment for secondary heterosexual transmission to non-drug-using sexual partners (that is, to women). The geographic distribution of HIV/AIDS cases and IV drug users in the United States was highly correlated. Women aged 19 years or younger had an HIV infection rate 3 times higher than the median rate for male teenagers. The CDC lists the following high-risk behaviors: (1) multiple sexual encounters; (2) anonymous sexual partners; and (3) participation in sexual activities that increase exposure to blood and semen. For biologic reasons, people with genital or anal ulceration may be at increased risk of acquiring and transmitting HIV.

Nemeroff, C. J., Brinkman, A., & Woodward, C. K. (1994). Magical contagion and AIDS risk perception in a college population. *AIDS Education and Prevention, 6*(3), 249–265.

This study explored the negative reactions and cognitive biases of people to indirect and noncontagion contact with people with AIDS. Specifically, general knowledge about AIDS transmission, personal worry about contracting AIDS, sex- and drug-related guilt, and actual risk behaviors were explored. A convenience sample of 600 undergraduate college students at Arizona State University were surveyed. A total of 402 (67%) questionnaires were returned; 399 were used in the final analysis of data. Of these, 225 were from women ages 18 to 48 (mean = 22.17).

Nolte, S., Sohn, M. A., & Koons, B. (1993). Prevention of HIV infection in women. *JOGNN, 22* (2), 128–134.

The authors summarized CDC statistics on women and HIV transmission. Over 50% of the women who tested HIV positive had had sex with an intravenous drug user. The CDC estimates that 0.2% of women in the United States are HIV positive. These authors recommend that nurses encourage use of latex condoms to prevent HIV transmission. Neumann's Health Care Systems Model was used to categorize care for women. The categories were: (1) primary prevention strategies aimed at promoting health and protecting women from contracting HIV; (2) secondary prevention, including early detection of HIV-infected women and educational efforts directed toward HIV-seropositive women, to prevent further transmission of the disease; and (3) tertiary prevention strategies, including early medical and psychiatric intervention after diagnosis. Women at risk should be offered testing for HIV transmission. Until there is a cure, perhaps only women who are at high risk for HIV and want to get pregnant should seek testing.

Phillips, D. M. (1994). The role of cell-to-cell transmission in HIV infection. *AIDS, 8,* 719–731.

This review article is an excellent starting point for serious study of HIV-1 virus transmission as well as a readable overview and discussion of the various theories. Basically, there are four theories about how HIV-1 enters the body and begins its destructive processes: (1) through free virions in body fluids; (2) through cell-to-cell fusion; (3) through cell-to-cell adhesion; and (4) through infected cell-releasing virus that enter epithelial cells. The authors state that some evidence exists for each of these theories. The article offers 111 references.

Smith, P. B., Weinman, M., & Mumford, D. M. (1992). Knowledge, beliefs, and behavioral risk factors for human immunodefiency virus infection in inner-city adolescent females. *Sexually Transmitted Diseases, 4,* 19–23.

This study was a joint effort of the Population Program at Baylor College of Medicine and the Graduate School of Social Work, University of Houston. In general, knowledge has not led to changes in behavior among teenagers. This study proposed to determine whether knowledge and beliefs are substantiated by high-risk behavior. A total of 565 women ages 12–20 were recruited from an adolescent family planning clinic in a public county hospital. The women were low-income; 13% were white, 62% were black, and 25% were Hispanic. Informed consent was obtained. Data from the Clemente et al. Knowledge and Attitude Scale, self-reported high-risk behaviors, and numbers of sexual partners were analyzed. Information on past STDs was obtained from medical records. Diagnostic laboratory testing for STDs was completed in 510 participants. The researchers found a significant difference in the reported number of sexual partners between women with current STD infection and women without current STD infection (P = 0.006, t test = 2.78). Similar differences were found between women who had a history of STDs and those with no such history. In questionnaire responses, 84% of the women reported that they were afraid of getting AIDS, and 59% believed they were at risk to get AIDS. Researchers found a significant difference in the number of sexual partners between women who were afraid of getting AIDS (84%) and those not afraid (26%). The mean number of sexual partners was 3.21 for those who were afraid and 2.33 for those not afraid (P = 0.02, t test = 2.24). Comparisons between ethnic groups were reported by the researchers, even though 62% of their sample were black.

Stein, Z. (1993). HIV prevention: An update on the status of methods women can use (editorial). *American Journal of Public Health, 83,* 1379–1382.

This author has summarized women's HIV transmission risks related to sexually transmitted diseases and has provided information about chemical and physical barriers. The author posited that prior or simultaneous infections with ulcerative organisms and nonulcerative organisms raise the risk of HIV transmission. The protective qualities of nonoxynol-9 in appropriate to lower doses, found in some infectious studies, were contrasted with findings that higher dosages were not found to be protective. In addition, higher dosages of nonoxynol-9 have been associated with abrasions of the vagina. The reviewer identified several factors that could confound these studies: the vehicle, the stage in the woman's menstrual cycle, the presence of low-grade infections, the woman's age, nutritional status, and the PH of the vagina. Three physical barriers other than condoms are available for women: (1) the diaphragm, (2) the cervical cap, and (3) the female condom recently approved by the Food and Drug Administration (FDA) for use in the United States. A concern is that the site of entry for HIV is unknown, and the vulva and vagina are not protected by these physical barriers. The cervix may play an important role in HIV transmission because cervical ectopy is common in adolescence. The use of oral contraceptives and the frequency of HIV infection has been reported to be higher both in younger women and in users of oral contraceptives. The article has 26 references.

Vlahov, D., Munoz, A., Solomon, L., Astemborski, J., Lindsay, A., Anderson, J., Galai, N., & Nelson, K. E. (1994). Comparison of clinical manifestations of HIV infection between male and female injecting drug users. *AIDS*, 8 (6), 819–823.

This is one of the first U.S. studies to examine symptoms, physical findings, and laboratory tests in women with HIV-1 infections. The study, conducted at the Johns Hopkins School of Hygiene and Public Health and the Johns Hopkins School of Medicine, included 562 men and 118 women who are HIV-infected IV drug users. Medians were compared using the Mann–Whitney test for medians; the means were calculated using Student's t-test; and P values were determined by Fisher's exact test (two-sided). The women in the study had a mean age of 33 years and median CD4+ lymphocyte counts of $480 \times 10.6/1$. Oral

candidiasis frequency increased as CD4 cell count decreased, in men as well as women. Women reported more outbreaks of genital herpes than men ($P < 0.05$), but the researchers found no significant difference between men and women on physical examination. The women in the study reported fatigue, weight loss, and shortness of breath as the three most common symptoms. Thirty-five percent of the 32 women with CD4 counts of less than 350 reported weight loss. The researchers concluded that, for men and women IV drug users in the early stages of HIV-1 infection, the signs and symptoms for men and women are similar. Data were collected prior to AIDS diagnosis in any of the study participants. The researchers predicted that women would probably have gynecological diseases related to HIV, bacterial infections, other sexually transmitted diseases, and possibly AIDS-defining diagnoses as the HIV infection progressed. This study reflects the need to design HIV/AIDS studies that examine the clinical manifestations for women rather than comparing the women with men. Studies should have larger numbers of women from the general population as well as female IV drug users.

Wilson, T. E., Jaccard, J., Endias, R., & Minkoff, H. (1993). Reducing the risk of HIV infection for women: An attitudinal analysis of condom-carrying behavior. *Journal of Applied Social Psychology*, 23 (14), 1093–1110.

This study aimed to examine the belief structure that determines women's attitudes toward carrying condoms. For the study, 971 sexually active women from Brooklyn, New York, were recruited. The women ranged in age from 15 to 45 (median age = 27); 75% were single and 90% were black. The women completed an interview and a questionnaire. Lisrel VII was used for a four-factor measurement model to map underlying factors. The main finding was that women perceived a social stigma attached to carrying condoms and thus were less likely to carry them.

Wood, R. W., Krueger, L. E., Pearlman, T. C., & Goldbaum, G. (1993). HIV transmission: Women's risk from bisexual men. *American Journal of Public Health, 83,* 1757–1759.

Although this secondary analysis of cross-sectional data from the AIDS Prevention Project of the Seattle–King County Department of Public Health included only men (n = 5,480), the purpose of the study was to examine the risk factors for women from bisexual men. The men were HIV seropositive and self-reported their sexual orientation: 77% were gay and reported almost no sex with women, 13% were bisexual, and 8.4% identified an average of 2.7% female sex partners in the previous year. In this study, 11% of the gay men, 20% of the bisexual men, and 34% of the men in the group that had female sex partners reported injection drug use. HIV testing was done using blood samples and enzyme immunoassay analysis. If reactive, the test results were confirmed by indirect fluorescence assay or Western Blot test. Categorical data were calculated using chi-square or Fisher's exact test, plus odds ratios with 95% confidence intervals. More injection drug users than nonusers reported having female sex partners (odds ratio = 4.2%, confidence interval 2.4–7.4). The men in the bisexual/female sex partners group reported unprotected vaginal sex. This study is typical in that the results of studies for HIV/AIDS are conducted with men and generalized to women. A replication of this study is needed from a woman's perspective. The behaviors that increase women's risk of HIV transmission should be identified, rather than the risk men pose to women.

Part VII

Mental Health/Illness

Chapter 12

Postpartum Depression in Hispanic Women

Lucy Martinez-Schallmoser

Postpartum depression affects the mother, the infant, and the entire family negatively. Early intervention with women at risk could decrease adverse outcomes. Despite its relatively common occurrence, estimated at 10% to 15% of postpartum women (Brown, 1979; O'Hara, 1987), a standardized clinical instrument does not exist to identify women at risk for postpartum depression, nor are there standardized protocols for the treatment of this serious problem. These discrepancies occur because researchers and clinicians have not agreed on the causes or factors associated with postpartum depression or even a standardized definition. If we could measure factors that may play a role in the etiology of postpartum depression, then we could predict its occurrence and intervene appropriately.

Because the United States is composed of diverse cultural groups, it is important to study cultural and social factors and their relationship to postpartum depression. Stressors, adaptive mechanisms, and predictive factors may differ. For example, cultural characteristics and socioeconomic factors related to Hispanic childbearing and postpartum mental health have not been studied. Most frequently, white, middle-income, married women have been the focus of research. Few studies have tried to ascertain whether factors related to postpartum depression in low-income women are different from those found in middle-income women. Prediction of postpartum depression necessitates an accurate measurement of factors that play a role in its etiology. Prospective and qualitative studies of minority women during pregnancy and the postpartum period have not been conducted, and are greatly needed.

Hispanics are the fastest growing minority group in the United States (Vega, Warheit, & Palacio, 1985). Within this group, Mexican American women have the highest fertility and birth rates (National Center for Health Statistics, 1989). Compared to Anglos, Hispanic women consistently report a higher rate of depression or psychological distress (Salgado de Snyder, Cervantes, Padilla, 1990); however, little is known about the mental health of Mexican American women during pregnancy or the postpartum period. A few studies of postpartum depression (Boyer & Van Der Leden, 1989; O'Grady, 1990) have included Mexican American women, but there are important gaps in our knowledge. Research that focuses on the social support networks of Mexican American women, especially during the perinatal period, is rare. Very few studies focus on the effects of social support, acculturation, stressful life events, and quality of life on their depressive symptomatology during the postpartum period. Therefore, for Hispanic women, basic questions about the relationship among these variables, from pregnancy throughout the postpartum period, remain unanswered.

REVIEW OF LITERATURE

Postpartum Depression

The literature describes numerous ways of categorizing postpartum psychological distress. Mood disorders during the postpartum period have recently been classified in the *Diagnostic and Statistical Manual of Mental Disorders* (DSM-IV; American Psychiatric Association, 1994). The onset must be within 4 weeks after delivery of a child. Postpartum major depressive, manic, or mixed episodes do not differ from symptomatology in nonpostpartum mood episodes, but may include psychotic features (American Psychiatric Association, 1994). The issues related to labeling of clients in the DSM-IV by the medical model are biased and potentially damaging to their future. In the case of postpartum depression, women's experiences are not seen as unique or affected by life experiences, culture, or socioeconomic factors. Therefore, treatment of women with this postpartum problem is based on general guidelines that are not experientially based. The time frame is too short to be able to treat women whose symptoms may appear after 4 weeks postpartum, which can cause legal and health insurance problems. At least women can now receive treatment for this disorder, but placing this postpartum mental health problem under the umbrella of non-postpartum disorders is a blind interpretation of this unique postpartum experience. Considering this problem as related to the childbearing experience is a valuable, yet belated step toward treatment and work in this area.

Commonly, postpartum psychiatric syndromes are described in three categories: (1) postpartum blues, (2) postpartum depression, and (3) postpartum psychosis (Hopkins, Marcus, & Campbell, 1984; Kumar, 1990). (Revised categories have been proposed; see Hamilton, Neel-Harberger, & Parry, 1992.) *Postpartum blues* is considered a transitory emotional lability with a rate of 50%–80%; it generally occurs 2–4 days postpartum. *Postpartum depression* has an undefined onset, from 2–8 weeks postpartum, with a rate from 3%–27% (Clarke & Williams, 1979; Tod, 1972). It may last for a few months or for more than a year. *Postpartum psychosis*, a relatively rare but severe disorder, has an incidence of 0.1%–0.2% and symptoms of manic-depressive illness, primary depression, or schizophrenia. Onset most often occurs in the first to third months postpartum. It is unknown whether these are three different illnesses or one illness with different degrees of severity. In addition, the etiology of these illnesses is unknown (Hamilton, 1989; Kumar, 1990; O'Hara, 1987). Hormonal, genetic, psychological, cultural, and situational theories have been proposed, but no definitive cause-and-effect relationships have yet been demonstrated.

Whereas postpartum blues are transitory and postpartum psychosis symptomatology is severe enough for the family to seek medical assistance, postpartum depression is frequently not identified. The health care provider may dismiss the symptoms as the "blues," or the woman may not disclose her symptoms. A female may be "minimally functioning in her role as a mother and suffering from a moderately severe depression for a long period of time" (Vandenbergh, 1980, p. 1106). Depressed mothers have been described as helpless, self-absorbed, overwhelmed, inwardly directed, overindulgent, overprotective, compulsive, guilty, resentful, and hostile—behaviors that impair their relationship with their infants, thereby possibly interfering with maternal–infant attachment (Anthony, 1983; Melhuish, Gambles, & Kumar, 1988). It appears that depressed women are unable to provide an environment that is conducive to infants' psychological development (Murray, 1988). The mothers may fail to establish mutuality and reflect back to their infants a depressed mood and rigid defenses that may promote insecurity in the infants (Anthony, 1983). Poor psychological, social, and behavioral outcomes as well as low birth weight, somatic complaints, accidents, nonaccidental injuries, poor growth, and cognitive difficulties can result (Lee & Gotlib, 1989; Zuckerman & Beardslee, 1987).

Postpartum depression may also produce untoward effects on the mother. Depressed mothers commonly experience disinterest in sex or usual activities, excessive fatigue, insomnia, or appetite disturbance (Boyer, 1990; Inwood, 1985; Vandenbergh, 1980). Women with severe depression may also be at risk for suicide (Boyer, 1990; Inwood, 1985; Vandenbergh, 1980).

Etiological Theories

In their review of the literature, Affonso and Domino (1984) classified fifteen causal theories of postpartum depression into three general types: (1) psychoanalytic, (2) personality, and (3) biophysical. Many etiologies have been suggested; most prominent are conflicts over the mothering role, inadequate personality structure, previous depressive episodes, attributional style, and the dramatic drop in hormones or change in chemical levels (Benedek, 1970; Cutrona, 1983; Dalton, 1980; Gelder, 1978; O'Hara and Zekoski, 1988; Steiner, 1979). However, additional factors have been cited as playing a role in the etiology of postpartum depression: environmental or cultural and interpersonal relationships (including stressful life events, cultural and social support, childbearing preparation, and spousal/partner relationship) (Gotlib, Whiffen, Wallace, & Mount, 1991; Harkness, 1987; O'Hara, 1987; O'Hara, Neunaber, & Zekoski, 1984; O'Hara, Schlechte, Lewis, & Varner, 1991; O'Hara & Zekoski, 1988; Paykel, Emms, Fletcher, & Rassaby, 1980; Stern & Kruckman, 1983).

Cultural and social factors, although rarely studied, must be considered when researching predictors of postpartum depression. A new mother's postpartum adaptation might be affected by cultural attitudes and practices surrounding the childbearing experience (Boyer, 1990; Harkness, 1987). Stern and Kruckman (1983, p. 1039) described the following broad cultural variations that are generally present in the structuring of the postpartum period and can affect postpartum depression:

1. Role expectations of the new mother and significant other;
2. Structure and organization of the family;
3. Recognition of a distinct postpartum period during which normal duties of the mother are interrupted;
4. Protective measures designed to reflect vulnerability of the new mother;
5. Social seclusion;
6. Mandated rest;
7. Assistance with tasks, mostly from other women;
8. Social recognition of the new status for the mother through rituals, gifts, or other means.

Such structuring of the postpartum period may affect postpartum depression, but most studies of postpartum depression have not looked at the effect of culture on postpartum depression. Stern and Kruckman (1983) hypothesize that postpartum depression in the United States may be associated with lack of social organization of postnatal events, instrumental aid and support of the new mother by extended family members, and social acknowledgment of role transition for the postpartum mother. It appears that the etiology of postpartum depression may be complex and multifactorial. Identification of characteristic predictive factors for other socioeconomic and cultural groups, such as low-income and Hispanic women, has been limited.

It is important to study the contributions of cultural and social factors to postpartum depression because the United States is multicultural, and predictive factors for postpartum depression may differ among the various populations. Research results are conflicting, regarding factors associated with postpartum depression. There has been little study of the cultural or socioeconomic variables related to postpartum depression, and the reports that do exist have focused on white, middle-income, married women. Few studies have tried to ascertain whether the predictive factors for postpartum depression in low-income women are different from those found in middle-income women.

Questionnaires, interviews, and observation are the standard methods used to identify valid and reliable predictors of postpartum depression. The validity and reliability of the instruments used have been questionable and/or reported with inconclusive results (Buesching, Glasser, & Frate, 1986; Frate, Cowen, Rutledge, & Glasser, 1979). Further testing is needed in low-income Hispanic and other minority women, to determine the validity of study results and instrumentation within these populations. Results such as those by Pitt (1968), in which the analysis considered social class, must be cautiously applied to low-income, urban, minority or Hispanic women because the Pitt study was conducted in England nearly 30 years ago.

Although this review deals primarily with issues related to postpartum depression in Hispanic women, knowledge deficits on Hispanic women and on poor, minority women were found in the literature. Therefore, it was important to touch on the literature that dealt with low-income Hispanic and other minority women and then to compare it with the literature on white, middle-income women.

For centuries, much anecdotal evidence has been observed and documented about the psychological disturbances in postpartum women. Only recently have prospective studies emerged. An abundance of literature pertains to inpatient women diagnosed as psychotic. Few systematic studies describe women during the pregnancy and postpartum periods. A major unanswered question is: Can postpartum depression be predicted during the antenatal period in women at risk for this psychological problem (Atkinson & Rickel, 1984; O'Hara et al., 1984; O'Hara, Rehm, & Campbell, 1982)?

Previous research has shown an association between several factors and postpartum depression. These factors have the potential of being incorporated in an instrument to screen for women at risk for postpartum depression. However, no cause-and-effect relationships have been established. Several weaknesses have been identified in previous studies of postpartum depression predictors.

This review will clearly establish the need to identify postpartum depression predictive factors in Hispanics because so little is known about the risk of postpartum depression in these women. Although past research has disclosed some associated factors that could be included in a prenatal questionnaire to screen women for risk of postpartum depression, testing is warranted in the specific population for which the questionnaire will be used. With demonstrated valid and reliable questionnaires, clinically based prevention and intervention programs can be initiated and evaluated for low-income women and/or Hispanics.

The fathers/partners and social support network members could be included in prenatal and breastfeeding classes, clinic appointments, and similar bilingual and bicultural educational efforts. Making the father/partner feel a part of the childbirth process could solidify or enhance the couple's relationship.

Postpartum hospital and home visits by bilingual and bicultural health care providers to primiparous and multiparous Hispanic women may also assist in the assessment of distressed postpartum women. Interventions such as home visits, phone calls, and advocacy programs by bilingual and bicultural personnel may decrease the potential devastating effects of postpartum depression on the women, their family members, and the newborns.

The results of this review clearly indicate the need to identify minority women at risk for postpartum depression. Early assessment and intervention, and continued follow-up throughout pregnancy and the postpartum period, may decrease the potential adverse outcomes of postpartum depression for childbearing women and their families. Assessment of acculturation, social support, quality of life, and depression in Hispanic women during the perinatal period is potentially important, and investigation may be warranted.

English-language journal articles were reviewed from years 1959 to 1994, including current and classic literature in the field. Articles were selected on the basis of predictive, methodological, instrumentation, cultural, and other related issues.

Recommendations and Implications

Pioneer research with minority women, especially Hispanic women, is needed to provide valuable guidelines for future researchers and clinicians. Beginning research should focus on the fastest growing minority group in the United States, Mexican Americans. Replication of studies with larger and more representative samples that reflect different socioeconomic levels, varied minority groups, and multiple sites would provide valuable information. In addition, a control group would lend validity to stated hypotheses. Improved research design would be useful in untangling pregnancy-related

and postpartum stressors, day-to-day stressful life events, and acculturation experiences that may determine the rate at which transient depressive
episodes occur. A new model could include additional data collection earlier
in the pregnancy and later in the postpartum period, as well as during well
gynecological checkups. Data collection methods using open-ended questionnaires or focus groups would provide richer data. Ideally, all interviews
should take place in the women's homes, for a truer picture of parenting
skills, interaction with family members, and the home environment. Interviewers should be bilingual and culturally sensitive to the different Hispanic cultures.

REFERENCES

Affonso, D., & Domino, G. (1984). Postpartum depression: A review. *Birth
11*(4), 231–235.

American Psychiatric Association. (1994). *Diagnostic and statistical manual
of mental disorders* (4th ed.). Washington, DC: Author.

Anthony, E. (1983). An overview of the effects of maternal depression on
the infant and child. In L. Morrison (Ed.), *Children of depressed parents:
Risk, identification, and intervention* (pp. 1–16). New York: Grune &
Stratton.

Atkinson, A., & Rickel, A. (1984). Depression in women: The postpartum
experience. In A. Rickel, M. Gerrard, & I. Iscoe (Eds.), *Social and
psychological problems of women: Prevention and crisis intervention*
(pp. 197–218). New York: Hemisphere.

Benedek, T. (1970). Motherhood and nurturing. In E. J. Anthony &
T. Benedek (Eds.), *Parenthood: Its psychology and psychopathology*
(pp. 153–165). Boston: Little, Brown.

Boyer, D. (1989). Prediction of postpartum depression. In A. McCormick
(Ed.), *NAACOG's clinical issues in perinatal and women's nursing*
(pp. 359–368). Philadelphia: Lippincott.

Boyer, D., & Van Der Leden, M. (1988). *Factors associated with postpartum
depression in low-income women.* Unpublished manuscript.

Brown, W. (1979). *Psychological care during pregnancy and the postpartum
period.* New York: Raven Press.

Buesching, D., Glasser, M., & Frate, D. (1986). Progression of depression in
the prenatal and postpartum periods. *Women and Health, 11*(2), 61–78.

Clarke, M., & Williams, A. (1979). Depression in women after perinatal
death. *The Lancet, 1*(8122), 916–917.

Cutrona, C. (1983). Causal attributions and perinatal depression. *Journal of Abnormal Psychology, 92*(2), 161–172.

Dalton, K. (1980). *Depression after childbirth.* New York: Oxford University Press.

Dalton, K. (1971). Prospective study into puerperal depression. *British Journal Psychiatry, 118*, 689–692.

Frate, D., Cowen, J., Rutledge, A., & Glasser, M. (1979). Behavioral reactions during the postpartum period: Experiences of 108 women. *Women and Health, 4*(4), 355–371.

Gelder, M. (1978). Hormones and postpartum depression. In M. Sandler (Ed.), *Mental illness in pregnancy in the puerperium,* (pp. 80–90). London: Oxford University Press.

Gotlib, I., Whiffen, V., Wallace, P., & Mount, J. (1991). Prospective investigation of postpartum depression: Factors involved in onset and recovery. *Journal of Abnormal Psychology, 100*, 122–132.

Hamilton, J. A. (1989). Postpartum Psychiatric Syndromes. *Psychiatric Clinics of North America, 12*(1), 89–103.

Hamilton, J. A., Neel-Harberger, P., & Parry, B. (1992). In J. A. Hamilton & P. Neel-Harberger (Eds.), *Postpartum psychiatric illness: A picture puzzle* (pp. 33–41). Philadelphia: University of Pennsylvania Press.

Harkness, S. (1987). The cultural mediation of postpartum depression. *Medical Anthropology Quarterly, 1*(2), 194–209.

Hopkins, J., Marcus, M., & Campbell, S. (1984). Postpartum depression: A critical review. *Psychological Bulletin, 95*, 498–515.

Inwood, D. G. (1985). The spectrum of postpartum psychiatric disorders. In D. G. Inwood (Ed.), *Recent advances in postpartum psychiatric disorders* (pp. 2–18). Washington, DC: American Psychiatric Press.

Kumar, R. (1990). An overview of postpartum psychiatric disorders. In A. McCormick (Ed.), *NAACOG's clinical issues in perinatal and women's health nursing* (pp. 351–358). Philadelphia: Lippincott.

Lee, C., & Gotlib, I. (1989). Maternal depression and child adjustment: A longitudinal analysis. *Journal of Abnormal Psychology, 98*, 78–85.

Melhuish, E., Gambles, C., & Kumar, R. (1988). Maternal mental illness and the mother–infant relationship. In R. Kumar & R. F. Brockington (Eds.), *Motherhood and mental illness 2* (pp. 191–211). Boston: Wright.

Murray, L. (1988). Effects of postnatal depression on infant development: Direct studies of early mother–infant interactions. In R. Kumar & R. F. Brockington (Eds.), *Motherhood and mental illness 2* (pp. 159–190). Boston: Wright.

National Center for Health Statistics, U.S. Public Health Service. (1989). Advance report of final natality statistics, 1987. *Monthly Vital Statistics Report, 38,* 1–45 (Supplement).

O'Grady, M. (1990). *Identifying women at risk for postpartum depression: The risk factor questionnaire.* Unpublished research project, University of Illinois at Chicago.

O'Hara, M. (1987). Postpartum "blues," depression, and psychosis: A review. *Journal of Psychosomatic Obstetrics and Gynecology, 7,* 205–227.

O'Hara, M., Neunaber, D., & Zekoski, E. (1984). Prospective study of postpartum depression: Prevalence, course, and predictive factors. *Journal of Abnormal Psychology, 93*(2), 158–171.

O'Hara, M., Rehm, L., & Campbell, S. (1982). Predicting depressive symptomatology: Cognitive-behavioral models and postpartum depression. *Journal of Abnormal Psychology, 91*(6), 457–461.

O'Hara, M., Schlechte, J., Lewis, D., & Varner, M. (1991). Controlled prospective study of postpartum mood disorders: Psychological, environmental, and hormonal variables. *Journal of Abnormal Psychology, 100,* 63–73.

O'Hara, M., & Zekoski, E. (1988). Postpartum depression: A comprehensive review. In R. Kumar & R. Brockington (Eds.), *Motherhood and mental illness 2* (pp. 17–63). Boston: Wright.

Paykel, E., Emms, E., Fletcher, J., & Rassaby, E. (1980). Life events and social support in puerperal depression. *British Journal of Psychiatry, 136,* 339–346.

Pitt, B. (1968). Atypical depression following childbirth. *British Journal of Psychiatry, 11,* 1325–1335.

Salgado de Snyder, V., Cervantes, R., & Padilla, A. (1990). Gender and ethnic differences in psychosocial stress and generalized distress among Hispanics. *Sex Roles, 22,* 441–453.

Steiner, M. (1979). Psychobiology of mental disorders associated with childbearing. *Acta Psychiatrica Scandinavica, 60,* 449–464.

Stern, G., & Kruckman, L. (1983). Multidisciplinary perspectives on postpartum depression: An anthropological critique. *Social Sciences and Medicine, 17,* 1027–1041.

Tod, E. (1972). Puerperal depression. In N. Morris (Ed.), *International Congress on psychosomatic medicine in obstetrics and gynecology* (pp. 338–340). Basel, Switzerland: Karger.

Vandenbergh, R. (1980). Postpartum depression. *Clinical Obstetrics and Gynecology, 23,* 1105–1111.

Vega, W., Warheit, G., & Palacio, R. (1985). Psychiatric symptomatology among Mexican-American farmworkers. *Social Science and Medicine, 20,* 39–45.

Zuckerman, B., & Beardslee, W. (1987). Maternal depression: A concern for pediatricians. *Pediatrics, 79,* 110–117.

Prediction of Postpartum Depression

Affonso, D., Mayberry, L., Lovett, S., Paul, S., Johnson, B., Nussbaum, R., & Newman, L. (1993). Pregnancy and postpartum depressive symptoms. *Journal of Women's Health, 2*(2), 157–164.

Boyer, D., & Van Der Leden, M. (1989). *Factors associated with postpartum depression in low-income women.* Unpublished manuscript.

Braverman, J., & Roux, J. (1978). Screening for the patient at risk for postpartum depression. *Obstetrics and Gynecology, 52*(6), 731–736.

Cox, J., Murray, D., & Chapman, G. (1993). A controlled study of the onset, duration and prevalence of postnatal depression. *British Journal of Psychiatry, 163,* 27–31.

Engle, P., Scrimshaw, S., Zambrana, R., & Dunkel-Schetter, C. (1990). Prenatal and postnatal anxiety in Mexican women giving birth in Los Angeles. *Health Psychology, 9*(3), 285–299.

Hayworth, J., Little, B., Carter, S., Raptopoulos, P., Priest, R., & Sandler, M. (1980). A predictive study of postpartum depression: Some predisposing characteristics. *British Journal of Medical Psychology, 53,* 161–167.

Leadbeater, B., & Linares, O. (1992). Depressive symptoms in black and Puerto Rican adolescent mothers in the first 3 years postpartum. *Development and Psychopathology, 4,* 451–468.

Little, B., Hayworth, J., Benson, P., Bridge, L., Dewhurst, J., & Priest, R. (1982). Psychophysiological antenatal predictors of postnatal depressed mood. *Journal of Psychosomatic Research, 26*(4), 419–428.

Martinez-Schallmoser, L. D. (1993, January). Perinatal depressive symptoms, quality of life, social support, and risk factors in Mexican-American women. *Dissertation Abstracts International, 53,* 2557.

O'Grady, M. H. (1990). *Identifying women at risk for postpartum depression: The risk factor questionnaire.* Unpublished master's project, University of Illinois, Chicago.

Playfair, R., & Gowers, N. (1981). Depression following childbirth: A search for predictive signs. *Journal of the Royal College of General Practitioners, 31,* 201–206.

Saks, B., Frank, J., Lowe, T., Berman, W., Naftolin, F., Phil, D., & Chen, D. (1985). Depressed mood during pregnancy and puerperium: Clinical recognition and implications for clinical practice. *American Journal of Psychiatry, 142*(6), 728–730.

Zayas, L., & Busch-Rossnagel, N. (1992). Pregnant Hispanic women: A mental health study. *The Journal of Contemporary Human Services, 73*(9), 512–515.

Braverman and Roux studied 120 randomly selected women over a six-month period. A special observation sheet was provided to the ward nurse on the day of discharge postpartum, and another was designed for the charge clinic nurse, to be completed during the routine postpartum visit at six weeks. Sixteen women were classified with postpartum depression. Two of the predictive items were: (1) Can you honestly say you don't want to have this child? and (2) Do you often feel unloved by your husband/partner? It appears likely that the "blues" rather than midlevel depression were predicted during an assessment performed on the fourth postpartum day. Rather than asking the women to describe their feelings, the study asked nurses to describe women's emotional reactions during the postpartum period, as an assessment of postpartum depression. A demographic description of the sample was not addressed.

Similarly, rather than using self-report, Playfair and Gowers utilized physicians' perceptions of depressive symptomatology with a convenience sample of 618 women. The women, from the British Isles, were recruited by the physicians during the antenatal period, as they presented for care. The physicians recorded information on a symptom checklist and made reports at the initial antenatal appointment, during the second trimester and the second week postpartum, as well as three months after birth—a total of 12 months. The mood of the mother and the presence or absence of 13 symptoms were recorded. Twenty-four percent had three or more symptoms of depression at (or about) three months after birth, and 10% had six or more symptoms. Perinatal and postnatal predictive factors of postpartum depression were: depressive symptoms at 22–30 weeks of pregnancy and at 6–20 days postdelivery—stress after the confinement but unrelated to the pregnancy, history of previous postpartum depression, number of past pregnancies of less than 28 weeks' duration, painful menstruation, previous psychiatric illness, and partner's employment status. They did not examine socioeconomic or cultural differences in the women.

A convenience sample of 4 black and 16 Anglo pregnant women without psychiatric histories were recruited for the study by Saks and colleagues; 5 of the women were multiparous and 15 were primiparous. Questionnaires were completed by the women during the 26th and 36th weeks of pregnancy and at two days and six weeks postpartum. Two psychiatrists interviewed the women at six weeks postpartum and rated them for depressive symptoms during the week before the interview and at any time during the previous six weeks. Two women (10%) were found to be depressed at six weeks postpartum in this very small sample of 20 women. The sample was too small to allow for meaningful analyses of relationships of demographic data and depression. Therefore, results must be generalized with caution.

The results of the research seeking predictive factors for postpartum depression have been conflicting. In their convenience sample of 166, Hayworth and associates had English women fill out three questionnaires during their antenatal visit. Most of the women successfully completed the antenatal questionnaires while waiting for their appointment; however, some of the women returned them the following week. A depression scale was mailed to the subjects six weeks after delivery. Over 76% (127) of the questionnaires were returned. There was a positive association between prenatal locus of control and postpartum depression. Those under 20 years of age tended to be depressed. Third-trimester measurements of anxiety were found to be highly and positively correlated with postpartum depression. There was no association between postpartum depression and socioeconomic, racial, gravidity, parity, and marital status.

Little and colleagues, in their subsample of 47 women from an original number of 108 women, found the first-trimester psychological variables of hostility and anxiety to be better predictors of postpartum depression than maternal physiological responses to a crying baby. The decision to select a subsample was based on an earlier pilot study in which women with high anxiety or hostility scores were shown to be more at risk for postpartum depression.

Cox, Murray, and Chapman selected 232 matched pairs of women to participate in a study of postnatal depression. The postpartum women were given depression questionnaires at some time closely following birth and during the six-month period thereafter. The control group of women were given the questionnaire at the same intervals. The groups were matched for marital status, number of living children, and income class, but the post-partum women were younger than the controls (25 years versus 27 years, respectively). The control group had children at least one year of age. (The postpartum group's neonates were approaching six months of age.) Analysis showed no significant difference between the two groups in the prevalence of depression dur-ing the first interview (9% postpartum group versus 8% control group, respectively) and the second interview at six months postpartum (14% postpartum group versus 13% control group, respectively). However, the depression lasted longer for the control group than for the postpartum women (50 weeks versus 36 weeks, respectively). No interviews were performed during pregnancy nor was the time of postpar-tum interviews given in the report. The results showed an increase in the incidence of depres-sion in both groups at six months. The post-partum women may have had increased depression because of their new roles, mater-nal stresses, day-to-day stresses, and life-event changes. Because these variables were not mea-sured, it is uncertain whether these variables or others are contributing to depression in both groups.

Affonso and colleagues performed a prospective, longitudinal, exploratory study aimed at examining the grouping of depressive symptoms of the Schedule of Affective Disor-ders and Schizophrenia (SADS) in women dur-ing their pregnancy–postpartum period. They used a convenience sample of women who were mostly white (76%), had an average age of 30 years (range = 20 to 40 years), had received an average education of 16 years (range = 11 to 24 years), were married (89%), had planned their pregnancy (80%), and verbally desired the pregnancy (99%). Interviews were performed at 10–14 and 30–32 weeks of pregnancy, and at 1–2 and 14 weeks postpartum. A specific but differing cluster of symptoms was found throughout the pregnancy and postpartum pe-riods. Symptom clusters at 10–14 weeks of pregnancy were: dysphoric mood, worrying, and psychic anxiety; and poor appetite, social withdrawal, psychomotor retardation, weight loss, and indecisiveness. A symptom cluster

during the second trimester and 1–2 weeks postpartum was: concern with the body, dis-couragement, and psychomotor retardation. The symptom cluster at 14 weeks postpartum was: quality of mood, dysphoric mood, nega-tive self-evaluation, self-reproach, guilt, and social withdrawal. Although this was a prelim-inary study, it is apparent that research efforts must continue to evaluate, during the preg-nancy and postpartum periods, depressive symptom assessment tools that are designed around women's childbearing experience.

Studies of psychological distress in Mexi-can American women during the pregnancy and postpartum periods have been rare. Boyer and Van Der Leden used a retrospective method to study 188 English-speaking and 40 Spanish-speaking women at their 4- to 6-week postpar-tum clinic visit. The English-speaking group consisted of 78% black, 12% non-Hispanic white, and 10% Hispanic women, with these characteristics: average age of 22 years, average of 11 years' education, 79% single, 50% primi-paras, and 85% with a yearly income of less than $10,000. Of the English-speaking women, 29% were 14 to 18 years old. The Spanish-speaking group consisted of 100% Hispanic, primarily Mexican, women, with an average age of 26 years, average of 8 years' education, 35% single, 21% primiparas, and 80% with a yearly income of less than $5,000. The study looked at depression and risk factors associated with postpartum depression. Thirty-three per-cent of the English-speaking group and 17.5% of the Spanish-speaking group exhibited post-partum depression. The incidence of depression was not significantly different between the groups. Within the English-speaking group, the incidence of depression was 33% for blacks, 57% for whites, 47% for Hispanics, and 26% for teens. Risk factors most predictive of post-partum depression for the entire sample were: feeling depressed or worried during the preg-nancy, being a nervous person or one who wor-ries, having had an unhappy childhood, and having life disrupted by the demands of caring for the baby. Analyses were performed to deter-mine the factors for the English-speaking and Spanish-speaking groups that were associated with postpartum depression. This study of poor, minority, and Anglo postpartum women helps mark the beginning of research in an area that lacks knowledge of these women, although it is hard to determine the significance of the incidence of postpartum depression in this sample in relationship to a study with randomized subjects or subjects as their own controls. One aim of the study was to construct a revised instrument that could identify women at risk for postpartum depression. Such an instrument would need continued validity for its use with English-speaking and Spanish-speaking Hispanic, other minority, and low-income women.

Engle and associates studied 291 Mexican American primiparous women, of whom 96% were born in Mexico. More than one-fourth of the women had been in the United States less than 1 year, and more than three-fourths had been in the United States 6 years or less. A preference for receiving explanations in Spanish was requested by 87% of the women. Age ranged from 15 to 38 years, with a mean of 22.6 years. The mean number of formal years of education was 7.6 years (range = 0 to 17). Based on occupation and education, the majority of the sample had low socioeconomic status. Sixty-six percent of the women were married.

These researchers found antenatal anxiety to be the strongest predictor of postpartum anxiety. Three other associated variables were: (1) negative attitude toward the newborn, (2) more complications during labor and delivery, and (3) less desire for control during labor and delivery. Depression was not measured in the study. Acculturation was not directly associated with prenatal or postnatal anxiety. Incidentally, for all women, the most important characteristic of doctors and nurses was that they explain what was happening (selected as "very important" by 90% of the women). The more anxious the women, the more they felt that physicians and nurses should be Hispanic and friendly.

O'Grady explored the concept of postpartum depression and risk factors with a beginning sample of 147 African American women during their pregnancy and a residual of 72 women during the postpartum period. Because approximately 51% of the subjects were lost during the postpartum data collection, the statistical analyses may have been compromised. The risk factor instrument used by O'Grady was the revised version used in the study by Boyer and Van Der Leden (see above). The age of the subjects ranged from 18 to 36 years; mean age was 23 years. Seventy five percent of the women were multiparous. Years of education ranged from 9 to 16 (average = 12 years). Seventeen percent were married, and 90% had a yearly income of less than $15,000. Antenatal depression was found to be significantly related to postpartum depression: the incidence of antenatal depression was 38% and 29% postnatally. Having an unplanned pregnancy, having housing or personal problems, having had a poor relationship with one's father, faulting oneself when bad things happen, and often feeling unloved by the husband/partner were risk factors significantly associated with postpartum depression for this sample. It is not known whether only data on subjects remaining in the study during the postpartum data-collection period were used for the final analysis. Although the risk factors differed in this sample as compared to Boyer and Van Der Leden's initial study, cultural differences and the sample's multiparous status may have affected the results.

Leadbeater and Linares studied depressive symptoms in 120 primarily primiparous adolescents. Approximately 54% were black and 43% were Puerto Rican. Their average age was 17 years; 67% of their families were on welfare and 72% of the new mothers lived with their own mothers. Initially, 49% were enrolled in school and 52% had completed high school. Depressive symptoms, stressful life events, and social support were assessed at 2–4 weeks postpartum, 6–7 months postpartum, 12–13 months postpartum, and 28–36 months postpartum. No significant ethnic differences in depression scores were found at any time or across depression group categories; data for the ethnic groups were therefore combined for analysis. Depression was positively related to stressful life events and negatively related to perceived social support and grandmothers' acceptance of the adolescent mothers at 2–4 weeks and 6–7 months postpartum. Baseline depression scores, life events, and social support during pregnancy may have shed some light on adaptation during pregnancy and the onset of depression postnatally.

Zayas and Busch-Rossnagel, in their pilot study, explored anxiety, depressive symptoms, and language preference in 86 pregnant Hispanic women whose ages ranged from 13 to 42 years (mean age = 22 years). Seventy-one percent of the women were Puerto Rican, and 29% were Dominican and Central and South American. All of them were from low socioeconomic backgrounds. Average education completed was 10 years (range = 4 to 14 years). Twenty-nine percent of the women were married, and 41% were primiparous. Teens (13 to 18 years) made up 31% of the sample. Almost 50% of this convenience sample of pregnant women exhibited depressive symptoms. The older women were slightly more depressed than the younger women.

Bilingualism was associated with lower levels of depression and anxiety in the older women. In the younger women, preference for English was associated with lower levels of depression and anxiety and bilingualism was associated with higher levels of depression and anxiety. Although this was a pilot study, the results provide valuable information on depression and language preference in Hispanic women during pregnancy. Data collected during the postpartum period would have provided even richer results. It is suggested that the main study have larger numbers in each Hispanic group and that data be analyzed separately, to determine group differences and similarities. It should not be assumed that the groups are alike. Use of a multidimensional acculturation instrument is suggested because the process of acculturation involves much more than language preference: cultural heritage, orientation of social conduct, ethnic identity, cognitive style, and perceptual behaviors are contributing factors.

The study by Martinez-Schallmoser explored acculturation, social support, risk factors, and quality of life, and their relationship to depressive symptomatology at 34–36 weeks of pregnancy and 4–6 weeks postpartum in a convenience sample of 66 multiparous Mexican American women. Age ranged from 20–39 years (mean = 28 years). Eighty-nine percent were first generation and primarily Spanish-speaking. The average length of time living in the United States was about 11 years (range = 2 months to 33 years). Sixty-eight percent of the women were married. All the women were multiparous; 14% had yearly income of less than $5,000, and 41% had yearly income of $5,000 to $10,000. Mean length of education was 9 years; nearly 49% had 8 years or less. Women who were more acculturated had higher third-trimester depression scores. A multidimensional acculturation instrument was utilized for the study. Thirty-eight percent of the subjects during the antenatal period and 53% during the postpartum period exhibited depressive symptoms. Antenatal depression was found to be the strongest predictor of postpartum depression.

The questionnaire assessing risk factors in this sample was used by O'Grady (1990) and had been validated for a pilot study prior to its use in this study. The following risk factors were associated with postpartum depression: having a history of miscarriage, having lost an unborn child, worrying about money or about housing or personal problems, and feeling depressed following the birth of an earlier child. The small sample size limits the generalizability of results to antepartum and postpartum Mexican American women. Without a control group, pregnancy-related and postpartum stressors, day-to-day stressful life experiences, and acculturation experiences that may determine the rate at which transient depressive episodes occur remain intertwined.

As with other studies of postpartum depression that have convenient samples, the results may represent a lower incidence of depressive symptoms because women with depressive symptoms who have young children at home or who lack resources for prenatal care may have been reluctant to leave their homes for health care. Thus, this group is underrepresented in the sample. The incidence rate may also be lower because postpartum depression may not occur within 4 to 6 weeks postpartum or may increase after this time.

Parity, Age, and Socioeconomic Variables

Cox, J., Connor, Y., Henderson, I., McGuire, R., & Kendell, R. (1983). Prospective study of the psychiatric disorders of childbirth by self-report questionnaire. *Journal of Affective Disorders, 5,* 1–7.

Foundeur, M., Fixsen, C., Triebel, W., & White, M. (1959). Postpartum mental illness. *Archives of Neurology and Psychiatry, 77,* 503–511.

Gotlib, I., Whiffen, V., Wallace, P., & Mount, J. (1991). Prospective investigation of postpartum depression: Factors involved in onset and recovery. *Journal of Abnormal Psychology, 100*(2), 122–132.

Grossman, F., Eichler, L., & Winiehoff, S. (1980). *Pregnancy, birth and parenthood.* San Francisco: Jossey-Bass.

Kumar, R., & Robson, K. (1978). Neurotic disturbance during pregnancy and the puerperium: Preliminary report of a prospective study of 119 primiparae. In M. Sandler (Ed.), *Mental illness in pregnancy and the puerperium* (pp. 40–51). New York: Oxford University Press.

Kumar, R., & Robson, K. (1984). A prospective study of emotional disorders in childbearing women. *British Journal of Psychiatry, 144,* 35–47.

Little, B., Hayworth, J., Benson, P., Bridge, L., Dewhurst, J., & Priest, R. (1982). Psychophysiological antenatal predictors of postnatal depressed mood. *Journal of Psychosomatic Research, 26*(4), 419–428.

O'Hara, M., Rehm, L., & Campbell, S. (1982). Predicting depressive symptomatology: Cognitive–behavioral models and postpartum depression. *Journal of Abnormal Psychology, 91*(6), 457–461.

Pop, V., Essed, G., De Geus, C., Van Son, M., & Komproe, I. (1993). Prevalence of postpartum depression or is it post-puerperium depression? *Acta Obstetrica et Gyncologica Scandinavica, 72,* 354–358.

Stein, A., Cooper, P., Campbell, E., Day, A., & Altham, P. (1989). Social adversity and perinatal complications: Their relation to postnatal depression. *British Medical Journal, 60,* 449–464.

Vandenbergh, R. L. (1980). Postpartum depression. *Clinical Obstetrics and Gynecology, 23*(4), 1105–1111.

Several authors disagree over whether parity, age, and socioeconomic status are associated with postpartum depression. Foundeur, Fixsen, Triebel, and White studied 200 women, evenly divided between a control group and an experimental group. Mean age in each group was approximately 31 years; approximate range was 19 to 44 years. The site of the observation was within a mental hospital after their admission as inpatients, which was judged to be precipitated by childbirth. Foundeur and colleagues found that 50% of the women had postpartum depression as a reaction to the birth of a later child versus their first child. Thirty percent of the women in both groups had a history of mental illness before this hospitalization. Approximately the same number in both groups had a previous admission to a psychiatric hospital.

Vandenbergh found that primiparous and older women were at risk for postpartum depression, as were women with a lengthy interval between their current and previous pregnancies. Yet parity was found not to be related in other studies (see Cox et al., Gotlib et al., and O'Hara et al.).

Cox and colleagues studied 230 women at 12 and 23 weeks of pregnancy and at 1 week and 5 months after childbirth. Utilizing visual analogues and scales, no association was found between depression or anxiety and marital status, social class, or gravity.

Using several measures via mail, Gotlib and associates studied a convenience sample of

730 primiparous and multiparous women during the second trimester of pregnancy and at approximately 4 weeks postdelivery. The depressed women had fewer years of formal education, and fewer were employed outside of the home. There was no significant difference in marital status, years married, number of children, or age between those women who became depressed postnatally and those who remained nondepressed. Analyses of potential differences between primiparous and multiparous women were not performed.

O'Hara and colleagues used several questionnaires during the second trimester of pregnancy and between 5 and 20 weeks postpartum in their study of 170 women. The convenience sample was made up of 87% white women of whom 85% were married. Their mean educational level was 13.9 years, and 45% of them were childless. Education and income levels, parity, and marital status were not predictive of postpartum depression.

Little and associates, who used a relatively small subsample of 47 women from an original number of 108 women, did not describe possible risk factors such as: parity, marital status, or cultural or socioeconomic characteristics. The decision to select a subsample was based on an earlier pilot study in which women with high anxiety or hostility scores were more at risk for postpartum depression.

Kumar and Robson, in 1978 and 1984, found women 30 years or older were more likely to exhibit postpartum depressive symptoms. O'Hara and colleagues found no relationship to age. Kumar and Robson (1984) interviewed 119 primiparous women and followed them up at 4 years. Clinical screening was performed at 12, 24, and 36 weeks of pregnancy, 3 and 6 months postpartum, and 1 and 4 years postpartum. Women older than 30 years were more likely to be depressed postnatally, but the number of women, time of onset, and duration are not clearly stated in the article. In their preliminary (1978) article discussing the same study, they discovered that women 30 years or older were more likely to be depressed at 3 months postdelivery.

Stein and associates, who followed 460 Oxford women up to 3 months postnatally, found that low-income women's odds of developing postpartum depression were increased by 3 ½ times, as compared to women with higher incomes.

Grossman, Eichler, and Winiehoff, using several instruments, followed 107 primiparous and multiparous women during the first trimester, at 8 months of pregnancy, during labor and delivery, at 2 months postpartum, and at 1 year postpartum. All the women were at middle-income levels. First-time mothers had a mean age of 27 years (range = 21 to 34 years) and were married a mean of about 3 years. Experienced mothers had a mean age of 28.9 years (range = 21 to 33 years) and were married a mean of 6.6 years. The study also included the women's partners. Women with higher socioeconomic status had a better marital adjustment. The relationship between socioeconomic status and depressive symptoms was not explored. Participation in a multiple measurement study may decrease the effects of postpartum depression or assist women in resolving distressful problems.

Pop and associates followed primiparous and multiparous women during 32 weeks of pregnancy, 4 weeks postpartum, and every 6 weeks until 34 weeks postpartum. They looked at the blues, depression, and premenstrual syndrome. The multiparous women were an average age of 31 years and the primiparous women, 27 years of age. Twenty-one percent, although not depressed during pregnancy, developed postpartum depression. Total sample incidence of postpartum depression was highest (approximately 14% at 10 weeks postpartum. Fifty-five percent of the primiparous women and 29% of the multiparous women reported the blues. Seventeen percent of the sample recalled having experienced premenstrual syndrome. Fifteen percent of the primiparous women and 18% of the multiparous women suffered from premenstrual syndrome. Social class, use of oral contraceptives, and age were not related to postpartum depression. Recall took place during the pregnancy. Recall of premenstrual syndrome may have been affected by time (32 weeks) into the pregnancy. In-depth analysis of the data was not presented.

Antenatal Depression

Braverman, J., & Roux, J. (1978). Screening for the patient at risk for postpartum depression. *Obstetrics and Gynecology, 52*(6), 731–736.

Campbell, S., Cohn, J., Flanagan, C., Popper, S., & Meyers, T. (1992). Course and correlates of postpartum depression during the transition to parenthood. *Development and Psychopathology, 4,* 29–47.

Foundeur, M., Fixsen, C., Triebel, W., & White, M. (1959). Postpartum mental illness. *Archives of Neurology and Psychiatry, 77,* 503–511.

Gotlib, I., Whiffen, V., Wallace, P., & Mount, J. (1991). Prospective investigation of postpartum depression: Factors involved in onset and recovery. *Journal of Abnormal Psychology, 100*(2), 122–132.

O'Hara, M. (1985). Psychological factors in the development of postpartum depression. In D. G. Inwood (Ed.), *Postpartum psychiatric disorders* (pp. 42–57). Washington, DC: American Psychiatric Press.

O'Hara, M., Neunaber, D., & Zekoski, E. (1984). Prospective study of postpartum depression: Prevalence, course, and predictive factors. *Journal of Abnormal Psychology, 93*(2), 158–171.

O'Hara, M., Rehm, L., & Campbell, S. (1982). Predicting depressive symptomatology: Cognitive-behavioral models and postpartum depression. *Journal of Abnormal Psychology, 91*(6), 457–461.

O'Hara, M., Schlechte, J., Lewis, D., & Varner, M. (1991). Controlled prospective study of postpartum mood disorders: Psychological, environmental, and hormonal variables. *Journal of Abnormal Psychology, 100*(1), 63–73.

Playfair, R., & Gowers, N. (1981). Depression following childbirth: A search for predictive signs. *Journal of the Royal College of General Practitioners, 31,* 201–206.

Antenatal depression has been found to be a predictive variable of postpartum depression. Gotlib and colleagues, as previously described, studied a convenience sample of 739 primiparous and multiparous women during the antenatal and postnatal periods. They found that antenatal depression was one of the strongest predictors of postpartum depression. O'Hara, Schlechte, and associates studied a sample of 182 pregnant women and 179 controls. Subjects had been asked to provide names of five acquaintances who were of similar age, marital status, and work status, and who had a similar number of children. Childbearing subjects had a mean age of 27 years; the control group, a mean of 27.5 years. The mean educational level for the pregnant subjects was 15 years; for the control group, 14.8 years. Years married for the pregnant women was a mean of 4 years; for the controls, 6 years. Forty-three percent of the childbearing women and 59% of the controls had one or more children. Socioeconomic levels were essentially equivalent but were not specifically described. The study looked at depression and other measures of both groups during the pregnancy and postpartum periods. Depression measures and diagnostic interviews were performed during the second trimester of pregnancy and at 9 weeks postpartum. Depression during pregnancy showed the strongest association with postpartum depression and was one of the significant predictors of postpartum depression.

In a study by O'Hara, Neunaber, and Zekowski, 99 women were interviewed twice for diagnostic purposes during the second trimester and at 9 weeks postpartum. Also, questionnaires were given to this convenience sample 6 weeks prior to their due dates and at 3, 6, and 9 weeks postpartum. Higher levels of depression were found during pregnancy than during the postpartum period. Depression during the second trimester of pregnancy significantly predicted postpartum depressive symptoms at 9 weeks postpartum. Previous familial history of depression was a strong predictor for postpartum depression diagnoses at 9 weeks postpartum. As previously described, O'Hara, Rehm, and Campbell also found antenatal depression to be strongly predictive of postpartum depression in their sample. Women exhibited significantly higher levels of depression during pregnancy than during the postpartum period. Although the Playfair and Gowers study had methodological flaws, one of the predictors of postpartum depression was depressive symptoms during the fifth and sixth months of pregnancy.

Women appear to be at risk for postpartum depression or psychiatric illness if there is a previous history of postpartum depression or psychiatric disturbance. In the previously described studies, Braverman and Roux and Playfair and Gowers, found a history of postpartum depression to be predictive of postpartum depression. Foundeur and colleagues, O'Hara (1985), and O'Hara, Schlechte, and colleagues found that a previous history of mental illness was predictive of postpartum depression. O'Hara, in the second prospective study, followed 99 women during their second trimester of pregnancy, approximately 9 weeks postpartum, and 6 months postpartum. Mental health history was a significant predictor of postpartum depression diagnosis. This history encompassed the number of previous episodes of depression and whether the subject had a depressed parent or sibling.

Campbell and colleagues performed a smaller study with postpartum depressed women and a matched control group of women from a larger main study. Depression as well as personal and family histories of psychopathology were analyzed for both groups. There was no difference in age, education, or occupation between the groups. Fifty-one percent of the depressed group, as compared to 25% of the controls, had parents with a history of psychopathology. A maternal history of affective disorder was one of the predictors of postpartum depression at two months postpartum.

Life Events, Childcare, Attributional Style

Cutrona, C. (1983). Causal attributions and perinatal depression. *Journal of Abnormal Psychology*, 92(2), 161–172.

O'Hara, M., Neunaber, D., & Zekoski, E. (1984). Prospective study of postpartum depression: Prevalence, course, and predictive factors. *Journal of Abnormal Psychology*, 93(2), 158–171.

O'Hara, M., Schlechte, J., Lewis, D., & Varner, M. (1991). Controlled prospective study of postpartum mood disorders: Psychological, environmental, and hormonal variables. *Journal of Abnormal Psychology*, 100(1), 63–73.

Paykel, E., Emms, E., Fletcher, J., & Rassaby, E. (1980). Life events and social support in puerperal depression. *British Journal of Psychiatry*, 136, 339–346.

Some research findings have shown an association among stressful life events, childcare-related stressors, and dysfunctional attributional style with increased postpartum psychological distress. Cutrona studied childcare stress and attributional style as predictors of postpartum depression in 85 pregnant women. Attributional style of a person involves the effects of how individuals discern the causes of events. The subjects were women who were giving birth to their first child, were married or in a committed relationship, had a mean age of 26 years, and were medically healthy. The sample's ethnic composition was 95% Anglo, 2% African American, and 2% Asian. The mean number of years married was three years. At least one year of college had been completed by 86% of the sample, and 59% had a bachelor's degree or graduate training. Interviews took place during the third trimester of pregnancy, approximately two weeks and eight weeks after delivery. Negative child-related events were strongly predictive of postpartum depression at eight weeks, as was attributional style. For those women depressed at two weeks postpartum, pregnancy-related attributional style was a significant predictor of postpartum depression at eight weeks after delivery. Results were based on a middle-income, highly educated sample as compared to other studies. The study should be replicated with a low-income, less educated sample, to measure any differences in the results.

O'Hara, Schlechte, and colleagues, as described earlier, also found that the number of stressful life events since delivery and the number of child-related stressors were significant predictors of postpartum depression in their sample. O'Hara, Neunaber, and Zekowski, as previously described, found life stress to be another significant predictor of postpartum depression diagnosis at 9 weeks postpartum.

Paykel and associates followed-up 117 postpartum Anglo women in England at 5 to 8 weeks postpartum and again 3 weeks later. Undesirable, recent life events were significant predictors of postpartum depression. However, it was not known whether postpartum depression occurred at the 5–8-week period or 3 weeks after that time. Because depression was not assessed during pregnancy, it is uncertain whether subjects were depressed during their pregnancy and, therefore, whether their depression was a new event, a continuation from pregnancy, or an increase or decrease in a continuing depressive level.

Turbulent or Interrupted Parent–Child Relationships

Buchwald, J., & Unterman, R. (1982). Precursors and predictors of postpartum depression: A retrospective study. *Journal of Preventive Psychiatry, 1*(3), 293–308.

Gotlib, I., Whiffen, V., Wallace, P., & Mount, J. (1991). Prospective investigation of postpartum depression: Factors involved in onset and recovery. *Journal of Abnormal Psychology, 100*(2), 122–132.

Kumar, R., & Robson, K. (1978). Neurotic disturbance during pregnancy and the puerperium: Preliminary report of a prospective study of 119 primiparae. In M. Sandler (Ed.),

Mental illness in pregnancy and the puerperium (pp. 40–51). New York: Oxford University Press.

Kumar, R., & Robson, K. (1984). A prospective study of emotional disorders in childbearing women. *British Journal of Psychiatry, 144*, 35–47.

Turbulent or interrupted parent–child relationships have been considered risk factors for postpartum depression. Buchwald and Unterman performed in-depth, open-ended interviews retrospectively with 31 postpartum women. Subjects were randomly chosen from postpartum and well-baby clinic clients. After initially answering a brief screening questionnaire, patients whose answers suggested the possibility of depression were interviewed at length by a psychiatrist. Patients for whom a clear diagnosis of postpartum depression was established were then given in-depth interviews. Women who experienced early physical or emotional separation from their mother or manifested an impaired subject–mother relationship and a disturbed subject–father relationship were identified as having risk factors for postpartum depression. No information is given on the reliability of the psychiatrists' assessments of postpartum depression nor on the criteria used to arrive at such a diagnosis. There is also no baseline information on the mental health of these women during pregnancy. Ninety-three percent of the women had a previous mental health problem—in particular, postpartum depression. Potentially faulty memory recall could also have affected the results of this study.

Gotlib and associates' study of primiparous and multiparous women revealed that these women had significantly more negative perceptions of the amount of caring they received from their mothers and fathers. Previously described studies by Kumar and Robson strongly suggest a link between subjects' difficulty in their parental relationships and postpartum depression. The studies suggest that a woman's perception of being cared for by her parents provides the confidence needed to adapt to the postpartum period, which may contribute to postpartum mental health.

Reactions Toward Pregnancy and Infertility

Braverman, J., & Roux, J. (1978). Screening for the patient at risk for postpartum depression. *Obstetrics and Gynecology, 52*(6), 731–736.

Kumar, R., & Robson, K. (1978). Neurotic disturbance during pregnancy and the puerperium: Preliminary report of a prospective study of 119 primiparae. In M. Sandler (Ed.), *Mental illness in pregnancy and the puerperium* (pp. 40–51). New York: Oxford University Press.

Pitt, B. (1968). Atypical depression following childbirth. *British Journal of Psychiatry, 11,* 1325–1335.

Women who have an unplanned or unwanted pregnancy or a prolonged ambivalent reaction toward pregnancy are more likely to become depressed after delivery. These were the findings in studies by Braverman and Roux and Kumar and Robson, previously described. The study by Pitt, also previously described, did not find a relationship between unplanned or unwanted pregnancy and postpartum depression. At the other end of the spectrum, women with a history of infertility for two or more years had a higher occurrence of postpartum depression. These findings were suggested in the study by Kumar and Robson. These women may have had long-awaited fantasies of childbirth and motherhood which, when untrue, increased the incidence of postpartum depression.

Social Support and Significant-Other Relationships

Campbell, S., Cohn, J., Flanagan, C., Popper, S., & Meyers, T. (1992). Course and correlates of postpartum depression during the transition to parenthood. *Development and Psychopathology, 4,* 29–47.

Collins, N., Dunkel-Schetter, M., & Scrimshaw, S. (1993). Social support in pregnancy: Psychosocial correlates of birth outcomes and postpartum depression. *Journal of Personality and Social Psychology, 65*(6), 1243–1258.

Cutrona, C. (1984). Social support and stress in the transition to parenthood. *Journal of Abnormal Psychology, 93*(4), 378–390.

Cutrona, C., & Troutman, B. (1986). Social support, infant temperament, and parent self-efficacy: A mediational model of postpartum depression. *Child Development, 57,* 1507–1518.

Hayworth, J., Little, B., Carter, S., Raptopoulos, P., Priest, R., & Sandler, M. (1980). A predictive study of postpartum depression: Some predisposing characteristics. *British Journal of Medical Psychology, 53,* 161–167.

Kendell, R., Rennie, D., Clark, J., & Dean, C. (1981). The social and obstetric correlates of psychiatric admission in the puerperium. *Psychological Medicine, 11,* 341–350.

O'Hara, M., (1986, June). Social support, life events, and depression during pregnancy and the puerperium. *Archives of General Psychiatry, 43,* 569–573.

Perez, R. (1983). Effects of stress, social support and coping style on adjustment to pregnancy among Hispanic women. *Hispanic Journal of Behavioral Sciences, 5*(2), 141–161.

Stemp, P., Turner, R., & Noh, S. (1986, May). Psychological distress in the postpartum period: The significance of social support. *Journal of Marriage and the Family, 48,* 271–277.

Turner, R. (1981). Social support as contingency in psychological well-being. *Journal of Health and Social Behavior, 22* (December), 357–367.

Social support measures have been shown to have specific effects on postpartum adjustment. The study presented by Turner included 292 women from three data sets. These women answered questionnaires on anxiety, depression, anger, social support, and stressful life events shortly after giving birth and at 6 months and one year after birth. Turner found that poor social support and increased life-event stress levels after birth were principal predictors of depression during the first 6 months postpartum. No description was given on the sample. Analyses did not include parity, age, or socioeconomic or marital status. Other studies of the postpartum period have also looked at the relationships between social support/marital status and postpartum depression. A retrospective review of 704 obstetric and psychiatric patients' records in an Edinburgh hospital was performed by Kendell and associates. They found an association between separated or unmarried status and increased psychiatric admission within 90 days after delivery. Limitations of using this technique are: representation of the existing records as constituting the entire set of all possible records for this phenomenon; the accuracy, authenticity, and authorship of records; and reliability of the coded data taken from the charts.

Hayworth and colleagues performed a prospective study with 176 women at 36 weeks of pregnancy and with 127 of the 176 women at 6 weeks postpartum. The women completed hostility, locus of control, and delusions questionnaires during pregnancy, and a depression self-rating questionnaire at 6 weeks postdelivery. Researchers found no relationship between marital status and postpartum depression. Absent or less perceived social support, or dissatisfaction with social support, was positively related to postpartum depression.

Cutrona studied 71 primiparous women at 33 weeks of pregnancy, at 2 and 8 weeks postpartum, and at 1 year postpartum. Depression, childcare stressors, and social support were investigated. Perceived social support during pregnancy was not a predictor of postpartum depression at 2 weeks postdelivery. However, it was a strong predictor of postpartum depression at 8 weeks postpartum. Results regarding the effect on postpartum depression of social support during pregnancy or at 2 and 8 weeks postpartum were not presented. Depression during pregnancy and at 1 year postpartum was not assessed and may have yielded additional information regarding the effects of perceived social support on depressive levels.

In the study by Cutrona and Troutman, 55 married women were followed with questionnaires on depression and social support during pregnancy and 3 months postpartum. Age of the women ranged from 19 to 38 years; average age was 27 years and the women had been married an average of 4.5 years. Fifty-five percent of the women were expecting their first child; the rest had at least one older child at home. Eighty-one percent had completed at least 1 year of college, and 63% had a bachelor's degree or graduate training. Infant temperament and self-efficacy questionnaires were given to the women at 3 months postdelivery. Social support and infant temperament did not predict postpartum depression. A path analysis appeared to show that social support exerted its effect on postpartum depression through the mediation of self-efficacy. In other words, the women's perceived positive social support from others appeared to increase their self-confidence to perform well as mothers, and that, in turn, effectively decreased levels of postpartum depression.

In O'Hara's study, 12% of the women in the sample had postpartum depression. The study involved 99 women; average age was 27 years, mean education level was 15 grades, and average length of marriage was 3 years. Of the sample, 98% were Anglo; 50% were nulliparous. Depression and depression histories, life stress, and social support measures were collected during the second trimester and at 9 weeks postdelivery. Less instrumental support was reported by depressed subjects than by nondepressed subjects. Depressed women also reported their spouses as less available, compared to those of nondepressed women. Although depressed women reported receiving less spousal support, they did not report any less marital satisfaction than did the nondepressed women. In general, women experiencing postpartum depression perceived excessively deficient spousal support. Depressed women felt less comfortable talking with their spouses and saw them as less available when needed. Women experiencing postpartum depression were less satisfied with their network support than were the nondepressed women.

Stemp and associates initiated an intervention study of 312 women in the early postpartum period, just after birth. Data were collected at 2 to 6 weeks postpartum, 6 months following the first interview, and 1 year following the initial interview. The women were randomly assigned to a volunteer intervention group or a control group. Psychological distress, marital intimacy, and social support were measured. The majority of women were multiparous (61%) and the average age was 27 years old. Marital intimacy within the context of social support was found to be significantly associated with postpartum psychological distress. The authors do not define the differences between concepts of postpartum depression and postpartum distress. However, the psychological distress questionnaire included measurements of depression, anxiety, anger, and aggression dimensions. The dimensions were not analyzed nor discussed separately but remained under the umbrella of psychological distress.

Studies of social support in Hispanic women have been limited. Perez failed to adequately operationalize the concept of support in a study of 93 mostly Spanish-speaking, third-trimester, Mexican American women. This seemed to result in insignificant interactions between social support and stress. Life stressors, coping style, anticipated delivery pain, anxiety, and social support were examined. The subjects, who had an average age of 26 years, came from poor financial backgrounds. Sixty-four percent were married and 49% were experiencing their first term pregnancy. Women reporting high life stress exhibited high antepartum anxiety levels.

In Campbell and associates' study of 67 postpartum depressed women and 59 women in a control group, described earlier, predictors of postpartum depression were found at 2 months. They included: a change in the relationship with their spouse and in the amount of spousal help with childcare and household tasks. At 6 months postpartum, those women who were still depressed did not differ from the nondepressed women. However, the depressed women still rated their husbands as having provided less help at 2 months postpartum.

A recent study by Collins and colleagues looked at a subset of data on a sample composed of 129 antenatal and postnatal women. Data on received social support, infant's father's support, health care provider's support, network sources, depression, prenatal life events, parity and medical risk, and labor and infant outcomes were obtained from each woman. Women were interviewed at each clinic visit throughout pregnancy or at least 10 days from the preceding interview, and 4 to 8 weeks postpartum. Because of a large number of missed postpartum clinic visits, interviews were performed via telephone. Subjects ranged in age from 18 to 42 years (average age = 28 years). Average education was 11 years. The subjects were primarily Hispanic (65%), with a small percentage of African Americans (20%), Anglos (13%), and others (2%). Sixty-eight percent were multiparous, and more than 50% were interviewed in Spanish. Fifty-eight percent were married, and 78% reported living with the infant's father at the time of entry into the study. Income information was not gathered on the sample. Women who reported higher prenatal quality of support had less depression prenatally. Support from the infant's father was associated with less antenatal depression. Women who received inordinate amounts of support reported feeling depressed. Lower quality of support and network resources was related to higher levels of depression, after controlling for antenatal depression. However, postpartum depression was unrelated to the amount of received antenatal support. Women who received more support but experienced high life events were significantly less depressed. Finally, postpartum depression was predicted solely by antenatal depression. It appears as though social support acts as a buffer against stressful life events. Reported analyses were not broken down according to the antenatal data collection times but were simply reported as prenatal in origin. Study replication would be difficult and clinical screening issues could be problematic.

Poor or Unsatisfactory Marital Relationship

Braverman, J., & Roux, J. (1978). Screening for the patient at risk for postpartum depression. *Obstetrics and Gynecology, 52*(6), 731–736.

Cogill, S., Caplan, H., Alexandra, H., Robson, K., & Kumar, R. (1986). Impact of maternal postnatal depression on cognitive development of young children. *British Medical Journal, 292,* 1165–1167.

Dimitrovsky, L., Perez-Hirshberg, M., & Itskowitz, R. (1986). Depression during and following pregnancy: Quality of family relationships. *Journal of Psychology, 121*(3), 213–218.

Gotlib, I., Whiffen, V., Wallace, P., & Mount, J. (1991). Prospective investigation of postpartum depression: Factors involved in onset and recovery. *Journal of Abnormal Psychology, 100*(2), 122–132.

Kumar, R., & Robson, K. (1984). A prospective study of emotional disorders in childbearing women. *British Journal of Psychiatry, 144,* 35–47.

O'Hara, M. (1985). Psycholgoical factors in the development of postpartum depression. In D. G. Inwood (Ed.), *Postpartum psychiatric disorders* (pp. 42–57). Washington, DC: American Psychiatric Press.

Paykel, E., Emms, E., Fletcher, J., & Rassaby, E. (1980). Life events and social support in puerperal depression. *British Journal of Psychiatry, 136,* 339–346.

Several studies found postpartum depression strongly related to a poor or unsatisfactory marital relationship. Coghill and associates studied 119 primiparous women during pregnancy, at 3 months postpartum, and at 1 year and 4 years postpartum. Depressed women were found to have marital conflicts and husbands with past psychiatric problems. The time of the pregnancy assessment was not provided nor were sample demographics.

Dimitrovsky and associates explored depression and quality of family relationships in 53 married, primiparous Israeli women with an average age of 27 years and average education of 12 years. Measurements were performed at 34–36 weeks of pregnancy and 4–8 weeks postpartum. A poor relationship with their husbands was a predictor of postpartum depression in this convenience sample. However, the husbands' role as active duty reservists in the war with Lebanon during the time the data were collected may have contributed to the poor marital relationship and postpartum depression.

In Gotlib and colleagues' study of 730 women, previously described, lower marital satisfaction was one of several variables that distinguished depressed from nondepressed postpartum women. In the study by Kumar and Robson, described earlier, two other groups of subjects were entered into the study during the postpartum period. These were 38 primiparous and 39 multiparous women. Both groups were followed at 1 year postpartum; only the multiparous women were followed at 4 years postpartum. The depressed, primiparous, and multiparous women of these two groups reported a higher degree of marital conflict than the nondepressed women.

O'Hara found, in a sample of 170 women, that depressed women reported more frequent marital problems and less happiness in their marriages. Poor communication with the husband and overall poor marital relationships were distinguishing variables in the undesirable events related to postpartum depression in 120 postpartum women studied by Paykel and associates, described previously. Feeling unloved by the partner was found to be associated with postpartum depression in 120 postpartum women assessed by the nursing staff, in the study performed by Braverman and Roux, presented earlier. The literature shows an apparent association between poor partner relationship and postpartum depression, but the effect of marital status is conflicting.

Chapter 13

The Experience of Depression in African American Women

Barbara Jones Warren

> . . . unconcerned, undisturbed by the commotion about her. Nothing reached her. Nothing penetrated the kind darkness into which her bruised spirit had retreated.
>
> —Larsen (1988)

Depression, one of the most prevalent mental health problems within the United States, has been defined by educators, religious writers, philosophers, and scientists as an "evil spirit, a malaise, a distress, a black bile melancholia, a medical disease" (Mahendra, 1986; DHHS (U.S. Department of Health and Human Services), 1993). However, African American women suffering from depression may not be able to define what they are suffering from because they are often unaware of its presence. When asked how they feel, depressed African American women may describe themselves as having a feeling of "fatigue, weariness, emptiness, loneliness, sadness, darkness, nothingness." Health care professionals, friends, family, and co-workers often tell these women that they "need more exercise, should eat a balanced diet, it's just your nerves" and that "in time, this will go away; it's just a fact of life for black women." Women are encouraged to "pray, ride it out, get rest, get a change of scenery." Medications for anemia, fatigue, or nervous exhaustion are often prescribed. Accessing and obtaining appropriate mental health treatment may be difficult for depressed African American women because society often discriminates against persons who have mental or emotional illness and because it may be difficult for these women to locate culturally competent health care providers (Campinha-Bacote, 1994; Warren, 1994).

This review addresses 19 literature sources about depression in African American women. Only sources that utilized African American women's experiences as the essence of their writings or presented information on a variety of ethnic/cultural minority groups have been included. This selection basis is important because little information has been written that incorporates these guidelines. Consequently, representative sources were chosen from 1979 to 1994 and were compiled from research papers and journals, educational books and journals, popular magazines, informational pamphlets and booklets, and a video. In addition, a listing of resources is included to provide women with more detailed information on depression.

African American women are at risk for depression because of their triple minority status; they are black, female, and positioned at the lower spectrum of the American political-economic order (Cannon, Higginbotham, & Guy, 1989; Taylor, 1992). This triple jeopardy status is based on socially devalued ethnic/racial/cultural/gender attributes. The jeopardy is intensified by the presence of African American women's multiple roles and of stressors that affect the development of their social support systems, self-esteem, and health care actions (Snapp, 1990; Taylor, 1992; Warren, 1994).

Past literature on depression has not yielded a clear definition of depression or delineated risk factors for depression in different classes of African American women. Yet information from this literature has been generalized to explain depression across all economic classes of African American women. The explanation given for depression in one African American social class may not be applicable for another social class, because of the different environments affecting each class (Coner-Edwards & Edwards, 1988; Warren, 1994). Most of the research on depression has focused on middle-income Euro-American populations (Barbee, 1992; McGrath, Keita, Strickland, & Russo, 1992). The findings of these studies have indicated that the lifetime depression rate for all populations of women is 8.7% as compared to 3.6% for men. The reported incidence of depression in African American women is ambiguous because of controversy regarding misdiagnosis and the lack of clinical research (Warren, 1994). It is estimated that 20% to 30% of African Americans experience depressive symptoms and that 4% to 6% are diagnosed with clinical depression (Brown, 1990; Kessler et al., 1994). The incidence of depression declines between the ages of 45 to 64 years and then increases after 65 years of age. African American women report more depressive symptoms than African American men, Euro-American women, or men across all marital categories (Brown, 1990).

The essential feature of depression is a disturbance of mood that produces a variety of human, emotional, and clinical responses that affect the ability to function (DHHS, 1993; Kessler et al., 1994). Depression can manifest itself as a single or recurrent episode, occur in conjunction with other emotional or physical disorders, and vary according to gender, race, and age (American Psychiatric Association, 1994; DHHS, 1993). As clinically described, the disorder of major depression is a syndrome of symptoms that occur, at a minimum, over a two-week period. A person must have a depressed mood, significant loss of interest in activities, and at least four of the following criteria:

1. depressed mood throughout the day (often every day);
2. lack of pleasure in life activities;
3. significant (more than 5%) weight loss or gain over a month;
4. sleep disruptions (generally every day);
5. unusual, increased, agitated, or decreased physical activity (generally every day);
6. daily fatigue or lack of energy;
7. daily feelings of worthlessness or guilt;
8. inability to concentrate or make decisions;
9. recurring death or suicidal thoughts (American Psychiatric Association, 1994).

Theories of depression include biological, psychosocial, and sociological perspectives (Abramson, Seligman, & Teasdale, 1978; Beck, Rush, Shaw, & Emery, 1979; Cockerman, 1992; Freud, 1957; Klerman, 1989). Biological theory focuses on changes within neurochemical and genetic structures within the body. Psychosocial theory examines a person's reaction to losses, perception of stressors, coping strategies, and feelings of control over his or her life. Sociological theory indicates that the development of depression may be contingent on a person's past conditioning and coping patterns with stress, the presence of positive social support systems, and the person's socioeconomic and political levels.

Clinical research on depression in African American women has focused on cognitive and analytic strategies within upwardly mobile (i.e., middle-income) African American women (Carrington, 1979, 1980; Snapp, 1990). Other studies have focused on symptomatology (Barbee, 1992; Brown, 1990; Fellin, 1989; Oakley, 1986; Tomes, Brown, Semenya, & Simpson, 1990) and epidemiology of depression, particularly in women of lower socioeconomic status (Brown, 1990; Cockerman, 1992; Oakley, 1986). Some researchers have examined gender roles, progression of depression, stressful life events, self-esteem, social support, marital status, and motherhood (Barbee, 1992; Beeber, 1987; Carrington, 1979, 1980; Oakley, 1986; Tomes et al., 1990; Woods, Lentz, Mitchell, & Oakley, 1994). There is no published literature regarding the influence of biological perspectives on African American women who are depressed. The American Psychological Association's National Task Force on Women and Depression has recommended that the following issues need to be examined by mental health care professionals who provide services for women suffering from depression: detailed physical and psychological history, medication usage, treatment of physical and psychological disorders, circadian rhythms, and "reproductive-related events" (i.e., menstruation, pregnancy, childbirth, infertility, abortion, menopause) (McGrath et al., 1992, p. 7).

Some social scientists have indicated that cultural influences (i.e., gender roles, community responsibilities, value system) affect the mental health of African American women (Carrington, 1979, 1980; Coner-Edwards & Edwards, 1988; Taylor, 1992). However, in most research of depression, cultural influences of African American women have not been considered. Specific cultural information on major depressive episode is discussed in DSM-IV (American Psychiatric Association, 1994) regarding Latino, Mediterranean, Chinese, Asian, and Middle Eastern cultures. However, information on African American cultures is lacking. Future revisions of the DSM should incorporate African American ethnic/racial/cultural information; because health care professionals look to this manual for guidelines in diagnosing mental health disorders across all genders, races, and classes.

A greater risk of depression is associated with African American mothers who have children under 18 years, as compared with African American women whose children are above 18 years (Brown, 1990). Similarly, the risk factor increases for working mothers (Avery, 1992; Brown, 1990). African American women who are widowed or divorced report the highest incidence of depressive symptoms (Brown, 1990; Gary, Brown, Milburn, Thomas, & Lockley, 1985).

It is unclear whether or how African American children's development may be affected if their mothers suffer from depressive symptoms or have been diagnosed with clinical depression. Some educators and researchers suggest that depressed African American women may be at risk for destructive life-style behaviors. These behaviors include the use of alcohol, other drugs, and cigarettes in order to alleviate stress and to decrease depressive symptoms (Avery, 1992; Brown, 1990; Carrington, 1980; Taylor, 1992). Taylor (1992) contends that the "health of one's mother begins with her mother's mother" and that the effect of African American mothers' detrimental health patterns may affect their children's psychological and physical health (p. 39). This connection between health and life-styles becomes clearer when one examines African American women's "both/and orientation" and the impact of gender, race, and class intersections on the women's lives (Collins, 1991; Taylor, 1992).

On various issues, African American women may simultaneously or alternatively support African American women and men, African American women, or women in general (Collins, 1991). The role of African American women has historically centered around family and group survival, as well as development of strategies that counteract oppressive conditions within American society (Collins, 1991). This both/and orientation has positive and negative outcomes. African American women may better understand life's contradictions and stresses because of their expanded orientation. However, African American women may be negatively affected and experience guilt when their role designations are in direct opposition to women's need to participate in "self-enhancing activities, either professionally or personally, that do not directly or indirectly include their families" (Carrington, 1980, p. 266).

In addition, it has been theorized that African American women may become depressed when they experience increased stressful, harmful daily hassles that occur because of their triple jeopardy status (Outlaw, 1993). The accumulation of stress creates an imbalance between demands and resources and precipitates illness (Lazarus & Folkman, 1984; Outlaw, 1993; Selye, 1973). In addition, African American women may have individual physical and psychological vulnerabilities that decrease their ability to manage stress appropriately (Outlaw, 1993). Damaging stress may result and can affect a woman's psychological and physiological health when she believes she possesses few resources (both material and emotional) to meet the demands of life (Outlaw, 1993). Ongoing stress may alter an African American woman's cognitive thinking so that she views each life event as being harmful or threatening and not just another challenge that she can manage (Outlaw, 1993; Warren, 1994).

Lena Wright Myers (1980), in her book *Black Women: Do They Cope Better?*, writes: "Feelings of self-worth lead to a greater ability to cope." She thereby suggests that a causal relationship exists between an African American woman's self-esteem and her ability to cope with stressful life events (p. 5). There is consensus in the literature that depression often occurs in conjunction with low self-esteem (Carrington, 1979, 1980; Outlaw, 1993; Rosenberg, 1981). If one has high self-esteem, one has a respect for oneself, an appreciation of one's merits, a sense of being worthy, and an ability to accurately measure one's weaknesses and strengths (Rosenberg, 1981). Persons with low self-esteem tend to view themselves as deficient and inadequate (Rosenberg, 1981). Myers (1980) also suggests that African American women's self-esteem is anchored by the women's social support network, composed of relationships with family, friends, church, and clergy. Myers (1980) defines social support, for African American women, as ". . . those helping agents or individuals within their environment whom black women identify as those who provide social support and feedback in solving problems or during periods of crisis" (p. 26).

This social support network helps African American women to assess the value of their interpersonal and social relationships, affects their physical and emotional status, and impacts on their ability to handle stress (McAdoo, 1982; Myers, 1980; Snapp, 1989; Warren, 1994). Overall, the social support network is thought to have a positive effect on emotional and mental health, which may prevent or buffer the negative effects of stress and the development of depression (Myers, 1980; Outlaw, 1993; Warren, 1994).

IMPLICATIONS OF THE LITERATURE

The discipline of nursing incorporates a focus on education, practice, administration, and therapeutics, which promotes and enhances clients' quality of life (Meleis, 1991). Theory and research form the foundation on which concepts, goals, and problems are delineated, solved, changed, and communicated (Meleis, 1991). The solutions for society's health problems and the growth and development of health care disciplines are contingent on each other (Laudan, 1978, 1984). Consequently, nurse researchers, educators, and practitioners must be aware of the interactive biopsychosocial dynamics involved in the phenomenon of depression in African American women. The aim of nursing protocols and interventions should be based on the nursing discipline's need to heal and renew the "retreated, bruised spirits" of those African American women who suffer from depression.

REFERENCES

Abramson, L. Y., Seligman, M. E. P., & Teasdale, J. D. (1978). Learned helplessness in humans: Critique and reformulation. *Journal of Abnormal Psychology, 87,* 49–74.

American Psychiatric Association. (1994). *Diagnostic and statistical manual of mental disorders* (*DSM-IV*) (4th ed.). Washington, DC: Author.

Avery, B. Y. (1992). The health status of black women. In R. L. Braithwaite & S. E. Taylor (Eds.), *Health issues in the black community* (pp. 35–51). San Francisco, CA: Jossey-Bass.

Barbee, E. L. (1992). African American women and depression: A review and critique of the literature. *Archives of Psychiatric Nursing, 6*(5), 257–265.

Beck, A. T., Rush, A. J., Shaw, B. E., & Emery, G. (1979). *Cognitive therapy of depression.* New York: Guilford Press.

Beeber, L. S. (1987). *The relationship of self-esteem, social support, and depressive symptoms in women.* Unpublished doctoral dissertation. University of Rochester (NY).

Brown, D. R. (1990). Depression among blacks: An epidemiological perspective. In D. S. Ruiz & J. P. Comer (Eds.), *Handbook of mental health and mental disorder among black Americans* (pp. 71–93). New York: Greenwood Press.

Campinha-Bacote, J. (1994). Cultural competence in psychiatric mental health nursing: A conceptual model. *Nursing Clinics of North America, 29*(1), 1–8.

Cannon, L. W., Higginbotham, E., & Guy, R. F. (1989). *Depression among women: Exploring the affects of race, class, and gender.* Memphis, TN: Center for Research on Women, Memphis State University.

Carrington, C. H. (1979). *A comparison of cognitive and analytically oriented brief treatment approaches to depression in black women.* Unpublished doctoral dissertation, University of Maryland.

Carrington, C. H. (1980). Depression in black women: A theoretical appraisal. In L. Rogers-Rose (Ed.), *The black woman* (pp. 265–271). Beverly Hills, CA: Sage.

Cockerman, W. C. (1992). *Sociology of mental disorder* (3rd ed.). Englewood Cliffs, NJ: Prentice-Hall.

Collins, P. H. (1991). *Black feminist thought: Knowledge, consciousness, and the politics of empowerment* (2nd ed). New York: Routledge.

Coner-Edwards, A. F., & Edwards, H. E. (1988). The black middle class: Definition and demographics. In A. F. Coner-Edwards & J. Spurlock (Eds.), *Black families in crisis: The middle class* (pp. 1–13). New York: Brunner/Mazel.

DHHS (U.S. Department of Health and Human Services). (1993). *Depression in primary care: Vol. 1. Detection and diagnosis.* DHHS Pub. No. 93-0550. Washington, DC: Government Printing Office.

Fellin, P. (1989). Perspectives on depression among black Americans. *Health & Social Work, 14*(4), 245–252.

Freud, S. (1957). *Mourning and melancholia.* In J. Strachey (Ed. and Trans.), *The standard edition of the complete psychological works of Sigmund Freud* (Vol. 14). London: Hogarth Press.

Gary, L. E., Brown, D. R., Milburn, N. G., Thomas, V. G., & Lockley, D. S. (1985). *Pathways: A study of black informal support networks.* Washington, DC: Institute for Urban Affairs and Research, Howard University.

Kessler, R. C., McGonagle, K. A., Zhao, S., Nelson, C. B., Hughes, M., Eshelman, S., Wittchen, H., & Kendler, K. S. (1994, January). Lifetime and 12-month prevalence of DSM-III-R psychiatric disorders in the U.S. *Archives of General Psychiatry, 51,* 8–19.

Klerman, G. L. (1989). The interpersonal model. In J. J. Mann (Ed.), *Models of depressive disorders* (pp. 45–77). New York: Plenum Press.

Larsen, N. (1988). *Quicksand and passing.* New Brunswick, NJ: Rutgers University Press.

Laudan, L. (1978). *Progress and its problems: Toward a theory of scientific growth.* Berkeley: University of California Press.

Laudan, L. (1984). *Science and values: The aims of science and their role in the scientific debate.* Berkeley: University of California Press.

Lazarus, R. S., & Folkman, S. (1984). *Stress, coping, and appraisal.* New York: Springer.

Mahendra, B. (1986). *Depression: The disorder and its associations.* Boston: MTP Press Ltd.

McAdoo, H. P. (1982). Stress-absorbing systems in black families. *Family Relations, 31,* 20–25.

McGrath, E., Keita, G. P., Strickland, B. R., & Russo, N. F. (1992). *Women and depression: Risk factors and treatment issues.* Washington, DC: American Psychological Association.

Meleis, A. I. (1991). *Theoretical nursing: Development & progress* (2nd ed.). Philadelphia: Lippincott.

Myers, L. W. (1980). *Black women: Do they cope better?* Englewood Cliffs, NJ: Prentice-Hall.

Oakley, L. D. (1986). Marital status, gender role attitude, and women's report of depression. *Journal of the National Black Nurses Association, 1*(1), 41–51.

Outlaw, F. H. (1993). Stress and coping: The influence of racism on the cognitive appraisal processing of African Americans. *Issues in Mental Health Nursing, 14,* 399–409.

Rosenberg, M. (1981). The self-concept: Social product and social force. In M. Rosenberg & R. H. Turner (Eds.), *Social psychology: Sociological perspectives* (pp. 593–624). New York: Basic Books.

Ruiz, D. S., & Comer, J. P. (Eds.), *Handbook of mental health and mental disorder among black Americans.* New York: Greenwood Press.

Selye, H. (1973, November–December). Evolution of the stress concept. *American Science, 61,* 692–699.

Snapp, M. B. (1989). *Toward race, class, and gender inclusive research on stress, social support, and psychological distress: A critical review of the literature*. Memphis, TN: Center for Research on Women, Memphis State University.

Snapp, M. B. (1990). *Occupational stress, social support, depression, and job dissatisfaction among black and white professional–managerial women*. Memphis, TN: Center for Research on Women, Memphis State University.

Taylor, S. E. (1992). The mental health status of black Americans: An overview. In R. L. Braithwaite & S. E. Taylor (Eds.), *Health issues in the black community* (pp. 20–34). San Francisco: Jossey-Bass.

Tomes, E. K., Brown, A., Semenya, K., & Simpson, J. (1990). Depression in black women of low socioeconomic status: Psychosocial factors and nursing diagnosis. *Journal of the National Black Nurses Association, 4*(2), 37–46.

Warren, B. J. (1994). Depression in African American women. *Journal of Psychosocial Nursing, 32*(3), 29–33.

Woods, N. F., Lentz, M., Mitchell, E., & Oakley, L. D. (1994). Depressed mood and self-esteem in young Asian, black, and white women in America. *Health Care for Women International, 15*, 243–262.

Barbee, E. L. (1992). African-American women and depression: A review and critique of the literature. *Archives of Psychiatric Nursing, 6*(5), 257–265.

As the title implies, Barbee's article focuses on how the literature critiques depression in African American women. Barbee is a nurse anthropologist and educator. This article was published in a professional psychiatric mental health nursing journal that is primarily read by educators, clinicians, researchers, and students within the mental health nursing profession. Barbee excludes a discussion of depression in children and elderly African American women ". . . because of their special circumstances" (p. 257). The article is insightful and evocative.

Barbee reviews the literature from a feminist perspective and discusses how gender, race, and class impact the development and progression of depression within African American women. This is a valuable viewpoint; these issues are rarely discussed in the literature.

Barbee begins the article with a brief overview of depression in African American women. Historical and statistical data are included. The remainder of the article discusses the philosophy underlying the development of assessment and diagnosis of depression.

Barbee critiques the traditional Euro-American depression assessment and treatment approaches that are utilized with depressed African American women, and provides information on two resources that may assist African-American women who suffer from depression: (1) the National Institute of Mental Health (NIMH) Depression/Awareness, Recognition and Treatment (D/ART) Program, an educational program developed for use by the general public and health care providers, and (2) the National Black Women's Health Project

(NBWHP), a self-help organization that promotes positive health care and political actions for African American women and their families. Barbee's discussion of violence, culture, and cultural sensitivity offers additional insights into the development of depression in African American women because it details a previously underexamined area and gives a contextual perspective for the development of depression in this population.

The article lacks a direct discussion and connection of the ideas and insights gained from the depression literature to the development of specific psychiatric mental health nursing protocols and interventions for depressed African American women. Space constraints may have been responsible, but this is an important omission because this journal is a resource for psychiatric mental health nurses. Barbee's discussion of Meleis's theoretical perspectives could have been expanded and might have provided a basis for the development of specific nursing protocols and interventions.

Brown, D. R. (1990). Depression among blacks: An epidemiological perspective. In D. S. Ruiz & J. P. Comer (Eds.), *Handbook of mental health and mental disorder among black Americans* (pp. 71–93). New York: Greenwood Press.

Brown's chapter is a synthesis and critique of the epidemiologic research (i.e., occurrence, distribution, and causes) on depression in adult African Americans. This chapter appears in a book whose purpose is to provide information and stimulate discussion among students, educators, practitioners, and administrators who study black mental health (Ruiz & Comer, 1990).

Brown describes how depression epidemiologic research is conducted. The chapter offers information on the definition, origins, and symptoms of depression; demographic factors (gender, income, age, education, employment status, occupation, marital status, and presence of children) affecting the development and progression of depression; stress and sociocultural factors involved in depression; a summary of the main points; and implications of

the research for African Americans. A table, summarizing community surveys (from 1973 to 1984) that include African Americans, provides a concise overview that includes names of the researchers, locations of the surveys, number of African Americans, instruments used to measure depression, and a summary of the findings.

Brown has given an excellent review and critique of the literature in relationship to individual adult African American women and men and the effect of depression on African American families and communities. However, no information is included about depression in African American children nor is any reason given for this exclusion. This information would be a good addition to any future updates of this chapter.

Cannon, L. W., Higginbotham, E., & Guy, R. F. (1989). *Depression among women: Exploring the affects of race, class, and gender.* Memphis, TN: Center for Research on Women, Memphis State University.

This is a report of an exploratory study that evolved from the work of sociologists and social workers at the Center for Research on Women. The relationship among race, class, gender, socioeconomic status, and psychological distress (i.e., depression) in full-time, employed, professional, managerial black women and white women aged 25–40 years is examined. Participants were 100 black and 100 white women. Information was gathered through face-to-face life-history interviews and the Center for Epidemiologic Studies Depression Scale [CES-D].

Results indicated that race, class, and socioeconomic status intersect to affect depressive symptoms in middle-income women. Women who had physical disabilities and illnesses reported higher levels of depression than women who were healthy. Higher depression levels were also found in women who used alcohol, had no leisure activities, and had experienced a "breakup of interpersonal relationships" (p. 24).

This paper may be confusing to persons not familiar with research jargon. However, the study adds important contextual information to the body of knowledge in research of depression, sociology, and women's studies.

Carrington, C. H. (1979). *A comparison of cognitive and analytically oriented brief treatment approaches to depression in black women.* Unpublished doctoral dissertation, University of Maryland.

Three groups of 30 "upwardly mobile" (i.e., middle-income) African American women aged 28–40 years were assessed by psychologists for their overall mental health status, depression level, and hopelessness level. Women were randomly assigned (10 each) to one of three therapy groups: the cognitive group (redirection of negative thinking), analytic group (use of reasoning), or wait list control group (no therapy during the conduct of the study). Treatment consisted of 30-minute sessions of individual therapy over a 12-week period.

Carrington found that women who were depressed had experienced physical or emotional losses of one or both of their parents during their childhood. In addition, the women perceived themselves as being worthless and not in control of their lives. Cognitive treatment strategies produced greater reduction of depressive symptoms than did traditional analytic therapy or no therapy.

This is a classic study: it represents the first published examination of depression within middle-income African American women. Carrington found support for two theories of depression (cognitive and learned helplessness) that had not been previously tested within middle-income African American women.

Carrington, C. H. (1980). Depression in black women: A theoretical appraisal. In L. Rogers-Rose (Ed.), *The black woman* (pp. 265–271). Beverly Hills, CA: Sage.

This chapter, an extension of Carrington's dissertation, is part of a collection of educational and research articles, written by psychologists, that focus on African American women's mental health status. Carrington discusses the sociological, psychoanalytic, and cognitive theories of depression. She also examines the effect of racism, gender, and class on the development of African American women's self-esteem and mental health. Carrington contends that African American women have strong nurturing responsibilities and needs in regard to their families and that this fact often places the women at risk for the development of guilt and depression when they realize that socioeconomic and political constraints may prohibit them from meeting the needs of their families or themselves.

Carrington discusses the role of the clinical practitioner in treating African American women who suffer from depression. She contends that cognitive interventions assist African American women to restore and develop their self-esteem and sense of worth. This is an interesting and valuable contribution because it connects clinical practice, research, and theory, which are often omitted in research articles. This connection is important because health care professionals often use traditional depression theory to develop protocols and interventions for African American women, yet these theories frequently have not been tested within this population. Carrington states that practitioners should help African American women identify detrimental thinking patterns, modify those thinking patterns, understand their interpersonal relationships, and develop positive self-esteem through the use of individual and group therapy sessions. The chapter is well written and readable.

Fellin, P. (1989). Perspectives on depression among black Americans. *Health and Social Work, 14*(4), 245–252.

Fellin's article is written to assist social workers in becoming more "ethnically sensitive" and in developing assessment skills for African American clients who may be depressed (p. 245). However, the information is valuable for any student, educator, researcher, or provider of health care for African Americans. This article is included even though Fellin does not focus exclusively on African American women. An excellent section on gender and depression incorporates ideas on the impact of race, gender, and class.

Fellin begins the article by emphasizing the need for culturally competent mental health care professionals because different meanings of symptoms and behaviors relate to mental health and mental disorders within different ethnic minority groups. He then reviews and critiques the literature on depression in African Americans in the areas of epidemiology, social class, unemployment, gender, sociocultural factors, misdiagnosis, service utilization, treatment and rehabilitation, and implications for social work practice. This concise, clear, and informative article also stresses the need for culturally sensitive research based on clinical practice.

National Mental Health Association & Eli Lilley (Producers). (1993). *Moving back into the light* (Video recording no. FL-1579-0). New York: NCM Publishers.

This video provides viewers with a clear profile of depression. A variety of persons from different ethnic minority and age groups discuss symptoms of depression, assessment strategies for depression, interpersonal relationships, theories of depression, and treatments for depression. Color and shading changes (from dark to light, from black-and-white to color) occur within the video as persons discuss the course of their depression. This technique captures the attention of the viewer and helps to intensify how appropriate treatment can improve a depressed person's life.

Other benefits of this video include its brevity (15 minutes) and the fact that women and men suffering from depression discuss their fears regarding societal stigma associated with their disease. Both of these features may make the video more accessible by depressed persons, who often have decreased attention spans and are sensitive to how others perceive them. Health care professionals are

represented by persons from different genders and races. Among the weaknesses of the video, it does not cover all the treatments for depression and it omits such treatments as diet, exercise, and light therapy and ECT. Overall, this video represents an additional or alternative visual aid for health care professionals when they discuss depression with their clients. Also, it could be used as an educational video for general audiences.

Oakley, L. D. (1986). Marital status, gender role attitude, and women's report of depression. *Journal of the National Black Nurses Association, 1*(1), 41–51.

This research study examined 51 African American women aged 18 to 45 years. The report is written from a professional nursing perspective. Through face-to-face interviews, information was collected in the areas of marital status, gender/role attitudes, and depression. Instruments included the Attitudes Toward Women Scale, the BEM Sex Role Inventory, and the Center for Epidemiologic Studies Depression Scale. Following a review and critique of the literature on depression, marital status, and gender role attitudes, study data are presented.

Oakley found that approximately 48% of the women studied were depressed and that approximately 55% of the women held very traditional views about women's gender roles. Women who had high traditional gender role attitudes and lower education and income levels also had high levels of depression. Marital status did not significantly correlate with depression levels. Oakley concluded that gender role attitudes seem to affect the mental health of some African American women and that African American women do not "naturally" exhibit feminist attitudes.

This well-written article presents some interesting findings and is one of the few studies that examines the influence of African American women's gender role attitudes on the development of depression. Information from the study is readily available to professional nurses and other health care providers because this journal is widely disseminated. Its circulation may stimulate additional questions and research as nurses critique the article's findings in conjunction with their clinical practices.

Oakley explains the practice implications for psychiatric mental health nurses but cautions that additional work is needed to examine the impact of marital status and gender role attitudes on depression in African American women. I would have liked a more in-depth review of the literature, and discussion of the literature in relation to the study findings. One source was omitted that I think should have been included: Christine Carrington's chapter, "Depression in Black Women: A Theoretical Appraisal" (Carrington, 1980). The chapter has a preliminary discussion on marital status and gender role attitudes in relation to the development of depression in African American women. This addition and an expanded literature review would have emphasized the need for and significance of Oakley's study.

Richardson, B. L. (1994). Talking to the walls. *Essence, 25*(3), 58–60, 114–116.

This article is written from the perspective of an African American woman whose sister suffers from bipolar depression (referred to in the article as "manic depression"). *Essence* is a popular magazine primarily read by African Americans. The article's publication in the popular press makes this information on depression more accessible to the general African American public. Richardson gives a brief explanation of how mental illnesses such as manic depression, anxiety disorders, panic disorders, and schizophrenia may manifest themselves within African Americans and how members within the community react to mental illness. She vividly and sensitively talks about what her sister was like prior to her mental illness and the family's frustration, embarrassment, and denial of the illness. She also discusses some of the assessment and treatment techniques that are available and the ill person's need for social support systems and, often, for spiritual guidance. Richardson provides a list of resources for African Americans—and their families and friends—who are affected by mental illness.

Snapp, M. B. (1990). *Occupational stress, social support, depression, and job dissatisfaction among black and white professional-managerial women.* Memphis, TN: Center for Research on Women, Memphis State University.

This paper discusses a portion of a larger study being conducted at Memphis State University's Department of Sociology and Social Work to examine social mobility, race, and women's health. Snapp's study focuses on the role of occupational stress, social support, and job dissatisfaction in the development of depression. One hundred black and 100 white professional women in managerial positions in the Memphis area participated in the study. Women were interviewed for purposes of gathering information about their race, economic background, supervisory role, marital and parental status, social supports, occupational stress, depression, and job dissatisfaction. The Center for Epidemiologic Studies Depression Scale was used to measure depression levels within the women. Multiple regression statistics were used for the analyses. Snapp included an in-depth discussion of the empirical & theoretical literature, as well as the study's methodology, results, and implications.

Findings indicated that occupational stress (i.e., trouble with a boss or subordinates) had an impact on job dissatisfaction and that women with occupational stress demonstrated higher levels of depression than women without occupational stress. Support from family, friends, or co-workers did not enhance the women's job satisfaction or mental well-being.

This paper may be too technical for some readers, but the literature review, summary, and discussion sections are readable for professional and nonprofessional audiences. In addition, Snapp examines some of the larger systems (work and social support) that may affect the development of depression in black and white women. Consequently, information

from this study adds to the depression literature because it emphasizes the influence of external influences on the development of
depression in women rather than an exclusive
focus on women's feelings and perceptions.
This contextual examination of depression is
often lacking in depression literature.

Taylor, S. E. (1992). The mental health status
of black Americans: An overview. In R. L.
Braithwaite & S. E. Taylor (Eds.), *Health issues
in the black community* (pp. 20–34). San Francisco: Jossey-Bass.

This chapter appears in a collection of contributions by health educators, clinicians, and
researchers. The book focuses on social issues,
critical health-related concerns in infants,
youth, and older adults, health education and
resource development, and future health care
concerns for black Americans. Taylor presents
a clear and concise examination of the impact
of social trends, service and treatment utilization, racism, socioeconomic status, and gender
on African Americans' mental health. Such a
contextual examination of mental health in
African American women and men is often ignored in the literature.

Taylor's discussion of gender is insightful
because she combines a review of the gender
literature with African Americans' perception
of society. She also discusses the impact of
African American women's multiple roles,
stressors, and social support systems on their
mental health. This is a readable and valuable
reference for any student, educator, researcher,
or practitioner who is concerned about mental
health in African American women.

Tomes, E. K., Brown, A., Semenya, K., & Simpson, J. (1990). Depression in black women of
low socioeconomic status: Psychosocial factors and nursing diagnoses. *Journal of the National Black Nurses Association*, 4(2), 37–46.

This study combines a nursing and sociology perspective in an examination of the
relationship among socioeconomic status,
attributional style, personality, racial identity,
and depression in a sample of 101 African
American women aged 18 to 59 years with
family incomes of less than $10,000 per year.
Information was obtained through face-to-face
interviews using the Beck Depression Inventory, Warheit Depression Syndrome Scale, Attributional Style Assessment Test, Modified
Inventory of Interpersonal Style, Taylor Nadi-
nalization Scale (measure of racial identity),
and a Bibliographical Data Form.

Findings indicated that 50% of the women
had mild to severe levels of depression. The depressed women exhibited a distorted view of
culture that included internalized negative
racial images, poor self-esteem, high anxiety
and aggression levels, difficulty handling pressure, and a lack of nurturing. The authors contend that these findings are supportive of the
cognitive theory of depression, which indicates
that depressed individuals perceive themselves
as being worthless and as having few enduring
relationships.

The study is an important addition to the
depression literature because it is the first study
that links racial identity to the development of
depression in African American women. The
authors conclude the article with an excellent
section on nursing implications and specific
nursing interventions for depressed African
American women. The one weakness is the article's lack of reliability (consistency) and validity (appropriateness) regarding the instruments
used to collect information.

U.S. Department of Health and Human Ser-
vices. (1991). Let's talk about depression.
DHHS Pub. No. ADM 91-1695. Washington,
DC: Government Printing Office.

This pamphlet, developed for use with
African American adolescents, discusses
symptoms of depression and provides helpful
resources. The pamphlet is colorful, the writing uses adolescents' language, and there are
pictures of African American adolescents who
discuss their feelings about their illness and
how others respond to them. The pamphlet has

been endorsed and promoted by the National Institutes of Mental Health's Depression/ Awareness, Recognition and Treatment Program (D/ART) and has been endorsed by celebrities and athletes such as Whitney Houston and Charles Mann. These features enhance the pamphlet's appeal to younger African Americans and may prompt these adolescents to ask questions about depression and to seek information about sources of support. In addition, the pamphlet is useful as an educational tool for adolescents from a variety of ethnic minority groups because it is written from adolescents' point of view.

U.S. Department of Health and Human Services. (1993). *Depression in primary care: Vol. 1. Detection and diagnosis.* DHHS Pub. No. 93-0550. Washington, DC: Government Printing Office.

U.S. Department of Health and Human Services. (1993) *Depression in primary care: Vol. 2. Treatment of major depression.* DHHS Pub. No. 93-0551. Washington, DC: Government Printing Office.

U.S. Department of Health and Human Services. (1993). *Depression in primary care: Detection, diagnosis, and treatment. No. 5.* DHHS Pub. No. 93-0552. Washington, DC: Government Printing Office.

U.S. Department of Health and Human Services. (1993). *Depression is a treatable illness: A patient's guide.* DHHS Pub. No. 93-0553. Washington, DC: Government Printing Office.

This series of booklets was developed by The Depression Guideline Panel, a group comprised of researchers, educators, practitioners, and consumers, in conjunction with The Agency for Health Care Policy and Research [AHCPR]. The AHCPR conducts and supports health care research, develops clinical practice guidelines, and disseminates research findings to health care professionals, government agencies, and the public. Volumes 1 and 2 are written in technical, medical language, are approximately 120 pages each,

and have extensive reference lists. Both volumes have comprehensive current information and are an extremely useful resource for educators, researchers, or practitioners.

Volume 1 provides information on detection and diagnosis of depression in the areas of definition of mood disorders, psychiatric and medical conditions affecting the development of mood disorders, medications affecting the development of depression, and assessment and diagnostic strategies for depression. Volume 2 describes treatment strategies for depression: the aims of treatment as well as acute and long-term interventions.

The fifth booklet is a quick reference guide for clinicians: it condenses the material from Volumes 1 and 2 into 20 pages. Use of blue-tinted bars, numbers, charts, and tables highlights the 12 main points and makes the information much more readable.

Depression Is a Treatable Illness is a 33-page patient's guide on depression that discusses depressive symptoms and what assessment and treatment approaches are available. The booklet begins with a section entitled "Finding Help" and offers suggestions on how to use the information. The booklet is user-friendly for persons who are experiencing depression as well as for their significant others. Important points are highlighted in blue-tinted bars and squares. Two valuable sections are intended to help a person with depressive symptoms prepare for a visit with a practitioner: one is a health history area, and the other is a weekly activity chart that the person can use to keep track of symptoms, daily activities, medications and their side effects, and any appointments with health providers.

Warren, B. J. (1994). Depression in African American women. *Journal of Psychosocial Nursing, 32*(3), 29–33.

This article provides a current review and critique of the literature on depression in adult African American women and incorporates information on cultural influences that affect the development and progression of depression in this population. The article is written from the perspective of a womanist and a psychiatric mental health nurse.

An overview of depression includes statistics, risk factors, and a discussion of the dynamics that impact African American women. The author examines the definition of depression and theories of depression as they relate to the *Diagnostic and Statistical Manual of Mental Disorders* (American Psychiatric Association, 1994). Information on African American cultural influences and implications for psychiatric-nursing practice incorporates data on physical, psychological, gender, race, and class issues that impact on the development and progression of depression in African American women. Specific, culturally competent, psychiatric mental health nursing intervention strategies are given.

Woods, N. F., Lentz, M., Mitchell, E., & Oakley, L. D. (1994). Depressed mood and self-esteem in young Asian, black, and white women in America. *Health Care for Women International, 15*, 243–262.

This research is an extension of a larger 1987 study, conducted by Woods and her associates, of perimenstrual symptoms in women. Information from the original study was collected via face-to-face interviews with women. The current study tested a model of depression and self-esteem, and examined the relationship among personal resources, socialization, and women's roles in a sample of 75 Asian, 91 black, and 295 white women aged 18 to 45 years. Self-esteem and depression were respectively measured by the Rosenberg Self-Esteem Scale and the Center for Epidemiologic Studies Depression Scale. Analyses was accomplished by descriptive, correlational, and regression statistics.

A discussion of the symptoms of depression in women is followed by description of the models of depression and self-esteem. These models include social disadvantage, social roles, socialization, social resources and social demands, developmental aspects, and ethnicity.

Findings indicated that social networks and life events were important for Asian, black, and white women. However, development of self-esteem was different for each subsample of women. Asian women's predictors of self-esteem included having children, having social support, avoiding conflicts, and experiencing positive life events. Important issues for black women included "positive effect of education and negative effect of conflicted network members"; those for white women included "number of negative life events, conflicted network, income, and attitudes toward women's roles" (pp. 258–259). The development of depression differed in each group of women. Asian women experienced less depression when they had an unconflicted network size and adequate income. Black and white women experienced higher depression levels when they incurred more negative life events, conflicted network size, lower education levels, and low religiosity. However, white women's depression was negatively associated with the number of children they had.

This study is unique and valuable for its examination of the theory of depression and self-esteem in women and its construction and testing of a model based on this knowledge in three ethnic minority samples. The study results are supportive of the models of depression and self-esteem in women. This reinforces the need for an integrative analysis of gender, race, and class issues when studying and researching depression in different ethnic minority classes of women. Finally, this article is readable for non-research-oriented people because the authors use limited research jargon. The study is more accessible to the general public and thus provides valuable information about the factors that foster depression in ethnically diverse women.

RESOURCES

Association of Black Psychologists
821 Kennedy Street, NW
Washington, DC 20005
(202) 722-0808

The American Psychiatric Association
1400 K Street, NW
Washington, DC 20005
(202) 682-6000

Depression/Awareness, Recognition and
    Treatment (D/ART) Program
Department of GL, Room 10-85
5600 Fishers Lane
Rockville, MD 20857
(800) 421-4211

National Alliance for the Mentally Ill
    (NAMI)
2101 Wilson Blvd., Suite 302
Arlington, VA 22201
(800) 950-6264

National Depressive and Manic Depressive
    Association (NDMDA)
730 N. Franklin St., Suite 501
Chicago, IL 60610
(800) 82-NDMDA

National Foundation for Depressive Illness,
    Inc. [NFDI]
P.O. Box 2257
New York, NY 10116-2257
(800) 248-4344

National Mental Health Association (NMHA)
National Mental Health Information Center
1021 Prince St.
Alexandria, VA 23314-2971
(800) 969-6642

Chapter 14

Sexuality, Sexual Orientation, and Violence: Pieces in the Puzzle of Women's Use and Abuse of Alcohol

Tonda L. Hughes
Jeanette Norris

T he history of research on alcohol use, alcohol abuse, and alcoholism among women is a short one. Hurley notes that, between 1929 and 1970, only 28 English-language studies focusing on alcoholism in women were published (1991, p. 255). Since the 1970s, significantly more research on women and alcohol has been published; however, much of this research has used male-biased models and has focused on a relatively narrow range of women and women's experiences. In the majority of existing studies, participants were predominantly white women or samples were obtained from treatment settings. Studies that have included other groups of women have often focused on the health problems of the fetus or infant whose mother drinks heavily or is alcoholic (Hughes, 1990; Hughes & Fox, 1993).

Alcohol use and abuse affects and is affected by many other aspects of women's lives, especially those related to intimate relationships. Within this context, the separate but often related areas of sexuality and violence appear to be particularly important, though research in both these areas has been limited.

As Teets (1994) has noted, sexuality for women encompasses a broad range of feelings, behaviors, and identity issues, which in turn affect many other areas of their lives. Although the evidence is not conclusive, sexual identity or sexual orientation appears to be associated with higher rates of alcohol use. Lesbians are less likely than heterosexual women to abstain and are more likely to drink on a daily or regular basis (Bradford & Ryan, 1987; McKirnan & Peterson, 1989a). This may be explained, in part, by lesbians' being less conventional and less constrained by traditional norms, roles, and responsibilities. Other factors related to lesbians' life-styles (e.g., greater reliance on bars, stress related to discrimination and homophobic attitudes) are thought to increase lesbians' risk for alcohol abuse and alcohol problems. We include research on lesbians primarily under the heading "Alcohol and Sexuality," but we wish to emphasize that sexuality is no more a defining characteristic of lesbians than it is of heterosexual women. However, because of the prevailing negative attitudes and discrimination toward women (and men) who choose same-gender partners, issues related to sexuality, and their effect on alcohol use and abuse, may be different for lesbians and heterosexual women.

With regard to violence, alcohol can serve both as a precursor that makes a woman vulnerable to victimization and as a consequence of experiencing traumatic events. Frequently, a history of childhood sexual victimization can lead an adult woman to self-medicate with alcohol, resulting in increased vulnerability to further violence. A circular pattern of drinking and victimization may then be enacted, and the woman may find it very difficult to extricate herself from that pattern.

In this chapter, we have chosen to focus on three understudied topics: (1) sexuality, (2) sexual orientation, and (3) violence. Each represents a particular interest or area of expertise of ours, and all are viewed as critically important in understanding women's use and abuse of alcohol.

Although a focus on intimate relationships could include a number of other subtopics, we have limited our discussion to those we believe are particularly important in the use and abuse of alcohol. For example, human immunodeficiency virus (HIV) is an important women's health problem that is closely related to sexuality and, to a lesser degree, violence. However, because the issues related to HIV are very broad and HIV is most clearly associated with the use of drugs other than alcohol, particularly injectable drugs, we elected to omit it as a topic in this chapter.

In addition, for each of the topics chosen, we have found it necessary to narrow our scope. Consequently, with regard to violence, we have considered mainly relationship violence—in particular, domestic violence, childhood sexual abuse, and acquaintance rape. Within these topics, we have focused on the woman as victim or as aggressor and on the dynamics of the relationship. In the context of a chapter on women's health, we felt that delving into the research on males as perpetrators or victims was beyond our scope. Thus, the material reviewed and discussed in this chapter is not intended as an exhaustive treatment of the topics covered. Rather, we hope to communicate to readers interested in women's health some of the most recent efforts to fill important gaps in the literature and to point out where gaps remain.

SEXUALITY

Alcohol and Sexuality

As is the case with research on women's drinking in general, research on the relationship of alcohol to women's sexuality has been understudied. This situation continues, at least in part, because much of the recent research on alcohol and sex has focused on behavior related to contracting HIV. Because of the disproportionately high rate of AIDS among gay men, attention has been drawn even further away from studying the relationship between alcohol consumption and women's sexuality. At this time, it cannot be stated with any certainty that alcohol consumption increases the likelihood that women will engage in increased sexual activity (Leigh, 1993; Leigh & Schafer, 1993).

Progress has been made in understanding some of the relationships between drinking and sex for women. In particular, outcome expectancies—that is, beliefs about the effects of alcohol—seem to play a key role in understanding this relationship. Early research indicated that men and women held essentially the same general expectancies regarding alcohol's effects (see Crowe & George, 1989 for a review). However, recent work on sex-specific expectancies has shown that males seem more likely than females to endorse expectancies related to disinhibition and risk-taking, although men and women still hold similar beliefs in the power of alcohol to enhance sexual experiences (Dermen & Cooper, in press). As Norris (in press) has noted in her review, expectancies related to the effects of alcohol on sex appear to have a major impact on women's use of alcohol; they may motivate heavy drinking in some women, especially those who are conflicted about sex.

Unfortunately, women who drink heavily because they believe that alcohol will enhance their sexual experiences ultimately find that alcohol has a deleterious impact on their sexual functioning. Norris (in press) points out the circular relationship between drinking and its effect on sexuality.

Women may initially drink to cope with sexual dysfunction, which may then worsen as a result of drinking. Further research is needed to better understand this relationship and to develop effective interventions aimed at breaking this cycle.

Use and Abuse of Alcohol among Lesbians

Although little research has been done, most available sources report that lesbians drink at higher rates or experience greater problems related to alcohol use than do women in the general population (Fifield, 1975; McKirnan & Peterson, 1989a; Saghir & Robins, 1973). This conclusion stems, in part perhaps, from the fact that much of the early data on alcohol use among gay women and men were collected from bar settings. For example, in one of the earliest and most frequently cited studies, Fifeld (1975) reported that 30% of her sample of lesbians from Los Angeles County drank heavily or were alcoholic. However, often not noted is the fact that Fifeld's sample was drawn primarily from gay-oriented bars or Alcoholics Anonymous (AA) groups. Saghir and Robins (1973) also used gay bars to obtain a portion of their sample; however, they attempted to deal with this source of bias by statistically controlling for "bar-going." In their sample of 57 lesbians, Saghir and Robins found that 35% of the women reported drinking at levels judged excessive or alcoholic. This rate is particularly striking when compared with matched heterosexual controls, only 5% of whom drank at similarly high levels.

More recently, McKirnan and Peterson (1989a, 1989b) studied a large sample of gay men and lesbians in Chicago. In an effort to overcome some of the sampling problems that characterize most studies of homosexuals' use and abuse of alcohol, respondents in this study were obtained from a wide variety of sources in Chicago: only 5% of the sample obtained questionnaires in bar settings. These methods proved more successful in obtaining gay men's participation (n = 2,652) than gay women's (n = 748). The investigators found that gay women and men, although less likely than heterosexual women and men in the general population to abstain from the use of alcohol (14% versus 29%), were more likely to be moderate users of alcohol (71% versus 57%) and were about equally likely to be heavy drinkers (15% versus 14% for men and women combined; 9% versus 7% for women only). A somewhat paradoxical finding was that, although not overrepresented among heavy drinkers, gay women and men reported rates of alcohol problems almost twice as high as those reported for heterosexual women and men (23% versus 12%). Further, the level of alcohol problems (e.g., loss of control over drinking, or dependency symptoms) was not significantly different for gay women and men. In contrast to findings from women and men in the general population, who tend to demonstrate substantial age differences related to alcohol problems, among gay women and men these problems do not appear to decline with age.

Like McKirnan and Peterson (1989a), Bradford and Ryan (1987) found that alcohol use among lesbians did not decline with age. In a study of 1,917 lesbians, the percentage of women who drank daily increased from approximately 3% for those younger than 34 years old to 7% for those 35 to 44 years old; 10% for those 45 to 54 years old; and 21% for those 55 years or older (Bradford & Ryan, 1987). This finding suggests a positive relationship between age and more frequent or heavier drinking. However, an alternative explanation based on generational differences is also plausible: younger cohorts of lesbians may be drinking less than older ones.

McKirnan and Peterson's (1989a) findings and those of Bloomfield (1993) indicate that alcohol and other drug (AOD) use, particularly alcohol abuse, may be declining in the gay community. Reasons for such a decline include the overall increased awareness and concern about health within American society, more moderate drinking among women and men in the general population in the past decade, increased dissemination of information about risk status (in part, stimulated by the AIDS epidemic) among gay groups and organizations, some lessening of the social stigma and oppression of gay people, and increased alternatives to gay bars for social interaction (Hall, 1993; Hastings, 1982; Paul, Stall, & Bloomfield, 1991).

Among the most frequently cited risk factors for alcohol problems among lesbians are (1) reliance on gay bars for socialization and (2) stress related to homophobic attitudes and discrimination (McKirnan & Peterson, 1989a; Sagir & Robins, 1973). These factors, particularly the influence of "bar-going," may be more important for gay men than for lesbians (Bloomfield, 1993; Norris, in press). Hughes and Wilsnack (1994) review a number of risk factors for alcohol abuse and alcohol problems that have been identified for women in the general population and that have implications for lesbians. Among these are life roles, such as employment status and intimate relationships; interpersonal violence; and psychological factors. For example, a well-established finding among women in the general population is that drinking behavior is affected by intimate partners' drinking. Because the lesbian population reportedly has lower rates of abstention and higher rates of alcohol problems than heterosexual women, lesbians may be at high risk for having a partner who abuses alcohol. Combined with other factors such as more opportunities to drink and fewer role restrictions, as well as the fact that lesbian relationships are characterized by greater intimacy and shared activities (Vargo, 1987), the influence of problem-drinking partners may be stronger on lesbians' drinking than on heterosexual women's drinking. More research is needed to explore the similarities and differences between lesbians' and heterosexual women's patterns of drinking in order to develop more effective prevention and treatment strategies for lesbians.

ALCOHOL AND VIOLENCE

Childhood Sexual Abuse

Like other stigmatized topics, childhood sexual abuse (CSA) continues to be understudied. Furthermore, although the number of studies focusing on this topic is growing, definitional and methodological problems common in this literature have made it difficult to draw conclusions. For example, because there is no standard definition of CSA, estimates of prevalence are meaningful only in the context of how the experience is defined in each study. Definitions vary considerably, based on type of sexual activity involved (e.g., fondling, intercourse), the relationship of the abuser to the child (e.g., relative, nonrelative, acquaintance, stranger), age difference between the abuser and the child, degree to which the sexual activity was forced, period of time the activity lasted, and amount of distress caused by the activity (Russell & Wilsnack, 1991, p. 61).

Much of what we know about the consequences of CSA comes from reports of women in treatment for substance abuse or psychiatric/mental health problems. Clinical studies, almost all of which have been conducted over the past 10 to 15 years, have reported higher rates of CSA among women with AOD problems or addiction than among women in the general population (Covington, 1982; Kovach, 1986; Miller, Downs, Gondoli, & Keil, 1987; Miller, Downs, & Testa, 1993; Pribor & Dinwiddie, 1992). In research for her doctoral dissertation, Covington (1982) compared 35 alcoholic women with a matched group of nonalcoholic women. She found that 34% of the alcoholic women and 17% of the nonalcoholic matched comparison group reported a history of CSA. Similarly, in a sample of 117 women participating in Alcoholics Anonymous, Kovach (1986) found that 27.8% of the women reported incest experiences during childhood. Miller, Downs, & Testa (1993) found that women in alcohol treatment reported significantly higher rates of CSA (70%) than did either women in a general household sample (35%) or women without alcohol problems who were receiving other mental health services (52%). These patterns held even after controlling for demographic characteristics and alcohol abuse among parents.

These and other studies have provided support for the suspected association between CSA and AOD abuse among women. However, because most studies have been conducted with women experiencing alcohol problems serious enough to prompt them to seek treatment, it is not clear whether CSA is also associated with alcohol use and abuse in women who do not seek treatment. In one of the few studies to explore the relationship between CSA and AOD abuse among women in the general population, Wilsnack, Vogeltanz, Klassen, and Harris (1994) found that CSA was strongly related to all measures of drinking behavior included in their survey (e.g., quantity/frequency, heavy episodic drinking, frequency of intoxication, number of drinking problems, number of alcohol dependence symptoms).

Studies of lesbians indicate that this population experiences CSA at about the same rate as heterosexual women. For example, in a study of lesbians admitted for AOD treatment, Neisen and Sandall (1990) found that nearly 70% of the women reported a history of CSA. Like those of women in the general population, studies of lesbians not in treatment reveal significantly lower rates of CSA. Using data from the National Study of Lesbian Health Concerns, Bradford, Ryan, and Rothblum (1994) found that 21% of the women surveyed reported being raped or sexually attacked during childhood. Rates of abuse varied by race: one-third of African American lesbians reported CSA as compared with one-fourth of Latina and one-fifth of white lesbians. White lesbians also had lower rates of incest (16%) than did Latina (29%) or African American (31%) lesbians. These findings are based on data obtained from a nonrandom sample and therefore cannot be generalized to all lesbians; furthermore, no attempt was made to determine whether CSA was associated with AOD abuse. Nevertheless, these findings raise important questions about cultural differences in experiences of CSA. Additional research is needed to explore these and other questions related to alcohol use and CSA among lesbians and other minority women.

Although studies support high rates of CSA among populations of women who abuse or are dependent on alcohol, it is not yet clear how CSA and alcohol abuse are related. The question of why some women who have experienced CSA later abuse alcohol and other women with similar victimization experiences do not abuse alcohol remains unanswered. A great deal of work has been done to document and describe the postabuse experiences of female victims of CSA (for review, see Harrison, Hoffman, & Edwall, 1989). Recent literature on CSA has drawn attention to a variety of potential long-term consequences. Among those that have received the most attention are anxiety, depression, sexual adjustment and function issues, eating disorders, and substance abuse (Briere & Runtz, 1987; Briere & Zaidi, 1989; Wilsnack et al., 1994).

Hurley (1991), in a comprehensive review of the research conducted on women alcoholics and on women who have experienced CSA, describes striking similarities in the characteristics of both. She discusses three interrelated areas—(1) sexual dysfunction, (2) drinking motives and perceived effects of alcohol, and (3) posttraumatic stress disorder (PTSD)—that support the view of alcoholism as a possible consequence of CSA. For example, the relationship between sexual dysfunction and alcoholism for the alcoholic incest-surviving woman may be related to expectancies that alcohol will have a positive effect on sexuality. This expectancy then leads to the use of alcohol as a means of self-medicating for possible sexual difficulties (p. 265). Hurley speculates that survivors of CSA who do not develop sexual dysfunction may be less likely to use alcohol in this manner. Further, among women who do develop sexual dysfunction, some may have negative expectancies of the effects of alcohol (e.g., loss of control), which lead them to choose other means of dealing with their sexual difficulties.

More research on the relationship between CSA and alcohol abuse is urgently needed. A greater understanding of the links between these two important women's health issues has important implications for both prevention and treatment.

Acquaintance Rape

The relationship between alcohol consumption and acquaintance rape is well-documented. It appears that approximately 50% of acquaintance rapes involve alcohol consumption (see reviews by Abbey, 1991; Abbey, Ross, & McDuffie, 1994; Benson, Charlton, & Goodhart, 1992; Rivinus & Larimer, 1993). Thus, investigation of the mechanisms through which alcohol consumption seems to increase the likelihood of sexual assaults by acquaintances is an important area of research.

Alcohol is believed to affect the occurrence of acquaintance rape through its psychologic as well as its physiologic effects on both the perpetrator and the victim. Abbey (1991) explored potential psychologic mechanisms, listing three that relate to the male perpetrator and four that focus on the victim. With regard to alcohol's physiologic effects on the victim, Abbey noted that excessive consumption can make it difficult to send and receive cues concerning refusal and physical resistance.

Psychologically, alcohol can affect both the victim's self-perceptions and others' perceptions of her. Abbey (1991) stated that consuming alcohol can enhance a victim's feelings of responsibility for an assault. She also noted that people stereotype drinking women as more sexually available than sober women. These beliefs may contribute to unwanted sexual advances toward a woman who drinks, and the effects of alcohol consumption may make it more difficult for the woman to resist such advances.

To explain how alcohol consumption affects sexual assault, Abbey and her colleagues (Abbey et al., 1994) have presented a theoretical model based on three sets of psychosocial variables. The first set is composed of predisposing belief systems, including gender-role norms about dating and sex, expectancies about alcohol's effects, and stereotypes about women who drink. These combine with interaction characteristics, such as men's misperceptions of women's sexual intent, which are enhanced by alcohol consumption and result in sexually forceful behavior on the part of men. Alcohol consumption decreases women's ability to correct men's misperceptions and to resist an assault. Finally, the model proposes that postinteraction factors play a role in explaining how alcohol operates within this context. First, alcohol consumption has historically been used to excuse or justify men's socially unacceptable behavior, including rape. Second, the authors believe that alcohol consumption makes women feel more, rather than less, responsible for a rape—a belief that men tend to subscribe to as well. Although untested empirically, this model may provide one means of integrating a number of diverse findings in this area. In addition, it presents a basis for a multivariate approach that can more effectively address the complexity of this women's health problem.

Domestic Violence

As noted in the debate between Flanzer (1993) and Gelles (1993), it is a matter of contention whether alcohol is a direct cause of or merely a contributing factor to domestic violence. Even the estimated number of domestic violence incidents that involve alcohol varies considerably across studies. Gelles (1993) notes that some early research reported approximately 50% of domestic violence cases involved alcohol, but he cites recent data from a national survey showing that alcohol was used in only about one-fourth of the cases. Given the lack of precise estimates of spouse abuse resulting from alcohol consumption, more research is clearly needed to better understand the ways in which alcohol contributes to domestic violence.

When partners drink together, it is difficult to ascertain whose drinking contributes most to acts of violence. Two recent studies have concluded that violent acts against women seem to result from either the man's general drinking habits (Leonard & Senchak, 1993) or from the man's drinking at the time of his assaultive behavior (Barnett & Fagan, 1993) rather than either aspect of the woman's drinking. These studies also demonstrate the importance of men's reasons for drinking. In the former study, men who believed that alcohol was an excuse for aggression were more likely to be violent than men who did not hold this belief; in the latter study, abusive men were more likely than nonabusers to drink for emotional reasons such as to cheer themselves up.

When abused women drink, they seem to do so in response to abuse (Barnett & Fagan, 1993; Downs, Miller, & Panek, 1993). Although they received information only from the male partners, Barnett and Fagan (1993) found that approximately 20% of female partners drank before an assault, compared with 48% who drank afterward. However, another study, focusing on abused women who killed their partners, found that these women were much more heavily involved with alcohol, as were their partners, than were abused women in a shelter (Blount, Silverman, Sellers, & Seese, 1994). Thus, heavier alcohol consumption on the part of abused women may be a spur to violence and lighter consumption more likely a response to it.

Violence in lesbian relationships is rarely mentioned in the literature. However, it is clear from the few studies that have explored this topic that lesbians are not exempt from violence in their intimate relationships. For example, in a small and geographically limited study, Schilit, Lie, and Montagne (1990) surveyed women belonging to a lesbian organization in Tucson, Arizona, about their experiences with abusive relationships. Of the 30% of women who responded, more than one-third (37%) reported that they had been or were currently involved in an abusive relationship with a female partner. Like findings related to battering in heterosexual women (e.g., Miller, Downs, & Gondoli, 1989), the majority of lesbians in abusive relationships (64%) reported that either they and/or their partners used alcohol or other drugs prior to or during incidents of battering.

Renzetti (1992) studied a larger group of lesbians from various parts of the United States and Canada. Only 35% of Renzetti's respondents reported that their partners were under the influence of alcohol or other drugs at the time battering occurred (28% reported that both they and their partners were under the influence). In a number of cases, both the respondent and her partner were near-abstainers. Much more information is needed to better understand and respond to the problem of battering in lesbian relationships. Because of the reluctance within the lesbian community to acknowledge domestic violence and because of lesbians' lack of trust in traditional service providers and sources of help, lesbians who are battered may be even less likely than heterosexual women to seek help.

One problem with most investigations of the relationship between alcohol use and domestic violence is the lack of specificity in the measures used, especially of alcohol use at the time of an assault. The Conflict Tactics Scale has provided a useful means of assessing specific types of violent acts, but assessments of alcohol use during an incident of domestic violence have remained quite global. Most studies do not examine whether drinking occurred before or after the incident, and some measure only global drinking habits. As the study by Barnett and Fagan (1993) has shown, more specific measures of timing of alcohol consumption in relation to incidents of violence will yield important insights into the dynamics of alcohol consumption and spouse abuse.

The studies discussed here suggest that men drink more heavily than their female partners and are more likely to do so before they become assaultive. Heterosexual abused women seem to drink less than their partners and are more likely to drink after they are attacked, except for those women who kill their abusers. Future research in this area should focus on specific interaction characteristics related to consumption before and after an abusive incident and on differences in the relationship between battering and alcohol consumption among heterosexual and homosexual populations. In addition, more work is particularly needed to improve our understanding of victims' drinking patterns, for instance, whether drinking may serve as a barrier to leaving an abusive relationship.

CLINICAL AND
RESEARCH IMPLICATIONS

Alcohol and Sexuality

It is apparent that sexuality is extremely important in women's lives, and is not just "frosting on the cake." Consequently, achieving satisfactory sexual functioning is a key component in a female alcoholic's recovery process. Because of the circular relationship between sexual dysfunction and alcoholism, both research and treatment programs need to focus on helping women to gain sexual self-esteem.

An area of particular importance in this regard is expectancies associated with alcohol's effect on sexual behavior. Research has already shown that positive expectancies may motivate heavy drinking in women who are conflicted about sex (see Norris, in press, for a review). To the extent that women believe that alcohol enhances their sexuality, women with low sexual self-esteem may attempt to use alcohol to bolster their sexual self-image. If they maintain this belief in the face of declining sexual functioning, their self-image may suffer even further, and they may in turn drink to cope with their disappointment. Thus, studies are needed to develop interventions aimed at changing women's beliefs about the beneficial effects of alcohol on sexual functioning. Such interventions then need to be implemented on a large scale in treatment programs.

Lesbians and Alcohol

The addicted lesbian carries a double stigma that likely affects both help seeking and treatment. Not only is alcohol use or alcoholism inconsistent with traditional roles and norms for women, both women and lesbians are devalued in our society. In light of this fact, it is not surprising that the literature reveals little about alcohol problems among lesbians. The paucity of research and the resultant inadequate theoretical base perpetuates the difficulties lesbians face in obtaining effective treatment for alcoholism.

Studies on lesbian health have been limited by small nonrepresentative samples and the lack of comparison groups. Lesbian samples, almost exclusively obtained through lesbian-oriented social organizations or activities, have contained disproportionately higher numbers of white, well-educated, professionally employed, and younger women, the majority of whom are at least somewhat open about their sexual orientation. These limitations undoubtedly provide a biased picture of lesbians' health, including its relationship to AOD use. For example, many, if not most, of the above socioeconomic characteristics have been found to be associated with higher levels of alcohol consumption.

Lack of comparison groups makes it difficult to draw conclusions about similarities and differences between lesbians and heterosexual women. Some efforts to compare data on these two groups have been made, but variations in the wording of questions and the likely inclusion of an unknown number of lesbians in general surveys of women's health limit the usefulness of such comparisons. Therefore, much more attention needs to be given to ways to improve research on lesbians. One relatively simple method is the inclusion of questions about sexual orientation in all major surveys of women's health. In addition, less traditional and more innovative strategies may be needed to ensure that adequate numbers, and more representative groups, of lesbians are included in general women's health surveys as well as in research focusing specifically on lesbians. It is especially important to obtain more representative samples of adolescent lesbians, lesbians of color, poor lesbians, lesbians with disabilities, and lesbians who are less open about their sexual identity. Findings indicate that, unlike alcohol use among heterosexual women, alcohol use among lesbians does not decline with age. Thus, there is a need to include greater numbers of older lesbians in studies of alcohol use and abuse. As in research on women generally, studies that explore patterns of use over time are particularly needed.

The changing political climate and increased media attention to issues affecting gay women and men may help to eliminate some of the stereotypes and stigma associated with the gay life-style and thus facilitate the development of more sensitive treatment alternatives. In the meantime, it is imperative that health care providers who work with lesbian or gay clients first explore their own attitudes, stereotypes, and myths about homosexual identity and experience. In addition, acquiring accurate information about the lesbian and gay life-style, as well as learning about common issues that confront persons who are gay, is essential to the process of coming to terms and dealing with homophobia.

Some of the common issues experienced by lesbians and gay men include "coming out," gender identity, relationship issues, alienation, oppression and discrimination, and unique friendship and kinship networks. For example, the gay woman or man is continually confronted with the decision of whether to acknowledge her or his identity. "Passing" involves the burden of a double identity that may lead to a sense of alienation and to unauthentic or deceptive interactions (Lowenstein, 1980). Health professionals who are heterosexual may be tempted to downplay the importance of society's homophobia and oppression of lesbians and gay men. Recognizing that every lesbian or gay client lives daily with such oppression is essential in understanding the context in which AOD problems develop and continue or are resolved. Finally, it should be recognized that lesbians who have alcohol problems, like heterosexual women who abuse alcohol, often have histories of physical and sexual abuse. Health professionals must be careful not to focus on issues related to sexual orientation at the expense of attention to issues related to violence and abuse that may be of equal or greater importance in the development of and recovery from AOD dependency or addiction.

Alcohol and Violence in Relationships

Although research has made significant progress in understanding the links between alcohol consumption and some aspects of relationship violence, several areas still require further attention. As noted earlier, alcohol consumption can be either a precursor or a response to victimization. For example, research has shown that a history of untreated childhood sexual abuse for many women may result in heavy, often alcoholic, drinking patterns. Treatment programs should assess clients for a history of such abuse at intake because many alcoholic women who have never sought help have nevertheless had such experiences (Downs, Miller, & Panek, 1993). It is unlikely that these women will be successful in their recovery unless they recognize and resolve the problems that these experiences have created in their lives. Further research is also needed to identify particular factors that may make some women more vulnerable to substance abuse as a result of victimization, as well as to develop interventions aimed at prevention.

Although acquaintance rape and domestic violence are types of relationship violence, alcohol's role in their perpetration appears to be quite different. Alcohol consumption seems to increase a woman's vulnerability to acquaintance rape (see Abbey, 1991; Abbey et al., 1994; Norris, in press, for reviews), but does not appear to be predictive of domestic violence (Leonard & Senchak, 1993). More in-depth studies are needed to answer these questions: Under what circumstances might women's drinking serve as a cue for partner violence and why does this occur? Are stereotypes associated with women's sexual availability primarily responsible for men's perpetration of sexual violence against women? Are there other aspects of male–female interaction that are key to spurring violence? Or, does the determination of violence lie solely within each man's belief systems and behavioral tendencies? Answers to these and other related questions can help to shed additional light on alcohol's contribution to different types of violence against women.

In addition to differences in the role of alcohol as a precursor in acquaintance rape and domestic violence, there also may be differences in the impact of these two forms of violence on alcohol consumption following victimization. Studies have now documented increased alcohol consumption among women following battering (see, e.g., Barnett & Fagan, 1993), but studies of acquaintance rape have mentioned alcohol consumption as one of several possible sequelae. Neither of these literatures has explored the role of alcohol in delaying recovery from victimization. More research is needed to explore these relationships, as well as to examine how alcohol consumption may act as a barrier to victims' seeking help. Does alcohol's "medicinal" effects cause women's help-seeking behaviors to decrease as levels of drinking increase? Is there a complex interaction in the relationship among alcohol consumption, help seeking, and self-esteem? That is, does a woman's self-esteem decrease as her drinking increases, making her feel less worthy of help? Because research has generally not addressed these potential connections, many questions remain unanswered.

The complexity of such relationships is further illustrated when viewed from various ethnic/cultural perspectives. We know very little about how race, ethnicity, or culture interacts with alcohol and violence. Although certain societal/cultural norms, such as those that support male dominance and female submissiveness, are believed to be primary factors contributing to violence against women, we lack a thorough understanding of these relationships, particularly in regard to the manner in which they are influenced by the use of alcohol or other drugs. Studies that explore alcohol use and domestic violence in various racial/ethnic groups could potentially help clarify some of the important factors influencing these relationships.

We also need to explore the similarities and differences in violence experiences for couples in married versus less traditional living arrangements, including gay and lesbian relationships. Not only are gay and lesbian relationships important to study in their own right, but exploring homosexual relationships may also provide an important comparison that could help us better understand the experiences of heterosexual couples as well. For example, same-gender relationships can provide a natural control group for exploring the impact of cultural attitudes and norms on the incidence of battering.

The questions raised here can be viewed as illustrative examples of the myriad issues that researchers have yet to tackle in attempting to put together pieces of the puzzle concerning women's use and abuse of alcohol.

REFERENCES

Abbey, A. (1991). Acquaintance rape and alcohol consumption on college campuses: How are they linked? *Journal of American College Health, 39,* 165–169.

Abbey, A., Ross, L. T., & McDuffie, D. (1994). Alcohol's role in sexual assault. In R. R. Watson (Ed.), *Drug and alcohol abuse reviews: Vol. 5. Addictive behaviors in women* (pp. 97–123). Totowa, NJ: Humana Press.

Barnett, O. W., & Fagan, R. W. (1993). Alcohol use in male spouse abusers and their female partners. *Journal of Family Violence, 8,* 1–25.

Benson, D., Charlton, C., & Goodhart, F. (1992). Acquaintance rape on campus: A literature review. *Journal of American College Health, 40,* 157–165.

Bloomfield, K. (1993). A comparison of alcohol consumption between lesbians and heterosexual women in an urban population. *Drug and Alcohol Dependence, 33,* 257–269.

Blount, W. R., Silverman, I. J., Sellers, C. S., & Seese, R. A. (1994). Alcohol and drug use among abused women who kill, abused women who don't, and their abusers. *Journal of Drug Issues, 24,* 165–177.

Bradford, J., & Ryan, C. (1987). The National Health Care Survey: Final report. Washington, DC: National Lesbian and Gay Health Foundation.

Bradford, J., Ryan, C., & Rothblum, E. D. (1994). National Lesbian Health Care Survey: Implications for mental health care. *Journal of Consulting and Clinical Psychology, 62*(2), 228–242.

Briere, J., & Runtz, M. (1987). Postsexual abuse trauma: Data and implications for clinical practice. *Journal of Interpersonal Violence, 2,* 367–379.

Briere, J., & Zaidi, L. Y. (1989). Sexual abuse histories and sequelae in female psychiatric emergency room patients. *American Journal of Psychiatry, 146,* 1602–1606.

Covington, S. S. (1982). Sexual experience, dysfunction, and abuse: A descriptive study of alcohol and nonalcoholic women. Unpublished doctoral dissertation, Union Graduate School.

Crowe, L. C., & George, W. H. (1989). Alcohol and sexuality: Review and integration. *Psychological Bulletin, 105,* 374–376.

Dermen, K. H., & Cooper, M. L. (in press). Sex-related alcohol expectancies among adolescents: Scale development. *Psychology of Addictive Behaviors.*

Downs, W. R., Miller, B. A., & Panek, D. D. (1993). Differential patterns of partner-to-woman violence: A comparison of samples of community, alcohol-abusing, and battered women. *Journal of Family Violence, 8,* 113–135.

Fifield, L. H. (1975). *On my way to nowhere: Alienated, isolated, drunk. Gay alcohol abuse and an evaluation of alcoholism.* Los Angeles: Gay Community Services Center.

Flanzer, J. P. (1993). Alcohol and other drugs are key causal agents of violence. In R. J. Gelles & D. R. Loseke (Eds.), *Current controversies on family violence* (pp. 171–181). Newbury Park, CA: Sage.

Gelles, R. J. (1993). Alcohol and other drugs are associated with violence—they are not its cause. In R. J. Gelles & D. R. Loseke (Eds.), *Current controversies on family violence* (pp. 182–196). Newbury Park, CA: Sage.

Hall, J. M. (1993). Lesbians and alcohol: Patterns and paradoxes in medical notions and lesbians' beliefs. *Journal of Psychoactive Drugs, 25*(2), 109–119.

Harrison, P. A., Hoffman, N. G., Edwall, G. E. (1989). Differential drug use patterns among sexually abused adolescent girls in treatment for chemical dependency. *International Journal of the Addictions, 24*(6), 499–514.

Hastings, P. (1982). Alcohol and the lesbian community: Changing patterns of awareness. *Drinking and Drug Practices Surveyor, 18*, 3–7.

Hughes, T. L. (1990). Evaluating research on chemical dependency among women: A women's health perspective. *Family & Community Health, 13*(3), 35–46.

Hughes, T. L., & Fox, M. L. (1993). Patterns of drug use among women: Focus on special populations. *Clinical Issues in Perinatal and Women's Health Nursing, 2*(4), 203–212.

Hughes, T. L., & Wilsnack, S. (1994). Research on lesbians and alcohol: Gaps and implications. *Alcohol Health & Research World 18*(4), 202–205.

Hurley, D. L. (1991). Women, alcohol and incest: An analytical review. *Journal of Studies on Alcohol, 24*(7), 655–673.

Kovach, J. A. (1986). Incest as a treatment issue for alcoholic women. *Alcoholism Treatment Quarterly, 3*, 1–15.

Leigh, B. C. (1993). Alcohol consumption and sexual activity as reported with a diary technique. *Journal of Abnormal Psychology, 102*, 490–493.

Leigh, B. C., & Schafer, J. C. (1993). Heavy drinking occasions and the occurrence of sexual activity. *Psychology of Addictive Behaviors, 7*, 197–200.

Leonard, K. E., & Senchak, M. (1993). Alcohol and premarital aggression among newlywed couples. *Journal of Studies on Alcohol* (Suppl.11), 96–108.

Lowenstein, S. F. (1980). Understanding lesbian women. *Social Casework, 64*, 29–38.

McKirnan, D. J., & Peterson, P. L. (1989a). Alcohol and drug use among homosexual men and women: Epidemiology and population characteristics. *Addictive Behaviors, 14*, 545–553.

McKirnan, D. J., & Peterson, P. L. (1989b). Psychosocial and cultural factors in alcohol and drug abuse: An analysis of a homosexual community. *Addictive Behaviors, 14*, 555–563.

Miller, B. A., Downs, W., Gondoli, D., & Keil, A. (1987). The role of childhood sexual abuse in the development of alcoholism in women. *Violence and Victims, 2*(3), 157–172.

Miller, B. A., Downs, W., & Testa, M. (1993). Interrelationships between victimization experiences and women's alcohol use. *Journal of Studies on Alcohol* (Suppl. 11), 109–117.

Neisen, J. H., & Sandall, H. (1990). Alcohol and other drug abuse in gay/lesbian populations: Related to victimization? *Journal of Psychology and Human Sexuality, 3*(1), 151–168.

Norris, J. (in press). Alcohol and female sexuality: A look at expectancies and risks. *Alcohol Health and Research World.*

Paul, J. P., Stall, R., & Bloomfield, K. A. (1991). Gay and alcoholic: Epidemiologic and clinical issues. *Alcohol Health and Research World, 15*(2), 151–160.

Pribor, E. F., & Dinwiddie, S. H. (1992). Psychiatric correlates of incest in childhood. *American Journal of Psychiatry, 149*(1), 52–56.

Renzetti, C. M. (1992). *Violent betrayal: Partner abuse in lesbian relationships.* Newbury Park, CA: Sage.

Rivinus, T. M., & Larimer, M. E. (1993). Violence, alcohol, other drugs, and the college student. *Journal of College Student Psychotherapy, 8,* 71–119. Simultaneously copublished in L. C. Whitaker & J. W. Pollard (Eds.), *Campus violence: Kinds, causes, and cures* (pp. 71–119). New York: Haworth Press.

Russell, S. A., & Wilsnack, S. C. (1991). Adult survivors of childhood sexual abuse: Substance abuse and other consequences. In P. Roth (Ed.), *Alcohol and drugs are women's issues: Volume 1. A review of the issues* (pp. 61-70) Metuchen, NJ/London: Women's Action Alliance/Scarecrow Press.

Saghir, M. T., & Robins, E. (1973). *Male and female homosexuality: A comprehensive investigation.* Baltimore: Williams & Wilkins.

Schilit, R., Lie, G., & Montague, M. (1990). Substance abuse as a correlate of violence in intimate lesbian relationships. *Journal of Homosexuality, 19*(3), 51–65.

Teets, J. M. (1994). Sexuality issues of chemically dependent women. In R. R. Watson (Ed.), *Drug and alcohol abuse reviews: Volume 5. Addictive behaviors in women* (pp. 263–278). Totowa, NJ: Humana Press.

Vargo, S. (1987). The effect of women's socialization on lesbian couples. In Boston Lesbian Psychologies (Eds.), *Lesbian psychologies* (pp. 161–173). Chicago: University of Illinois Press.

Wilsnack, S. C., Vogeltanz, N. D., Klassen, A. D., & Harris, T. R. (1994, May). *Childhood sexual abuse and women's substance abuse: National survey findings.* Paper presented at the American Psychological Association Conference on Psychosocial and Behavioral Factors in Women's Health: Creating an Agenda for the 21st Century. Washington, DC.

Sexuality

Blume, S. B. (1991). Sexuality and stigma. The alcoholic woman. *Alcohol Health and Research World, 15*(2), 139–146.

The link between alcohol and sexuality is deeply ingrained in American culture. This article summarizes historical, anecdotal, and scientific evidence describing a societal stereotype that leads to the stigmatization of alcoholic women. This stereotype differs from that of the alcoholic male in that it contains a culturally ingrained expectation of hypersexuality and sexual promiscuity. The research discussed describes potential consequences of such societal perceptions for women who drink, and examines whether the stereotype can be supported in terms of real physiologic and behavioral changes that result when women drink. Blume concludes by offering strategies for altering prevailing negative attitudes and stereotypes. She notes that if inaccurate sexual stereotypes lead to stigmatization of alcoholic women and to such consequences as physical and sexual violence, then it is in the interest of society to find ways to alter these views. The challenge is to preserve the protection afforded women by cultural expectations that they will drink less than men while changing inaccurate perceptions of alcohol's effects on sexual responsiveness.

Dermen, K. H., & Cooper, M. L. (in press). Sex-related alcohol expectancies among adolescents: Scale development. *Psychology of Addictive Behaviors.*

Sex-related alcohol expectancies are one important component in individuals' reasons for drinking and the circumstances under which they do so. This research presents the development of a scale measuring sex-related alcohol expectancies in male and female adolescents, a group for whom the association between drinking and sex may be especially important. A large random sample (n = 916) of black and white 13- to 19-year-olds participated, 47.4% of whom were female. An excellent response rate of 81% was achieved. Confirmatory factor analyses were conducted and resulted in three domains of items: (1) enhancement (5 items); (2) risk taking (5 items); and (3) disinhibition (8 items). Multivariate analyses of variance showed that males were more likely to endorse items concerned with disinhibition and risk taking. This was especially true of older and of black males. On the other hand, white females were more likely to endorse risk-related and disinhibition expectancies than were black females. Although it is unfortunate that the scale was not standardized on older age groups, it has several strengths and will probably be useful in future research.

Gavaler, J. S., Rizzo, A., Rossaro, L., Van Thiel, D., Brezza, E., & Deal, S. R. (1993). Sexuality of alcoholic women with menstrual cycle function: Effects of duration of alcohol abstinence. *Alcoholism: Clinical and Experimental Research, 17,* 778–781.

This study examined sexual functioning in two groups of 58 abstinent (long- and short-term) alcoholic women. All women had retrospectively reported low sexual functioning. Even after a short period of abstinence, both groups reported significant improvement in sexual desire, capacity to be aroused, and sexual responsiveness. This is an important, albeit preliminary work; previous studies had confounded findings by including postmenopausal women. The need for addressing sexual issues in treatment and recovery is highlighted, and hope is provided for alcoholic women in recovering sexual functioning.

Leigh, B. C. (1993). Alcohol consumption and sexual activity as reported with a diary technique. *Journal of Abnormal Psychology, 102,* 490–493.

The question of how alcohol consumption affects sexual behavior is still open. This study engaged 118 men and women to maintain daily logs of their drinking and sexual activities for 10 weeks. In general, alcohol consumption was associated with a decreased likelihood of sexual activity and unrelated to the use of a condom. Thus, although previous research using other methods has demonstrated a relationship between alcohol consumption and sexual activity, closer examination of individuals' behavior, using themselves as controls, calls the relationship into question. The author calls for future research that examines the role of possible mediators of the relationship.

Leigh, B. C., & Schafer, J. C. (1993). Heavy drinking occasions and the occurrence of sexual activity. *Psychology of Addictive Behaviors, 7,* 197–200.

Most research examining the relationship between alcohol use and sexual activity involves questioning respondents about their alcohol consumption for a particular sexual event. This study does the opposite: subjects were asked about heavy drinking occasions and whether sexual activity occurred. This technique allowed assessment of sexual variability

as a function of drinking. Data were drawn from a local mail survey, as well as a national in-person survey. In general, the likelihood of engaging in sex increased with the amount of alcohol consumed. In addition, those who drank most heavily were somewhat more likely to have sex with a new or casual partner (this was more true of men than women). The authors note several possible theoretical interpretations for these findings and see a need for additional research to explore them further.

Teets, J. M. (1994). Sexuality issues of chemically dependent women. In R. R. Watson (Ed.), *Drug and alcohol abuse reviews: Volume 5. Addictive behaviors in women* (pp. 263–278). Totowa, NJ: Humana Press.

It is worth noting that this book on addictive behaviors in women contains a chapter on issues related to sexuality. Until recently, sexual functioning, except in relation to reproductive capacity, was considered "icing on the cake," rather than an important integral component of an addicted woman's recovery. The chapter covers a wide range of sexuality-related issues, including violence and abuse, sexual behavior while using alcohol or other drugs, gender-role enactment, sexual orientation, and sexual health issues. Given its brevity, it is more noteworthy for its breadth than its depth of analysis. Nonetheless, the topics discussed are critical in the life of a chemically dependent woman, and just calling them to attention is an important step toward their inclusion in treatment protocols.

Wilsnack, S. C. (1991). Sexuality and women's drinking. *Alcohol Health and Research World, 15*(2), 147–150.

Although clinical reports as well as cultural and historical beliefs have suggested important links between women's drinking and their sexual experience, few serious studies of such links were undertaken until the past decade. The National Study of Health and Life Experiences of Women, a longitudinal study of the causes and consequences of women's drinking, provides information about how various aspects of women's sexual experience relate to changes in drinking habits and drinking problems over time. The sample includes 917 women and explores a large number of variables that potentially influence women's drinking.

This article summarizes major findings regarding relationships between sexuality and alcohol consumption. Variables related to sexuality have consistently been found to be among the strongest predictors of drinking behavior. For example, more than twice as many problem drinkers as nonproblem drinkers reported experiencing at least one incident of sexual abuse before the age of 18 years old. Furthermore, a history of sexual abuse also predicted the onset of problem drinking over a 5-year follow-up period; that is, 51% of sexually abused women versus 19% of the women with a history of sexual abuse and with no signs of problem drinking in 1981 reported one or more alcohol problems in 1986. History of childhood sexual abuse was also associated with a variety of other consequences, including depressed mood, feelings of worthlessness, suicidal thoughts, use of other drugs, and involvement in violent or conflicted relationships. Wilsnack notes that these findings support earlier clinical reports that childhood sexual abuse increases women's risks for many long-term, adverse consequences, including alcohol abuse.

Sexual dysfunction not only was related to women's drinking in cross-sectional analyses, but was also found to be a consistent predictor that a drinking problem would continue over time. The author suggests that women use alcohol to "treat" their sexual problems—for example, to reduce sexual distress or increase sexual pleasure. However, because heavy use of alcohol depresses physiologic sexual functioning, a vicious cycle may develop, in which heavy drinking becomes both a cause and an effect of sexual difficulties.

Sexual Orientation

Bloomfield, K. (1993). A comparison of alcohol consumption between lesbians and heterosexual women in an urban population. *Drug and Alcohol Dependence, 33,* 257–269.

This researcher found no significant difference between lesbians and heterosexual women on a number of measures related to alcohol consumption, including drinking status, heavy drinking, drinking prior to or during sexual encounters, and frequency of going to bars. Using data collected from a larger study on alcohol and risky sexual behavior among a random sample of households in San Francisco, this is the first study of lesbians' use of alcohol to report such findings.

For the original study, a random sample of 4,000 households containing adults aged 18–50 years was drawn from a San Francisco household directory. This sample was meant to be representative of age groups that are most sexually active and, thus, at greatest risk for HIV transmission. Among the 844 persons (23%) who agreed to participate in the study, 445 (48%) were women. Of those women, 85% reported being primarily or exclusively heterosexual and 15% reported being primarily or exclusively lesbian (n = 52) or bisexual (n = 6). The majority of women (heterosexual, lesbian, and bisexual) were white (82%), 8% were Asian, 4% were Hispanic, and 3% were African American. Most of the women were well educated; 69% were college graduates or had postgraduate education. Interestingly, the only demographic variable on which the two groups of women differed significantly was family/household income. Lesbian and bisexual women reported an average of $27,000 a year compared with more than $37,000 per year reported by heterosexual women.

As mentioned earlier, no significant differences were found between the two groups on self-reported drinking status (e.g., nondrinker, light drinker, moderate drinker, heavy drinker). Only the category "recovering alcoholic" differed. Significantly more lesbian and bisexual women (13%) than heterosexual women (3%)

reported being in recovery. It could be argued that because no definitions of these terms were provided, different standards may exist between the two groups concerning what is "light," "moderate," and "heavy" drinking; however, no significant differences were found for other measures of drinking. For example, total volume, frequency of drinking, and mean number of drinks per day were the same for both groups of women. Similarly, in further analysis controlling for differences in background variables (e.g., age, income, relationship status), no significant differences were found. Only frequency of bar-going had any significance in predicting the total number of drinks; yet, this variable was not influenced by sexual orientation. Finally, no differences were found in patterns of drinking before or during sexual encounters.

Despite the limitations of the overall low response rate and the fact that this sample is, at best, only representative of younger, urban, white lesbians, the design used in this study is an improvement over many previous studies of lesbians' use of alcohol. These results, along with those of McKirnan and Peterson (1989a, 1989b) suggest that rates of alcohol use among lesbians and bisexual women may not be as high as previously thought. Unfortunately, Bloomfield's data do not contain information related to alcohol problems (which McKirnan and Peterson found were higher among their gay subjects than among heterosexuals in the general population). It is hoped that these findings will serve to stimulate more rigorous research that will further unravel the complexities of this important women's health issue.

Bradford, J., Ryan, C., & Rothblum, E. D. (1994). National lesbian health care survey: Implications for mental health care. *Journal of Consulting and Clinical Psychology, 62*(2), 228–242.

The National Lesbian Health Care Survey is the largest study of lesbian health to date. The authors present data on demographic, life-style, and mental health variables for 1,925 lesbians. Particularly interesting in this data set are the responses to questions related to substance abuse and violence. The majority (83%) of the women who responded to the survey drank alcohol at least occasionally. Almost one-third of the sample reported regular use of alcohol: 6% drank every day, and daily drinking tended to increase with age. Another 25% drank more than once a week, and 14% were worried about their use of alcohol.

A smaller percentage of white women (40%) than Latinas (46%) and African American women (51%) reported that they were raped or sexually abused at least once in their lives. Almost a quarter of all the women (21%) reported that they had been raped or sexually attacked during childhood. Racial/ethnic differences were particularly apparent for childhood sexual abuse: one-third of African American lesbians had been sexually abused as children, compared with one-fifth of white and one-fourth of Latina lesbians. White lesbians also had lower rates of incest (16%) than did Latina (29%) or African American (31%) lesbians.

About three-fourths of the women had received counseling at some time, and one-half had done so for reasons of sadness and depression. Most lesbians in the survey were socially connected and reported a variety of social supports, mostly within the lesbian community. Few, however, had disclosed their sexual orientation to all family members and coworkers. Greater levels of openness about lesbianism were associated with less fear of exposure, a greater likelihood of receiving therapy, and more choices about mental health counseling. The authors compare the findings with existing data on the mental health of heterosexual women and discuss similarities and differences. Although this study, like most studies of lesbians, offers data collected from predominantly white, well-educated, professionally employed women between 25 and 44 years old, it is an important contribution to an area of women's health that has heretofore been largely ignored.

Hughes, T. L., & Wilsnack, S. C. (1994). Research on lesbians and alcohol: Gaps and implications. *Alcohol Health and Research World*, *18*(3) 202–205.

Despite the growing concern about alcohol and other drug use among women, researchers have paid relatively little attention to lesbians as a group. This gap remains despite persistent claims in the literature, over the past two decades, that as many as one-third of all women who self-identify as lesbian drink excessively or experience alcohol problems. This article briefly reviews and discusses some of the limitations of existing literature related to the prevalence of alcohol use among lesbians. Despite the limitations in research, several findings are surprisingly consistent. The most notable include the following: (1) fewer lesbians than heterosexual women abstain from alcohol; (2) although rates of heavy drinking among lesbians and heterosexual women are reasonably comparable, lesbians' rates of problem drinking are higher than those of heterosexual women; and (3) the relationships between some demographic characteristics and drinking behaviors differ for lesbians and heterosexual women. This difference is particularly striking in relation to age: in contrast to heterosexual women, lesbians' rates of drinking, heavy drinking, and problem drinking do not appear to decrease with age. This finding suggests a positive relationship between age and more frequent drinking. However, an alternative explanation based on cohort or generational differences is also plausible: younger cohorts of lesbians may be drinking less than older ones.

Potential influences on drinking that may help explain lesbians' possible higher risk status are briefly highlighted. The authors note that, despite some gains in knowledge about lesbians' drinking in recent years, there are still major gaps in this area of research. There is a clear and pressing need for studies that will more accurately document alcohol use patterns and problems as well as help to identify specific risk factors that contribute to alcohol problems among lesbians.

Paul, J. P., Stall, R., & Bloomfield, K. A. (1991). Gay and alcoholic: Epidemiologic and clinical issues. *Alcohol Health and Research World*, *15*(2), 151–160.

This article is organized around the following questions: (1) Do elevated rates of alcoholism exist in the gay community? (2) Are rates of alcohol abuse in the gay community changing? (3) What are the risk factors for alcohol abuse in the gay community? (4) Is there a need for gay-sensitive alcoholism treatment programs? (5) How can existing treatment programs respond to the needs of gay alcoholics? and (6) How can gay alcoholics obtain the social support necessary to maintain sobriety? The authors review available information related to these questions but acknowledge that significant gaps exist in the research literature. They also point out that much less is known about the drinking practices of lesbians than those of gay men. Despite the disproportionate focus on gay men, this review article provides an excellent summary of the literature on alcohol use and abuse among gay women and men in the United States.

Ryan, C., & Bradford, J. (1993). The National Lesbian Health Care Survey: An overview. In D. Garnets & D. C. Kimmel (Eds.), *Psychological perspectives on lesbian and gay male experiences* (pp. 541–556). New York: Columbia University Press.

This chapter describes the results of a large-scale, comprehensive study of lesbian health, the National Lesbian Health Care Survey, which was conducted under the coordination of Caitlin Ryan and Judy Bradford through the National Lesbian and Gay Health Foundation (NLGHF) from 1983 to 1988. The purpose of the survey was to expand knowledge about the health care needs and concerns of women.

Findings related to substance abuse include the use of cigarettes, alcohol, marijuana, cocaine, tranquilizers, heroin, and "uppers." Of the respondents who smoked (40%), 30% smoked regularly and 11% did so occasionally. Among these smokers, approximately one-half reported feeling worried about their smoking. Most of the women (83%) drank alcohol at least once a month. Thirty-one percent said they drank regularly: 25% more than once a week, and 6% every day (drinking daily was most common among women in the $40,000 or higher income bracket). Almost one-half of the sample (47%) reported using marijuana at least occasionally. Younger lesbians and African American lesbians were more likely than other respondents to use marijuana. Twenty percent of the sample had tried cocaine and were more likely to be African American, Hispanic, and young. Only 1% of these respondents reported regular use. Few of the women reported use of tranquilizers, heroin, or uppers.

More than one-third of the women (37%) reported having been severely beaten or physically abused at some point in their lives; 6% had been physically abused both in childhood and adulthood. Among those abused as adults, more than one-half (53%) had been abused by a lover and about one-fourth (27%) by their husbands. White women were less likely than ethnic minority women to have been abused. Although the rate of sexual abuse in adulthood was similar among whites, African Americans, and Hispanics, one-third of all African American women, one-fourth of the Hispanic women, and one-fifth of the white women had been abused as children. Only one-third of the women who were sexually abused had sought help.

Data reported in this chapter are based on bivariate analysis. The authors do not report, for example, whether lesbians who had been sexually or physically abused were more likely to report use of alcohol or other drugs. The findings do emphasize, however, the limitations of the current health care delivery system for lesbians.

Underhill, B. L., & Osterman, S. E. (1991). The pain of invisibility: Issues for lesbians. In P. Roth (Ed.), *Alcohol and drugs are women's issues: Volume 1. A review of the issues* (pp. 71–77). Metuchen, NJ/London: Women's Action Alliance/Scarecrow Press.

The authors cite estimates that between 25% and 35% of lesbians and gay men have serious problems with alcohol and other drugs. They argue that, despite the gains made by the Women's Movement and the Gay Rights Movement in addressing issues of sexism and social justice, lesbians continue to be the object of considerable prejudice by the dominant culture. The social factors with which every lesbian must contend, consciously or unconsciously, on a daily basis provide fertile ground for the development of alcohol and other drug problems. This chapter examines some of the ways in which American culture transmits antilesbian messages to individuals as well as the eroding effect of this discrimination on self-esteem. The focus is on factors such as stigma, denial, alienation, and discrimination, which place lesbians at high risk for the development of alcohol and other drug problems. Finally, some guidelines for working with lesbians and incorporating their needs into existing projects and programs are presented, as is a list of resources useful to clinicians who work with lesbians.

Violence

Childhood Sexual Abuse

Hurley, D. L. (1991). Women, alcohol and incest: An analytical review. *Journal of Studies on Alcohol, 52*(3), 253–266.

Although increasingly recognized among clinicians and researchers, the links between childhood sexual abuse and the development of alcohol problems have been explored in relatively few studies. This author provides a comprehensive review of empirical research on the topics of women and alcohol and women and incest. Specifically addressed are family background and characteristics, childhood and adolescent experiences, self-esteem and self-concept, depression, and sexuality. Similarities in the characteristics of alcoholic women and women who have experienced incest are strikingly illustrated in a table that juxtaposes research findings from each area.

The author also reviews the limited information on incest-surviving women who are alcoholic, and explores characteristics that may differentiate between incest survivors who develop alcohol problems and those who do not. This review provides a strong argument for the necessity of multidisciplinary research and practice to more effectively identify, diagnose, and treat women who are survivors of incest and are alcoholic.

Miller, B. A., Downs, W. R., & Testa, M. (1993). Interrelationships between victimization experiences and women's alcohol use. *Journal of Studies on Alcohol* (Suppl. 11), 109–117.

Controlling for background variables, these researchers examined the link between childhood victimization and women's later development of problem drinking. Alcoholic women, when compared to heavy drinkers not in treatment and women sampled from the general population, reported more severe victimization in several areas. Almost half had experienced sexual abuse involving penetration, as opposed to less than 10% of the other two groups. Nearly half had also experienced severe physical violence by both parents. Even after controlling for demographic and family background differences, analyses showed that alcoholic women had experienced higher levels of sexual abuse, as well as verbal aggression and severe violence by their fathers. Increasingly, research is indicating that the treatment of alcoholic women must address childhood victimization if recovery is to be effected.

Russell, S. A., & Wilsnack, S. C. (1991). Adult survivors of childhood sexual abuse: Substance abuse and other consequences. In P. Roth (Ed.), *Alcohol and drugs are women's issues: Volume 1. A review of the issues* (pp. 61–70). Metuchen, NJ/London: Women's Action Alliance/Scarecrow Press.

A link between childhood sexual abuse (CSA) and substance abuse is increasingly being recognized by clinicians and researchers. As the authors note, however, it is not yet clear whether substance abuse comes first and is a factor in the development of consequences such as depression and sexual dysfunction, or whether such consequences come first and, in an effort to cope, alcohol and other drug use follows. Because there is no standard definition of CSA, estimates of prevalence are meaningful only in the context of how each study defines the experience. Researchers interested in this area must grapple with such questions as the relationship of the abuser to the girl (relative or nonrelative, type of relative, stranger or acquaintance), the age difference between the victim and her abuser, whether the abuse involved physical contact, to what degree the advances were forced, whether the advances caused distress and, if so, how much and for how long. This chapter provides an excellent review of the literature related to the consequences of CSA, including substance abuse. A unique contribution is an overview of the limited information related to women of color and an assessment of the relationship between CSA and social class. Considering racial differences, it is interesting to note that, although prevalence rates are similar, the degree of trauma experienced differs across racial and ethnic groups: compared to white and Asian women, more Latinas and African American women report considerable or severe trauma. The authors conclude with recommendations for how women's services can be more responsive to women who have experienced childhood sexual abuse.

Swett, C., Cohen, C., Surrey, J., Compaine, A., & Chavez, R. (1991). High rates of alcohol use and history of physical and sexual abuse among women outpatients. *American Journal of Drug and Alcohol Abuse*, 17(1), 49–60.

Recent research has begun to show a high rate of physical and sexual abuse among female patients in clinical settings. This study explored the relationship between physical and sexual abuse and alcoholic drinking among 189 women at an adult psychiatric outpatient clinic. Using a self-administered questionnaire on abuse history and the Michigan Alcoholism

Screening Test (MAST), the investigators found that 120 women reported physical and/or sexual abuse at some time in their lives and that the mean scores on the MAST were significantly higher among women who reported past physical or sexual abuse than among women who had no prior history of abuse. The highest rates of alcohol use were among women who reported a history of both physical and sexual abuse. Nevertheless, in a stepwise multiple regression analysis, physical and sexual abuse and having a blood relative with a substance abuse problem accounted for only 12% of the variance in MAST scores. This indicates that other factors also influence drinking level.

Another interesting finding of this study was the relatively high number of women who were heavy drinkers (14% as measured by a score of 10 or more on the MAST). Of concern is the fact that alcoholism was diagnosed in only two of these women on admission and only 16 (8%) were later given a DSM III-R diagnosis of alcoholism. As the authors note, this finding indicates that the MAST may be a useful screening measure for identifying alcohol problems among clients on admission or early in treatment. In addition, MAST scores can be used as indicators of when more information on alcohol intake and alcohol problems should be obtained.

Perpetrators of sexual violence against the majority of these women were men. It was not clear whether the perpetrators, the victims, or both had consumed alcohol prior to the abuse. Because women alcoholics appear to experience more severe sexual abuse, it is important that more research be done to disentangle the relationship between sexual abuse and alcohol abuse.

Watts, W. D., & Ellis, A. M. (1993). Sexual abuse and drinking and drug use: Implications for prevention. *Journal of Drug Education,* 23(2), 183–200.

Data for this study were collected as part of an ongoing evaluation of a substance abuse school-based prevention program in a predominantly white, wealthy suburb of a large city in the southwestern United States. Students in grades 7 through 12 were surveyed anonymously about drug use, sexual abuse and molestation, delinquency, and a number of social psychological factors. The analyses reported by these investigators focus on responses from 670 female students from the six grade levels.

A significant number (14.5%) of the female students reported past abuse or molestation (questions about sexual abuse by a family member or close relative were not asked). An additional 7.5% reported having been raped or molested on a date. It is not clear whether the terms "molested" or "raped" were defined in the questionnaire.

Significant but weak correlations were found between sexual molestation and almost all drugs included in the survey (e.g., alcohol, marijuana, hallucinogens, crack cocaine, steroids, amphetamines, barbiturates, and inhalants) for a lifetime, past-year, and past-month use. Use of designer drugs and cocaine did not differ between students who had been abused or molested and those who had not. Interestingly, young women in the 7th, 8th, and 9th grades who reported sexual abuse or molestation were more likely to use alcohol and other drugs than students in the 10th through 12th grades who had been abused or molested. The investigators present several tables of correlations between sexual abuse and delinquency as well as between sexual abuse and a variety of family, peer, and psychosocial variables. Again, although a number of the relationships are statistically significant, many of the correlations are weak.

The major strength of this study is its focus on a nonclinical, noninstitutionalized sample of adolescents. Given the salience of both sexual abuse and substance abuse to the health of adolescent and young women, research exploring the links between these problems is greatly needed.

Acquaintance Rape

Abbey, A. (1991). Acquaintance rape and alcohol consumption on college campuses: How are they linked? *Journal of American College Health,* 39, 165–169.

This article reviews the relevant literature and explores the possible links between alcohol consumption and acquaintance rape. Three of the possible explanations focus on the male perpetrator: (1) men's expectancies concerning the effects of alcohol; (2) misperceptions of women's intentions; and (3) using alcohol as a justification for violence. Four explanations focus on the victim: (1) alcohol consumption interfering with the ability to send and receive cues; (2) alcohol consumption interfering with the ability to resist; (3) stereotypes about women who drink; and (4) alcohol consumption enhancing women's sense of responsibility. Although the author provides support for each of these contentions, the available research was not necessarily designed to test each one. Prevention strategies and ideas for future research are also discussed.

Abbey, A., Ross, L. T., & McDuffie, D. (1994). Alcohol's role in sexual assault. In R. R. Watson (Ed.), *Drug and alcohol abuse reviews: Volume 5. Addictive behaviors in women* (pp. 97–123). Totowa, NJ: Humana Press.

This chapter reviews the empirical literature documenting the relationship between substance abuse and sexual assault, with particular emphasis on alcohol. The extensive support provided draws from criminal justice data, survey data, and substance abuse treatment data. The authors present a theoretical model that describes three categories of psychosocial explanations of the relationship between alcohol consumption and sexual assault. Predisposing belief systems include: gender-role norms about dating and sex, including beliefs about forced sex, individual differences in gender-role beliefs, and how alcohol affects the enactment of these norms; expectancies about alcohol's effects; and stereotypes about women who drink. The second component of the model focuses on aspects of interaction, including how alcohol affects men's perceptions of friendliness as sexual intent; women's ability to rectify these misperceptions; and women's ability to resist

sexual assault. Finally, the model discusses postinteraction factors: how alcohol is used as a justification for men's sexual aggression, how alcohol increases women's sense of responsibility for an assault, and how substance abuse is linked to childhood sexual assault. The authors also provide prevention and treatment implications and suggestions for future research.

Benson, D., Charlton, C., & Goodhart, F. (1992). Acquaintance rape on campus: A literature review. *Journal of American College Health, 40,* 157–165.

This article documents the incidence of acquaintance rape and provides an extensive literature review on several issues related to acquaintance rape on college campuses. These include: the cultural context, legal issues, adolescent attitudes and development, alcohol, what is known about assailants and victims, and recommendations for institutions' response to sexual assault. With regard to alcohol's involvement, the authors relate it to the use of alcohol as a social "disinhibitor." They also note that alcohol is frequently used, on the one hand, to excuse a perpetrator who drinks, but, on the other, to increase the culpability of the victim. Women who drink excessively often become more vulnerable to assault because of their inability to respond to aggressive cues and resist them. The authors unfortunately do not provide recommendations specifically related to alcohol.

Frintner, M. P., & Rubinson, L. (1993). Acquaintance rape: The influence of alcohol, fraternity membership, and sports team membership. *Journal of Sex Education and Therapy, 19,* 272–284.

The question of fraternity and sports team involvement in campus acquaintance rape has been hotly debated, but scant data have been put forth to clarify this relationship. Thus, this research is an important attempt to address the issue. Mail surveys were obtained from 925 undergraduate women for a response rate of 62%. Seventy-five percent of the women were white, 24% belonged to a sorority, and participants were equally spread across years in college. The questionnaire was designed to assess experiences of sexual victimization; items assessed the most sexually stressful experience and were followed by open-ended questions related to the experience. Twenty-seven percent of the sample reported at least one experience of victimization; 83% were committed by an acquaintance. Of those victimized, 55.3% reported that they had been drinking and that 67.5% of the male perpetrators had been drinking at the time of the assault. Twenty-one percent of the victims of sexual assault (which involved penetration) or attempted sexual assault felt that the man had encouraged them to drink to make them more vulnerable. The study also reports that fraternity and sports team members were overrepresented in the commission of these acts. Although the information provided by this research is useful and informative, it is unfortunate that the authors did not perform additional analyses to determine the relationships between the victimization variables and alcohol or group membership.

Kalof, L. (1993). Rape-supportive attitudes and sexual victimization experiences of sorority and nonsorority women. *Sex Role, 29,* 767–780.

Whether some women are more vulnerable to acquaintance rape by virtue of their personality characteristics or group membership is a contentious issue. Feminists and other victim advocates are very sensitive to the problem of "victim blaming." This issue, combined with whether members of campus "Greek" organizations are overrepresented in incidents of sexual assault, presents a particularly difficult research problem. Kalof has attempted to explore potential differences in sorority and nonsorority women's attitudes that might make sorority women more vulnerable to sexual assault. Using responses from a university campus mail survey, she compares the two groups

on their ratings of rape-supportive attitudes, as well as their experiences of different types of sexual assault. Multivariate analyses showed that sorority members were more likely than nonsorority women to accept both rape myths and interpersonal violence in general. In addition, sorority women were more likely to have experienced physical coercion and alcohol-related nonconsensual sex. Some provisos regarding these findings are in order. First, of the total 216 women who returned questionnaires, only 21 were sorority members. Thus, caution must be taken in generalizing findings from these individuals to the larger population of sorority members. Noting this, Kalof interprets her data very conservatively. Also, the relationship between the attitude differences found in the sorority women and the nonsorority women is not known. It is tempting to draw an inference in the direction of attitudes causing, or at least preceding, victimization, but it is possible that rape-supportive attitudes might develop as a response to victimization in order to justify it psychologically, or that the two are completely unrelated. Kalof provides some provocative results that serve as an impetus for further research in this area.

LeJeune, C., & Follette, V. (1994). Taking responsibility: Sex differences in reporting dating violence. *Journal of Interpersonal Violence, 9,* 133–140.

Although alcohol consumption is not a main focus of this work, it does shed light on the use of alcohol by men and women when engaging in violent behavior. Mail surveys were obtained from 465 undergraduates (response rate of 52%), of whom 58% were male. The overwhelming majority were white and heterosexual. Thirty-one percent reported experiencing physical violence in their current relationships. Among women who engaged in violence, 42% reported that they usually initiate the violence. Among men, only 14% reported that they usually initiate a violent act. The authors suggest that women are more likely to take responsibility for violent acts.

Approximately 35% of males and 30% of females reported using alcohol when violent. Men who admitted to initiating violence reported more alcohol or drug use than women who initiated violent behavior. This finding is notable because it suggests: (1) men have a harder time than women admitting violence against a partner and (2) when they do admit violence, they seem to engage in "deviance disavowal." Interventions are needed that encourage men to disclose violent tendencies, identify the underlying causes, and effect a change in their behavior.

Norris, J., & Kerr, K. L. (1993). Alcohol and violent pornography: Responses to permissive and nonpermissive cues. *Journal of Studies on Alcohol* (Suppl. 11), 118–127.

Violent pornography and alcohol consumption have independently been implicated as contributors to the sexual victimization of women. However, their exact relationship to each other has not been sufficiently examined. This study employed a balanced placebo design to determine whether learned expectancies or the physiological effects of alcohol had a greater impact on men's and women's judgments of a violent pornographic story. In addition, the drinking status of the characters in the story was varied, to investigate the possibility that the presence of alcohol could serve as a permissive cue for the acceptance of violent sexual behavior.

For ratings of the male story-character's behavior, multivariate analyses showed that female subjects who had been drinking perceived less force and more acceptability on the part of the male character. Male subjects who had been drinking rated the female character as more deviant and less socially acceptable. In addition, intoxicated women who read the story version in which the characters consumed alcohol were most likely to rate themselves as likely to behave like the female story-character. Among male subjects, those who were drinking or who read the story version containing alcohol consumption tended to

rate themselves as likely to behave like the male story-character, compared to nondrinking male subjects who read the no-alcohol story.

Secondary analyses of male subjects showed several differences between those who were split on the trait known as hypermasculinity, a "macho" personality constellation. Compared to men low on this trait, hypermasculine males in general viewed the female character as typical of most women; believed other men would behave similarly; said they would themselves behave like the man in the story; and were less likely to believe that the male character had committed rape. This research demonstrates ways in which alcohol can affect individuals' judgments of sexual violence, as well as the importance of certain personality traits.

Norris, J., & Cubbins, L. A. (1992). Dating, drinking, and rape: Effects of victim's and assailant's alcohol consumption on judgments of their behavior and traits. *Psychology of Women Quarterly, 16,* 179–191.

Alcohol not only affects those who consume it, but a drinking context can act as a cue for engaging expectancies associated with alcohol. This scenario study varied whether a man, a woman, both, or neither drank alcohol on a date. The man subsequently raped the woman. Male and female subjects then rated the characters' behaviors and traits, and judged several potential outcomes. Multivariate analyses of variance showed that when the man and the women had been portrayed as drinking together, the man's behavior was least likely to be viewed as rape; he was most likely to be viewed as sexual/romantic and was liked most. In addition, in this situation, the woman's reactions were seen as least negative, and the couple was judged most likely to date again within a week. The analyses controlled for positive rape attitudes. Thus, it appears that when a man and a woman drink together, sexual violence is more likely to be viewed as sex than violence, compared to when either drinks or when no alcohol is consumed. These findings have implications both for the prevention and treatment of acquaintance rape and for establishing assailant accountability.

Rivinus, T. M., & Larimer, M. E. (1993). Violence, alcohol, other drugs, and the college student. *Journal of College Student Psychotherapy, 8,* 71–119. Simultaneously copublished in L. C. Whitaker & J. W. Pollard (Eds.), *Campus violence: Kinds, causes, and cures* (pp. 71–119). New York: Haworth Press.

This article/chapter provides a comprehensive review of the research literature establishing the link between substance abuse and violence in general, with a focus on the college student. The authors present a theoretical systems model explicating the links among a number of factors purported to be associated with acquaintance rape. They also thoroughly discuss both the psychologic and physiologic effects of various substances related to violent behavior. In a substantial section on sexual violence, they focus on alcohol's role in increasing the likelihood of sexual assault, as well as in establishing blame and responsibility. A discussion of sexuality describes how stereotypes about drinking women, expectations about alcohol's effects on sexuality, and misperceptions of women's intentions may increase vulnerability. The authors also describe how alcohol interferes with rape prevention and discuss special issues related to treatment of an intoxicated rape survivor. This is a thorough and sensitive treatment of issues that are becoming increasingly prominent on college campuses.

Domestic Violence

Barnett, O. W., & Fagan, R. W. (1993). Alcohol use in male spouse abusers and their female partners. *Journal of Family Violence, 8,* 1–25.

One piece of the alcohol-and-family-violence puzzle concerns the relative contributions of the abuser's versus the abused's drinking. This study, although it obtained information only from abusers, helps to clarify the role of victims' drinking in the occurrence of domestic violence. Furthermore, it compares counseled and uncounseled batterers with two groups of nonabusive men, happily and unhappily married (n = 181). Several standardized measures of abuse, marital satisfaction, and alcohol consumption were employed, and the groups were matched on a number of demographic variables.

Although the groups did not differ in their frequency of alcohol consumption, abusers drank greater amounts, for different reasons, than nonabusers—that is, compared with nonabusers, abusers were more likely to drink for emotional reasons (e.g., to relax, to forget, to cheer up). By their husbands' accounts, abused women drank greater amounts than nonabused, although, like the men, their frequency of consumption did not differ. Female partners drank less than their male partners. During abusive incidents, 28% of the men reported drinking "often" or "very often," compared with about 20% of the women. In contrast, after an abusive incident, 48% of abused women reported drinking versus 24% of abusers. Abusers were more likely to have been abused as children and to be unsatisfied with their marriages.

A number of findings are notable in this study. First, only about one-quarter of the abusers report drinking while engaging in violence. This finding conflicts with other studies that report greater levels of drinking during a violent episode. One might also expect these men to "blame the booze" for their violence. Thus, the relationship of alcohol consumption and spouse abuse remains in question. Second, it is also notable that abusers drink more, for different reasons, than nonabusers. Assuming that there is some relationship between consumption and violent behavior, this pattern suggests interventions directed at teaching stress reduction or other coping mechanisms. Third, few studies have addressed the relative contributions of abusers' and victims' drinking. When violence occurs in conjunction with drinking, it is apparently the result of the man's drinking, whereas women drink to cope with the abuse. It is unfortunate that this study did not obtain reports from the partners of these men to corroborate these findings. Future research should address this issue. Finally, the authors provide a post hoc explanation for their findings based on the "alcohol myopia" model. This model, like other social learning models, shows promise for testing the role of alcohol in domestic violence.

Blount, W. R., Silverman, I. J., Sellers, C. S., & Seese, R. A. (1994). Alcohol and drug use among abused women who kill, abused women who don't, and their abusers. *The Journal of Drug Issues, 24,* 165–177.

The main question addressed by this research was: Does alcohol or other drug use by abused women, their partners, and/or their family of origin discriminate women who kill their abusers from those who seek help from a battered women's shelter? The researchers interviewed 42 incarcerated women who had killed their abusers and 59 abused women in shelters. The two groups were matched on level of abuse—the overwhelming majority had experienced severe abuse, including burns and other injuries requiring hospitalization.

The groups were equivalent on most demographic variables, but, compared to the shelter group, the incarcerated women were more likely to be white, to have fewer children, and to believe that religion is important. With regard to family of origin, shelter women were more likely to have suffered sexual abuse after age 12, although approximately 40% of the total sample had experienced such abuse before age 12. Shelter women were more likely to have witnessed physical abuse in their families, as had their partners, and to report that their partners had been abused as children.

Controlling for demographic and family-of-origin differences, a discriminant analysis employing the alcohol and drug abuse variables as predictors correctly classified 89% of the cases. The analysis showed that both the partners of the women who had committed homicide and the women themselves were more heavily involved with alcohol. The incarcerated women were also more likely to use other drugs, whereas shelter women were more likely to have had someone in their family of origin use drugs. Although these findings are enlightening, it is important to note that general alcohol and drug use were measured but were not assessed in relation to particular incidents of abuse. Therefore, it is not known whether the women who killed their abusers did so when they or the abusers were drinking, or whether these women drank in response to the abuse. Nevertheless, these findings demonstrate the importance of AOD use in the commission of homicide.

Downs, W. R., Miller, B. A., & Panek, D. D. (1993). Differential patterns of partner-to-woman violence: A comparison of samples of community, alcohol-abusing, and battered women. *Journal of Family Violence, 8,* 113–135.

This study compared the frequency and type of partner abuse of 45 alcoholic women, 38 battered women, and 40 randomly selected community women. Three subscales of the Conflict Tactics Scale were developed to measure negative verbal interaction, moderate violence, and severe violence. Complex patterns of abuse were found. As might be expected, multiple regression analyses showed that, in general, battered women experienced the greatest range of negative verbal interaction, as well as moderate and severe violence. However, alcoholic women experienced a high frequency of negative verbal interaction and moderate violence. The authors note that women may only seek help after they experience severe violence. Alcoholic women may suffer victimization as a result of the stigmatization associated with being alcoholic and may also drink more as a way to cope with their victimization. The study also showed that the Conflict Tactics Scale is a multidimensional instrument that can be used to assess complex patterns of abuse.

Flanzer, J. P. (1993). Alcohol and other drugs are key causal agents of violence. In R. J. Gelles & D. R. Loseke (Eds.), *Current controversies on family violence* (pp. 171–181). Newbury Park, CA: Sage.

Gelles, R. J. (1993). Alcohol and other drugs are associated with violence—they are not its cause. In R. J. Gelles & D. R. Loseke (Eds.), *Current controversies on family violence* (pp. 182–196). Newbury Park, CA: Sage.

These chapters present an interesting and provocative set of arguments on the controversy concerning the role of alcohol in family violence. Flanzer presents the perspective of a committed practitioner with a wealth of first-hand experience in the field. From this view of alcohol and family violence as a dynamic process, alcohol consumption is not a critical proximal element in the perpetration of violence, but is involved more globally in the family dynamics. Gelles, one of the most recognized and respected researchers on the topic of family violence argues more from a scientific point of view. He points out the lack of evidence for the notion that alcohol is a physiologically based disinhibitor, as well as the importance of learned expectancies associated with alcohol's effects. He also notes that a small proportion of violent acts actually involve drinking at the time of the incident. Ultimately, the only way to resolve the issue will be through the development and testing of causal models that incorporate factors known to be associated with violence. Such research may determine that there is no single cause of family violence, and that both views are correct. In some instances, alcohol may be the key causal agent; in others, it may not even be present. Nevertheless, these two chapters provide important insights into the different perspectives that shape how the problem of violence is approached and treated.

Leonard, K. E., & Senchak, M. (1993). Alcohol and premarital aggression among newlywed couples. *Journal of Studies on Alcohol* (Suppl. 11), 96–108.

Most research in the area of family violence focuses on well-established couples and frequently obtains data from only one member of the pair. Thus, this work is especially noteworthy in examining aggressive behavior relatively early in intimate relationships, from the perspective of both the victim and the aggressor. Other strengths of the study are its large sample and its substantial representation (more than 25%) of minorities. The researchers take a social learning perspective. They hypothesize that heavy drinking should be more strongly related to domestic violence in men who hold strong beliefs that alcohol facilitates aggression. In addition, they examine the role of the partner's drinking and several different characteristics among individuals. Results show a complex set of relationships between prior beliefs and how they facilitate aggression. The belief that alcohol serves as an excuse for aggression can increase aggressive behavior among men who drink heavily but who are not generally predisposed to violence. However, even among men who do not hold this belief, a high degree of marital dissatisfaction was also associated with violence among heavy drinkers. Thus, expectancies about alcohol's effects on aggression appear to be an important but not necessary precursor of violence in men who have consumed alcohol. Noteworthy in this study was that, after controlling for the man's drinking, neither the woman's drinking nor the interaction of the husband's and wife's drinking was important in predicting aggression. These researchers assessed general patterns of alcohol consumption, not drinking associated with particular acts of violence. Future research would benefit from a closer examination of this possible connection.

Renzetti, C. M. (1992). *Violent betrayal: Partner abuse in lesbian relationships.* Newbury Park, CA: Sage.

This book reports the results of one of the most comprehensive studies of partner abuse in intimate lesbian relationships. Renzetti used a feminist participatory research model to design and study the experience of battering from the perspective of 100 lesbians whose partners were physically violent. Although the women who responded came from all parts of the United States (95%) and from Canada (5%), the author notes that the sample is limited in a number of important respects. First, and most importantly, the study used a nonrandom sampling strategy. Persons who volunteer to participate in research studies, particularly studies concerning sensitive topics such as lesbian battering, may differ in important ways from women who do not volunteer. In addition, as in most studies of lesbian health issues, participants tended to be young (most were 26 to 35 years old), white (95%), and well educated. As the author notes, however, despite the limitations of the sample, the study helps to refute the myth that violence is more common among working-class than among well-educated middle- and upper-class lesbians. A final caveat: the data reported represent the experience of lesbian battering only from the victims' perspective (lesbians who batter were not asked to participate in this study).

The author provides a comprehensive review of literature on violence in intimate lesbian relationships, including research and theory that can be used to better understand this problem. Chapters describe the correlates of abuse, seeking and receiving help (a chapter that might better be called "difficulties battered lesbians have in receiving help"), and providing help to battered lesbians. Included at the end of the book are the questionnaire and interview schedule used to collect data, as well as a list of resources for battered lesbians.

Chapter 3, reviews two of the most popular explanations for domestic violence in heterosexual relationships: (1) substance abuse and (2) intergenerational violence. In this chapter, Renzetti explores research concerning the relationship between substance abuse and violence, as well as research that focuses on the transmission of violence from one generation to the next. Each of these perspectives is discussed in terms of its relevance to battering in lesbian relationships. In discussing the

relationship between substance abuse and violence, Renzetti reviews similarities and differences between lesbians' and heterosexual women's use of alcohol and other drugs. Also described are other studies of both lesbians and heterosexual women that can be used to better understand the violence/substance abuse link in lesbian relationships. The author concludes that, as in violent heterosexual relationships, alcohol and other drug abuse is often, but not always, present in violent lesbian relationships. For example, only 35% of the respondents in this study reported that their partners were under the influence of alcohol or other drugs at the time of the battering incident; 28% reported that both they and their partners were under the influence. In a number of cases, both the respondent and her partner were near-abstainers.

The research and information compiled in this book provide an important and valuable resource for researchers, educators, and clinicians who are interested in women's health, domestic violence, or substance abuse.

Sommer, R., Barnes, G. W., & Murray, R. P. (1992). Alcohol consumption, alcohol abuse, personality and female perpetrated spouse abuse. *Personality and Individual Differences, 13,* 1315–1323.

Partner abuse by women is undoubtedly an understudied phenomenon. Thus, this article is an especially important contribution. The researchers employed a random sample of adults, albeit limited geographically (Winnipeg, Manitoba) and culturally (92.3% white), and attained a relatively high response rate of 63.5%. The measures of personality, alcohol consumption, and physical abuse are well recognized and standardized. In addition, the researchers provide theoretically derived hypotheses based primarily on Eysenck's personality theory, as well as the sociological literature. That is, spouse abusers were expected to: score high on measures of psychoticism, extraversion, and neuroticism; be young; be alcohol consumers, especially when violent;

and, in general, have demographic characteristics typical of those in a lower SES. These hypotheses do not differ from those that would be expected of male spouse abusers.

The authors found that approximately 39% of the women studied had engaged in an act of spouse abuse with their current partner. However, 38% of the total number of acts were classified as minor violence (e.g., throwing or threatening to throw something, but not at their partner), and only about 16% were classified as severe (e.g., hitting). As with other studies of this phenomenon, these researchers did not take into account whether the violence perpetrated by these women was in self-defense, nor the consequences—that is, even though hitting can be viewed as a severe act of violence, a man hitting a woman is more likely to result in serious injury than when a woman strikes a man. The authors mention these points, but their study would have been much more enlightening if the data had directly addressed them.

The hypotheses were supported, for the most part, although, unlike in male spouse abusers, alcohol consumption was only weakly correlated with abuse, and only for measures of dependence. This study may help to identify some of the personality factors evident in the subgroup of women who are violent toward their spouses, but the social dynamics of domestic violence by women remain largely unexplored.

Part VIII

Economics, Ethics, Policy, Legislation

Chapter 15

Reproductive Options and Women's Rights: An International Perspective

Joan Woods

The current struggle for women's right to control their fertility and sexuality arose largely in response to the powerful population control movement. Feminists argue that reproductive rights are fundamental: that every woman has the right to bear children if, when, and with whom she chooses; the right to be sexually free from disease and unplanned pregnancy; the right to successfully carry a wanted pregnancy to term and raise healthy children; and the right to live free from violence. To make these fundamental rights meaningful, women need, among other things, access to safe, sensitive family planning services.

Throughout history, women have developed traditional folk methods of birth control and abortion. They often practiced these secretively, hidden from disapproving partners (Brody, 1988). In the past few decades, modern methods such as hormonal birth control have been developed to control fertility. These developments have the potential to increase women's reproductive autonomy.

The regulation of fertility has been a topic of public discourse, most often among men. Seventeenth- and 18th-century mercantilists, arguing that large populations yielded economic and political benefits, encouraged high fertility. Utopians believed in the capacity of modern science to provide for ever-larger populations. In 1798, Thomas Malthus published an opposing view in his *Essays on the Principles of Population*. He believed that food production could not keep up with population growth and the growing numbers of people would result in greater poverty and hunger. These beliefs led to the 19th-century movement for birth control in Europe and North America (Dixon-Mueller, 1994).

The modern population control movement began after World War II. Post-Malthusians have various theories of the causes and consequences of population growth but generally agree that population pressure from high fertility leads to poverty, environmental degradation, and political instability (Dixon-Mueller, 1994). In fact, political considerations have had an influence on the inclusion of population control programs in U.S. foreign policy. A brochure by Hugh Moore, published in 1954 and reprinted over the next ten years, stated that "there will be 300 million more mouths to feed in the world four years from now—most of them hungry. Hunger brings turmoil—and turmoil, as we have learned, creates the atmosphere in which communists seek to conquer the earth" (Gordon, 1976).

There has not been universal agreement about the Malthusian theory that large numbers of people cause chaos and suffering. At the 1974 World Population Conference in Bucharest, there was disagreement between northern and southern countries on population control. Those from developed countries stated that limiting fertility was necessary in order for southern countries to achieve an acceptable standard of living. Many representatives from southern countries, on the other hand, thought the north was ignoring deeper causes of poverty and instability: the inequities in consumption and distribution of resources. Rather than family planning programs, they argued, "development is the best contraceptive." However, by 1984, when the World Population Conference was held in Mexico City, there was an international debt crisis and the concept of population control was accepted by most policymakers, north and south. Many women observers felt that the consensus reached in Mexico City ignored women's reproductive rights focusing primarily on demographic outcomes (Bunch, 1990).

Women's reproductive rights advocates realize that reproductive decisions have a societal effect on population, development, and the environment. According to Bongaarts, there are likely to be 10 billion people on the earth by the year 2100 despite current fertility declines (Bongaarts, 1994b). This undoubtedly contributes to environmental degradation (although individuals in the less populated countries of the north consume, waste, and pollute much more than their southern neighbors).

Although women bear a disproportionate burden in fertility regulation and childbearing, they have been denied a voice in policies aimed at lowering fertility. They have also been the target of coercive and abusive policies aimed at controlling women. An example of such abuse is the eugenics movement of the late 19th and early 20th centuries. Heredity was used by eugenicists to explain social problems and to place doubt on the efficacy of social programs. Crime, insanity, poverty, prostitution, and other "degenerate behaviors" were believed to be inherited diseases and non-Europeans were thought to carry undesirable genes. This belief in the innate inferiority of certain members of society perpetuated racial and class hierarchies. This was manifest in policies of immigration restriction, compulsory surgical sterilization, and the encouragement of poor women to use contraception in order to decrease the numbers of "inferior" persons. Between 1907 and 1945, 45,000 persons were involuntarily sterilized, half of them mentally ill, most of them poor women (Gordon, 1976, pp. 121–136; Petchesky, 1984, pp. 85–87).

In 1975, Germain argued that in addition to providing women access to contraception, the status and role of women must be improved in order to have a substantial impact on societal fertility levels. Rather than developing population policies based on a view of women simply as reproductive agents, she argued for a change in pronatalist cultural norms and the creation of economic alternatives to childbearing.

Over the next two decades, feminists have come to view this approach primarily as a fulfillment of women's fundamental rights rather than as a means of population control. They have challenged population control programs because such programs blame women for "excess fertility" and exclude a focus on empowering women. Women's rights advocates recognize the sexual power dynamics that subordinate women and believe that family planning programs must attempt to change these dynamics (Dixon-Mueller, 1994). However, to suggest that feminists around the world are in agreement about women's needs is to oversimplify reality. Women from developed and developing nations often have very different ideas about what the empowerment of women means and how it should be achieved.

RISKS ASSOCIATED WITH LACK OF REPRODUCTIVE OPTIONS

Although the rights of individuals to control their fertility have been recognized by the United Nations (UN), many women around the world are denied this right because governments continue to neglect women's reproductive health. This is part of the wider societal problem of discrimination against women, which has serious consequences for women's health.

The lack of reproductive options is associated with maternal and infant mortality and morbidity (Cook, 1991). Half a million women die each year from pregnancy-related illnesses, 99% of them in developing countries. Between 25% and 50% of these deaths are due to complications arising from clandestine abortion (Eschen & Whittaker, 1993). Several million more suffer disabling illnesses (Jacobson, 1993). Maternal mortality occurs most commonly at the extremes of reproductive ages: younger than 20 and older than 35 or 40. Further, mortality also increases with parity greater than four and is slightly increased for first births (Winikoff & Sullivan, 1987). Maternal mortality and morbidity commonly results directly from hemorrhage, obstructed labor, hypertensive disorders, and septic pregnancies. In addition, many women are at high risk of sexually transmitted diseases (STDs), including HIV and reproductive cancers. Many of these adverse health effects are preventable and are the indirect results of gender discrimination (Koblinsky, Campbell, & Harlow, 1993).

The lifetime risk to women of dying during pregnancy or childbirth is 1 in 6,000 in the United States and 1 in 20 in sub-Saharan Africa (Dixon-Mueller, 1990). Maternal mortality is 200 times higher in developing countries than in Europe and North America (Lowenson, 1993). The risk factors for maternal mortality often begin in childhood. In developing countries, young girls often have less access to food and health care than their male counterparts. Those who survive childhood often have stunted growth and nutritional deficiencies (Cook, 1991). Adolescent marriage and pregnancy are common, and having many children, especially boys, is often the only way that women can become respectable and secure members of society. This leads to childbearing patterns commonly referred to as "too early, too close, too often, too late." The fact that women often resort to dangerous clandestine abortions in an effort to stop this pattern demonstrates how desperate they are. Combined with heavy physical workloads, poor nutrition, and loss of iron through menstruation, this reproductive pattern puts women at risk for poor health outcomes and even death (Koblinsky et al., 1993).

Women who begin childbearing as adolescents and have many closely spaced pregnancies suffer economically as well as physically. Women who become pregnant during adolescence are unlikely to finish school and thus have less education and training to obtain jobs that will support themselves and their children. Additionally, in all societies, certain types of work are culturally and socially unacceptable for women to perform. Those that are acceptable are less remunerative than traditional "men's work." Such differences in access to wealth and income decrease the bargaining power of women within the family. Men are allowed to impose on their wives their decisions regarding family size and contraceptive practice. Women's lack of economic power also makes it possible for men to shift the work of raising children onto mothers, usually in the form of longer work hours for women (Folbre, 1983).

BARRIERS TO REPRODUCTIVE OPTIONS

Legal systems often limit women's autonomy. In parts of Africa and the Middle East, women cannot legally own property, inherit wealth or divorce their husbands (Orubuloye, Caldwell, & Caldwell, 1993). In many countries, women are still considered legal minors (Freeman, 1990) and do not have a right to contract for health services (Cook & Maine, 1987). Some laws require girls to be at a younger minimum age than boys at the time of marriage. This reinforces the stereotype regarding women's childbearing roles and further limits women's access to education (Lowenson, 1993). Within this context of economic and legal lack of power, women's ability to make fertility-related decisions is severely limited.

Laws specifically relating to reproductive control also restrict women. Contraceptive services are often available only to married women, denying unmarried and adolescent women their reproductive rights. In Papau New Guinea, Niger, and several other countries, women cannot legally get contraceptives without their husbands' permission. In Turkey, women must have their husbands' consent to have abortions. Legal reproductive options may be out of reach of many women. According to the World Fertility Survey, only 23% of African women who do not want any more children use contraception. The numbers for Asia and Latin America are 43% and 57%, respectively (Eschen & Whittaker, 1993).

More than 1 billion people live in countries where abortion is strictly limited or prohibited. Moderately wealthy women can still usually get access to safe abortions. However, poor women are barred from access to safe abortions. As discussed above, clandestine abortions have a huge impact on maternal mortality and morbidity worldwide. Even in countries where abortion is legal under specific circumstances, access is often limited because of a lack of service providers and prohibitive costs. India and rural areas of the United States are good examples of such regions (Dixon-Mueller, 1990).

In addition to legal rights, availability, utilization, and efficiency of reproductive health services are important determinants of women's reproductive health status (Fathulla, 1991), and are often limited because of lack of resources or the low priority given to reproductive health. At least 100 million women have unmet needs for contraception. Many women do not receive services because they have no access or have access only to low-quality family planning programs, lack knowledge about the availability of services, worry about side effects of fertility regulation, or cannot afford the time away from work and family required to obtain reproductive health services. (Bongaarts, 1994a).

There are also important cultural and traditional barriers to reproductive self-determination. In agricultural societies, children are often a valuable source of labor and support for aging parents. Many cultures support the belief that men have ownership over their wives' fertility (Cook & Maine, 1987) and that the primary function of women is to produce and raise children. In these circumstances, women who are "barren" or have few children are often social outcasts. Failure of a wife to bear sons can lead to culturally sanctioned divorce, abandonment, or the taking of another wife by the husband. In such cultures, women who bear many children gain a place of respect in the family and the community.

The population control movement has been accused of being unaware of or unconcerned with women's lack of legal, economic, and social power. Women all over the world have increasingly called for rethinking "the population problem." This had been defined by the population control movement as a problem of women: they are simply having too many children. The solution, then, is to limit women's fertility. Rather than look at the cultural, economic, and legal reasons for high fertility, this definition reduces women to demographic statistics and leads to abuses and coercive policies.

In calling for a redefinition of the problem, women argue that they have been excluded from policymaking roles in the population control movement. According to Dixon-Mueller (1993), most policymakers show little awareness of the impact of policies on women's lives. They are more interested in macrolevel analyses of population growth, economics, the environment, and political stability. Women are demanding that their own experiences and desires be taken into account and have recently mobilized around issues of quality of care in family planning programs and improvement and protection of women's health and rights (Dixon-Mueller, 1993).

INTERNATIONAL HUMAN RIGHTS LAW

In an attempt to redress the legal barriers to reproductive health, women's groups have entered the arena of legal analysis. They are developing radical legal theories that question the supposed neutrality and objectivity that give law its authority. It is argued that laws made and enforced by politically and economically powerful men perpetuate the subordination of women. Feminist legal scholars believe that legal theories cannot be separated from history, culture, and politics. Because distinctive women's experiences are factored out of the legal process, laws lack universal validity (Charlesworth, Chinkin, & Wright, 1990).

International law has been affected by women's questioning the unassailability of human rights law. Women's advocates have built on ambiguous early United Nations declarations to develop a body of law that recognizes women's reproductive rights. In 1948, the United Nations Universal Declaration of Human Rights failed to mention reproductive rights but did recognize the right of women and men to "the free and full development of personality." Women have used this to argue for a right to education, literacy, and reproductive freedom (Brody, 1988).

Twenty years later, the international human rights conference in Teheran asserted that "parents have a basic human right to decide freely and responsibly on the number and spacing of their children" (Freeman, 1993) and that individuals have the right to "access to the relevant information, means and methods for implementation of such decisions" (Brody, 1988).

The most important UN document in terms of women's human rights is the Convention on the Elimination of All Forms of Discrimination Against Women (the "Women's Convention"). This was adopted in 1979; to date, 132 countries* have ratified it (Amnesty International, 1994). The Women's Convention provides a framework for the participation of women in economic and political development (Rahman, 1990). Article 12(1) states that appropriate measures must be taken to "eliminate discrimination against women in the field of health care in order to ensure . . . access to health care services, including those related to family planning" (Cook & Maine, 1987). It is interesting to note that the rights discussed are not passive; that is, they are not rights to be free from something such as torture or religious oppression. Rather, the reproductive rights as stated are positive: governments are obligated to take action so that these rights are meaningful. The Women's Convention requires state parties to make family planning services available to all who want them, to remove barriers that restrict unmarried individuals from obtaining family planning services, and to eliminate spousal authorization requirements for abortion and voluntary sterilization (Cook & Maine, 1987).

International standards, declarations, and conventions are meaningless if they have no effect on women's lives. The Women's Convention has no binding effect; it is only an articulation of ideals (Rahman, 1990). Moreover, states have made numerous revisions of the Convention, limiting its effect even further. (Charlesworth, et al., 1990). However, women's rights advocates around the world use the Women's Convention as a statement of intent and to push for women-centered reproductive policy. According to Dixon-Mueller (1994), national and international women's groups are motivated and united by the Convention. Citizens whose governments have ratified the Convention can hold their leaders accountable for fulfilling its requirements.

CONCLUSION

At the base of the differences between population control advocates and feminists who are concerned primarily with women's rights is a fundamental question: Should family planning programs primarily be means of controlling population size or should the primary focus be to allow women to exercise their basic right to control fertility? How policymakers, legal experts, and women answer this question is important in determining what reproductive health services are available to women and in what context.

Family planning programs that allow women to limit and space births benefit the health of women and children. However, accessible family

* The United States has not ratified the Women's Convention.

planning methods alone are not enough to ensure reproductive health. Women must be offered a variety of choices of methods and have adequate information about each. They need methods that protect them from STDs as well as unwanted pregnancy. Women need sensitive and effective care when they contract STDs. Safe and legal abortion services are necessary when contraceptive methods fail or are not used.

To achieve all of these goals and to ensure women's reproductive health, women must be allowed to make decisions that affect their bodies, their health, and their lives. As Olivia Cousins says, "There can be no true and valid discussion of women's health until we first address the issue of empowerment." All of the clinics and health services in the world will not improve women's lives if they are not free to use them.

REFERENCES

Amnesty International. (1994, Spring). *INTERact: A Bulletin about Women's Human Rights* (Susan Roach, ed.), p. 6.

Bongaarts, J. (1994a). Population policy options in the developing world. *Science, 263,* 771–776.

Bongaarts, J. (1994b). Talk at NCIH Conference. June 26–29, 1994, Arlington, Virginia.

Brody, E. (1988). Culture, reproductive technology and women's rights: An intergovernmental perspective. *Journal of Psychosomatic OB/Gyn, 9,* 199–205.

Bunch, C. (1990). Women's rights as human rights: Toward a re-vision of human rights. *Human Rights Quarterly, 12,* 486–498.

Charlesworth, H., Chinkin, C., & Wright, S. (1990). Feminist approaches to international law. *American Journal of International Law, 85,* 613–645.

Cook, R. J. (1991). International protection of women's reproductive rights. *International Law and Politics, 24,* 645–727.

Cook, R. J., & Maine, D. (1987). Spousal veto over family planning services. *American Journal of Public Health, 77*(3), 339–344.

Dixon-Mueller, R. (1990). Abortion policy and women's health in developing countries. *International Journal of Health Services, 20*(2), 297–314.

Dixon-Mueller, R. (1993). *Population policy and women's rights: Transforming reproductive choice.* Westport, CT: Praeger.

Dixon-Mueller, R. (1994). Talk at NCIH Conference. June 26–29, 1994, Arlington, Virginia.

Eschen, A., & Whittaker, M. (1993). Family planning: A base to build on for women's reproductive health services. In M. Koblinsky, J. Timyan, & J. Gay (Eds.), *The health of women: A global perspective.* San Francisco: Westview Press.

Fathalla, M. F. (1991). Reproductive health: A global overview. *Annals of the New York Academy of Sciences, 626,* 1–10.

Folbre, N. (1983). Of patriarchy born: The political economy of fertility decisions. *Feminist Studies, 9*(2), 261–284.

Freeman, M. A. (1990). Measuring equality: A comparative perspective on women's legal capacity and constitutional rights in five commonwealth countries. *Berkeley Women's Law Journal, 5,* 110–138.

Germain, A. (1975). Status and roles of women as factors in fertility behavior: A policy analysis. *Studies in Family Planning, 6*(7), 192–200.

Hartmann, B. (1987). *Reproductive rights and wrongs: The political politics of population control and contraceptive choice.* New York: Harper & Row.

Jacobson, J. (1993). The price of poverty. In M. Koblinsky, J. Timyan, & J. Gay (Eds.), *The health of women: A global perspective* (p. 3–32). San Francisco: Westview Press.

Koblinski, M., Campbell, O., & Harlow, S. (1993). Mother and more: A broader perspective on women's health. In M. Koblinsky, J. Timyan, & J. Gay (Eds.), *The health of women: A global perspective* (p. 32–62). San Francisco: Westview Press.

Lowenson, R. (1993). Defining fundamental rights in reproductive health. *Progress, 1*(1), 35–43.

Orubuloye, I. O., Caldwell, J., & Caldwell, P. (1993). African women's control over their sexuality in an era of AIDS: A study of the Yoruba in Nigeria. *Social Science and Medicine, 37*(7), 859–872.

Petchesky, R. P. (1984). *Abortion and women's choice: The state, sexuality, and reproductive freedom.* New York: Longmans.

Rahman, A. (1990). Religious rights versus women's rights in India: A test case for international human rights law. *Columbia Journal of Transnational Law, 28,* 473–498.

Winikoff, B., & Sullivan, M. (1987). Assessing the role of family planning in reducing maternal mortality. *Studies in Family Planning, 18*(3), 128–143.

The Argument for Reproductive Rights as Human Rights

Cook, R. J. (1991). International protection of women's reproductive rights. *International Law and Politics, 24*, 645–727.

Government neglect of women's reproductive health leads to maternal morbidity and mortality. According to Cook, such neglect reflects women's political, economic, and social powerlessness and is a part of systematic discrimination against women. Laws that limit women's ability to control fertility as well as governmental failure to provide women with reproductive health services are violations of women's human rights.

The challenge, according to Cook, is to achieve such widespread respect of women's right to regulate entry into reproduction and parenthood that access to fertility regulation is recognized as a fundamental human right. She discusses the role of feminist legal methods and the Convention on the Elimination of All Forms of Discrimination Against Women in achieving this.

Dixon-Mueller, R. (1993). *Population policy and women's rights: Transforming reproductive choice.* Westport, CT: Praeger.

Dixon–Mueller is a leading proponent of women's reproductive health, and this book is essential for those with an interest in the subject. It is a compilation of essays in which she develops a framework to view women's rights. In Part 1, the author discusses the evolution of concepts of human rights, including reproductive and sexual rights, and important UN declarations that attempt to articulate these rights. Part 2 presents the contradictory views of the population control movement and women's rights advocates in a historical context. Part 3 examines women's lives and the conditions in which they make (or are prevented from making) reproductive and sexual choices. Data from southern countries are comparisons to the north.

Finally, Dixon-Mueller proposes that the "population policy" that blames women for "excess fertility" must be redefined from the feminist perspective, which recognizes that the exercise of women's reproductive rights depends on the exercise of all other human rights—economic, social, and political. Because women around the world define their needs differently, such a perspective must include minimal but essential components of such a perspective. These include "building on women's shared and diverse social experiences in program design, and recognizing that girls and women everywhere are subject . . . to oppression under patriarchy. Policies and programs must incorporate systematic means of recognizing the risks women face and strengthening alternative bases of survival, security, and empowerment."

Freedman, L. P., & Issacs, S. L. (1993). Human rights and reproductive choice. *Studies in Family Planning, 24*(1), 18–29.

The authors propose a woman-centered approach to reproductive health, emphasizing women's autonomy and decision-making powers. This approach would address reproductive health in the way that women experience it, rather than as isolated biomedical "problems." It would take into account the larger social situation and would acknowledge the fact that, currently, in most of the world, "men have the power to shape the world in which women live."

The interrelationship of international law, national law, culture, and individuals is discussed. A history of reproductive choice as a human right is presented, from the World Population Conference in Bucharest, Romania, in 1974, to current World Bank and International Monetary Fund policy statements.

Incentives and disincentives and their potential conflict with reproductive autonomy are also discussed.

Lowenson, R. (1993). Defining fundamental rights in reproductive health. *Progress, 1*(1), 35–43.

Although written from the perspective of life in Zimbabwe, the issues in this article are applicable to women in developing countries everywhere. Lowenson believes that reproductive health rights include the right to: (1) information, (2) control over sexual patterns, (3) control over fertility, (4) freedom from disease and illness due to reproduction, and (5) freedom from negative economic and social discrimination due to reproductive roles. Each of these rights is complex and the author addresses each, putting it in the context of AIDS, sexual harassment and rape, the breakdown of the extended family, and decision-making power.

According to Lowenson, maternal and child health, family planning, and AIDS programs disseminate information about reproductive health in a verticalized manner rather than as a holistic system. Services should be integrated with other health and rights functions so that the complex issues that affect women's reproductive health can be adequately addressed. The link between health and human rights is an area of change and struggle. It demands a shift in the power relationships between men and women and is therefore not neutral.

Macklin, R. (1989). Liberty, utility, and justice: An ethical approach to unwanted pregnancy. *International Journal of Obstetrics and Gynecology* (Suppl. 3), 37–49.

The author uses the three principles in the title of her article to develop a moral framework in which to assert women's right to reproductive health and freedom. This includes both the natural right to make reproductive decisions without interference and a social right, which requires governments to provide services that make those decisions meaningful—family planning and abortion services.

Macklin recognizes that these ethical principles are not applied in a vacuum; they are applied within particular cultures at particular moments in history and therefore conflicts among principles arise. In addition, in developing countries, there is often competition in allocating resources. The right to reproductive health may be subordinated to the right to food and housing where resources are limited. While clearly outlining the major conflicts that arise when applying the ethical principles of liberty, utility, and justice to reproductive rights, the author does not attempt to develop definitive solutions to these conflicts.

Analysis of Legal Theory

Bunch, C. (1990). Women's rights as human rights: Toward a re-vision of human rights. *Human Rights Quarterly, 12*, 486–498.

While not specifically addressing issues of reproductive rights, this paper examines the separation of human rights and women's rights in treaties and in practice. This separation arises from the belief that oppression of women is personal or cultural rather than political—a reflection of power, domination, and privilege in all aspects of life. Bunch argues that states are responsible for abuses of women, even for acts conceived by many as "private," because governments condone or sanction these acts.

In combination with poverty and poor health services, women's lack of control over reproduction is deadly, leading to illegal abortions, early childbirth, and dangerously high parity.

Bunch describes four related approaches to viewing women's rights in order to link them to human rights: (1) women's rights as political and civil rights, (2) women's rights as socioeconomic rights, (3) women's rights and the law, and (4) the feminist transformation of human rights. These are interrelated and build on each other. Women's issues should incorporate gender perspectives into other issues (race, class, religion), in order to prevent isolation from and competition with other groups.

Callahan, D., & Clark, P. (Eds.). (1981). Population policy, universal rights and national sovereignty in ethical issues of population aid: Culture, economics and international assistance. New York: Irvington.

The conflict between "universally recognized" individual rights and national sovereignty is discussed. This conflict affects family planning programs because nations and international groups often have targets of decreased (or increased) population size. If it is determined that decreasing the number of children born in each family will benefit the nation, the potential for outright coercion and violation of individual rights exists.

Callahan believes that conflict is inevitable because the United Nations has developed a list of rights without prioritizing them. In this situation, national sovereignty rights can be used to justify limiting individual human rights. The author suggests that the rights recognized by the United Nations be prioritized so that more individual rights supersede national sovereignty rights.

However, Callahan does not mention women's rights to control their bodies and does not seem to view this conflict in terms of gender.

Charlesworth, H., Chinkin, C., & Wright, S. (1990). Feminist approaches to international law. *American Journal of International Law*, 85, 613–645.

The authors question the abstract rationality that gives law its authority. Feminist analysis examines the role of the legal system in creating and perpetuating women's lowered status. The immunity of international law to feminist scrutiny is questioned and the author proposes that we look behind the "abstract entities of states" to examine the impact of international laws on women's lives. Currently, women's experiences are factored out of the international legal process so the laws do not have universal validity. Men dominate political power nationally and internationally. They control the structures of international law-making and the content of the rules of law. The male perspective of the international legal order ensures male dominance.

The authors distinguish public from private life. The public realm includes the workplace, law, economics, politics, and cultural life. These are considered the natural province of men. Women occupy the private realm of home and children, and their needs in this area are often made invisible. Society places greater significance on the public arena, justifying as natural the unequal distribution of labor and allocation of resources. Certain principles of international law reproduce this private/public dichotomy. The feminist perspective challenges the artificial division and the notion that states are responsible for only the public sphere.

Cook, R. J. (1993). International human rights and women's reproductive health. *Studies in Family Planning*, 24(2), 73–86.

Cook describes a feminist legal approach to explain paternalistic laws designed to control women. The theory inherently rejects the idea that laws are gender- and politically neutral. This approach should be applied to international laws that do not explicitly discriminate against women by asking "the woman question": How does the law fail to take into account the experiences and values of women and how does this place women at a disadvantage?

The author discusses the 1979 Convention on the Elimination of All Forms of Discrimination Against Women. She analyzes women's rights through other international treaties that guarantee rights to life, liberty, and security of person; the right to marry and found a family; the right to private and family life; rights of access to information and education; the right to reproductive health and health care; and the right to the benefits of scientific progress. The link between each of these rights and reproductive health is demonstrated.

The fact that national laws are needed to protect women's rights is acknowledged, and the author discusses committees established to monitor compliance with treaties and nongovernmental organizations that make reports regarding compliance. The paper does not fully address the inadequacies of such "enforcement" methods or offer alternatives.

Freeman, M. A. (1990). Measuring equality: A comparative perspective on women's legal capacity and constitutional rights in five commonwealth countries. *Berkeley Women's Law Journal, 5,* 110–138.

This study examines the legal status of women in Kenya, Tanzania, Zimbabwe, Jamaica, and Canada. In many countries, women do not have full legal capacity; they are considered minors under the guardianship of their father, husband, brother, or other male relative. Freeman uses the concept of capacity as a basic measure of equality. This is the recognized ability of one to carry out the responsibilities and have access to the rights of an adult in society. In order for this to be legally relevant, the work done by women, paid and unpaid, must be acknowledged as contributing to the family and to society.

These five countries are at different stages with regard to the legal capacity of women. In the Commonwealth African countries, relevant equality issues involve women's status as family members. The rights to consent to marriage, to inherit property, and to have custody of their children are relevant. In Jamaica and Canada, where women have had the status of legal adults for decades, equality issues are framed as the right to equal pay for equal work and a recognition of women's unpaid contribution to the economy.

Lacey, N. (1987). Legislation against sex discrimination: Questions from a feminist perspective. *Journal of Law and Society, 14*(4), 411–421.

This paper analyzes the British Sex Discrimination Act of 1975 from a feminist perspective. Lacey raises important questions regarding national and international laws affecting women.

- Does the law take into account the fact that women's disadvantage is not solely the result of individual acts but of structural discrimination embedded in social institutions?

- Does the law promote equality of opportunity or equality of results? Is there an underlying assumption (perhaps in enforcing the law) that men and women make different choices, so that women's lack of opportunity is their decision? Are "natural sex differences" legitimated?

- Does the law present the problem as sex discrimination rather than discrimination against women? (According to Lacey, this renders the actual social problem invisible.)

These and other questions raised in the article lead Lacey to question whether the courts are the appropriate arena for dealing with issues of women's rights. Males dominate the personnel of legal systems and the legislatures and interest groups that influence them. Lacey argues that feminists should also focus on changes at the policy level.

Reproductive Options and Women's Health

Bongaarts, J. (1994). Population policy options in the developing world. *Science, 263,* 771–776.

Bongaarts is a well-known population scholar and his discussion of family planning is from a population control perspective. He suggests ways of decreasing fertility such as: increasing the educational levels of everyone, especially girls and women; improving the status of women; decreasing child mortality; and increasing the population's exposure to different life-styles through the media. He argues for improvements in the economic, social, and legal status of women in order to reduce desired fertility. He also makes the curious statement that "most governments already pursue these socially desirable objectives [raising the status of women] independent of their potential role in lowering the rate of childbearing."

Brody, E. (1988). Culture, reproductive technology and women's rights: An intergovernmental perspective. *Journal of Psychosomatic OB/Gyn, 9,* 199–205.

Women have developed and passed on traditional methods of fertility regulation throughout history. The social control of women's sexuality and fertility is analyzed. Brody also offers an interesting discussion of the unique position of representatives to the U.N. General Assembly from developing countries and how their position affects international law. They must balance a desire for their countries to be recognized and respected internationally with pressures at home to maintain traditional practices that may violate U.N. definitions of human rights. The author briefly presents the U.N. Declaration on Human Rights and the Convention on the Elimination of All Forms of Discrimination Against Women. Also, the author examines the implications of newer reproductive technologies such as in vitro fertilization and surrogate motherhood and the impact of biomedical research on human rights.

Cook, R. J., & Maine, D. (1987). Spousal veto over family planning services. *American Journal of Public Health, 77*(3), 339–344.

According to the authors, there are often situations in which husbands are allowed to veto their wives' fertility control choices. Where spousal veto over reproductive health care exists, it is a serious threat to the lives and health of women and children. Spousal veto violates national and international laws that guarantee personal privacy and autonomy and the right to health care. Courts in several countries have ruled that spousal veto regulations are illegal. In addition, they violate the Convention on the Elimination of All Forms of Discrimination Against Women.

Spousal veto regulations appear in national ministry of health guidelines, clinic guidelines, or customary practice. In many cases, spousal veto regulations persist because of misperceptions of laws or out of fear of offending local customs. However, the authors argue that spousal veto is contrary to the professional ethics of health care providers, whose primary responsibility is toward the health and well-being of clients, not their spouses. In fact, refusal to give care may constitute negligence or abandonment punishable by law. In cases of cultural support of spousal veto, the authors recommend involving men in family planning decisions and educating them about the adverse health effects on women and children of frequent pregnancies closely spaced.

Dixon-Mueller, R. (1990). Abortion policy and women's health in developing countries. *International Journal of Health Services, 20*(2), 297–314.

Dixon-Mueller discusses the global problem of clandestine abortion in terms of maternal death and the physical and emotional cost to all women. National laws may not reflect reality; some countries with nominally restrictive laws may in fact have abortion readily available for those who can afford it. In addition, in countries such as India, abortion laws are liberal, but many women lack access because of a severe shortage of trained personnel and facilities. Dixon-Mueller points to lack of access to integrated reproductive health services and poor quality of care as leading to unwanted pregnancy and limiting access to abortion. To remedy this, she recommends community-based primary health care services utilizing family planning workers, village health workers, and nurse-midwives from the community. Such workers should be trained to terminate pregnancy by vacuum aspiration.

International conferences on maternal and child health, human rights, population, and the status of women seldom discuss issues of abortion; when they do, it is in terms of maternal mortality and morbidity caused by clandestine abortion. Participants have been reluctant to press for legalization of abortion and increased access to safe services. The author argues that abortion is implied in documents that guarantee safe and accessible family planning services to all women. In the absence of safe, universally effective, acceptable contraception, women use abortion as a method of family planning to regulate the number or spacing of their children. Abortion should be fully legalized, and restrictions, such as special approval of physicians, should be removed. In countries where abortion is legal only when the health of the mother is endangered, health care providers can adopt the WHO definition of health that includes mental and social as well as physical well-being.

Fathalla, M. F. (1991). Reproductive health: A global overview. *Annals of the New York Academy of Sciences, 626*, 1–10.

Basing her definition of reproductive health on the WHO definition of health in general, Fathalla argues that "reproductive health is accomplished in a state of complete physical, mental, and social well-being and is not merely the absence of disease or disorders of the reproductive process." This implies that people must have the ability to regulate their fertility and enjoy sexual relationships.

Women's socioeconomic status is closely intertwined with women's health. In general, women carry a disproportionate burden in fertility regulation. The methods used by women are those that are associated with potentially harmful side effects. Fathalla argues that availability, utilization, and efficiency of health services are important determinants in reproductive health, and improvement must be made in these areas.

Germain, A. (1975). Status and roles of women as factors in fertility behavior: A policy analysis. *Studies in Family Planning, 6*(7), 192–200.

While not specifically discussing women's reproductive health rights, Germain argues in this article for increasing the status of women. She presents the idea that family planning programs have had limited success in decreasing fertility because access to services does not guarantee contraceptive use. Motivation to limit fertility is constrained by cultural, social, and economic factors, which must be addressed. Women must have access to education, employment, and roles other than motherhood.

Several barriers to increasing the status of women are presented and addressed. These include economic limitations and the fear of imposing Western ideals on developing countries. The author explains several actions that can be taken to broaden women's roles.

Gordon, L. (1976). Woman's body, woman's right: A social history of birth control in America. New York: Grossman.

This is an excellent and comprehensive history of birth control, from methods used in ancient times to those in use in the mid-1970s. Methods are discussed in terms of religious, economic, medical, and social views. Much of the book analyzes the birth control movement in the United States and prohibition of birth control as a defense of class and gender privileges. This movement evolved into population control policies that were included in U.S. foreign policy. Gordon distinguishes between birth control and population control. Birth control is defined as methods used by individuals to control fertility; population control is policy imposed on individuals from the ruling elite to limit societal fertility. Gordon points out that the latter can often be coercive and discusses examples.

Hartmann, B. (1987). Reproductive rights and wrongs: The political politics of population control and contraceptive choice. New York: Harper & Row.

Hartmann gives a comprehensive history of the population control movement from a women's rights perspective, including a discussion of abuses and coercion of women. The perception of a "population problem" went from being a concern with fertility in North America and Europe to a concerted international effort to limit women's fertility worldwide because of political and economic factors.

The author analyzes the causes and consequences of rapid population growth and describes why many women lack control over their reproduction. She discusses controversies surrounding different birth control methods, such as the IUD, sterilization, and abortion, and suggests why women continue to choose these methods. The final section of the book, entitled "The Way Forward," suggests that the traditional demographic transition theory used to explain fertility declines in developed countries is not directly applicable to currently developing countries. Before fertility will decline, positive steps must be taken toward equality: women must have access to education, employment opportunities, and general and reproductive health services. There must be income and land redistribution and the legal age of marriage must be raised.

Koblinsky, M., Timyan, J., & Gay, J. (Eds.). (1993). *The health of women: A global perspective.* San Francisco: Westview Press.

This book gives a broad overview of the global status of women's health, with frequent mention of reproductive health and women's rights. This collection of writings was assembled by participants of the NCIH International Health Conference on Women's Health held in 1991. The first chapter, by Jodi Jacobson, gives an excellent explanation of the effect of poverty on the health of women, with special reference to reproductive health. Women's lack of access to resources and funds, despite their contributions to the family and society, is described. Andrea Eschen and Maxine Whittaker discuss reproductive health in a chapter on family planning. Methods of improving the quality of care, including providing broad health services beyond pregnancy care, are presented.

Petchesky, R. P. (1984). Abortion and women's choice: The state, sexuality, and reproductive freedom. New York: Longmans.

Petchesky analyzes the history and politics of abortion in the United States from a feminist perspective. Access to abortion is discussed in terms of race, class, and right-wing attacks on feminists, women in general, and

the poor. Petchesky argues that abortion is a basic health care need rather than a "choice," which implies that it is unnecessary. She also takes issue with the idea that abortion is a "necessary evil that will disappear." Because there always will be contraceptive failure and barriers to contraceptive methods, abortion is an integral part of any humane and just women's health care service.

Winikoff, B., & Sullivan, M. (1987). Assessing the role of family planning in reducing maternal mortality. *Studies in Family Planning,* 18(3), 128–143.

The effect of high fertility and lack of access to reproductive health care on women's mortality is presented. Winikoff suggests that a combination of family planning services and primary maternity care is the most effective service delivery method of reducing maternal mortality. This combination, if accessible to all women, would prevent the need for clandestine abortions, decrease the number of high-risk births, decrease parity, and lessen the spread of STDs.

Winikoff discusses risk factors for maternal mortality in terms of age, parity, and general health status. She also acknowledges and addresses the risks associated with pregnancy prevention methods.

Specific Cultures/Geographic Areas

An-Na'im, A. (1987). The rights of women and international law in the Muslim context. *Whittier Law Review,* 9, 491–516.

The author contends that, in a historical perspective, Muslim law, Shari'a, has had a positive impact on the rights of women. Shari'a guaranteed all Muslim women the capacity to hold and dispose of property, a specific share in inheritance, access to education (in facilities separated from males), and some participation in public life. At the family level, Shari'a restricted polygamy, guaranteed a wife's right to maintenance and decent treatment, and provided for the right of women to divorce on specific grounds. However, a woman's share of inheritance is half that of a man of similar relationship to the deceased. Women can seek divorce (before male judges) on only limited grounds; a man can divorce at will. Polygamy is restricted to the taking of four wives. Moreover, the access of Muslim women to the means by which rights become meaningful is limited by segregation, requirements of the veil, and confinement to the home.

An-Na'im stresses the need for an "alternative Islamization" that would reform Shari'a based on alternative interpretations of the Qur'an and Sunna regarding women's rights. However, this reform must come from within the Islamic tradition and Muslim society. This internal debate must demonstrate that rights of women are Islamic values, not alien Western notions.

Fickle, J., & McIntosh, A. (Eds.). (1994). The politics of population: Conflict and consensus in family planning. New York: Population Council.

This collection of articles is concerned primarily with population policy and politics. Four chapters on specific geographic areas are concerned with family planning program policy rather than reproductive rights:

1. A chapter on Africa describes the cultural and political predeterminants of high fertility on the continent.

2. The history of family planning programs in India is presented, along with a discussion of the difficulties of ensuring reproductive health in a country with great ethnic and caste diversity and a democratic structure.

3. Mexico's current family planning program is described, along with a history of past attempts at increasing access and use of family planning methods.

4. Ruth Dixon-Mueller and Adrienne Germain examine the activism of women's organizations in Brazil, Nigeria, and the Philippines. They discuss the different levels of political autonomy and the relationships between

women's groups and the political, religious, and medical institutions in each country, examining the different effects women's groups have had on reproductive rights policies and programs.

Kerr, J. (Ed.). (1993). *Ours by right: Women's rights as human rights.* London: North–South Institute.

The writings in this compilation are based on speeches given at the "Linking Hands for Changing Laws" international conference on women's rights. The conference was held in September 1992, in Toronto, Canada. Probably the greatest asset of this book is the geographic and philosophical range of its 23 authors, who are experts in women's legal rights.

The book is divided into four parts. (1) "Setting the Agenda" introduces a human rights framework and describes the challenges facing women. (2) "Women's Rights—Country Experiences" has discussions on the legal status of women in Africa, Canada, Latin America, and some Muslim countries. The similarity of women's subordination by state, industry, and individuals across world regions is striking. (3) "Mechanisms for Change" presents analysis of potential change agents, from international conventions to grass-roots organizations to feminist analysis and challenge of the basic premises of international law. (4) "Strategies and Action" discusses strategic approaches to gaining recognition of women's rights as human rights.

Orubuloye, I. O., Caldwell, J., & Caldwell, P. (1993). African women's control over their sexuality in an era of AIDS: A study of the Yoruba in Nigeria. *Social Science and Medicine, 37*(7), 859–872.

The authors discuss the differences across sub-Saharan Africa in women's ability to refuse sex with their husbands or long-term partners. In east and central Africa, women have little control of their sexuality. Several factors are suggested to account for this: a patrilineal tradition in which women cannot own land and are no longer part of the family of origin at marriage; the payment of bride-price; limited access of women to urban trading; and lack of ability for women to control their own earnings. In this setting, women generally cannot deny their husbands sex under any circumstances.

The Yoruba in coastal west Africa represent a very different position of women. Here, women are always members of their family of origin. If a marriage falls apart, they can return and get land to farm. Women are involved in trading and controlling their earnings. In addition, the Yoruban culture places responsibility on women to ensure that no sexual relations take place during menstruation or the postpartum period, after becoming a grandmother, or after reaching menopause. It is believed that ignoring postpartum abstinence can cause the death of a child. Women are socially supported in refusing sex under these circumstances.

The authors talked to several Yoruban women about STDs and whether having an infected husband justified refusal of sex. Nearly all of the women said that this was a valid reason to refuse sex, until the husband is cured. The authors speculate that this right to refuse may be transferable to other situations, such as having a husband with HIV. However, many of the women had misperceptions about HIV, saying that they would not have sex with their husbands until he was cured, and most thought this would be a short period of time. When a woman refuses sex over an extended period of time, she risks a breakup of the marriage. The chief constraint of Yoruban wives' refusing sex is the ease with which their husbands can seek sex elsewhere.

Part IX

Research/Theoretical Issues

Chapter 16

Prostitution

Susan T. Misner
Randy Spreen Parker
Beverly J. McElmurry

"More prostitutes have received fictional immortality than any other class of working girl, and, perhaps it is unfair that the 'good' girls in other traditionally female occupations have not been given their fair share of the heroines' roles. Nurses and teachers might be considered more worthy and deserving of recognition because their services are more humanitarian.

That, of course, is open to debate."

Jan Hutson, *The Chicken Ranch*

The "oldest profession" invokes a wide variety of descriptive phrases: lady of the night, courtesan, call girl, kept woman, mistress, sex worker, prostitute, hooker—and worse. The language characterizing prostitution reflects the conflicted perceptions and attitudes in our society about the exchange of sex for economic gain. For some, female prostitution challenges deeply held religious beliefs and morals or philosophies such as those of personal equity and freedom. Regardless, during the period from childhood to adulthood, views are developed about prostitution. How then do we realize a thoughtful analysis of prostitution and a personal comprehension of the lived experiences of female prostitutes? These questions are important because knowledge about the lives of prostitutes is quite limited for many people, especially those of the so-called helping professions.

Why has the subject of prostitution not been a focus of concern among health professionals? Why are relatively few articles found in the professional health literature about this topic? Whatever beliefs readers may hold about these questions, we hope that the material presented in this chapter will increase understanding of prostitution as a serious public health concern. Prostitution affects more women than men. From a variety of perspectives, prostitution may be considered as a form of violence that must be given attention and brought out of its taboo status as a topic of concern for women's health.

In considering prostitution as a women's health issue, the concept of social ethics is useful. Fowler (1993) has written that social ethics is the area of ethics that deals with what is good or right in the organization of human communities and the shaping of social policies. An activity that she finds important in social ethics is the communication (epidictic discourse) that occurs within a group as it strives to reaffirm or reinforce the values that the community embraces. Thus, the position of the authors of this chapter is that issues must be raised about the nature of prostitution in our current society, including the fundamental reasons for its endemic persistence and the social response to the health of female prostitutes. The primary focus of this chapter is on women, but it must be remembered that prostitution is not an activity that involves only females. There are male prostitutes, and the users of prostitutes are predominantly males. Yet, in spite of concerns about the impact of prostitution on public health, prostitutes themselves have rarely been included in dialogues about the social good, either within or outside of the health professions.

One unique example of participation by prostitutes in social discourse is reflected in Bell's editing (1987) of proceedings of a 1985 conference in Canada, which brought so-called "good girls" (feminists) together with "bad girls" (sex trade workers). A key issue raised by the prostitutes attending the conference was that, in their view, most feminists have formulated positions about prostitution without a working knowledge about the lives of prostitutes.

Written materials available to interested readers address a social response to prostitution, as well as the thoughts, experiences, and living conditions of prostitutes. Hobson (1987) has written an interesting political history of prostitution in the United States. The irrepressible Margo St. James gives an interesting introduction to Pheterson's edited (1989) conference proceedings about the rights of prostitutes. Carment and Moody (1985) present the perspectives and lives of some New York City prostitutes. One can even find qualitative, participatory observation studies about the lives of prostitutes such as Dalby's (1983) description of the Geisha traditions of Japan. However, the writings of literate, articulate prostitutes or those who study them rarely capture the abject poverty and racial prejudice that encompass the lives of many prostitutes. Some authors may espouse the perspective that prostitution is an occupation entered into by choice, but many examples in the literature, especially studies by those who work with adolescent prostitutes, portray a life-style entered into through coercion or desperation.

Attempts to understand the nature of prostitution and its reciprocal social consequences lead to questions about intimate, sexual relationships; the issues of individual choice and responsibility in the context of sexual relationships; socially defined gender-based roles; sexual and emotional abuse; and economic equity. With disparate viewpoints about prostitution likely to continue, a review of societal responses to the existence of prostitution is worthwhile and will be considered in this chapter.

INTIMATE RELATIONSHIPS

What is the nature of a sexual relationship for the primary, if not exclusive, purpose of economic gain? It is a characteristic of the human community that a sexual relationship is not always an intimate relationship. Conversely, an intimate relationship does not require engaging in sex. However, in the exchange of sexual services for goods or money, the sexual relationship is viewed as the exploitation of people through their sexual activities (Durkin, 1983, p. 146). This view is consistent with the sexual morality of Kant, described by Cook (1991), in which relationships limited to "sexual love" consider one agent to be using the other as an object of personal ends, thus subordinating the principle of humanity. This view not only considers the assumed exploitation of those seeking to purchase sexual services, but also takes into account the correlative corruption and stigmatization of the provider of those services, as in the "fallen woman" image. Most current laws on "sexual deviance" in the Western world can be traced to Judeo-Christian sexual prohibitions intended to preserve morality according to religious tradition (Masters, Johnson, & Kolodny, 1986). Thus, this notion holds that if relationships restricted only to sexual passion diminish the human condition, sex outside of true intimacy and commitment is undesirable.

Yet, the taboo regarding sexual relationships specifically for economic benefit is applied selectively. Today, it is not uncommon to hear discourse, however lighthearted, in which busy women make reference to a desire to be "rescued" from the stress of multiple responsibilities by becoming a "kept woman." In reality, some marital relationships are bound primarily by economic expedience rather than personal intimacy, but rarely are those relationships viewed in the context of prostitution. Pheterson (1990) discusses the stigma associated with the concept of sexual labor and the fact that few researchers examine sexual-economic exchanges occurring outside the label of "prostitution." However, some research is beginning to consider long-term relationships "in which sex is exchanged in combination with domestic and reproductive services as in marriage" (Pheterson, 1990, p. 399).

A contrasting conceptualization of prostitution, apart from the notion of exploitation, applies the standard employment doctrine of the "master-servant" relationship, thus implying a mutually consenting, contractual agreement (Jenness, 1990). Here, sexual activity is viewed as a legitimate service provided by one consenting party to another willing to purchase that service. In this concept, prostitution is viewed as a service occupation or business for employment or independent contracting. Customer payment may be in cash or, in some instances, credit card. Where legalized in the United States, stock options have been offered for companies operating brothels (Prospectus, 1989).

The notion of sex as commerce for legitimate trade has been promulgated by COYOTE (an acronym for "Call Off Your Old Tired Ethics"). COYOTE, a prostitutes' rights organization in the United States, has tried to move social discourse about prostitution from sin, crime, and illicit sex to discussion of work, choice, and civil rights (Jenness, 1990).

However, the concept of sex as a commodity is thought by some to perpetuate subordination of women. This concern has stimulated much controversy regarding prostitution among feminist authors (Jenness, 1990; Shrage, 1989; Walkowitz, 1983). According to Walkowitz (1983), the controversy harkens to the infancy of the suffrage movement, when prostitution was attacked as "undifferentiated male lust" but prostitutes were defended because of legal attempts to control "vice," which included mandatory "sanitary inspection" of prostitutes under regulatory legislation. This campaign incorporated dialogue regarding the conditions of commercial sex—including the degradation of women's sexuality, and violence against women—and the societal restrictions placed on women's social and economic activities. These remain concerns today among feminists and others, some of whom contend that prostitution perpetuates patriarchal hierarchy (Shrage, 1989). Others warn that limiting the discussion to the social problems that affect prostitution will cast women as victims, subject to male protection and control.

PERSONAL CHOICE AND RESPONSIBILITY

Much of the debate regarding prostitution centers on the value of personal choice and responsibility. In question is the nature of constraints on freedom of choice as it applies to one's personal sexual activity. Traditionally, standards of sexual morality have reflected socially and culturally determined norms, which include the powerful and, at times, mysterious interaction of beliefs about sexuality, reproduction, and perpetuation of the species. These associations have contributed to the position that sexual activity holds a correlative duty related to its procreational possibilities, linking the necessary morality of commitment between sexual partners. Therefore, from this perspective, it is posited that the choice of prostituting oneself for economic purposes requires an unacceptable moral psychology (Green, 1989).

It has been argued, however, that individual choice of adult consensual sexual activity and occupation is based on the right to privacy and freedom of expression. In the United States, arguments have been made that there is constitutional protection against selective criminal law enforcement and discrimination against prostitutes. Specifically, these arguments are based on the First Amendment protection of freedom of speech, the Fourth Amendment privacy requirement of probable cause for government action, and the Fourteenth Amendment guarantee of equal protection against gender discrimination and unreasonable interference of government in personal matters. Historically, much of case law has limited the extent of application of these rights to prostitutes. However, many Americans do not believe the choice of engaging in prostitution is inherently immoral (Rio, 1991).

Some prostitutes in the United States claim to have freely chosen prostitution as a "career," though they recognize and deplore the existence of coerced prostitution. Carment and Moody's (1985) interviews reflect this claim. As one prostitute stated, "No one, in my opinion, can really be forced to do anything; if they are, there is always a way out" (p. 102).

Yet, when one considers gender-associated roles and economics, belief in the power for unconstrained freedom of choice of livelihood for many women and for some men must be viewed with skepticism. Although wide differences exist in culturally defined gender roles, every culture guides the determination of the sexual development of its members. In Western cultures, traditional expectations of women in their sexual role have been that they are coy and flirtatious, if not passive and submissive. The devaluing of women's sexual and economic contribution has created limitations of personal choice for those seeking equity in sexual and work relationships, even within monogamous relationships and nuclear families. Bound by reproductive biology, women almost universally share a disproportionate responsibility for childrearing. The failure of society to support women in their childrearing role is reflected by the cases of unpaid child support in the United States (Keegan, 1992).

Organized prostitution has purported to renew the claim on sexual equity and power for women, through insistence on occupational and sexual choice, protection of civil rights, and unbiased consideration by social institutions such as the health care system. According to these prostitute groups, many of the stereotypical perceptions and some of the real hazards related to commercial sex activity are results of societal constraints on prostitution rather than of the exchange of sex for money or goods. For instance, where centralized business locations can be legally operated, street solicitation is limited or absent. Prostitutes are at a greater risk of violence because of their inability to report crimes without fear of their own prosecution. The risk of incarceration with the need to post bond makes living in the psuedofamily structure of the "life" with "pimps" a distinct benefit for street-hustling prostitutes (Romenesko & Miller, 1989).

Although the topic of AIDS is covered extensively in other chapters in this annual review, it is important to debunk a common societal perception that a prostitute is a "pariah in the age of AIDS" (King, 1990). As Huddleston points out in Chapter 11, male-to-female transmission of the HIV virus is the primary mode of heterosexual transmission of AIDS. Ironically, more concern is expressed about the health of the consumer of prostitution than about the health of prostitutes at risk for AIDS. In reality, research data suggest that prostitutes are at greatest risk for acquiring HIV not through the delivery of sexual services to clients, but through sharing needles to support a drug habit or engaging in unprotected sex with a lover or spouse (Jackson, Highcrest, & Coates, 1992).

Prostitution can be viewed as maintaining gender-related subordinated power. Dominelli (1986) has identified four factors contributing to this viewpoint: (1) prostitution endorses the ethos of consumerism; (2) prostitution complies with male dictates of women's sexuality; (3) prostitution perpetuates sexuality as an apolitical, private concern; and (4) income generation for women from prostitution depends on men's discretionary income. Though there is little knowledge based on any objective research, most women currently engaged in prostitution are subject to risks of stigmatization, incarceration, violence, exposure to the drug culture, sexually transmitted disease, and limited long-term economic benefits.

The financial benefits of prostitution are questionable. Many prostitutes must turn over a substantial amount of earnings to their "man," pimp, or brothel owners. Even where legalized in the United States, prostitutes receive no sick leave, vacation pay, or workers' compensation, and they must pay as much as 40% of their earnings plus room and board to the brothel owners. When no longer "in demand," few prostitutes have any career alternatives (Campbell, 1991).

Perhaps then, given the disparity of views regarding prostitution, it is necessary to identify areas of common social concern. Questions regarding the inherent morality or immorality of prostitution should be subjugated to questions regarding the nature of society's response to the existence of prostitution, or, in the case of the health professions, the lack of a response to or recognition of prostitution as a health concern. How should we respond to those prostitutes who claim free occupational choice, who have been attracted to prostitution by the lure of financial opportunity where other opportunities were not in sight, who have been coerced by those who claimed to love and care for them, or who have made a conscious choice to sell or trade sex for drugs or, tragically, to meet their families' basic needs? Does it make sense to use limited societal resources to implement punitive responses, which have questionable deterrence value and, at worst, expose those engaged in prostitution to additional exploitation and violence? It makes more sense for us to use resources for health screening and treatment of prostitutes and their clients, education for alternative employment opportunities for prostitutes, support to needy families, and substance abuse rehabilitation.

It is not in the moral interest of society or of the prostitute to be engaged in commercial sex because of a lack of other alternatives or outright coercion related to a complex set of economic, discriminatory, and personal history factors (Romenesko & Miller, 1989). We must begin to consider anew how societal resources will be used to address these common concerns. In response to prostitution, societal efforts are best directed toward efforts that will lead to improved personal, sexual, and occupational choice, the elimination of gender bias and other forms of discrimination, and the assurance of economic equity in employment situations.

IMPLICATIONS

The paucity of professional health literature on prostitution may well exist because this complex topic deeply divides us as women and as health professionals. Even feminist lawyers, philosophers, and educators are divided on the issue. However, among all these groups, there has been little concerted effort to enter into a dialogue with sex workers, find common ground, and unite with a mutual agenda for reform. The end result is that prostitution is ignored as a taboo topic while, within our society, the behavior of those who perpetuate and benefit from the sex trade continues to be tolerated.

The authors of this chapter agree with other feminists who assert the need to change social norms and power inequities among men and women. Whether addressing female or male prostitution, no person's body should be sold for sexual favors. We believe women have a right to control their bodies; however, we question the degree of autonomy (i.e., freedom of choice) available to the majority of women who enter prostitution given the realities of poverty, childhood histories of abuse/violence, drug abuse, and the economic devaluation of women's work. We share the conclusion of many feminists that significant changes in social values, beliefs, and practices that oppress women would result in the elimination of prostitution as it exists today. Yet the sex trade is unlikely to disappear in the near future; the problem defies simplistic solutions. As authors, we don't pretend to have any short-term solutions; nevertheless, we believe concrete strategies can be developed and implemented that begin to address the root causes of prostitution.

Some key areas to address in considering well-being of female prostitutes include:

- **Educational programs that will destigmatize women involved in prostitution and inform both the public and professionals about pathways into the life-style of prostitution.** Many fallacies endure about women's motivation for becoming involved in prostitution. Public education is needed regarding potential long-term outcomes of the sexual exploitation of children and adolescents. Curricular content on the social and health aspects of prostitution must be included in educational programs for health and social services professionals, as they are for law enforcement and criminal justice personnel. For those programs providing health and social services to women at risk for or involved in sex trade, personnel training content should include substance abuse, child abuse, posttraumatic stress due to violence, hopelessness, and cultural diversity.

- **Public policy amendments that will change the emphasis from law enforcement and judicial processing of prostitution cases to diversion into nonjudicial intervention.** Mechanisms must be identified to divert funds and resources currently allocated for punitive legal actions against prostitutes to programs focusing on child abuse prevention, runaway intervention, and substance abuse treatment. Law enforcement, judicial, and public health agencies need to work together to develop treatment and placement alternatives to the arrest, incarceration, and court processing of prostitutes. Intensive and comprehensive programs for homeless youth who are participating in survival sex should incorporate a multidisciplinary team approach that coordinates interventions across a variety of public service sectors, such as child welfare, education, public health, and juvenile justice. Rape cases and other acts of violence against prostitutes must be thoroughly evaluated, and women should be informed of their legal rights to pursue criminal investigation and prosecution of the perpetrator.

- **For women who want to leave the life of prostitution, expanded support services that offer mental health counseling, vocational training, and rehabilitation programs.** Program initiatives need to be developed in high-incidence community areas to prevent entry into prostitution and assist women who want to exit sex work. For homeless and runaway adolescents, health and social service providers should evaluate the risk factors that lead to entry into the sex trade. Opportunities for education and job training are necessary components for the rehabilitation of women previously involved in prostitution. Without economic means of support, recidivism is a serious risk, even for those women truly seeking escape from the dangers and degradation of survival sex. Rehabilitation programs should involve, as leaders and advisers, women who have successfully exited prostitution.

- **Research that evaluates the impact of prostitution on women's health.** Studies are needed to investigate methods that will assist women who wish to leave prostitution; for example, how effective are present interventions specifically for substance abuse in the context of the sex trade? Methadone maintenance programs for prostitutes should be evaluated. Qualitative research might focus on methods to overcome barriers faced by women who attempt to leave the sex industry. Intervention methods that prevent recidivism need to be developed and evaluated. Social policy research is needed to evaluate the deterrent effect of vocational training programs and services for youths in crisis situations. Research that will increase knowledge of the health beliefs of prostitutes, particularly their perceptions about health risk behavior, is essential.

- **To address adolescent prostitution, intervention services that are located in places frequented by youth.** Access to substance abuse treatment and transitional housing should be made available to adolescent prostitutes. Long-term placement for youth with serious psychological illness must be available to all local communities. Programs must be directed toward meeting individualized needs of youth, based on underlying contributing factors like substance abuse, need for shelter, or issues of sexual identity (Lagloire, 1990). Adolescent prostitutes should be screened for risk of suicidal ideation.

Also, efforts to ensure gender equity in educational opportunities and employment compensation must continue. Programs are needed that provide material support to families and children in "run away" situations.

REFERENCES

Bell, L. (1987). *Good girls/bad girls.* Seattle: Seal Press.

Campbell, C. A. (1991). Prostitution, AIDS, and preventive health behavior. *International Philosophy Quarterly, 31*(1), 3–13.

Carment, A., & Moody, H. (1985). *Working women: The subterranean world of street prostitution.* New York: Harper & Row.

Cook, V. M. (1991). Kant, teleology, and sexual ethics. *International Philosophy Quarterly, 31*(1), 3–13.

Dalby, L. (1993). *Geisha.* New York: Vintage Books.

Dominelli, L. (1986). The power of the powerless: Prostitution and the reinforcement of submissive femininity. *Sociological Review, 34*(1), 65–92.

Durkin, M. G. (1983). *Feast of love: Pope John Paul II on human intimacy.* (p. 146) Chicago: Loyola University Press.

Fowler, D. M. (1993). Professional association, ethics and society. *Oncology Nursing Forum* (Suppl.), *20* (10), 13–19.

Green, K. (1989). Prostitution, exploitation and taboo. *Philosophy, 64,* 525–534.

Hobson, B. M. (1987). *Uneasy virtue: The politics of prostitution and the American reform tradition.* Chicago: University of Chicago Press.

Hutson, J. (1980). *The chicken ranch.* NJ: A.S. Barnes.

Jackson, L., Highcrest, A., & Coates, R. (1992). Varied potential risks of HIV infection among prostitutes. *Social Science Medicine, 35* (3), 281–286.

Jenness, V. (1990). From sex as sin to sex as work: COYOTE and the reorganization of prostitution as a social problem. *Social Problems, 37* (3), 403–420.

Keegan, A. (1992, March 8). Artful dodging. *Chicago Tribune Magazine,* 12–20.

Lagloire, R. (1990, June). *Growing up too fast: An ethnography of sexually exploited youth in San Francisco.* San Francisco: Office of Criminal Justice Planning.

Masters, W. H., Johnson, V. E., & Kolodny, R. C. (1986). *Masters and Johnson on Sex and Human Loving.* Boston: Little, Brown.

Pheterson, G. (Ed.). (1989). *A vindication of the rights of whores.* Seattle: Seal Press.

Pheterson, G. (1990). The category "prostitute" in scientific inquiry. *The Journal of Sex Research, 27* (3), 397–407.

Prospectus: Prostitution goes public. (1989). *Harper's, 278* (1668), 21–22.

Rio, L. M. (1991). Psychology and sociology research and the decriminalization or legalization of prostitution. *Archives of Sexual Behavior, 20* (2) 205–218.

Romensko, K., & Miller, E. M. (1989). The second step in double jeopardy: Appropriating the labor of female street hustlers. *Crime and Delinquency, 35* (1), 109–135.

Shrage, L. (1989). Should feminists oppose prostitution? *Ethics, 99* (2), 347–361.

Walkowitz, J. R. (1983). Male vice and female virtue: Feminism and the politics of prostitution in nineteenth-century Britain. In A. Snitow, C. Stansell, & S. Thompson (Eds.), *Powers of desire: The politics of sexuality* (419–438). New York: Monthly Review Press.

Substance Abuse and Prostitution

Feucht, T. E. (1993). Prostitutes on crack cocaine: Addiction, utility, and marketplace economics. *Deviant Behavior, 14* (91), 91–108.

In a qualitative study of female prostitutes and their use of crack cocaine, the author reports an inductive analysis of interviews conducted with 39 women recruited by outreach workers of a drug-counseling agency in Cleveland, Ohio. All of the women reported use of cocaine at least three times and a minimum of three different sex partners during the week prior to their interview. The average age was 32, roughly half of the women had less than a high school education, and the average monthly income was approximately $2,000. Only one woman was legally employed.

The interviews covered the subjects' drug history and experiences in prostitution. The author identifies three characteristics of drug use by women: (1) addiction, (2) utility, & (3) marketplace economics (p. 96). The subjects' involvement in prostitution was secondary to their cocaine addiction; however, it "rarely appeared to be the dominant factor in a respondent's initiation into prostitution" (p. 97). The number of subjects in this study who began their involvement in prostitution prior to becoming drug addicted was not reported. Some respondents had first exchanged sex for money as a means to support themselves. Additionally, some women viewed cocaine use as pragmatic to their lives as prostitutes. This focus on utility included subjects' perceptions of cocaine use for its effects on their sexuality or that of their sex partners, or as a coping mechanism to endure difficult circumstances or to facilitate trade activities related to prostitution. Market-place economics involved the survival skills learned through exposure to the competition of illegal street culture. Here, the roles of the prostitute are as collaborators with crack dealers, consumers in the drug markets, and providers of prostitution. All of these dimensions must be considered in public health prevention programs.

The anecdotal excerpts in this article are poignant. Within the limitations of a small, nonprobability sample and the potential for coding bias, this study provides an understanding of the complex relationship of cocaine use and the exchange of sex for money.

Gossop, M., Griffiths, P., Powis, B., & Strang, J. (1993). Severity of heroin dependence and HIV risk. I. Sexual behavior. *AIDS Care, 5* (2), 149–157.

As part of the Drug Transitions Study of the National Addiction Centre in London, England, the level of dependence on heroin was studied in relation to the frequency of sexual behaviors that increase the risk for HIV transmission. Community settings were used to recruit 408 participants who reported use of heroin within the month preceding the study. A structured interview conducted by specially trained interviewers and a self-administered questionnaire on sexual behavior, returned to the interviewer in a sealed envelope, were the methods used to collect data. The Severity of Dependence Scale (SDS) was used to determine the level of dependence. The average subject was 27.7 years old; 38% were females, and the first use of heroin ranged from age 11 to age 38. In the total sample, at the time of the interview, 58% had a regular sex partner. Women with serious levels of addictive behavior reported more sexual partners in the previous month and more frequent participation in anal sex. A significant positive relationship was found between SDS scores and the number of sex-for-money and sex-for-drugs transactions. Of the women studied, 17% had provided sex for either money or drugs during the preceding year, and 8% had provided sex for both money and drugs. The women who traded sex for drugs or money had a significantly higher SDS score. The severity of heroin addiction was positively related to the frequency of sex transactions. However, the women who traded sex were more likely to use condoms. Though not statistically significant, SDS scores were higher for women who perceived they were at risk of becoming infected with HIV (9.0 versus 8.2). The authors concluded that the severity of drug dependence has a more specific association with prostitution for women and men.

Health Risks

Centers for Disease Control. (1988). Relationship of syphilis to drug use and prostitution—Connecticut and Philadelphia, Pennsylvania. *Morbidity and Mortality Weekly Report, 37,* 755–758, 764.

Rolfs, R. T., Goldberg, M., & Sharrar, R. G. (1990). Risk factors for syphilis: Cocaine use and prostitution. *American Journal of Public Health, 80,* 853–857.

Hibbs, J. R., & Gunn, R. A. (1991). Public health intervention in a cocaine-related syphilis outbreak. *American Journal of Public Health, 81,* 1259–1262.

Balshem, M., Oxman, G., van Rooyen, D., & Girod, K. (1992). Syphilis, sex and crack cocaine: Images of risk and morality. *Social Science and Medicine, 35,* 147–160.

This group of articles informs readers of concerns involving the transmission of syphilis and prostitution, especially in the context of cocaine use. In 1988, the Centers for Disease Control analyzed interview data from newly

diagnosed patients with early syphilis, as well as some patients with secondary and latent syphilis. For female subjects, the proportion of cases reporting involvement in prostitution increased threefold over the three-year study period. The proportion of women with syphilis and past drug use increased more than sixfold.

In Philadelphia, Rolfs et al. conducted a case-control study comparing newly diagnosed patients with syphilis with control subjects recruited from patients of a sexually transmitted diseases clinic. Cocaine use and exchange of drugs for sex were found to be risk factors for syphilis. Women who used cocaine were more likely to report prostitution than women who did not use cocaine. The authors concluded that trading sex for drugs, rather than for money, was more strongly associated with risk for syphilis.

Hibbs and Gunn reported on control efforts for a town with a fivefold increase in syphilis cases between 1987 and 1988. The public health officials selected screening and treatment locations based on prostitutes' reported use of these sites for the sale of sex and drugs. Recruitment of candidates for screening took place at community sites, and treatment was provided to consenting participants at the time of screening, unless they reported no sexual contacts during the previous year. Followup was conducted with reported sexual contacts, but the multiple anonymous sexual contacts limited the capacity for partner notification. Of the 136 clients who were screened, the risk of syphilis was 27% for females and 13% for males. Also, 15% of the participants screened reported involvement in prostitution and 28% reported cocaine use. The success of such screening programs is determined by: site identification, training and background of investigators, determination of times to conduct the screening program, and use of mobile vans. However, such screening and treatment programs do not address the underlying risk factors for sexually transmitted diseases.

Balshem et al. (1992) reported an analysis of in-depth interviews with a convenience sample of 40 women and men at high risk for syphilis, who were recruited from numerous community sources. The average age of the respondents was 33; range was from 16 to 50 years. More than half of the respondents were female, and 44% did not have a high school diploma. Of the participants, 12 (10 women and 2 men) reported having provided sex services. Of the 31 respondents with a history of crack cocaine use, 7 had traded sex for crack cocaine and 11 had traded sex for other commodities. Despite reluctance about reporting prostitution activities, 26 of the 31 respondents who had used cocaine either had seen or had engaged in the trading of sex and crack. The authors noted the issue of truthfulness in such sensitive subject matter, but found that many of the respondents believed their insights had relevance to matters of public policy. A poignant example of the discrepancy between the scientific model of risk and the respondents' perceptions of risk for syphilis was the respondents' identification of moral decline and deterioration. The authors suggest that eliminating the stigmatization of groups at risk for syphilis, including the stigmatization of these groups by health care professionals, could be an important step in improving public policy. Collectively, these articles emphasize the risk of syphilis for women engaged in the trade of sex, particularly when they trade for drugs.

Kline, A., & Strickler, J. (1993). Perceptions of risk for AIDS among women in drug treatment. *Health Psychology, 12* (4), 313–323.

This cross-sectional study examined three areas of interest: (1) the association of perceived risk with actual risk for HIV infection; (2) which risky behaviors were associated with risk perception; and (3) which psychological or contextual factors were associated with perceived high risk for HIV infection. Data were obtained from 152 women in drug treatment (primarily methadone maintenance clinics) who reported a primary male sex partner for the four weeks preceding data collection and who reported negative HIV status for themselves and their partners.

Data were collected on perceived susceptibility to HIV drug use behavior, age, race or ethnicity, marital status, education, and five aspects of sexual behavior: (1) condom use, (2) multiple partners, (3) anal intercourse, (4) partner's HIV risk factors, and (5) change in sexual behavior. Psychosocial factors associated with perception of susceptibility to AIDS were also measured.

The analysis of data considered perceived risk and each of the explanatory factors in a stepwise multiple logistic regression. In this study, 71% of the women were African American, had an average age of 35 years, and were, on average, high school graduates. About 33% of the women were either married or cohabitating with their sex partner, and 66% of these women reported never using condoms. Overall, only 5.9% of the women reported having sex with multiple partners and 47.5% did not know their partners' HIV status. The measures of sexual behavior did not have a significant association with perceived risk, and the crack cocaine use had no association with risk perception from exchanging sex for drugs or money. However, the low number of women in this study may explain the lack of association with these behaviors. The findings reflect a need for educational interventions for women who participate in the exchange of sex for money.

Child and Adolescent Prostitution

Deisher, R. W., Farrow, J. A., Hope, K., & Litchfield, C. (1989). The pregnant adolescent prostitute. *American Journal of Disadvantaged Children, 143,* 1162–1165.

Deisher, R. W., Litchfield, C., & Hope, K. (1991). Birth outcomes of prostituting adolescents. *Journal of Adolescent Health, 12,* 528–533.

These articles are based on a year-long study, initiated in January 1987, of 61 Seattle female prostitutes between the ages of 13 and 18. The authors represent medicine, social work, and nursing, and are associated with the adolescent medicine program at the University of Washington, Seattle. The clinic has a 15-year history of providing health care through a network of free night clinics dispersed throughout the metropolitan area. The earlier article describes an exemplary model for the provision of health care to this population and presents two case studies to illustrate the clients served. The review of literature identifies areas that have been studied relative to adolescent prostitutes and notes relatively little literature on their pregnancy and pregnancy outcomes. The investigators' sensitivity to young women is illustrated by the statement that ". . . those professionals who work with children and adolescents must be made aware of the victimization of these young people, not only by their families, pimps, and clients, but by a society to whom they are almost totally invisible, and by whom, if recognized, they are held responsible for their life situation." The picture for this group of pregnant teens is grim. In addition to the usual concerns health workers have with pregnant teens, this group presented issues of sexual abuse, drug dependence, malnutrition, a violent street-based lifestyle, sexually transmitted diseases, potential exposure to AIDS, and lack of coping and social skills for dealing with the stress associated with the life-style.

For the second article, the authors conducted a retrospective chart review of 54 of the 61 prostitutes who delivered infants between November 1987 and November 1989. Here, the authors differentiated prostitution (engaging in sexual conduct for a fee) from survival sex (exchange of sexual acts for necessities such as shelter, food, drugs, and companionship). The demographic data collected on each subject included age, ethnic group, substance abuse history, number of prenatal visits, maternal complications, and parity. Outcome data collected were birth weight, occipitofrontal head circumference, length, Apgar scores, and neonatal complications. The group studied had high rates of maternal and infant complications: preterm births (22%), precipitous delivery (15%), pregnancy-induced hypertension (16%), positive toxicology screens (28%),

meconium staining (30%), infant hypertonicity (30%), and small (for gestational age) infants (14.5%). In discussing the outcomes of their study, the authors are realistic in their appraisal of the limitations of retrospective chart analysis, but their grasp and understanding of this population are impressive. A diverse range of innovative and nontraditional services are urged for these adolescents, and essential aspects of their care include outreach, individual assessment, case management, referral, and long-term follow-up.

Kruks, G. (1991). Gay and lesbian homeless/ street youth: Special issues and concerns: *Journal of Adolescent Health, 12,* 515–518.

This article is based on data collected by the Youth Services Department (YSD) of the Los Angeles Gay and Lesbian Community Service Center. The Center provides services for street youth and has been in existence for almost two decades. Both gay- and nongay-identified youth use the Center. About 70% of the youth identify as gay, and the majority of these youths are males. The author indicates that the numbers of lesbians may be more difficult to discern because of their invisibility and reluctance to self-identify. The YSD collects data on roughly 2,500 individuals each year, and case manages about 800 of these youths after a detailed intake interview. From this experience, it has been observed that gay and bisexual-identified male youths are at increased risk for homelessness after being forced from their homes because of their sexual orientation. Such youth are more likely to engage in survival sex and to have attempted suicide. The tragedy for many of these youths is that, while they are struggling to achieve a personal identity and social acceptance, they are often emotionally and physically abused rather than provided with the support they need.

Pennbridge, J., Mackenzie, R. G., & Swofford, A. (1991). Risk profile of homeless pregnant adolescents and youth. *Journal of Adolescent Health, 12,* 534–538.

Yates, G. L., Mackenzie, R. G., Pennbridge, J., & Swofford, A. (1991). A risk profile comparison of homeless youth involved in prostitution and homeless youth not involved. *Journal of Adolescent Health, 12,* 545–548.

Yates, G. L., Pennbridge, J., Swofford, A., & Mackenzie, R. G. (1991). The Los Angeles system of care for runaway/homeless youth. *Journal of Adolescent Health, 12,* 555–560.

Cohen, E., Mackenzie, R. G., & Yates, G. L. (1991). HEADSS, a psychosocial risk assessment instrument: Implications for designing effective intervention programs for runaway youth. *Journal of Adolescent Health, 12,* 539–544.

These articles are from a group of investigators with the Division of Adolescent Medicine, Children's Hospital of Los Angeles and The University of Southern California, Los Angeles. They are included in this review of literature because of the frequent association of homeless/runaway youth with prostitution. However, we caution readers not to *assume* the association when working with homeless youth, but only to be sensitive to the possibility.

Pennbridge et al. compared 55 pregnant homeless youths with 85 pregnant youths who lived with their families. During their examination in a primary health care clinic, the High Risk Youth Clinic, the study participants were interviewed about their life-style. The major differences between the homeless and those living with their families were that the homeless were more often white, younger, from outside Los Angeles County, depressed, drug abusing, and had histories of sexual and physical abuse as well as suicide attempts. Although most of the women did not describe themselves as prostitutes, they did admit to survival sex. It is emphasized that providing care to homeless youths requires aggressive outreach efforts to contact them. When they are in the clinics, intensive efforts are made to provide comprehensive services and referrals.

Yates, Mackenzie, et al. reviewed the initial health clinic visits of 620 runaway/homeless youths during a 12-month period from July 1988 to June 1989. Of this group, 153 of the youths were prostitutes, and their adolescent risk profile included a wide variety of medical problems, health-compromising behaviors, drug abuse, suicide, and depression. The authors provide extensive data in terms of demographics, common medical diagnoses, and psychosocial variables. Roughly 25% of the prostitutes had their first sexual activity by the age of 10. Grave concern is expressed by the authors about the history of sexual abuse that the youths experienced before becoming homeless. Readers are reminded that juvenile prostitution is technically a form of child sexual abuse that has moved with the youths from the home to the streets. A plea is made for nontraditional, vigorous efforts to serve these youths and to attain their active involvement with the child welfare system.

Yates, Pennbridge, et al. present a description of the program model that they developed over several years of working with runaway/homeless youth in Los Angeles. The long-term goal of the group is to realize a comprehensive system of care that covers the entire county. The five major components of the model are: (1) networking and consolidation, (2) outreach, (3) short-term crisis shelter, (4) comprehensive medical and psychosocial care, and (5) long-term shelter and case management. The development of a comprehensive data collection system has proven important for the efforts in Los Angeles to better understand the characteristics of the teens being served as well as to formulate policy and evaluate the outcomes of services. Some successes with this model of care have returned youths to productive activity. Although it is very difficult to establish a primary health care system like this one, it is an excellent example of the merits of working toward a strong primary health care model or community-based health care model.

Cohen et al. provide more information about HEADSS, a special assessment tool developed for use with adolescents. The HEADSS instrument covers *h*ome, *e*ducation, *a*ctivities, *d*rug use and abuse, *s*exual behavior, and *s*uicidality and depression. In addition to the characteristics of the Los Angeles homeless youths described in the above articles, the authors note that, of the 1,015 youths who were interviewed, the 63% who were homeless were 6 times more likely to be at risk of HIV infection. The assessment form was first developed in 1974 and has been used by Los Angeles investigators since 1982. It is designed to begin with less emotionally charged areas and then move to questions in areas that teens find more difficult to discuss with health professionals, such as sexual behavior or depression. The assessment takes from 5 to 20 minutes to administer. It has much utility in structuring the questions asked by the interviewer and helping to ensure a common database useful to all health team members. Among all of the uses for data that are discussed, it was of most interest that the data are used to define areas for community workshops targeted for health professionals from various disciplines. Although specific data on the psychometric properties of the tool are not provided, the authors note that continued work is planned for further standardization of the tool.

Schram, D. D., & Giovengo, M. A. (1991). Evaluation of Threshold: An independent living program for homeless adolescents. *Journal of Adolescent Health, 12,* 567–572.

The Threshold Project, a replication of the Boston Bridge Project, was designed to serve homeless Seattle women involved in or at risk of involvement in prostitution. Threshold is a community-based model of care conducted as a collaborative effort of the State of Washington Department of Child and Family Service, the University of Washington Adolescent Clinic, and Youth Care. The 16- to 18-year-old women were provided progressively independent living experiences that emphasized education, employment, budgeting, and adherence to rules. This article describes outcomes after the initial group of 24 women had participated in the program for 2 years. The follow-up data revealed that 42% of the women had met the desired outcomes: lived independently in stable settings, attended school and/or were employed, were not engaged in prostitution, and

did not abuse alcohol or other substances. Given the documented evidence that it is very difficult to reach this population, the success rate for this demonstration project is noteworthy. Other interesting aspects of this article are the perspective on traumatizing events experienced by the women who become prostitutes, and the listing of educational interventions provided for the group. In addition to the value of this article as a description of a community-based model, the investigators identify their plans for a statewide dissemination of the demonstration project.

Sereny, G. (1985). *The invisible children: Child prostitution in America, West Germany and Great Britain.* New York: Knopf.

Like the author of this book, who states that the book should not need to be written, one wishes that child prostitution did not have to be considered a factor in American society. However, Sereny is a journalist who makes the children she writes about in her documentary only too vivid and tragic. The sources of this sordid business are the enormous profits that some can make from commerce in sex—profits that generally exclude the child being used to make those profits. The research for the book took 18 months' travel and dialogue with children in three countries. In the narrations of the stories of the children interviewed, the reader learns a great deal about the children, the families from which they came, and the pimps who use them. The impressions that Sereny draws from interviewing 69 children include, in all cases, a breakdown in communication between the parents and the child. Often, the juvenile expresses a need for love by running away and, in the process, falls under the illusion that a pimp will care for him or her and will provide the sought-after affection. Most importantly, the author asks how we can be unaware of child prostitution or not see its existence in everyday life, whether in media advertisements or its blatant presence on the streets. Writing the book was the author's attempt to make the public more aware of the child prostitution problem and thus more prepared to demand that actions be taken to correct this serious individual and societal health problem. The story of each child/juvenile, whether male or female, is heartbreaking. Very few juveniles escape the life-style once they slide into it.

Shah, P. M. (1984). The health care of working children. *Child Abuse and Neglect, 8,* 541–544.

The author, a physician, indicates that child prostitutes are an at-risk category of child workers. The author's claim that the adverse effects of child labor have not been scientifically studied is hard to refute when one thinks about child prostitutes. At some points, perhaps unknowingly, we find that science does not rule our hearts; it is difficult to think about improving child labor laws if we believe that child prostitution should be abolished. Although there is only brief mention of prostitution, the author provides a useful categorization of the detrimental factors often associated with child labor: poverty, malnutrition, communicable disease, physical damage, restricted psychosocial development, and limited social interaction. Interestingly, the author suggests that alternative approaches to the health care of child workers are: the implementation of primary health care, the use of community workers, providing access to health surveillance at times convenient to the child worker, and involvement of the community and the employer in efforts to provide health care. Overall, this is a pragmatic response for a professional health worker who has to deal with conditions that do not go away.

Legal Aspects

Baldwin, M. A. (1992). Split at the root: Prostitution and feminist discourses of law reform. *Yale Journal of Law and Feminism, 5,* 47–120.

Rio, L. M. (1991). Psychological and sociological research and the decriminalization or legalization of prostitution. *Archives of Sexual Behavior, 20* (2), 205–218.

Shuster, K. (1992). On the "oldest profession": A proposal in favor of legalized but regulated prostitution. *University of Florida Journal of Law & Public Policy, 5,* 1–31.

The issue of decriminalization versus legalization of prostitution has taken on new significance in the context of the AIDS crisis. One must ask whether the recent social attention to prostitution stems from disproportionate concern about transmission of AIDS by female prostitutes rather than a public interest in limiting the risks for women's becoming involved in the life of prostitution or the desire to prevent health risks for women related to sex trade. These three articles, while applying somewhat different perspectives, provide the reader with comprehensive discussions regarding many related issues, including cost versus benefit (Rio, 1991), legal interventions for violence against women (Baldwin, 1992), and constitutionality (Shuster, 1992). Collectively, these authors submit a call for change—some type of change—based on noted illogic in the current social response to the needs of women who participate in the trade of sex and the resultant consequences, both for the women of prostitution and for all members of our society.

Kandel, M. (1992). Whores in court: Judicial processing of prostitutes in the Boston Municipal Court in 1990. *Yale Journal of Law and Feminism, 4*(2), 329–352.

Lindquist, J. H., White, O. Z., Tutchings, T., & Chambers, C. D. (1989). Judicial processing of males and females charged with prostitution. *Journal of Criminal Justice, 17,* 227–291.

Lindquist et al. reviewed the processing by prosecutors and courts for 2,859 cases of male and female prostitution occurring between 1973 and 1985 in south central Texas. Females comprised 63.1% of the study's cases. The statistical analysis used in this study permitted evaluation of the effects of gender, ethnicity, sexual orientation related to the charge of prostitution, and a prior offense. These factors were evaluated for the judicial processing—including case disposition, judgment, and sentencing—as well as for consideration of the interaction of these factors. Women were more likely to be found not guilty; over 87% of the women (compared to over 62% of males) were repeat offenders. However, minority status was a significant factor in being sent to jail and in length of sentence. In this study, gender was not related to sentencing.

In a more recent study of cases of prostitution in Boston, Kandel reported that 163 women were arrested for 263 different case charges of prostitution and common nightwalking/common streetwalking during the year 1990. However, the author stated that this is likely to be an underestimate because many prostitutes are arrested under the Massachusetts disorderly conduct statute. Twenty percent of these cases were dismissed, and an additional 16% continued without a finding. Suspended sentences and/or probation were the outcomes for another 38% of these women. Only about 10% of the women were sentenced to serve time in jail. Repeat offenses (at least two arrests in the same year) accounted for more than one-third of the cases, leading the author to question the rationale of the deterrent effect of arrest. Forty-three percent of the cases against males were dismissed, compared to only 19% for females. No male customer/client was arraigned during the entire year, in spite of a state statute that makes buying of sex an offense. Only 11 cases in all 263 listed a "witness" who was not a police officer, perhaps reflecting, as suggested by Kandel, the use of mostly male police decoys. The author concludes, based on the data and critical analysis, that the judicial processing of prostitution cases in the Boston Municipal Court "serves no effective protective, rehabilitative or deterrent function." Decriminalization is proposed by Kandel, because the funds that support the cost of these cases, which comprise about 15% of the court's caseload, might be allocated for counseling and intervention programs. Together, these two articles point to the difficulties in the criminal justice approach to limiting sex trade and inform readers of the realities involved in legislative and law enforcement efforts to restrict prostitution.

Feminist Literature on Prostitution

Cooper, B. (1989). Prostitution: A feminist analysis. *Women's Rights Law Reporter, 11* (2), 99–119.

Cooper, a graduate of Yale Law School, applies feminist insights to a legal analysis of prostitution. She describes conservative moralist, liberal individualist, and feminist views on prostitution, and demonstrates how statutory and case law in the United States continues to reflect a conservative moralist discomfort with prostitution. In examining liberal approaches to prostitution, specifically those used in Nevada and West Germany, the author critiques these approaches and offers her own feminist alternative. Cooper asserts that prostitution should be decriminalized and placed under the control of women, that government regulation should be kept at a minimum, and that feminists should support these efforts to ensure that the terms of legalization are drawn up in cooperation with prostitutes themselves. She claims that prostitution is tolerable in the short run, not because it involves the free choice of autonomous women, but because the harm to women in outlawing prostitution is greater than the harm of decriminalizing it. The long-term goal is to change the current value system of our society so women are not forced to choose between the lesser of these two evils. Cooper's proposal is not endorsed by all feminists, but her analysis is thorough, pragmatic, and representative of the feminist camp that is in favor of decriminalization. Legal issues aside, the author recommends that prostitutes should be provided opportunities to leave the profession, be given the chance to train for desirable and decently paying jobs, and the financial means to survive this transition period. Moreover, retraining programs should be undertaken in cooperation with prostitutes' organizations.

Dominelli, L. (1986). The power of the powerless: Prostitution and the reinforcement of submissive femininity. *The Sociological Review, 34* (1), 65–92.

Dominelli uses a feminist sociological perspective to analyze and critique Liazos' concept of power as it applies to the experiences of prostitutes. In examining the complex nature of power, the author covers a breadth of information on sources of power, gender roles, society norms, and the association among power, the legal process, and prostitution. Dominelli's detailed theoretical critique is informative and thought-provoking. However, this material is dense with terminology that may not be reader-friendly to a lay audience.

The second half of the article describes one effort among prostitutes to organize collectively. The Programme for the Reform of the Law on Soliciting (PROS) is a client-centered group aimed at improving conditions for prostitutes and developing links between prostitutes and other women. Dominelli discusses PROS's strengths and political successes but also notes that groups like this have a reformist agenda that reinforces the myth that progress for women can occur without a major restructuring of society and of the underlying power inequities between men and women. Dominelli asserts that prostitutes can become more powerful by organizing themselves, forming a collective identity, and developing a coherent political agenda; however, prostitution by its very nature supports existing social relations in which women are subordinate to and dependent on men. For meaningful change to occur, society must challenge existing social norms and the distribution of power between the sexes.

O'Neil, M. (1992). Women at work: Prostitution and feminism in the context of late modernity. *Phoebe, 4* (1), 25–35.

O'Neil argues that the feminist movement needs to join forces with the whores' movement to explore possibilities for social change. She correctly observes that the debate on whether women freely choose to enter prostitution is unfruitful without examining the wider social, economic, and cultural aspects of women's lived experiences—specifically, the contradictions of women's oppression and the feminization of poverty. Most feminists would agree with O'Neil that viewing prostitution through a moral lens (ideology) or a justice lens (which criminalizes and stigmatizes the whore but not her client) skirts the real issues of gender and power. The exchange of money for sex sanctions inequalities and a dual standard of morality in law. The byproduct, O'Neil asserts, is the objectification of women's bodies as commodities to be bought and sold.

O'Neil's discussion of the relationship between prostitution and late modernity may be interesting to an academic audience, but her interview data with current and former prostitutes are compelling material for any reader. O'Neil interviewed an unspecified number of sex and ex-sex workers in an effort to capture their views on choice, power, and control over their own and other's bodies. She details the lived experience of a 15-year-old who, living in poverty, was sexually abused and subsequently fled from home into prostitution, hoping to escape the violence, make some money, and buy herself freedom. Now an ex-prostitute, this woman claims that decriminalizing prostitution is a "red herring" that offers a superficial answer to the problem. O'Neil tells this story to demonstrate how women's choices are determined by the economic and emotional resources available to them. She suggests that the decriminalization of prostitution lets the government "off the hook" regarding issues of poverty, and further sanctions the role of the state as a pimp while simultaneously ignoring the need to create economic and social alternatives for women. O'Neil concludes that prostitutes are women first, and the fight for women's rights should not be divided; prostitutes must be given a voice that is listened to and acted on by feminists. This collaboration is essential to the development of a critical feminist praxis where feminist theory not only reflects women's lived experiences but informs practice and policy changes.

Overall, C. (1992). What's wrong with prostitution? Evaluating sex work. *Signs: Journal of Women in Culture and Society, 17* (4), 705–741.

Overall writes a comprehensive and impressive analysis of the similarities and differences between prostitution and other forms of paid labor in a capitalistic society. To the author's credit, she admits her biases up front, alerting the reader that she believes prostitution is wrong and bad for women and that, as a feminist, she supports sex workers' demands for human rights but does not respect sex work itself. Among the many insights Overall presents are: prostitution is a classist, ageist, racist, and sexist industry in which the disadvantaged sell services to the more privileged; like rape, incest, and sexual harassment, prostitution is inherently gendered; and, a continuum of labor performed by women reflects varying degrees of oppression. Some forms of sex work are at the far end of the continuum, but, as Overall observes, others are not: "Doing housework for a battering spouse might be worse." The author recommends that feminists and sex workers challenge the good girl/bad girl dichotomy that appears to divide them, beginning with the recognition that, from a patriarchal perspective, all women are "bad girls" (feminists, in particular). She also observes that women can profit from the patriarchy; however, if, as some prostitutes claim, many sex workers choose their profession freely, then they carry the responsibility to evaluate its meaning, implications, and effects on other women.

Overall asserts that what is wrong with prostitution is not limited to the servicing of sexual needs; rather it is women's servicing of men's sexual needs under capitalist and patriarchal conditions—conditions that create both the male needs themselves and the ways in which women fill them. Under these conditions, women sell sex exclusively for the benefit of men. In our capitalistic society, it is implausible to conceive of men selling their sexual services to women; this type of sexual equality is unthinkable. Overall maintains that it may make sense to defend prostitutes' entitlement to do their work, but not to defend prostitution as a practice. As other authors have concluded, fundamental changes must take place in our society before prostitution will be eliminated.

Shaver, F. M. (1988). A critique of the feminist charges against prostitution. *Atlantis*, 14 (1), 82–89.

Many feminists reject the criminalization of prostitution because they believe that what is needed is a nonsexist policy that will reduce the economic disparity between men and women and eliminate the double standard of sexual morality. Shaver notes that some studies show that up to 80% of prostitutes are victims of incest, rape, or other forms of physical or sexual abuse in their childhood. Moreover, for many women living in poverty, prostitution is a viable alternative to criminal activity, welfare, or low-paying jobs. Yet many feminists stop short of embracing the legalization of prostitution, arguing instead that such a policy sanctions a dangerous, sexually degrading, and morally abhorrent business. Ultimately, most feminists are hesitant to defend prostitution as a legitimate business in the hope that it will be abolished in the future through social and political change. To the contrary, Shaver's thesis is that the business of prostitution is defensible; that the risk of physical violence is no greater than the risk of abuse among nonprostitutes; and that social change should foster the development of an egalitarian form of prostitution where the buying or selling of sexual services is equally available to women and men. Shaver asserts that if women could get past their moral outrage over prostitution, prostitutes and nonprostitutes could form an alliance aimed at eradicating the socioeconomic disparity between men and women and the double standard of sexual morality.

One can only be dumbfounded with Shaver's thesis and recommendations. This article is included in this review because the flaws in logic, the abundance of contradictions, and the lack of insight regarding gender roles and power all fuel the very moral outrage among women that Shaver wants to eliminate. She points out the high prevalence of childhood abuse among prostitutes, ignores (among other things) the high prevalence of drug addiction among these women, skirts the risk of the spread of AIDS and other STDs, and then suggests that prostitution is not a hazardous business! Perhaps equally disconcerting is that, apparently, the author not only views women's bodies as commodities to be bought and sold, but believes we ought to objectify men's bodies as well. Shaver suggests that women should have an equal opportunity to consumers of prostitution. For anyone hesitant to become proactive on the issue of prostitution, this article is likely to remove any doubt.

***

Shrage, L. (1989). Should feminists oppose prostitution? *Ethics, 99,* 347–361.

Shrage's well-written article describes the salient issues that feminists must attend to if prostitution is to be eliminated. Her careful analysis of the topic demonstrates why prostitution is problematic and what factors contribute to the social construction and meaning of prostitution. She notes that prostitution is not a social aberration but a result of longstanding beliefs and values that form an essential part of our social institutions and practices. Shrage claims that if feminists direct their efforts toward overcoming all discriminatory aspects of our society—in the family, at work, and in our political institutions—then they will succeed in challenging the cultural presuppositions that sustain prostitution. Basically, prostitution requires no unique solution if progress is made in altering patterns of beliefs and practices that oppress women in all facets of their lives. Nevertheless, Shrage asserts that, although there is no unique social cure, important strategic feminist goals will be served by politically opposing prostitution and pushing for a consumer boycott of the sex industry.

Glossary

analysis. Separation or breaking up of any whole into its parts so as to find out their nature, proportion, function, or relationship.

anonymity. Protection of the participant in a study such that even the researcher cannot link him or her with the information provided.

assumptions. Basic principles that are accepted as being true on the basis of logic or reason, without proof or verification.

causal relationship. A relationship between two variables such that the presence or absence of one variable (the "cause") determines the presence or absence, or value, of the other (the "effect").

coding. The process of taking raw data and transforming it into a form that can be analyzed.

confidentiality. Protection of participants in a study such that their individual identities will not be linked to the information they provided and publicly divulged.

control group. Subjects in a study who did not receive the experimental treatment and whose performance provides a baseline against which the effects of the treatment can be measured.

convenience sampling. Selection of the most readily available persons as subjects in a study.

data. The pieces of information obtained in the course of a study.

descriptive statistics. Statistics used to describe and summarize a researcher's data.

ethics. The quality of research procedures with respect to their adherence to professional, legal, and social obligations to the research subjects.

experiment. A research study in which the investigator controls the variable under study and randomly assigns subjects to different conditions.

experimental group. The subjects who receive the experimental treatment or intervention.

exploratory research. A preliminary study designed to develop or refine hunches (hypotheses), or to test and refine the data collection methods.

hypothesis. A guess or hunch about the relationship between two phenomena.

informed consent. An ethical principle that requires researchers to obtain the voluntary participation of subjects, after informing them of possible risks and benefits.

instrument. A tool that assists in the process of securing observations that are to compose the data for a research study.

interview. A method of data collection wherein one person asks questions of another person; interviews are collected either face-to-face or by telephone.

longitudinal study. A study designed to collect data at more than one point in time.

phenomenon. Any fact, circumstance, or experience that is apparent to the senses and that can be scientifically described or appraised.

population. A general group or category of individuals represented in a study.

qualitative analysis. The nonnumerical organization and interpretation of observations for the purpose of discovering important underlying dimensions and patterns of relationships.

quantitative analysis. The manipulation of numerical data through statistical procedures for the purpose of describing a phenomenon or assessing the relationships among variables.

questionnaire. A method of gathering self-report information from respondents through self-administration of questions in a "paper-and-pencil" format.

random sampling. The selection of a sample such that each member of the population (or subpopulation) has an equal chance of being included.

reliability. The degree of consistency or dependability with which an instrument measures what it is designed to measure.

replication. The duplication of research procedures in a second investigation for the purpose of determining whether earlier results can be repeated.

research. Systematic inquiry that uses orderly scientific methods to answer questions or solve problems.

research design. The overall plan for collecting and analyzing data, including specifications for enhancing the validity of the study.

sample. A subset of a population selected to participate in a research study.

sampling. The process of selecting a portion of the population to represent the entire population.

sampling bias. Distortions that arise from the selection of a sample that does not represent the population from which it was drawn.

self-report. Any procedure for collecting data that involves a direct report of information by the person who is being studied (e.g., by interview or questionnaire).

significance level. The probability that a relationship could be caused by chance; significance at the .05 level indicates the probability that a relationship would be found by chance only 5 times out of 100.

statistical significance. A term indicating that the results obtained in an analysis of sample data are unlikely to have been caused by chance, at some specified level of probability.

subject. An individual who participates and provides data in a study.

survey research. A type of nonexperimental research that focuses on obtaining information regarding the status quo of some situation, often by direct questioning of a sample of people.

theory. An abstract generalization that presents a systematic explanation about the relationships among phenomena.

treatment. A type of intervention.

validity. The degree to which a test or instrument measures what it is intended to measure.

variable. A characteristic or attribute of a person or object that varies (i.e., takes on different values) within the population under study.

REFERENCE

Polit, D., & Hungler, B. (1991). *Nursing research: Principles and methods.* Philadelphia: Lippincott.